MW00388262

RECLAIMING THE PETITION CLAUSE

RECLAIMING THE PETITION CLAUSE

Seditious Libel, "Offensive" Protest, and the Right to Petition

the Government for a Redress of Grievances

Ronald J. Krotoszynski, Jr.

Yale
UNIVERSITY PRESS
New Haven & London

Published with assistance from the foundation established in memory of
Calvin Chapin of the Class of 1788, Yale College.

Copyright © 2012 by Yale University.
All rights reserved.
This book may not be reproduced, in whole or in part, including illustrations,
in any form (beyond that copying permitted by Sections 107 and
108 of the U.S. Copyright Law and except by reviewers for the public press), without
written permission from the publishers.

Yale University Press books may be purchased in quantity for educational,
business, or promotional use. For information, please e-mail
sales.press@yale.edu (U.S. office) or sales@yaleup.co.uk (U.K. office).

Set in Electra type by IDS Infotech Ltd., Chandigarh, India.
Printed in the United States of America.

Library of Congress Cataloging-in-Publication Data

Krotoszynski, Ronald J., 1967–
Reclaiming the petition clause : seditious libel, "offensive" protest, and the right to
petition the government for a redress of grievances / Ronald J. Krotoszynski, Jr.
p. cm.
Includes bibliographical references and index.
ISBN 978-0-300-14987-6 (cloth : alk. paper) 1. Petition, Right of–United States.
I. Title.
KF4780.K76 2012
323.4'80973–dc23

2011037233

A catalogue record for this book is available from the British Library.

This paper meets the requirements of ANSI/NISO Z39.48–1992
(Permanence of Paper).

10 9 8 7 6 5 4 3 2 1

This book is dedicated to the memory of Judge Frank M. Johnson Jr. (1918–1999), for whom I had the privilege of serving as a law clerk. Judge Johnson served with great distinction—and courage—on the federal bench in Montgomery, Alabama, during some of the most tumultuous years of the civil rights movement. As a district court judge, Johnson presided over many of the most important civil rights cases aimed at securing federal constitutional rights in Alabama.

Judge Johnson firmly believed that, if permitted to operate freely and openly, the democratic process could be relied upon to correct many constitutional injustices through the regular functioning of the legislative process. For example, his opinion in *Williams v. Wallace*, 240 F. Supp. 100 (M.D. Ala. 1965), in which he issued an injunction permitting the iconic Selma-to-Montgomery March to go forward, reflects and incorporates this deep-seated faith in democracy and the democratic process. Judge Johnson appreciated the centrality of petitioning to the project of democratic self-government, and from the bench he worked to ensure that government would remain both accessible and accountable to its citizens through peaceful petitioning activity seeking a redress of constitutional grievances.

Judge Johnson's faith in the possibility of peaceful social reform through the operation of the democratic process, at a time when tempers ran high and political violence constituted an omnipresent—albeit despicable—reality, can and should serve as an example to us today. No one can deny the real and pressing security issues that exist in the post-9/11 world; indeed, we can, should, and must take seriously the threat of political violence as an illegitimate means of seeking to alter government practices and policies. For a democratic people effectively to oversee the government and its officers, however, citizens must have the ability to access and engage their government and its officials about matters of public concern. Moreover, government has a duty to engage its citizens and respond to their concerns and criticisms. Judge Johnson understood that petitioning activity lies at the very heart of this democratic feedback loop.

Judge Johnson's remarkable opinion in *Williams* stands as a testament to this important truth; his unwavering commitment to safeguarding the right of petition, even if exercised in a hybrid form that annexed speech, assembly, and association rights, provided significant motivation—indeed, inspiration—to me in pursuing this project. Accordingly, I dedicate this book as a tribute to Judge Johnson's remarkable judicial contributions to helping secure constitutionally protected expressive freedoms in the most difficult of times and places. His life's work and legacy can and should inspire us all to consider carefully the importance of safeguarding fundamental expressive freedoms, including the right of petition, in the contemporary United States and also in the larger world.

CONTENTS

PREFACE

This book argues that the Petition Clause of the First Amendment should secure a right of access by ordinary Americans to their government and its officers, and that this right of access should include the ability to communicate in real time, and in person, with these officers as an incident of the Petition Clause. At its core, the Petition Clause represents the framers' view that a democratic government must be both open and accessible, not only to its citizens, but to all persons residing within the polity. And, as a historical matter, the ability to petition the government included a right of personal access to government officials for the purpose of petitioning—and also a concomitant duty on the part of the government to receive, consider, and answer *all* petitions.

To be sure, petitioning has fallen into near-total desuetude in the contemporary United States. No serious person expects Congress, a state legislature, or even a city council (beyond small towns in New England) to receive, consider, and answer the random submissions of ordinary people. Classic petitioning, that is, petitioning aimed at securing some sort of legislative or executive action, today constitutes, at best, a feature of fringe politics. (Petitioning incident to the initiative and referendum process in the states, however, presents a different case entirely.)

Moreover, to the extent that scholarship on the Petition Clause exists, legal scholars, political scientists, and historians routinely dismiss the clause and the act of petitioning as an imperfect form of democratic politics necessary only in times and places where universal suffrage does not exist. Under this view, then, with all adults enjoying voting rights in the contemporary United States, there is simply no institutional need to maintain petitioning as an imperfect alternative form of participation in the process of democratic deliberation.

This book challenges both the standard historical account and the view that petitioning is simply a relic of a less enlightened time and place. At its core, petitioning involves a democratic feedback loop, in which ordinary people can seek and obtain access to the government and its officers to press directly their concerns, in hopes of securing some redress of their grievances. Indeed, the iconic Selma-to-Montgomery march, of March 21–25, 1965, provides perhaps the best modern example of petitioning in action. To be sure, the march involved the mass exercise of speech, assembly, and association rights, but all in the service of seeking changes in government policy at the state and federal levels. Indeed, the Southern Christian Leadership Conference's plans for the march involved presentation of petition to Governor George C. Wallace seeking recognition and respect for the political and civil rights of Alabama's African American citizens.

Simply put, if "We the People" are to hold government accountable, we must have the ability to access and engage our government. However, the ability of ordinary people to access their government through peaceful protest, of a petitioning character, seeking a redress of grievances is becoming more and more difficult. In the name of security, access to government officials has been highly limited, and sometimes completely abolished.

Over time, and with increasing speed and vigor since the horrific attacks of September 11, 2001, the United States has experienced more and more restrictions on the exercise of civil liberties in the name of promoting security. Indeed, a few years earlier, the riots in downtown Seattle, during the 1999 World Trade Organization meeting, focused the attention of event planners and law enforcement agencies on the need to protect the meeting's delegates and the meeting venues themselves from disruption (including even violent attack). No reasonable person could deny the reality of dangers associated with the presence of large crowds near major political events or government meetings. In a very real sense, security concerns are simply part of the "new normal" in the contemporary United States.

At the same time, however, the process of democratic deliberation requires public deliberation in order to function. The Internet and the computer age certainly provide new and wonderful opportunities for ordinary people to engage both each other and their government, but the availability of the Internet should not imply the closure of older, more traditional means of communication within the body politic and between the citizenry and their government. Yet, there seems to be a growing trend toward banishing speech in traditional public forums, usually in the name of security, in order to safeguard both government officials and those invited to attend the particular event.

The quadrennial presidential nominating conventions provide an extreme example of this phenomenon: the entire downtown areas of large U.S. cities are closed completely to "protest" activities, and those wishing to engage in peaceful protest activity must repair to "designated protest zones" located at great removes from the event venues. These restrictions, then, have the effect of denying would-be protestors access to their preferred audience, an audience that usually includes incumbent government officials and senior leaders of the major political parties.

Again, the government's interest in security is both real and pressing. The assassination of President John F. Kennedy, during a Dallas, Texas, motorcade event open to the public on November 22, 1963, provides a chilling cautionary note, as does John Hinckley's attempted assassination of President Ronald Reagan, on March 30, 1981, in Washington, D.C., outside the Washington Hilton hotel. More recently, the horrific attempted assassination of Representative Gabrielle Giffords, on January 8, 2011, while she was conducting an open air public meeting with her constituents, called "Congress on Your Corner," provides yet another striking example of the reality of the threats faced by public servants and the unfortunate, but very real, risk of political violence.

Yet, it seems dubious—and far too easy—simply to assume that all would-be protestors constitute terroristic threats. It also seems convenient to equate dissent with danger, and to banish it from eyesight and earshot of those attempting to hold the media's attention to propagate a particular—and uninterrupted— message. Moreover, Lee Harvey Oswald, John Hinckley, and Jared Lee Loughner were not protestors but would-be assassins. The difficulty, of course, is that the same access that facilitates access by protestors also could facilitate access by those wishing to disrupt an event (or worse).

I readily accept the proposition that limits on expressive activity are necessary to secure the safety of both government officials and those invited to participate in meetings at which government officials appear. However, flat bans on all speech activity proximate to these events cannot be justified in the name of security, if access to an intended audience enjoys any serious First Amendment protection. If local, state, and federal law enforcement agencies can success- fully conduct background checks and physically screen more than seventy thousand people, including guests, media representatives, and support workers, who attend a presidential acceptance speech in a modern NFL football sta- dium, it simply is not plausible to suggest that these same officers have no resid- ual ability to screen even a dozen would-be protestors. Those organizing these events simply do not want the protestors to register their dissent near the event; moreover, they wish to avoid having the media disseminate a mixed message to the larger national political community. The interest in enjoying uncontested access to the voting public seems rather far removed from the initial claim that the demands of effective security require a flat proscription on protest in an area that otherwise constitutes a traditional public forum, such as a sidewalk, street, or park.

I do not pretend to have all of the answers to these difficult questions. The existence of clear and present dangers to the safety and security of government officers and the general public is a pressing, indeed compelling, government interest. At the same time, however, courts cannot simply accept any and all restrictions on expressive activity, particularly of a petitioning cast, applicable to public streets and sidewalks. Taken to its logical extreme, the security rationale would justify complete bans on all expressive conduct near any and all government buildings, banks, and other financial institutions, and the buildings used by major international corporations. Indeed, the entire downtown areas of most major U.S. cities could be closed completely to expressive activity, of any sort, if the security rationale were given full flower.

This is not hyperbole on my part. In the litigation involving speech bans proximate to the 2008 presidential nominating conventions in Denver, Colorado, and St. Paul, Minnesota, the federal district courts deciding the lawsuits credited the risk of a suicide bomber as a basis for closing dozens of blocks proximate to the convention venues to any and all forms of protest. If the abstract risk of a suicide bomber provides a sufficient predicate for closing downtown Denver to protest during the Democratic National Convention, shouldn't this same concern apply with equal force when workers are present at an IRS building, a federal courthouse, or a Fortune 500 corporate headquarters? Yet, the effect of such a ban on the process of democratic deliberation would be extreme and unjustified. Simply put, a commitment to democratic self-government implies accepting the risk of serious social costs when necessary to facilitate the process of democratic engagement. Elections, to be meaningful, require the ability to engage both incumbent government officers and one's fellow citizens about matters of public concern.

My hope is that this book will help to open a dialogue about the relevance and meaning of the Petition Clause to contemporary politics and governance in the United States. The Petition Clause, at its core, requires government to be accessible and accountable to the people. This value is no less relevant in 2012 than it was in 1791, when the First Amendment became part of the U.S. Constitution. Finally, even if one contests my specific arguments for how the clause should apply in the contemporary United States, the question of adequately safeguarding meaningful access to the government and its officers will still remain and require serious attention by legal academics, judges, and practicing lawyers. A democratic government must be both accessible and accountable to We the People, and the imperatives of security and public safety must not be permitted to completely displace these democratic values.

ACKNOWLEDGMENTS

A scholarly project of this scope requires the active support and encouragement of many persons to succeed; accordingly, I owe significant debts of grati-
tude to a number of people and institutions for their active support and
encouragement. First, I should acknowledge the significant contributions of
Clint A. Carpenter, Esq., W & L '07, who, after graduating and while clerking
for Judge Norman K. Moon, collaborated with me as a coauthor on *The Return
of Seditious Libel*, 55 UCLA L. Rev. 1239 (2008), an earlier iteration of some of
the arguments contained in this book. Clint was a terrific coauthor, and the
book has benefited directly from his outstanding legal research and writing
skills. In addition, several excellent student research assistants contributed to
the success of this project, including John Martin, W & L '08, Michael
McCarthy, W & L '09, Emily White, W & L '09, Holly Chesnut, Alabama '09,
Josh Christensen, Alabama '11, and Sean Fahey, Alabama '12.

Reclaiming the Petition Clause required access to a rather large number of
obscure historical sources; the esoteric nature of the subject—the Petition
Clause and petitioning more generally—greatly complicated the task of
researching the book. My labors benefited greatly from the active assistance of
two outstanding research librarians, Robert Marshall, of the Bounds Law
Library at the University of Alabama School of Law, and Kerry Fitz-Gerald, of
the law library at the Seattle University School of Law.

Dean Ken Randall, of the University of Alabama School of Law, provided
consistent and unwavering support for this project, including financial support,
but also including affirmative efforts to ensure that I had the necessary time and
space to complete this book. Moreover, *Reclaiming the Petition Clause* would
not have been possible without the financial support of the University of

Alabama Law School Foundation, which provided generous summer research grant support over the past four years.

I also wish to acknowledge the active and unfailing support of the Seattle University School of Law, which has hosted me as a visiting scholar in residence for the past several summers. Dean Mark Niles and the administrators, faculty, and staff at Seattle University all helped to facilitate this project by providing comprehensive research support during my periods in residence in Seattle, Washington. In particular, I should mention the consistent support and friendship of Ms. Lori Lamb, who unfailingly has gone out of her way to help make my time in Seattle as productive as it can possibly be.

Several law school faculties contributed to this research project by hosting workshops at which I presented one or more chapters of this book. I am grateful to the law faculties at Brooklyn Law School, the University of Georgia, the University of Illinois at Urbana-Champaign, the University of Oregon, Washington University at St. Louis, the University of Western Ontario, and the University of Windsor for helping me refine my claims and arguments. *Reclaiming the Petition Clause* also benefited from the thoughtful comments and suggestions of the faculties and graduate students at the University of Georgia's Grady College of Journalism and Mass Communication and the University of Oregon School of Journalism and Communication, which both hosted colloquiums at which I presented portions of the working draft of this book.

Finally, portions of *Reclaiming the Petition Clause* first appeared in print as:

(1) Ronald J. Krotoszynski Jr., "Celebrating Selma: The Importance of Context in Public Forum Analysis," 104 *Yale Law Journal* 1411 (1995) (portions of chapter 6). Reprinted by permission of The Yale Law Journal Company and Fred B. Rothman & Company from the *Yale Law Journal*, vol. 104, pp. 1411–1440.

(2) Ronald J. Krotoszynski Jr. and Clint A. Carpenter, "The Return of Seditious Libel," 55 *UCLA Law Review* 1239 (2008) (portions of chapters 2, 3, 4, and 5).

I should note, however, that the material drawn from these earlier published works has been substantially revised—and expanded—for inclusion in this book.

The Growing Marginalization of Dissent and the New Seditious Libel

The right to petition for the redress of grievances has an ancient history and is not limited to writing a letter or sending a telegram to a congressman; it is not confined to appearing before the local city council, or writing letters to the President or Governor or Mayor. Conventional methods of petitioning may be, and often have been, shut off to large groups of our citizens. Legislators may turn deaf ears; formal complaints may be routed endlessly through a bureaucratic maze; courts may let the wheels of justice grind very slowly. Those who do not control television and radio, those who cannot afford to advertise in newspapers or circulate elaborate pamphlets may have only a more limited type of access to public officials. Their methods should not be condemned as tactics of obstruction and harassment as long as the assembly and petition are peaceable, as they were here.

—*Justice William O. Douglas, Adderley v. Florida*[1]

I. INTRODUCTION: BARRING THE DOOR AGAINST WOULD-BE DISSENTERS AND DISSENT

During the summer and fall of 2009, a remarkable series of confrontations took place between members of Congress and their constituents. Although often misinformed about the precise content of pending national health care legislation, thousands of average citizens took the time and trouble to attend town hall meetings featuring their local member of Congress or senator in order to express their opposition to pending federal health care reform legislation. This, however, was not how these town hall meetings were supposed to proceed: "The politicians, every one of them, seemed taken aback—shaken and unprepared."[2] The media images were iconic, and it was clear that the incumbent legislators did not anticipate, or very much enjoy, being publicly challenged by their constituents—with the local television stations' cameras rolling.

Alas, these scenes were not repeated in 2010, and they may not be repeated very often going forward.[3] As one newspaper reporter observing this change wryly put it, "If the time-honored tradition of the political meeting is not quite dead, it seems to be teetering closer to extinction."[4] Many, but by no means all, incumbent politicians have abandoned the open town hall format in favor of ticketed events likely to generate favorable local media coverage, rather than images of angry constituents confronting incumbent legislators.

Evidently, the town hall meetings were intended to serve as a form of positive political theater, not as an opportunity for members of the public to register their support for, or opposition to, particular government policies direct, and in person, to their elected member of Congress.[5] From the perspective of many incumbent legislators, an ideal town hall would have involved the local member of the House of Representatives proudly reporting on federal largesse secured in the last session for the benefit of the district's residents via the herculean efforts of their hardworking member of Congress, coupled perhaps with reports on major legislation pending in the chamber, and finished off with a few nonconfrontational questions from concerned, but largely supportive and appreciative, constituents. During the summer of 2009, however, things plainly did not go according to plan at these town hall meetings.[6]

The difference between then and now is nothing short of extraordinary. A year later, in summer 2010, "[o]f the 255 Democrats who make up the majority in the House, only a handful held town-hall style forums" in a recent congressional recess.[7] Here is a rather telling, and representative, account of the radical change in approach to constituent meetings from summer 2009 to summer 2010: "The reception that Representative Frank Kratovil Jr., a Democrat, received here [in Bel Air, Maryland] one night last week as he faced a small group of constituents was far more pleasant than his encounters during a Congressional recess last summer. Then, he was hanged in effigy by protesters. This time, a round of applause was followed by a glass of chilled wine, a plate of crackers, and crudités as he mingled with an invitation-only audience at the Point Breeze Credit Union, a vastly different scene than last year's wide-open televised free-for-alls."[8]

As a consequence of this change in strategy, many average citizens have been unable to engage personally their members of Congress, regardless of whether the constituent's precise concern is the new health care legislation, the federal government's response to the Deepwater Horizon oil spill disaster, or economic stimulus policies within the G20 group of nations.[9] Thus, one of the last long-standing means of securing direct communication with an incumbent federal government legislator has now been lost.[10]

Moreover, contemporary efforts to squelch dissent are hardly limited to canceling town hall meetings open to the public. Instead, with increasing regularity, government officials from both major political parties seek to limit, if not banish, political dissent proximate to major speeches and meetings, such as presidential appearances and the national presidential nominating conventions.[11] "Designated speech zones," often surrounded by mesh-covered fencing and festooned with razor wire, and routinely located at great distances from presidential appearances and national political conventions, have become the norm rather than the exception.

Average citizens should have the ability to communicate their views to their elected representatives effectively, and, in the age of autobots and spam filters, simply writing a letter or sending an e-mail is a relatively poor means of ensuring effective communication with a government officer. We know with certainty that President George W. Bush was well aware of Cindy Sheehan's views on the Iraq War, not because a staff member responded to an e-mail from Sheehan sent to www.whitehouse.gov, but rather because of her vigil outside the president's ranch in Crawford, Texas, in August 2005.

Increasingly, however, incumbent government officials wish to avoid unflattering media coverage of dissent. To be clear, I do not suggest that government seeks to censor the messages themselves; instead, government seeks to avoid having messages of disagreement conveyed contemporaneously with the government's own message, relying on the media presence generated by the appearance of a senior government official. Because, happily, it is not possible to prevent media coverage of dissent in the United States (as opposed to, say, in contemporary China or Cuba), the government seeks to banish dissenters from the physical proximity of its officials. This is done not in the name of censorship, but rather in the name of security.

Since the 1988 Democratic National Convention in Atlanta, Georgia, and at every subsequent national presidential nominating convention, both political parties have sought to banish protestors from the vicinity of the meetings. This has been accomplished, with growing effectiveness, by denominating any visible sign of protest a security threat and removing would-be protestors to venues far removed from the conventions (and from the delegates and government officials attending these meetings).

Shocking as it might seem, expression of a dissenting viewpoint leads local law enforcement and the Secret Service to classify a protestor as a "demonstrator," and, by definition, "demonstrators" constitute a security threat. By way of contrast, wearing a T-shirt emblazoned with "I ♥ Obama" or "I ♥ McCain" is perfectly acceptable and will not lead to forced relocation or arrest. In fact, the Secret Service's *Presidential Advance Manual* in force during George W. Bush's administration provided that if a protestor was within eyesight or earshot of the president, that person constituted a security threat and had to be removed, even from a public street or sidewalk that otherwise constitutes a classic traditional public forum.

Although government does not formally prohibit critical speech, by invoking security concerns as a basis for extraordinary limits on where and when such speech may occur, it seeks to remove dissenting speech from within eyesight and earshot of incumbent government officials—thereby both prohibiting direct petitioning of such officials and also making it far less likely that protest will garner much, if any, media coverage.[12] Indeed, even daring to speak to a government officer, such as the vice-president, in a critical fashion in a public place can and does lead to an arrest for "assault" if the vice president, or his Secret Service security detail, deems the words offensive.[13]

These efforts at suppressing dissent also lack subtlety, often bordering on the facially pretextual. For example, the *Presidential Advance Manual* used during George W. Bush's administration expressly provides that "[i]f it is determined that the media will not see or hear [the demonstrators] and that they pose no potential disruption to the event, they can be ignored," but otherwise demonstrators must be removed to a "protest area" designated by local law enforcement authorities (on pain of arrest).[14] Although a threat of disruption to a presidential event obviously constitutes a relevant security consideration, a non-disruptive protest that the media could "see or hear" also plainly comes within the letter of the rule.

The manual also calls for local police and event planners to organize "rally squads" who will "spread favorable messages using large hand held signs, placards, or perhaps a long sheet banner," with the express purpose of using these signs as shields between the demonstrators and the media's press platform.[15] And, to be clear, efforts to suppress media coverage of dissent enjoy bipartisan support.[16]

II. THE POTENTIAL RELEVANCE OF THE PETITION CLAUSE AS A MEANS OF SECURING A MEANINGFUL RIGHT TO EXPRESS DISSENT TO INCUMBENT GOVERNMENT OFFICIALS

One might reasonably ask: Doesn't the First Amendment guarantee some sort of right of access to the government and its officers? The answer to this question might come as something of a surprise: existing precedents squarely hold that the Free Speech and Assembly Clauses of the First Amendment *do not* secure a right of access to a preferred audience, even if this audience consists of government officials.[17] As the U.S. Court of Appeals for the First Circuit has explained with unmistakable clarity, "the Constitution neither recognizes nor gives special protection to any conversational distance," "handbilling is not specially protected," and "[t]ime-place-manner restrictions routinely make particular forms of expression impracticable without raising constitutional concerns."[18] Precisely because "there is no constitutional guarantee of any particular form or mode of expression" on public property,[19] there is also no constitutional guarantee of access to any particular intended audience. In other words, reasonable time, place, and manner regulations that are content neutral and viewpoint neutral may constitutionally have the effect of denying a would-be speaker access to an audience of her choosing, even if the desired audience consists entirely of popularly elected government officials and senior political party leaders.[20]

The First Amendment, however, contains more than just the Speech and Assembly Clauses—it also contains the Petition Clause. In relevant part, the Petition Clause provides that "Congress shall make no law . . . abridging . . . the right of the people . . . to Petition the Government for a redress of grievances."[21] The text of the Petition Clause itself is intriguing, for the clause appears to be annexed to the Assembly Clause: "Congress shall make no law . . . abridging . . . the right of the people peaceably to assemble, and to petition the Government for a redress of grievances."[22]

In contrast, when James Madison introduced the Bill of Rights in the House of Representatives on Monday, June 8, 1789, the Speech and Press Clauses were in a separate provision from the Assembly and Petition Clauses. Madison proposed an amendment that provided: "The people shall not be restrained from peaceably assembling and consulting for their common good; nor from applying to the Legislature by petitions, or remonstrances, for redress of their grievances."[23] The immediately preceding, entirely separate, and wholly independent clause would have secured the rights of free speech and press: "The people shall not be deprived or abridged of their right to speak, to write, or to publish their sentiments; and the freedom of the press, one of the great bulwarks of liberty, shall be inviolable."[24] Thus, Madison linked the fundamental expressive freedoms of speech/press, on the one hand, and the rights of assembly/petition, on the other. Nor was Madison's linkage of assembly with petition a mere accident: assembly enjoys protection precisely because it is an antecedent activity to petitioning.[25] This linkage between assembly and petitioning had roots in British law at the time of the framing and simply carried over to the United States.

In Anglo-American legal history, the right of petition encompassed, literally, the right of the people to lay complaints "at the foot of the throne, that the king with the advice of his council or of his lords might redress them."[26] The right of petition also included not merely the right to be heard but also a right to a formal response from the government.[27] In other words, at its core, the right of petition protects a personal right to bring complaints about public policy directly to officers of the government, up to and including the king himself, and to receive some sort of response. Moreover, petition was an exception to the doctrine of seditious libel: one could not be convicted of seditious libel based on the content of a petition. In fact, during the first Adams administration, when the Sedition Act of 1798 was being used systematically to silence prominent political opponents of the president and his Federalist Party, petitions to Congress remained the *only* available avenue of expressing dissent without risking a criminal conviction and prison.[28]

Thus, the Petition Clause, as a matter of the original understanding and Anglo-American legal history, provides an entirely plausible independent source of protection for a right to protest government policies directly, and even in person, to high government officers and those who control the means of selecting them. In addition, as chapter 5 demonstrates, strong normative and public policy reasons also exist for reclaiming and renewing the Petition Clause as a means of reinvigorating the process of democratic self-government.[29]

If the federal courts were to approach the Petition Clause purposively, as they have when interpreting its first cousin, the Free Speech Clause,[30] the Petition Clause's key contribution to the universe of expressive freedom and democratic self-government would be securing *access* to the government and its agents. More than anything else, the Petition Clause stands for the proposition that citizens should enjoy meaningful direct access to their government and its officials.

When considered in historical terms, petitioning has always involved the ability of average people, including those lacking the right to vote—women, noncitizens, and even, in at least some instances, human chattel slaves—to enjoy meaningful access to the agents of the government for the purpose of raising concerns about public policy and governance. Historically, petitioning also has encompassed a duty on the part of the government to hear, consider, and answer concerns brought forward through petitioning activities. Thus, one could add the concept of *engagement* to access as resting at the core of the First Amendment's express protection of petitioning. This book argues that these two concepts—access and engagement—should inform our contemporary understanding of the Petition Clause and its doctrinal contours.

The easy answer to arguments about access and engagement, however, is that in the post-9/11 world, the concept of access, much less engagement, is at best naive and at worst affirmatively dangerous. This potential response implicates another important historical parallel that exists between the treatment of protestors at presidential appearances and national nominating conventions and the original understanding of the Petition Clause. As a historical matter, seditious libel, the concept that the state could prohibit criticism of the government, was grounded in national security concerns. If government was not protected from false accusations of corruption or incompetence, it might not be able to effectively conduct the affairs of state.[31] The efficacy of the government, the argument runs, requires that the dignity of the government be protected.[32] Indeed, the Federalist Party even argued, in defense of the Sedition Act of 1798, that criminal proscription of seditious libel enhanced the democratic legitimacy of government by creating the conditions necessary for democratically elected officials to work the will of the people.[33]

Thus, the advancement of security concerns represents the very heart of the doctrine of seditious libel; and although cloaked in the nomenclature of security, incumbent politicians essentially create two material equivalencies that are remarkably self-serving: the first is between "security" and the dignity of the government and the second is between the dignity of the government and those holding public office. Hence, in practice, seditious libel worked to protect the dignitarian interests of incumbent politicians, ostensibly to protect the security of the government and to ensure that elected officers could work the will of "We the People."

The recent growth in unprecedented and highly disturbing limits on public dissent proximate to elected government officials arguably rests on precisely the same footing as the doctrine of seditious libel and arguably represents the return of seditious libel (albeit in a substantially weaker form). Unlike its older, more robust cousin, this new seditious libel is not as far-reaching or as all-encompassing as the old seditious libel; rather, the new seditious libel works merely to marginalize rather than absolutely banish speech. Yet, it does so for the same reason—security—and has the ancillary effect of protecting incumbent politicians from facing the calamity of having the television cameras that they conjure by their mere presence at a speech, meeting, or other function purloined by those seeking to oppose them and their policies.

Even in the era of the Sedition Act, however, petitioning remained a viable means of accessing incumbent government officials and engaging them on matters of popular concern. The Federalist Congress received, considered, and answered petitions on myriad topics, including highly contentious issues, such as slavery, industrial policy, and U.S. foreign relations with France and the United Kingdom.[34] Moreover, the level of solicitude afforded petitions and petitioners in this period would be shocking to most incumbent members of Congress — ordinary people precipitated floor debates on petitions often lasting weeks or more.[35] Thus, the original understanding of petitioning involved levels of access and direct engagement that are difficult to imagine in today's United States.

Of course, it is true that the under the modern variant of seditious libel, protestors will not face jail for the content of their speech (at least directly),[36] but by marginalizing their ability to share the media spotlight generated by those holding public office, the net effect on the marketplace of ideas is really not much different. In fact, between making martyrs of political opponents, as the first Adams administration did in the late eighteenth century, and simply rendering political opponents effectively invisible (and thereby irrelevant), "sedition lite" has much to recommend it to would-be censors over the use of old-school seditious libel.

To be clear, however, I do not claim — or even suggest — that any and all invocations of security as a basis for limiting access to public officials and public buildings represent mere pretext. Unfortunately, security concerns are not always and everywhere chimerical, and "security" is not invariably a shibboleth invoked by federal judges to sustain unreasonable restraints on the exercise of expressive freedoms.

The tragic events of January 8, 2011, in suburban Tucson, Arizona, demonstrate quite concretely the reality that public service can involve significant personal risks. More than most members of Congress, of either party, Representative Gabrielle Giffords is strongly committed to remaining accessible to her constituents. In fact, her "Congress on Your Corner" event at a local grocery store in her congressional district was only one of several public events that she planned to conduct while in the area during the House's recess. As a congressional colleague, Paul Kanjorski, noted in the aftermath of the attack: "Despite numerous threats, Ms. Giffords took that risk [of meeting constituents in public, with minimal security-based limits on access] and welcomed her constituents at a grocery store in Tucson. She recognized, as we did, that accepting the risk of violence was part of the price of freedom."[37] As Representative Kanjorski observes, the attempted assassination "was especially shocking, because it was so personal."[38] He explains that "[s]he was hunted down far from the halls of power while performing the most fundamental responsibility of her job, listening to her constituents."[39]

A deranged and psychologically unbalanced young man, Jared Lee Loughner, was unsuccessful in his attempt to assassinate Representative Giffords, but he succeeded in shooting nineteen people and murdering six, including John M. Roll, a Tucson federal district judge, and Christina Green, a nine-year-old girl.[40] Security at this event was essentially nonexistent; Representative Giffords did not use a local security detail at this event or at other "Congress on Your Corner" events.[41]

It bears noting that, on January 5, 2011, just a few days before the shooting in Tucson, Representative Giffords read the text of the First Amendment from the well of the House of Representatives, incident to a reading of the U.S. Constitution that was part of the ceremonies associated with the House of Representatives opening its new session.[42] This demonstrates quite clearly that Representative Giffords's commitment to being accessible to her constituents, and her willingness to engage them in public, with no holds barred, reflects a considered commitment on her part;[43] she obviously possesses a deep-seated appreciation for the value and importance of democratic deliberation in a nation that practices democratic self-government. Moreover, she personally works to facilitate that process by welcoming—indeed, affirmatively seeking out—real-time, in-person interactions with her constituents.[44] In this respect, Representative Giffords models and exemplifies the values safeguarded by the Petition Clause.

The issue of access, accordingly, is complicated. No reasonable person would suggest that the Petition Clause (or any other provision of the Bill of Rights, for that matter) guarantees an unqualified or unrestricted right of access to government officers and government buildings. At the same time, however, the pretextual invocation of security as a basis for squelching any and all public expression of dissent near government officials or public buildings plainly goes too far.

In advocating for a right of access to government officials as an incident of the Petition Clause, I do not seek to avoid or minimize the difficulties facing a federal court tasked with ascertaining whether bona fide security concerns justify a particular restriction on protest in an otherwise available traditional or designated public forum. The problem, however, is that contemporary First Amendment doctrine does not require reviewing courts to entertain seriously this question. Because there is no First Amendment interest in communicating directly with a particular audience (even if the audience consists of government officials or party leaders who control the primary election process and thereby access to the general election ballot), the lower federal courts have imposed almost no meaningful burden of justification on local governments that adopt protest-free zones that encompass almost the entire downtown area of a major U.S. city. Surely the appropriate line requires more effort to accommodate peaceful protest and the modern imperatives of security. As former Representative

Paul Kanjorski noted in the aftermath of the tragic Tucson attack, "it is impossible to eliminate the risks faced by elected officials when they interact with their constituents."[45]

III. THE SCOPE OF THE TASK: RECLAIMING THE PETITION CLAUSE WILL NOT BE EASY BECAUSE THE PETITION CLAUSE HAS LARGELY BEEN FORGOTTEN

In the contemporary United States, the Petition Clause has little practical legal effect, and the Supreme Court has not attempted to delineate its doctrinal and jurisprudential contours independently of its cousins, the Free Speech and Assembly Clauses. The Petition Clause serves as the basis for a constitutionally mandated exemption from the Sherman and Clayton Acts for lobbying efforts that might otherwise violate antitrust principles,[46] and it secures a right of access to the federal courts.[47] Beyond this, the Petition Clause has virtually no independent legal force or effect. This book questions whether this state of affairs should continue. The Petition Clause, unlike the Speech, Assembly, and Press Clauses, presupposes a right of access by average citizens to a particular audience (viz., incumbent government officials), at least for the purpose of "petitioning" this audience for a redress of grievances; historically, it has secured access to the government and its officers and required government to engage the concerns brought to its attention via petitions and petitioning.

Although it might come as a surprise to persons who lack any concept of petitioning as a well-used tool in the engaged citizen's civic tool box, petitioning flourished in the colonial, prerevolutionary, and early years of the Republic. In fact, Congress received petitions from its inception in 1789—well before the submission of the First Amendment to the states for ratification.[48] Petitions started to arrive in the House of Representatives less than a week after it began meeting.

The most prominent early petitioners were Quakers, who, seeking an early end to at least some aspects of the slave trade, petitioned Congress to close international and interstate commerce to the importation of human chattel slaves.[49] These Quaker abolitionists were not only among the first federal petitioners, they were also the first organized lobbyists.[50] The Quakers rented rooms in boarding houses proximate to Federal Hall in New York City, and began plying federal legislators with food and drink, using the opportunity to impress upon their guests the importance of an early end to the importation of slaves. "At the same time, their petitions were published in the newspapers, and New York seemed suddenly awash in antislavery pamphlets and broadsides."[51]

What might come as an even greater surprise: Congress itself felt not only an obligation to receive petitions but also a corresponding duty to respond to petitions on the merits. To be sure, Congress did not always agree to grant the request sought in a petition. Nevertheless, simply ignoring a petition was not considered consistent with the legislature's responsibilities to the citizenry. As I explain in greater detail in chapter 4, from 1789 to 1836, after receiving a petition, Congress almost invariably would refer it to an appropriate committee for review and a proposed response, and the house that received it would in fact respond to the petitioners.

Petitioning constituted a primary means of political organization not only for abolitionists in the early nineteenth century but also for women's suffragists in the later nineteenth century, for those advancing the legal rights of Native Americans, for veterans, and also for proponents and opponents of Prohibition. Moreover, these mass petitioning campaigns also used speech, mass assembly, and association as part and parcel of their law reform efforts; petitioning was part of synergistic exercises of expressive freedom. In fact, petitioning at the federal level of government retained cultural and political salience well into the nineteenth century. But, relatively soon after the turn of the twentieth century, petitioning fell into relative desuetude, preempted, at least in part, by the Progressive movement's successful advocacy of initiative and referendum as a means of securing direct democratic change through a plebiscite in about two dozen states.[52]

One might ask whether petitioning actually encompassed a right of access to government officers. The short answer is that it did. As noted earlier, the historical model of petitioning, going back to the thirteenth century in England, literally involved laying a petition at the foot of the king while in the royal presence. Although it is true that the seat of government served as the locus of petitioning activity, it would not require much of a departure from the historical model to extend the right of petitioning to locations where government officials happen to be conducting business on a given day (just as the king might relocate his court from place to place, thereby altering the locus of petitioning). Thus, if the president is attending a NATO meeting in Colorado Springs, Colorado, or a member of Congress is hosting a town hall meeting in Toledo, Ohio, logically a citizen should be able to engage in petitioning activity in that location, rather than solely in Washington, D.C.

It also bears noting, in thinking about the wisdom of a renewed social, political, and legal commitment to the right of petition, that a democracy cannot function as a democracy if average citizens lack meaningful access to their elected officials. Most citizens simply cannot afford to make $2,400 campaign contributions to their incumbent members of Congress as a means of securing access to them. Yet, if citizens can be removed from motorcade routes and side-walks proximate to convention centers where political meetings will occur, what other effective means of communication exist for citizens who wish to ensure that their congressman or senator knows their view on the Iraq War, the Deepwater Horizon oil spill disaster, or the growing federal debt?

In addition, the ability of a citizen to confront power has a powerful effect in facilitating democratic discourse. If the president makes a speech before an adoring audience, the media images help to build and maintain support for those policies. However, if the evening news coverage also includes large groups of protestors outside the venue demonstrating against the president's policies, reportage of the event has a very different social and political effect. The fact of public dissent becomes part of the story, and the story in turn helps to facilitate a larger discussion of the relevant questions within the body politic. Recall that, toward the end of his presidency, Lyndon B. Johnson made all of his major speeches either from the Oval Office or from military bases before a captive audience of stone-faced armed services members; he generally did not speak from public venues, because his presence would generate mass demonstrations that would, and often did, overtake the president's own message.[53] Thus, the very fact of dissent helps to generate a dialogue within the citizenry that might otherwise not exist in the absence of dissent reported by the media to the general public.

The iconic Selma-to-Montgomery march, of March 1965, provides perhaps the best example of this phenomenon. It is certainly true that the march itself constituted core speech and assembly, as well as association (an unenumerated expressive freedom that nevertheless enjoys greater judicial solicitude at present than petitioning). At the conclusion of the march, in Montgomery, Alabama, the Southern Christian Leadership Conference (SCLC) planned to hold, and in fact held, a rally on the steps of the Alabama state capitol building, after which a delegation of twenty SCLC leaders intended to enter the building and present Governor George C. Wallace with a petition seeking recognition of and respect for the civil and political rights of African American citizens of Alabama.[54] The delegation did attempt to deliver the petition after the rally, but Governor Wallace refused to receive them; the petition was delivered to his official office in the state capitol about a week after the rally incident to a personal meeting between Governor Wallace and around twenty representatives of the SCLC.[55]

In a very real sense, then, the march itself and the rally served as a framing device for a petition to the executive branch of government in the state of Alabama. The event was a synthesis of speech, assembly, association, and *petition.* Moreover, national media coverage of the march and rally helped to generate crucial public support for enactment of the Voting Rights Act of 1965, which secured the right to vote without regard to race in the United States. Judge Frank M. Johnson Jr.'s remarkable opinion in *Williams v. Wallace* clearly recognized the petitioning nature of the SCLC's proposed multiday march from Selma to Montgomery and subsequent mass rally at the state capitol building, and it accorded the SCLC broader access to public property, including public streets, highways, and sidewalks, than might otherwise have been available for speech activity that lacked a petitioning character.[56]

Judge Johnson strongly believed that the petitioning element of the expressive activity justified a greater margin of constitutional solicitude for the march and rally than would have existed in the absence of the petitioning characteristic.[57] In other words, synergies exist when citizens seek to exercise multiple expressive freedoms contemporaneously; the sum might well justify a level of constitutional solicitude exceeding that afforded by the individual parts on a disaggregated basis.

To say that exercises of expressive freedom that annex speech, assembly, and association to a petition for a redress of grievances exist and merit special judicial solicitude does not answer or resolve a host of very difficult questions, which, moreover, the federal courts would need to address in order to give meaningful jurisprudential effect to the Petition Clause as an independent source of an expressive freedom that secures a right of access to the government and its officers. How much access does the Petition Clause require? And on what precise terms and conditions? The government's interest in the security and safety of its officers and buildings, as well as the safety and security of the general public, will also require careful consideration in setting the metes and bounds of a Petition Clause–based right of access. Obviously, to ask these questions is not to answer them definitively.

The goal of this book is to open a public dialogue on the potential relevance and importance of petitioning to contemporary process of democratic deliberation. Just as Professor Owen Fiss asked pressing and important questions about the threat to democratic self-government presented by the systematic loss of public space available for the exercise of expressive freedoms,[58] I argue that we also need to focus time and attention on the growing limits that govern access by ordinary people to their government.

If, as Alexander Meiklejohn so powerfully argued, the existence and maintenance of democratic self-government demand an active and engaged body politic,[59] the ability of persons living within the polity—citizen and noncitizen alike—to access and engage the government and its officers constitutes an essential condition for the process of democratic self-government. Petitioning speech helps to maintain a democratic feedback loop: average people share their concerns over matters of public policy and governance with those holding the reins of power within the government, and the government's responsiveness (or lack thereof) then becomes a central electoral issue in the next election season.

IV. CONCLUSION: THE PETITION CLAUSE CONSTITUTES AN INTEGRAL PART OF THE FIRST AMENDMENT AND SHOULD BE SO RECOGNIZED

If citizens are to enjoy a constitutional right of access to government officials, the Petition Clause provides the most likely—and most natural—textual basis to secure such a right. Moreover, it makes little sense to ignore a clause of the First Amendment entirely, particularly when it has an independent legal and political history. It seems very strange indeed to elevate an unenumerated expressive interest, the right of free association, to constitutional status while simply ignoring the Petition Clause, yet this is precisely how matters currently have come to rest.[60]

This book represents a fresh attempt to reclaim the Petition Clause and to restore it to our pantheon of expressive freedoms. As citizens, we should have the right to communicate our views with democratically accountable government officials in a manner that is likely to be effective. Theodore Woolsey, a political scientist and former president of Yale University, wrote in his treatise *Political Science or the State* that citizen petitioning "is needed in constitutional representative governments, because opinions change, new wants arise, and the representative may act on the base principle that he represents a party only."[61] Moreover, Woolsey embraced the concept of citizen access to elected officials in a democratic policy as an incident of the right of petition. Citizens and foreigners alike, Woolsey argued, "ought thus to have free access not only to the courts but to legislatures and magistrates, either in reference to public affairs or to such as affect their own industry and calling."[62] In other words, petitioning secures a right of access to help facilitate effective democratic governance, and it initiates a process of engagement that, at least in theory, makes government more accountable to We the People.

These concerns remain salient, even as the average citizen's effective access to elected government officials has steadily decreased over time. Today, a public protest on a street or sidewalk along a motorcade route might well constitute the only potential means available to an ordinary citizen to communicate a message of either support or opposition regarding an administration policy directly to the president; yet, in the name of security, even this means of communication appears to be in danger of extinction.

This is not to say that security concerns are irrelevant or that any citizen has a right to speak anytime, anywhere, to any government official she pleases. I am not advocating anarchy or a free-for-all in the guise of petitioning. I am arguing for a baseline presumption in favor of access to government officials from public spaces that otherwise constitute public forums, in tandem with a serious burden of justification resting on the government before it may banish dissent and dissenters from the sight and hearing of government officials with some measure of responsibility for the policies at issue.

In order to establish a need for reclaiming the Petition Clause, the argument begins by documenting the increasing marginalization of dissent in the contemporary United States and the (at best) tepid response to this trend by the federal courts.[63] Government officials, invoking open-ended and ill-defined security concerns, have successfully convinced the federal courts that any protest proximate to major political events, such as the national presidential nominating conventions, risks chaos and anarchy, if not serious injuries or deaths.

Local and federal law enforcement officials, citing the 1999 World Trade Organization riots in Seattle, routinely argue that the problems that took place in Seattle, more than a decade ago, will surely recur unless *all* organized protests are removed from the immediate vicinity of the political event. Moreover, the U.S. courts of appeals have consistently sustained security-based restrictions on protests nearby major political events on the theory that the restrictions are content and viewpoint neutral, constitute sufficiently tailored reasonable time, place, and manner restrictions on speech on public property, and leave open ample alternative channels of communication.[64]

The security rationale, as noted earlier, is plainly not entirely pretextual.[65] Nevertheless, the relationship between limits on expressive freedom and security has found legal traction before, primarily incident to the doctrine of seditious libel.[66] The refusal of both major political parties to accommodate any protest whatsoever at venues such as the national presidential nominating conventions reflects a desire to banish dissent, and potential media coverage of this dissent, from the electorate, rather than solely legitimate security concerns. Accordingly, it reflects the return of a kind of junior varsity version of the doctrine of seditious libel.

Unlike the doctrine of seditious libel, which punished those who deigned to criticize the government or its incumbent officers with imprisonment, this less obvious form of censorship is arguably more pernicious precisely because it is less transparent. For democracy to function, the citizenry needs to be able to openly and plainly discuss issues of the day and to critique the government's policies without fear of retribution. Indeed, whatever the potential outer scope of the free speech project, everyone agrees that political speech is essential to democratic self-government.[67]

Chapter 3 argues that the ability of citizens to register dissent by petitioning incumbent government officials to alter their policies, and to make the fact of this dissent known through local and national media, constitutes crucial elements of the democratic process. To be clear, government does not seek to imprison protestors today (although some protestors are, in fact, arrested). Instead, the main goal is to make it difficult, if not impossible, for the media representatives sent to cover a senior government officer or major political event from also covering dissent near official political events. The goal is not to punish speech per se (as was the case with seditious libel) but rather is to avoid national media coverage of public dissent from the positions and policies of the official or party conducting the meeting (whether a national presidential nominating convention, a presidential appearance, or a congressional town hall meeting).

Having demonstrated that existing First Amendment doctrine does not afford sufficient breathing room for public dissent,[68] and that petitioning could provide a theoretical basis for thwarting the return of a junior varsity version of seditious libel,[69] the analysis next considers the history of the Petition Clause in the United Kingdom, the United States, and New Zealand.[70] After all, if we are to reclaim the Petition Clause, we need to know precisely the metes and bounds of the right of petition as they once were.

Petitioning has its origins in English law, dating back to the Magna Carta and before. Colonists brought petitioning with them from the United Kingdom, and colonial governments, revolutionary period and postrevolutionary state governments, and the federal government in its first forty years of existence all took petitions and petitioning very seriously. However, in the 1830s, legislative attitudes toward petitioning changed drastically, not only in the United States, but also in the United Kingdom, and an important aspect of the right of petition—the duty of a legislative body to respond on the merits to a properly presented petition—fell into desuetude in both nations.

Although there is always some danger in oversimplifying the causes of radical legal and political changes, it seems safe to say that in the United Kingdom, Chartist efforts to promote universal suffrage and annual elections (among other Chartist agenda items) precipitated Parliament's decision to cease taking petitions seriously as a means of achieving legislative changes in public policy. In the United States, petitions seeking the abolition of slavery in the District of Columbia had the same effect, more or less contemporaneously with Parliament's decision to cease considering and responding to petitions on the merits.

One might question, in fact, whether a political culture that relies on petitioning remains viable in modern society. After all, in an age of universal suffrage and immediate access to mass audiences via the Internet, is a classically eighteenth-century form of political expression still plausible or even potentially relevant to contemporary politics and governing? Commentators in both the United States and the United Kingdom have, since the 1950s, relegated petitioning in its classic form to little more than an interesting historical footnote. As it happens, however, New Zealand maintains an active petitioning culture, and its example suggests that, contrary to the assumptions of legal scholars and historians writing about petitioning in the United States and the United Kingdom as a dead letter, it would be possible to maintain a functioning petitioning culture in the twenty-first century.

In my view, there is precious little reason to believe that relitigating speech, assembly, and association claims in the future will secure meaningful judicial protection for the expression of dissent directly to incumbent government officials; instead, would-be protestors must demonstrate a constitutional interest in their preferred audience. Chapter 5 presents an extended argument that the Petition Clause can and should serve to support such a claim; this chapter also considers the doctrinal implications of a renewed commitment to enforcing the Petition Clause.[71] At a minimum, the Petition Clause means that average citizens must enjoy meaningful access to government officials to express support or opposition to government policies for which the officers bear some measure of responsibility.

At the outset, I will concede that my argument focuses more on a hybrid right than exclusively on the right of petition by itself: the conflation of petitioning with the exercise of speech, assembly, and association rights. When citizens exercise their speech, assembly, and association rights for the purpose of petitioning for a redress of grievances, federal courts should recognize a First Amendment interest in access to a particular audience, namely, government officials and senior political party leaders. Moreover, this access to government officials must be susceptible to coverage by the mass media if it is to facilitate a broader discussion and engagement of the issues raised by the petitioners within the polity, an essential condition if petitioning is to return to its former importance as a means of direct democratic action.

In thinking about how a reclaimed Petition Clause might actually work in practice, Judge Johnson's iconic opinion in *Williams v. Wallace*[72] serves as an ideal case study of the proposed hybrid right to engage in "petitioning speech."[73] When would-be speakers seek to engage in petitioning speech in a traditional public forum, the presumption should be that government has an obligation to accommodate the expressive conduct, even if doing so requires government to address and resolve potential security issues. If local law enforcement and the Secret Service can successfully screen the tens of thousands of persons who attend mass rallies in professional sports arenas, as was the case for Barack Obama's nomination acceptance speech at Invesco Field, home of the Denver Broncos NFL football team franchise, which is capable of seating more than seventy-five thousand persons, it stands to reason that it must be possible also to screen some finite number of protestors who wish to communicate their views to the delegates, public officials, and party leaders attending the event.

By reclaiming the Petition Clause and its promise of access to those who hold government power, we may restore the ability of average people to speak truth, at least as they understand it, to power. Make no mistake: confronting power in public is a powerful means of challenging the status quo and provoking wider discussions of the wisdom of government policies. Anyone who has seen the iconic image of the Chinese student protestor confronting an army tank in Tiananmen Square, during the 1989 student uprising, understands how even a single person's message of dissent can reverberate powerfully within the national, and indeed global, marketplace of ideas.

Properly theorized and operationalized, petitioning involves access and engagement not only between petitioners and government officials but also engagement more broadly within the larger political community. Petitioning once served as a means of generating national conversations on such topics as slavery, women's suffrage, Prohibition, and even federal income taxation. In the nineteenth century, the media's participation in the petitioning process was an important, indeed essential, part of the process of civic engagement. To deny or impede the mass media's ability to report to the larger community on petitioning activity is to compromise, perhaps fatally, petitioning's function as a means of generating broad based civic conversation about important questions of the day.[74]

Consider, for example, the effect of Gillian Duffy's public criticism in the United Kingdom of the Labour Party's policies on immigration, which she expressed directly to a clearly startled Prime Minister Gordon Brown on national television.[75] Mr. Brown subsequently referred to Ms. Duffy as a "bigot" and railed at his staff members over the embarrassing public confrontation, telling them: "You should never have put me with that woman."[76] "Speaking while unaware that his comments were being broadcast live on television, Mr. Brown snapped at aides over being put in the 'ridiculous' situation of meeting a member of the public who disagreed with him."[77] Although one should hesitate before ascribing fundamental importance to a single event in a national political campaign, this gaffe plainly undermined Brown's chances for reelection. Democracy is enhanced, not degraded, when incumbent government officials have to defend their policies and priorities, not only to a single petitioner or group of petitioners, but to the body politic as a whole. For this to occur, however, the media must play an active role as a conduit of the fact of petitioning speech activity, of dissent from the government's policies and priorities, to the larger political community.

In sum, the Petition Clause once had coequal status with voting as a fundamental means of securing accountability from government officials—starting with British monarchs and running forward through history to thin-skinned Federalist Party presidents. We have lost this tradition and we must reclaim it. Petitioning for a redress of grievances, up close and personal, is a central bulwark of ensuring that, in a representative democracy, the rulers actually know what the citizenry thinks about particular questions of public policy.

When government officials, with the blessing of the federal courts, come to view average citizens seeking to petition the government for new or different policies as presumptive terrorist threats and, in consequence, banish these citizens to remotely located cages and pens that are little more than jails, the notion of democratic self-governance has been utterly and completely betrayed. The Petition Clause offers a new way of thinking about the question of citizen access to government officials and an important means of renewing and enhancing American democracy.

The Growing Loss of Public Space for Collective Expression of Dissent and the Failure of Contemporary First Amendment Doctrine to Address This Problematic Phenomenon

I. INTRODUCTION: THE ACCELERATING LOSS OF PUBLIC SPACE FOR COLLECTIVE EXPRESSIONS OF DISSENT TO GOVERNMENT OFFICIALS

In anticipation of hosting the 2004 Democratic National Convention (DNC), then only days away, the city of Boston erected a temporary structure nicknamed "the DZ." Disquieting, yet oddly fitting, the moniker was short for "designated demonstration zone," the area set aside as the only lawful place proximate to the Fleet Center, site of the DNC, for groups of more than twenty to engage in political protest speech.[1] Judge Woodlock, the district court judge who heard the First Amendment challenge to this speech restriction, described the DZ as follows:

> A written description cannot begin to convey the ambience of the DZ site. . . . Most—at least two-thirds—of the DZ lies under unused Green Line tracks. The tracks create a space redolent of the sensibility conveyed in Piranesi's etchings published as *Fanciful Images of Prisons.* It is a grim, mean, and oppressive space whose ominous roof is supported by a forest of girders that obstruct sight lines throughout . . . .
>
> The DZ is surrounded by two rows of concrete jersey barriers. Atop each of the jersey barriers is an eight foot high chain link fence. A tightly woven mesh fabric, designed to prevent liquids and objects from being thrown through the fence, covers the outer fence, limiting but not eliminating visibility. From the top of the outer fence to the train tracks overhead, at an angle of approximately forty-five degrees to horizontal, is a looser mesh netting, designed to prevent objects from being thrown at the delegates.

On the overhead Green Line tracks themselves is looped razor wire, designed to prevent persons from climbing onto the tracks where armed police and National Guardsman [*sic*] will be located.[2]

As if there could be any mistake, Judge Woodlock added, "Let me be clear: the design of the DZ is an offense to the spirit of the First Amendment."[3]

He then upheld the city's use of the DZ.[4]

Several days later, the U.S. Court of Appeals for the First Circuit affirmed.[5]

What can explain the bizarre circumstance of a speech regulation that is simultaneously both constitutional and "an offense to the spirit of the First Amendment"? Facially, the city of Boston claimed, and the lower federal courts accepted, the proposition that bona fide security needs justified the remarkably broad restrictions on protests conducted physically proximate to the 2004 DNC. Even though "security is not a talisman," the First Circuit ruled that "[w]e do not believe that a per se rule of barring the government from using past experience to plan for future events is consistent with the Court's time-place-manner jurisprudence."[6] Despite the lack of any concrete evidence that those seeking to protest at the 2004 DNC would engage in any unlawful activity, the court endorsed forcing would-be protestors to remain in a cage of chain-link fencing topped with razor wire, separated from the delegates by an opaque mesh wall, as a reasonable time, place, and manner restriction because other protestors, in other cities, seeking to advance other causes, engaged in unlawful behavior.[7]

In some respects, it is unfortunate that Governors George C. Wallace of Alabama, Orval Faubus of Arkansas, and Eugene Talmadge of Georgia did not have the benefit of the incumbent First Circuit bench as the local federal judges during the civil rights era. For, on the very same logic, the mass protests of the American civil rights movement could have been shut down or entirely marginalized on the theory that the protests or some number of the protestors might break the law.[8] The actions of the radical few, such as the Black Panther Party, could have been taxed against the nonviolent many in a form of mindless guilt by association.[9] Yet the First Circuit is hardly alone in permitting local governments to engage in broad-based guilt by association. The Ninth Circuit and a local Seattle district court followed the same logic to sustain a virtual ban on all protests proximate to a World Trade Organization meeting, regardless of whether any credible evidence existed to support the notion that a particular group of protestors would engage in unlawful conduct. Remarkably, the Ninth Circuit went even further and seemed to endorse the city's concerns that the protests might adversely affect the positive public relations benefits that might otherwise be garnered from hosting such a prestigious international group.[10]

Even though the Supreme Court has not itself directly addressed the issue, the verdict from the lower federal courts is clear: local governments may adopt draconian speech restrictions to ensure that mass political meetings do not result in mixed media messages—at least if they adopt them in the name of advancing interests rooted in "security."[11] If a city wishes to silence those opposed to the official meeting sponsors, it may do so, provided that it banishes all speakers (at least as a formal matter). As I explain in this chapter, the doctrinal requirement of content neutrality and viewpoint neutrality is easily met, even in circumstances where speech restrictions appear to be adopted in order to target specific viewpoints.[12]

Other important aspects of the *Ward v. Rock Against Racism* test, including the narrow tailoring and ample alternative channels of communication requirements, do not seem to prevent the adoption of speech bans on public property either.[13] Indeed, fairly obvious forms of viewpoint discrimination, because they are cloaked in the sheep's clothing of a generic time, place, and manner regulation, routinely pass constitutional muster in circumstances where the basis for the government regulation, invariably vague "security" concerns, plainly borders on naked pretext. These decisions demonstrate concretely the abject failure of the Supreme Court's traditional time, place, and manner jurisprudence to protect core political speech of a dissenting cast.

To be sure, the scholarly commentators addressing these decisions to date unanimously have deplored them.[14] It is rare indeed when the scholarly community speaks in such a clear, unified voice. Yet, decisions continue to grow in the lower federal courts permitting abstract, entirely hypothetical security concerns to justify what Judge Woodlock described as "a space redolent of the sensibility conveyed in Piranesi's etchings published as *Fanciful Images of Prisons.*"[15] Moreover, federal court challenges to limits placed on protests near the 2008 Democratic National Convention, in Denver, Colorado, and the 2008 Republican National Convention, in St. Paul, Minnesota, both failed to secure any meaningful relief in the form of enhanced access to the government officials, party leaders, and delegates attending those meetings.[16]

Although the matter is not entirely free from doubt, the scholarly pleas for federal courts to enforce the traditional *Ward* content-neutral, reasonable time, place, and manner regime seem doomed to failure.[17] Experience teaches that federal judges—faced with abstract claims that failure to endorse cages guarded by razor wire will lead to public chaos—are simply not going to apply the narrow tailoring requirement in a more demanding fashion or require a higher degree of equivalence with respect to "ample alternative channels of communication."[18] Instead, if core political speech proximate to public officials and senior political party officials is to survive, more than mere doctrinal tinkering around the edges is needed. Simply put, the playing field must be reset to resemble something closer to level.

As explained in subsequent chapters, the best means of reorienting the decisional logic of the lower federal courts would be to relocate the right to protest at events featuring government officials and senior party leaders from the Speech and Assembly Clauses to the Petition Clause.[19] The Petition Clause, it is true, has become something of a constitutional appendix. Most contemporary casebooks on the First Amendment do not bother to provide the Petition Clause with any independent coverage,[20] and the main constitutional law treatises treat the Petition Clause as a dead letter. There is no good reason why this should be so. Just as each and every part of the Fifth Amendment and the Fourteenth Amendment enjoy individualized exegesis,[21] there is no good reason why any independent clause of the First Amendment, including the Petition Clause, should fall into total desuetude.

Chapter 2 considers in some detail the formal First Amendment doctrines that ostensibly work to prevent the use of government power to squelch dissent based on its content and viewpoint, as well as the general rule against prior restraints. It concludes that, at least in the context of protest physically proximate to government and party officials, these doctrines are incapable of securing more than a modicum of protection for those seeking to petition the government for a redress of grievances.

II. A GENERAL REVIEW OF FIRST AMENDMENT JURISPRUDENCE RELATED TO GOVERNMENT REGULATION OF SPEECH BOTH GENERALLY AND ON PUBLIC PROPERTY

In theory, the First Amendment provides remarkably broad protection for core political speech—even speech of a strongly dissenting cast.[22] To some extent this proposition does hold true. Thus, in the post–*Brandenburg v. Ohio* era, as a general proposition, one may advocate the violent overthrow of the government without facing criminal sanctions.[23] But protecting meaningless abstract advocacy does not go very far in protecting speech when the government thinks that the speech might actually matter (i.e., have some serious effect on shaping or moving public opinion). Permitting a group of racist lunatics to inveigh against the government on a remote suburban Cincinnati, Ohio, farm is one thing.[24] Protecting speech that contradicts the president's "message of the day" is quite another. The federal courts—at least the lower federal courts— have not proven to be consistent allies of those engaged in dissenting speech, at least in contexts where dissent might prove embarrassing to the government (whether local, state, or federal).[25]

The resulting free speech jurisprudence features a very wide gap between the theoretical commitment to protecting dissent and the real-world commitment to protecting dissent in certain contexts. This part explores both sides of the equation: the formal, theoretical commitment to protecting political speech on the broadest possible basis and the countervailing de facto regime of suppression that exists in some important contexts. To be clear, I do not insist on a particular normative outcome with respect to the toleration of speech that imposes (or might impose) high social costs. It does seem reasonable, however, to ask for a jurisprudence that treats risk in a consistent fashion: if average citizens must tolerate the social risks associated with the public dissemination of racist, sexist, homophobic, and religiously bigoted speech, it seems odd to sustain rules that have the effect (and perhaps purpose) of protecting incumbent politicians from public embarrassment.[26]

A. The Theory: The First Amendment Conveys Robust Protection on Even Highly Offensive or Potentially Dangerous Speech Without Regard to Viewpoint or Content

Since 1969 (or perhaps 1964),[27] the Supreme Court of the United States has generally disallowed the regulation of core political speech because it poses risks to peace, good order, and security. The pre-*Brandenburg* free speech jurisprudence, represented by decisions like *Dennis v. United States*,[28] permitted government to regulate speech based on the possibility that speech might have "bad tendencies."[29] The "bad tendencies" doctrine tracks the intellectual foundations of the doctrine of seditious libel; seditious libel was a form of constructive treason, constructive because the speaker or writer might not directly call for the overthrow of the government but engaged in speech or publishing that government feared might increase the possibility of such an outcome.[30] *Brandenburg* put to rest the idea that government could squelch speech if the risk of harm, however remote, was of a sufficiently grave character.[31]

1. The Rules Against Viewpoint and Content Discrimination

The Supreme Court has built two central pillars to ensure that government does not regulate or suppress speech on a merely pretextual basis. The first, and most absolute, is a rule against government regulations based on the viewpoint of the speaker. Thus, government may not permit pro-choice speakers to hold a rally in the public square while denying pro-life advocates access to the same public space for a rally advocating their position on abortion. As Professor Cass

Sunstein has explained, "[w]hen government regulates on the basis of viewpoint, it will frequently be acting for objectionable reasons."[32]

The second, somewhat less categorical, doctrinal pillar on which modern free speech doctrine rests is the rule against content discrimination. As a general matter, government may not exclude particular subjects or topics (regardless of viewpoint) from the marketplace of ideas. Thus, government could not prohibit discussion of immigration issues in the public square simply because it feared that any discussion of immigration policy might lead to "trouble" (i.e., public disorder or violence).

What do these doctrines mean for the dignity of public officials and officers? At least in theory, government cannot suppress speech based on its content, even if that content is highly offensive and constitutes a targeted insult of a government officer. It also means that government must tolerate potentially dangerous speech—speech that could cause public unrest or anger, perhaps because of its viewpoint (e.g., a pro–Al Qaeda rally near the World Trade Center site) or because of its content (e.g., a rally includes the use of offensive words and phrases, including strong profanity). The dignity of the government and its minions must give way to the paramount value of full and free political expression.[33] Moreover, the state must assume some risk to peace and public order as the price of a vibrant and functioning public marketplace of ideas.[34] Hence, the First Amendment affords constitutional protection if one were to call a police officer a "motherfucking pig" or hurl the f-bomb at the local school board president at a public meeting.[35] Or, as Dr. Ben Marble did post Hurricane Katrina in Gulfport, Mississippi, tell the vice president of the United States to "go fuck yourself."[36]

Why should such uncivil public discourse enjoy constitutional protection? Because the motivation to ban the speech relates directly to viewpoint and content: the motivation to punish relates to the dissenting character of the speech (few are arrested for telling the president, "Fucking A on bombing those terrorists!") and because the content of the speech, the use of vulgar idiom, leads to selective punishment, often under generic laws against disturbing the peace.[37] Core principles of U.S. free speech doctrine preclude the government from restricting speech because of antipathy toward its viewpoint or banning speech because of its content. And, in most cases involving average citizens or low-level government functionaries, these commitments hold firm.[38]

Beyond this, the doctrines work to protect low-value, high-risk speech, such as calls to race wars or the extermination of particular religious, racial, or sexual orientation minorities. Since *Beauharnais*[39] and *Dennis*,[40] both decided in the 1950s, the Supreme Court essentially has told minority groups to meet hate speech with counterspeech, rather than to seek government proscriptions against generic threats that lack an imminent risk of producing harm. Federal courts have been consistent and vigilant in disallowing laws aimed at protecting minorities from offense based on the viewpoint or content of speech.[41]

Thus, at a formal level of abstraction, the Free Speech Clause privileges speech over the dignity interests of public officials and public figures, and also over the security interests of minority groups. The nation's commitment to an "uninhibited, robust, and wide-open"[42] public debate requires that both high government officers and average citizens pay the social cost of highly offensive speech activity, even activity overtly designed to cause offense.[43]

2. The Rule Against Prior Restraints

Although related to the rules against viewpoint and content discrimination, a separate legal doctrine generally disallows the use of prior restraints on speech. Indeed, prior restraints are presumptively void.[44] Government cannot ban speech before the fact, even for good reasons, like national security. The proscription against prior restraints has a long and deep history, running back to Blackstone's conception of "the" freedom of speech (which was limited to a categorical ban on prior restraints and a rule against licensure of the press).[45]

As other legal commentators have noted,[46] however, the rule against prior restraints is less absolute in actual contemporary practice than it is in theory. Here's why: the Supreme Court's doctrine regarding content neutral, reasonable time, place, and manner restrictions on speech taking place on government property sanctions a great deal of prior restraint. In other words, for government to regulate speech activity before the fact, incident to a time, place, and manner scheme, is to say that government may enact prior restraints against speech that fails to meet the requirements of the regulatory rules. The Supreme Court has never explained why reasonable time, place, and manner restrictions do not constitute a form of prior restraint, but has instead simply argued from necessity that civic life could hardly go on without some reasonable limits on the use of public spaces for expressive activity.[47]

The aggressive use of time, place, and manner restrictions can do more than simply regulate speech—the doctrine opens up the possibility of actually banishing speech from inconvenient venues (from the government's perspective) to more convenient venues (again from the government's perspective). The problem, of course, is that the convenience of a venue might reflect censorial motives as much as legitimate regulatory concerns about traffic flow or preserving a public park as a place of peace, quiet, and rest. The only protection against the use of time, place, and manner restrictions as a means of silencing unpopular speakers is the requirement of content neutrality. Yet, the federal courts, including the Supreme Court, routinely have required only facial, or superficial, content neutrality in order to find this requirement satisfied.[48]

B. The Standards Governing Time, Place, and Manner Restrictions Provide Insufficient Protection for Dissenting Speech and Assembly

As the Supreme Court explained in *Ward v. Rock Against Racism*: "[E]ven in a public forum the government may impose reasonable restrictions on the time, place, or manner of protected speech, provided the restrictions 'are justified without reference to the content of the regulated speech, that they are narrowly tailored to serve a significant government interest, and that they leave open ample alternative channels for communication of the information.'"[49] On its face, the time, place, and manner doctrine appears fairly protective of free speech. A standard of review that is, in essence, intermediate scrutiny presents a high bar indeed. As the doctrine has evolved over time, however, the criteria set forth by the Supreme Court often present the government with only minor impediments—mere speed bumps along the path to suppression of even core political speech at times, and in places, that might be inconvenient at best and terribly embarrassing at worst.[50] "[W]hat once were rules to protect speech [have] now become rules to restrict it."[51]

1. Existing Time, Place, and Manner Rules Underprotect Speech and Assembly

There are two principal ways in which the time, place, and manner doctrine is less protective of speech than first appears. The first is in the requirement of "narrow tailoring."[52] As the Court explained in *Ward*, in the context of time, place, and manner restrictions, "narrowly tailored" is not synonymous with "least restrictive means."[53] "Rather, the requirement of narrow tailoring is satisfied 'so long as [the] regulation promotes a substantial government interest that would be achieved less effectively absent the regulation.' . . . So long as the means chosen are not substantially broader than necessary to achieve the government's interest . . . the regulation will not be invalid simply because a court concludes that the government's interest could be adequately served by some less-speech-restrictive alternative."[54] Redefining "narrow" to mean "not substantially broader than necessary" clearly weakens the facially stringent requirement of narrow tailoring, but that is not the end of the story. According to the *Ward* Court, lower courts must give deference to the government's own "reasonable determination" of how its interest will best be achieved.[55]

The practical effect of these principles on the requirement of narrow tailoring was aptly summarized by Justice Marshall, writing in dissent in *Ward*: "The majority thus instructs courts to refrain from examining how much speech may be restricted to serve an asserted interest and how that level of restriction is to be achieved. If a court cannot engage in such inquiries, I am at a loss to understand how a court can ascertain whether the government has adopted a regulation that burdens substantially more speech than is necessary."[56]

Perhaps even more invidious than the substantial weakening of the narrow tailoring requirement is the Supreme Court's application of the rule against content (and viewpoint) discrimination.[57] The strictness with which the Court polices this rule is vital to the protection of speech activity because the presence or absence of content neutrality determines the level of scrutiny to which a speech restriction will be subjected.[58] Regrettably, the Court's application of the neutrality requirement reflects a pattern of willful blindness.[59]

2. The Supreme Court's Inconsistent Application of the Content Neutrality Rule

The "fundamental principle" underlying the neutrality requirement appears highly protective of speech: the "government may not grant the use of a forum to people whose views it finds acceptable, but deny use to those wishing to express less favored or more controversial views."[60] Yet despite the seemingly strict requirement of neutrality, a speech regulation may be found "content-neutral" regardless of its discriminatory real-world effects or the government's discriminatory intent in enacting it.[61]

For example, in *Hill v. Colorado*,[62] the Court considered a Colorado statute making it a misdemeanor for a person to "knowingly approach another person within eight feet of such person . . . for the purpose of passing a leaflet or hand-bill to, displaying a sign to, or engaging in oral protest, education, or counseling with such other person . . . within a radius of one hundred feet from any entrance door to a health care facility."[63] The legislative history of the statute strongly suggested that highly visible and highly unpopular antiabortion protests near family planning clinics offering abortion services largely, if not entirely, motivated the Colorado legislature's enactment of the law. Applying the *Ward* standard, the majority held that the statute was content neutral (and therefore subject to intermediate rather than strict scrutiny) for two principal reasons.[64] First, the majority relied on the Colorado courts' construction of the statute and their interpretation of the legislative history to conclude that "it was not adopted 'because of disagreement with the message [protesting near health care facilities] convey[ed].'"[65] Second, and most important, the majority argued that "the State's interests in protecting access and [patients'] privacy, and providing the police with clear guidelines, are unrelated to the content of the demonstrators' speech."[66] The majority then went on to apply intermediate scrutiny, upholding the statute as narrowly tailored to serve a significant government interest and leaving open ample alternative channels of communication.[67]

Only from a purely theoretical level, however, can one say that a ban on abortion clinic picketing is content neutral and viewpoint neutral; if a pro-choice group wished to picket a clinic to support abortion rights, such a picket would fall within the proscription. Yet, we all know that pro-choice groups simply do not picket women's health clinics. To call the Colorado statute content neutral requires willful blindness of a sort not used in other areas of the law, such as equal protection, where the Supreme Court routinely looks behind the face of the law to seek out discriminatory intent. Where discriminatory intent motivates a law with discriminatory effects, the law is subject to heightened judicial scrutiny, even if it is otherwise facially neutral.[68] In contrast, the Supreme Court's formulaic application of the content neutrality requirement ignores both the intent of the enacters and the real-world effects of the law.

This practice, if not gutting the content neutrality requirement, surely undermines it a great deal. Is it plausible to think that if a school board under a desegregation order simply voted to close the public schools (denying children of all races access to public educational facilities) that the Supreme Court would not look behind the face of the law to the intent of the board and the effect of the law? We need not engage in mere speculation to answer this question—the Supreme Court would not hesitate to disallow such a change in policy.[69]

Turner Broadcasting System, Inc. v. FCC[70] provides another example of the Court's willful blindness toward content discrimination. *Turner* concerned Sections 4 and 5 of the Cable Television Consumer Protection and Competition Act of 1992,[71] which Congress enacted in response to concern that cable television was "endangering the ability of over-the-air broadcast television stations to compete for a viewing audience and thus for necessary operating revenues."[72] Among other things, the act required cable systems to set aside up to one-third of their channels to carry any local broadcast television stations requesting carriage.[73] The dissent succinctly summarized the issue in *Turner*: "There are only so many channels that any cable system can carry. If there are fewer channels than programmers who want to use the system, some programmers will have to be dropped. . . . By reserving a little over one-third of the channels on a cable system for broadcasters, [Congress] ensured that, in most cases, it will be a cable programmer who is dropped and a broadcaster who is retained. The question presented in this case is whether this choice comports with the commands of the First Amendment."[74]

As in *Hill*, the resolution to the First Amendment question in *Turner* turned on whether or not the provisions were content neutral and therefore subject to only intermediate scrutiny. The majority reasoned that "[n]othing in the Act imposes a restriction, penalty, or burden by reason of the views, programs, or stations the cable operator has selected," and that the burden imposed on cable programmers by virtue of the reduction in the number of available cable channels "is unrelated to content, for it extends to all cable programmers irrespective of the programming they choose to offer viewers."[75] As a result, the majority held that "the must-carry rules, *on their face*, impose burdens and confer benefits without reference to the content of speech" and are therefore subject only to intermediate scrutiny.[76]

Once again, the Court's finding of content neutrality flew in the face of reality. After reciting the laundry list of justifications for the act, as stated in the act itself, Justice O'Connor concluded: "Preferences for diversity of viewpoints, for localism, for educational programming, and for news and public affairs all make reference to content. They may not reflect hostility to particular points of view, or a desire to suppress certain subjects because they are controversial or offensive. . . . But benign motivation, we have consistently held, is not enough to avoid the need for strict scrutiny of content-based justifications."[77] Even if the majority correctly construed Sections 4 and 5 as facially content neutral, a dubious proposition to begin with, Congress's findings, codified as part of the act itself, make clear that the intent and likely actual effects of the act are not only content based, they are also viewpoint based, in that they prefer local points of view over national ones: "The interest in ensuring access to a multiplicity of diverse and antagonistic sources of information . . . is directly tied to the content of what the speakers will likely say."[78]

To its credit, the majority in *Turner* did acknowledge that "even a regulation neutral on its face may be content based if its manifest purpose is to regulate speech because of the message it conveys."[79] After unpersuasively attempting to distinguish the congressional findings, however, the majority found no such manifest purpose in the challenged regulations.[80] Thus, the Supreme Court subjected the must carry regulations to only intermediate scrutiny, despite Congress's clearly discriminatory intent and the benefit conferred on one group of speakers (local broadcasters) at the expense of others (cable programmers).

3. *Ward* Makes It Relatively Easy for Government to Restrict Speech in Ways That Limit Access to Intended Audiences

Between the relaxed application of the narrow tailoring requirement and the willful blindness associated with application of the content neutrality requirement, the Supreme Court has greatly eroded the time, place, and manner doctrine's bulwark against government regulation of disfavored or unpopular speech. To be clear, this does not mean that government may proscribe speech it does not like; rather, it means that government can use its ability to regulate access to public spaces to limit access to times and places when dissenting speech will be less likely to be noticed. Thus, if one wishes to communicate with women considering having an abortion, a blanket ban on protest on public streets and sidewalks proximate to a reproductive health clinic, during the hours of operation, might pass constitutional muster on the theory that all speech, regardless of content or viewpoint, has been banished, and the regulation leaves open ample alternative public spaces, away from the family planning clinics, in which to express the same message.

Provided that government is willing to restrict all speakers alike, the time, place, and manner doctrine, as explicated in *Ward* and subsequent cases, imposes relatively few absolute limits on such regulations. And the weak application of the content neutrality rule means that proscribing speech at particular times and places passes First Amendment scrutiny, even if the effects of the regulation fall disproportionately on one group of would-be speakers, such as pro-life demonstrators outside a family planning clinic, or antiwar demonstrators outside the 2008 Republican National Convention. Pro-choice advocates simply do not picket abortion clinics, and pro-Republican citizens do not protest outside GOP national nominating conventions.

As the cases discussed in the next section demonstrate, with respect to at least one form of core political expression—dissent proximate to the national presidential nominating conventions, presidential appearances, and major international meetings—the dam has now burst under the added weight of the government's post-9/11 interest in security. The result has been not only government regulation but also criminalization of disfavored speech in what is, in effect, a qualified return to the law of seditious libel.

III. FREE SPEECH AS HOSTAGE TO SECURITY CONCERNS

In *Hill*, Justice Scalia was of the opinion that the Court's exceptionally weak application of the time, place, and manner requirements in that case was more a result-oriented product of the pro-abortion rights views of the majority than a principled attempt to apply First Amendment doctrine.[81] As he boldly asserted, "I have no doubt that this regulation would be deemed content based *in an instant* if the case before us involved antiwar protestors."[82] The Supreme Court has yet to test his hypothesis, but if the decisions of the federal circuit courts are any indication, Justice Scalia was woefully mistaken. Indeed, nowhere have the weaknesses of the time, place, and manner doctrine been exploited in a more striking or troubling fashion than in recent U.S. courts of appeals decisions upholding total bans on protest activity of *all* stripes proximate to national and international political events.

Such bans on protest speech take the form of "no-protest zones" or "free speech zones" and occur at large-scale political events, such as presidential appearances and the quadrennial Democratic and Republican National Conventions.[83] Orchestrated by local law enforcement, often with the participation or at the direction of the U.S. Secret Service,[84] no-protest and free speech zones are a fairly recent phenomenon, appearing to date back to the 1988 Democratic National Convention in Atlanta.[85] Sometimes these zones are simply designated areas that otherwise appear completely open; at their worst, they are virtual cages, like the designated protest zone in *Bl(a)ck Tea Society.*[86]

Protest activity within a no-protest zone or outside a free speech zone is forbidden and subjects violators to criminal sanctions. Although these speech restrictions are ostensibly content neutral, the evidence is virtually indisputable that they are often used to marginalize petitioning speech by physically moving protestors away from an event and, hence, making media coverage of the protest much less likely.[87] This suppression of dissent is, however, decidedly nonpartisan[88] and is invariably justified by reference to the government's undeniably strong interest in the security of these large-scale national and international political events.[89]

Given the weakness of the Supreme Court's application of the time, place, and manner doctrine, protestors seeking to challenge the use of no-protest and free speech zones have always been at a disadvantage in the courts. However, since the 1999 riots at the World Trade Organization conference in Seattle and, especially, the 9/11 terrorist attacks in New York City and Washington, D.C., the governmental interest in security has become a virtual blank check for the imposition of total speech bans and the use of degrading limits on legitimate protest activity.[90] Although protestor plaintiffs have occasionally succeeded at the trial level,[91] the federal appellate courts have been unanimous in upholding even the most egregious uses of no-protest and free speech zones as reasonable time, place, and manner regulations, as illustrated by the cases discussed below. Moreover, the most recent cases, arising from limits on protests and marches at the 2008 national presidential nominating conventions, have simply continued this trend.[92]

A. *Bl(a)ck Tea Society v. City of Boston*

In 2004, the First Circuit decided *Bl(a)ck Tea Society v. City of Boston*, which arose out of the "designated protest zone" created for the 2004 Democratic National Convention.[93] The appalling character of "the DZ" was detailed earlier in this chapter;[94] suffice it to say here that the DZ was, as the district court stated, "an offense to the spirit of the First Amendment."[95] The district court had nonetheless upheld Boston's use of the DZ, denying the plaintiff's request for an injunction, and the First Circuit affirmed.[96]

In assessing the validity of the DZ as a time, place, and manner regulation, the court quickly dispensed with the requirements of content neutrality, stating without further elaboration that "the challenged security precautions are plainly content-neutral and there can be no doubting the substantial government interest in the maintenance of security at political conventions."[97] The court did not address the practical reality that the DZ would house far more anti–Democratic Party demonstrators than pro–Democratic Party demonstrators.[98]

Proceeding to the narrow tailoring requirement, the court acknowledged that the DZ "dramatically limited the possibilities for communicative intercourse between the demonstrators and the delegates."[99] And even though the court stated that "[s]ecurity is not a talisman that the government may invoke to justify *any* burden on speech (no matter how oppressive)," it nevertheless affirmed the district court's determination that the DZ was narrowly tailored.[100]

The court then turned to the appellant's contention that there were no other alternative channels of communication "within sight and sound of the delegates assembled at the Fleet Center [the site of the convention]."[101] The court addressed this issue only indirectly. First, the court noted (without citing any authority) that "there is no constitutional requirement" that demonstrators be granted direct access to the delegates "by, say, moving among them and distributing literature."[102] Even if true, however, this response ignores the vast middle ground of possibilities that lie between the "brutish"[103] DZ and unrestrained one-on-one physical access to convention delegates.

The court's only other answer to the appellant's alternative channels claim was that the claim "greatly underestimates the nature of modern communication."[104] As the court explained, "[a]t a high-profile event, such as the Convention, messages expressed beyond the first-hand sight and sound of the delegates nonetheless have a propensity to reach the delegates through television, radio, the press, the internet, and other outlets."[105] In other words, the plaintiffs lacked a valid constitutional interest in real-time communication with the delegates because the delegates might randomly see a newspaper article or YouTube video post about the protestors and their message. The key doctrinal point here is that the Free Speech and Free Assembly Clauses apparently do not afford *any* protection to a would-be speaker's interest in speaking to a particular audience in real time, even if he seeks to do so by utilizing a classic traditional public forum, such as a street, sidewalk, or park.

The possibility of access to the preferred audience through means other than expressive activity proximate to the convention venue satisfied the First Amendment as interpreted in *Ward*. Finding the ample alternative channels requirement satisfied and the DZ therefore a reasonable time, place, and manner regulation, the court affirmed the district court's denial of an injunction.[106] Moreover, the First Circuit's application of *Ward* seems legally correct: *Ward* simply does not take into account any interest in communicating one-on-one, in real time, with a particular person or group, even if the proposed communication will take place in a classic public forum. This is so because *Ward* focuses on the First Amendment interest in using a particular public space for expressive activity, and not at all on the interest in reaching a particularized audience.

B. Menotti v. City of Seattle

Although protestor riots at the WTO conference in Seattle occurred in 1999, a First Amendment challenge arising from those events did not reach the Ninth Circuit until the 2005 case of *Menotti v. City of Seattle*.[107] Despite the notoriety of the anti-WTO riots at this meeting, one must keep in mind that the vast majority of the protest activity in Seattle was peaceful;[108] nevertheless, violence had broken out as early as three weeks prior to the start of the conference, beginning with a Molotov cocktail attack on a Gap store in downtown Seattle.[109] Violent protest activity continued intermittently until the opening of the conference, at which point it intensified. "The disruption of normal city life was so extreme in some locations that it bordered on chaos."[110]

In response, the mayor of Seattle declared a civil emergency and signed "Local Proclamation of Civil Emergency Order Number 3."[111] "The effect of Order No. 3 was that all persons, subject to limited exceptions, were prohibited from entering the portion of downtown Seattle" surrounding the conference.[112] Within this "restricted zone," which covered twenty-five square blocks in Seattle's downtown core,[113] were the conference sites and the hotels where WTO delegates were staying.[114] Exceptions to the prohibition on entering the restricted zone were granted for WTO delegates and personnel, employees and owners of businesses within the restricted area, and members of the press, among others.[115] The practical effect of these exceptions, as well as the manner in which the local police enforced the restrictions created by Order No. 3, was that only protestors were prevented from entering the restricted zone.[116]

In *Menotti v. City of Seattle*, persons who had been arrested for violating the restricted zone sought "damages for the constitutional rights that were alleged to be violated by the emergency order."[117] The district court had granted the defendants' motion for summary judgment, and the Ninth Circuit affirmed, upholding Order No. 3 as a constitutional time, place, and manner restriction on speech.[118]

To do so, the Ninth Circuit first found that the order was content neutral.[119] Because *Ward* requires only facial neutrality, the court had little difficulty finding that the city's policy met this requirement.[120] Again, as interpreted and applied by the Supreme Court and lower federal courts, the content neutrality requirement can be satisfied with obviously pretextual blanket prohibitions on speech; the fact that groups with a particular viewpoint are likely to be the only persons affected by particular temporary speech regulations (including the creation of speech bans on public property otherwise constituting a traditional public forum) simply does not matter to the analysis.

The court then considered whether Order No. 3 was narrowly tailored to serve a significant government interest. The focus of the court's inquiry into Seattle's interest was on the city's clearly significant interest in safety and maintaining public order.[121] Several times in its opinion, however, the court also argued that the city had a significant interest in attracting the future business of international conferences, stating at one point that "[t]he City also had an interest in seeing that the WTO delegates had the opportunity to conduct their business at the chosen venue for the conference; a city that failed to achieve this interest would not soon have the chance to host another important international meeting."[122] To suggest that such an interest is significant is to suggest that it has the potential to outweigh First Amendment speech rights. One has to wonder whether an interest in attracting occasional convention business can ever carry such weight.[123]

Surely a city's interest in avoiding "bad press" cannot count as a "significant government interest" under *Ward*, yet, in this instance, it appears that the *Menotti* court considered it a potentially valid "significant government interest" in adopting a massive no-protest zone in the heart of downtown Seattle. Clearly, few mass protests are likely to make a city *more* desirable as a potential convention site, and this is doubly so when a major convention is itself the object of the protest activity. Thus, if the potential economic effects of adverse publicity constitute a significant government interest, local governments will have very little, if any, difficulty meeting this aspect of the *Ward* test. Protests are by their very nature disruptive of the community and involve diverting streets and sidewalks from their regular use for the purpose of facilitating expressive conduct.[124] If an interest in avoiding this dislocation can constitute a substantial government interest, this aspect of *Ward* is utterly meaningless as a limit on the ability of government to banish the use of classic public forums for speech activity.

Strictly speaking, the court's application of the narrow tailoring requirement asked whether Order No. 3 was narrowly tailored to serve the city's interest in security, to which the court responded in the affirmative.[125] Most of the court's discussion focused on the expansive size of the no-protest zone, which was justified, according to the court, by the large area over which the WTO delegates were housed, and more important, the fact that the order arose in response to pervasive violence that had already occurred.[126]

Finally, much as in *Bl(a)ck Tea Society*, the court gave short shrift to the ample alternative channels of communication requirement. At best, the evidence was unclear on the existence of alternative channels for use by the peaceful, nonviolent protestors to communicate their message effectively to the WTO delegates and, through the intermediation of the media representatives reporting on the conference, to the body politic at large.[127] Nevertheless, the court found that the ample alternative channels of communication requirement was satisfied and upheld Order No. 3 as a reasonable time, place, and manner regulation.[128]

C. CITIZENS FOR PEACE IN SPACE V. CITY OF COLORADO SPRINGS

As the saying goes, "bad facts make bad law," and that may explain, to at least some extent, the outcomes in *Bl(a)ck Tea Society* and *Menotti*. Unlike most situations in which no-protest and free speech zones are used, the no-protest zone in *Menotti* was established in response to violence that had already begun and was ongoing. Even if Seattle overreached in its reaction to the violence, it is perhaps somewhat understandable that the Ninth Circuit might have been inclined to be forgiving, given the extent of the chaos facing the city. In *Bl(a)ck Tea Society*, both the district and the circuit courts faced very real time limitations in deciding the case. Because the plaintiffs did not file suit seeking an injunction until July 21, 2004, with the DNC scheduled to begin in Boston on July 26, 2004, the case was both tried and appealed in the space of only five days.[129] The effect of this time limitation was addressed in both the district and the circuit court opinions and was at least partially responsible for the extraordinary deference accorded to the city.[130]

The 2007 case *Citizens for Peace in Space v. City of Colorado Springs*,[131] however, presented neither of these disabilities, making it an ideal test case for the application of the time, place, and manner doctrine to security-justified speech restrictions. It is therefore all the more surprising that the Tenth Circuit's decision is the most egregious example yet of a court blindly accepting an asserted, but largely unproven, security interest and applying an unwarranted level of deference to sustain a large no-protest zone in the center of an urban area otherwise open to the public.

The First Amendment claim in *Citizens for Peace in Space* arose out of a conference hosted by the secretary of defense at the historic Broadmoor Hotel in Colorado Springs, Colorado.[132] Invited to the conference were the defense ministers of nineteen member nations of NATO, as well as nine invitee nations.[133] Among the security preparations for the conference was the creation of a large "security zone" that "surrounded the Broadmoor and extended across public and private property for several blocks in all directions."[134] Only persons affiliated with the conference or the Broadmoor, accredited members of the media, and persons residing in the security zone and their guests were allowed inside the zone, all of whom were subjected to screening at security checkpoints on the perimeter of the zone.[135]

The Citizens for Peace in Space are peace activists, whose principal concerns are the militarization of space and the prevention of war, and who sought to hold a six-person, one-hour-long, fixed-point protest vigil across the street from the main conference center.[136] After the city denied their request, the Citizens filed suit, alleging that the prohibition on protesting in a public forum violated their First Amendment rights. The district court found in favor of the city, and the Tenth Circuit affirmed the district court's decision, upholding the security zone as a reasonable time, place, and manner restriction.[137]

Because the Citizens conceded that the city's use of the security zone was content neutral and that its interest in security was significant, the court addressed those factors only briefly. The "primary security concern was the threat of a terrorist attack utilizing explosives. . . . Accordingly, the breadth of the security zone ensured that the blast from any such detonation would not get close enough to the Broadmoor to endanger any of the delegates."[138] The court also credited a security interest based on "the threat posed by disorderly and violent protestors."[139] One must keep in mind, however, that the plaintiffs had sought only a *six-person fixed vigil*; they were not seeking to conduct a mass protest march or picket.[140] Indeed, the amount of law enforcement effort necessary to screen and monitor the proposed six-person vigil was minuscule relative to the security personnel needed to enforce the no-protest zone more generally. Screening and monitoring the proposed vigil would have imposed only the most minimal of additional burdens on local law enforcement services.

Before proceeding to the narrow tailoring requirement, however, the court stated a principle which had been percolating below the surface of such decisions as *Bl(a)ck Tea Society* and *Menotti*, but which no court—certainly not the Supreme Court—had yet been bold enough to make explicit: "[T]he City's security interest is of the highest order and *guides our determination* of whether the security plan was narrowly tailored and whether there were ample alternative channels of communication."[141] Indeed it did, as the court's application of the narrow tailoring and alternative channels requirements makes clear.

In the court's view, the security zone was narrowly tailored simply because it worked.[142] Although the court acknowledged the Supreme Court's statement in *Ward* that "[g]overnment may not regulate expression in such a manner that a substantial portion of the burden on speech does not serve to advance its goals,"[143] its application of that principle completely ignored the previous sentence of *Ward*, which forbids regulations that "burden substantially more speech than is necessary to further the government's legitimate interests."[144] Instead, the court selectively cited Supreme Court precedent to, in effect, suggest that time, place, and manner regulations are *presumptively* narrowly tailored: "[A] restriction 'may not be sustained if it provides only ineffective or remote support for the government's purpose.'"[145] From this skewed perspective, a speech restriction is narrowly tailored if it merely accomplished the government's goals, regardless of how much speech was suppressed in the process.[146]

Having found the narrow tailoring requirement satisfied, the Tenth Circuit then turned to the requirement of ample alternative channels of communication. Relying on *Menotti*, the court brushed aside the clear inadequacy of the alternative of protesting at a great distance from the conference center, delegates, and media representatives: "The ample alternative channels analysis cannot be conducted in an objective vacuum. . . . Thus, we must ask whether, given the particular security threat posed, the geography of the area regulated, and the type of speech desired, there were ample alternative channels of communication. To treat the ample alternative channels analysis as wholly independent disconnects it from reality and diminishes the emphasis courts have traditionally placed on the importance of the government interest."[147] Under this formulation of the ample alternative channels requirement, it was inevitable that the court would find the requirement satisfied, given that "the City's security interest [was] of the highest order and guide[d] [the court's] determination."[148]

Because the Tenth Circuit viewed the security zone as narrowly tailored and leaving open ample alternative channels of communication, it upheld the zone as a reasonable time, place, and manner regulation. Accordingly, the city of

Colorado Springs did not violate the Free Speech and Free Assembly Clauses by refusing to accommodate a fixed protest by six persons across the street from the NATO meeting venue. If such a small-scale protest can be prohibited consistent with *Ward*, plainly *any* and *all* protests may be banished to distant designated protest zones.

Even a single fixed protestor, subject to a background check and security screening, would constitute a security threat, and local law enforcement personnel would be justified in prohibiting the proposed protest. This is so notwithstanding the fact that federal, state, and local law enforcement officers presumably will screen hundreds, if not thousands, of delegates, staff, media representatives, local area workers, and even members of the public seeking to patronize local businesses. The government's claim, reduced to its core, is simply implausible, yet it still seems to satisfy *Ward*. Absent some constitutional interest in access to a particular audience, those seeking to express dissent directly to those holding public office must settle instead for sending an e-mail or writing a letter to the editor of the local newspaper.

D. The Federal District Court Decisions Arising from the 2008 Democratic and Republican National Conventions

The Democratic and Republican National Conventions in 2008 once again led to federal court litigation regarding draconian restrictions on both parades and demonstrations using streets and sidewalks near the convention venues; neither case has yet produced a decision from the court of appeals. The district courts rejected demands for greater access to the delegates through parades and protests closer to the meeting spaces. Neither case incorporates or reflects any new thinking or legal analysis and both, accordingly, simply represent a continuation of the preexisting jurisprudential trend line.

1. *American Civil Liberties Union of Colorado v. City and County of Denver*[149]

The Denver case broke very little new doctrinal ground, even though Denver's approach to suppressing dissent at the 2008 Democratic National Convention was not significantly less zealous than Boston's efforts in 2004—including concentration camp accouterments such as concrete jersey barriers and chain-link fences.[150] Denver also established a very large "protest free zone." The "designated protest zone," it bears noting, although quite large at forty-seven thousand square feet, was essentially composed of a distant parking lot that was literally an Interstate exit or two removed from the Pepsi Center, the site of the convention. At its closest point to one of the delegate entrances, the zone was about two hundred feet, or almost seventy-five yards, distant.[151] Fencing and a buffer zone prevented any possibility of leafleting or direct contact of any kind between a delegate and protestor within the zone.[152] Thus, there was, literally, no chance of delegates or media representatives finding themselves at the designated protest zone unless they were badly lost.

The city also refused to grant parade permits for marches proximate to the Pepsi Center or its grounds. The city-approved parade routes came no closer than 450 feet (i.e., 150 yards) from the Pepsi Center building.[153] Parades would be permitted before and after the DNC sessions, but not during the meeting itself.[154]

The ACLU challenged the security regulations, specifically complaining that the designated protest zone was "outside 'sight and sound' of delegates and the Pepsi Center building itself, render[ing] it an inadequate alternative to offset the closure of some public streets to First Amendment users," and also that the routes, terminus, and timing of protest marches to take place during the DNC minimized, if they did not completely deny, the ability of protestors to deliver their message to the government officials, party leaders, and delegates attending the meeting.[155] The district court sustained all of the restrictions, and did not require any modifications whatsoever.[156]

After reviewing the *Ward* test criteria,[157] and also canvassing other recent federal court decisions involving protests at the national presidential nominating conventions and major government meetings (including *Bl(a)ck Tea Society, Citizens for Peace in Space, Menotti,* and the recent *Coalition to March on the RNC and Stop the War* decision from St. Paul),[158] Judge Marcia Krieger held that Denver's restrictions on both demonstrations and parades were content neutral, advanced a significant government interest in a narrowly tailored way, and left open ample alternative channels of communication.[159]

With respect to the creation of protest free zones and designated protest zones, Judge Krieger found them to be content neutral,[160] justified by a significant interest in security,[161] and narrowly tailored.[162] Regarding the government's interest, she noted that "every court to consider First Amendment challenges in these circumstances has found that the governmental interest in protecting attendees at high-profile political functions and the public in general against terrorist attacks and violent demonstrations is a significant one."[163]

On the question of narrow tailoring, in a particularly distressing analysis, the court pointed out that "[t]he requirement of narrow tailoring does not require, however, that government officials are limited to the development of security measures only in response to specific, known threats, nor that they are required to lay bare their intelligence and assumptions when security measures are challenged."[164] The government's evidence at trial involved general testimony about potential "attacks by explosive devices," including both suicide bombings and the use of motor vehicles to "carry and detonate large amounts of explosives, causing damage to buildings and injury to persons in and around those buildings."[165] Judge Krieger concluded that "[a]lthough the record on this point is less-developed than it might be, the Court finds that there is a sufficient fit between the concern for explosive-based attacks and the closure of some of the streets within the Pepsi Center grounds."[166] Simply put, "the First Amendment does not require the Defendants to create an ideal, or even the least-restrictive, security plan."[167]

The court also rejected the possible alternative of screening persons without credentials who wished to enter public areas comprising or adjacent to the Pepsi Center complex grounds. Its reason: "[S]uch screening would undoubtedly impose significant additional burdens on the Defendants for staffing and equipment," and so "the decision to close the specified streets has been narrowly tailored to fit the substantial governmental interest in protecting buildings and people on the Pepsi Center grounds from the use of explosives and firearms."[168]

Tens of thousands of delegates, guests, and media representatives had to be screened for admission to the Pepsi Center itself; moreover, Barack Obama's acceptance speech took place at Invesco Field at Mile High Stadium, home of the Denver Broncos NFL football team, with a seating capacity of more than seventy thousand persons. Thus, local officials found it possible and feasible to screen more than seventy thousand invited guests and media representatives, but evidently lacked the capacity to screen *any* would-be protestors or demonstrators. This claim simply lacks any credibility; it is not the inability of government but rather a lack of will that prevents the admission of even a single person lacking credentials from the secure zones that surround meeting venues.

The *ACLU* court's rationale for sustaining the speech bans—a generic potential threat of human or vehicular suicide bombers, or persons armed with firearms, or "unruly demonstrators"—exists even when the Democratic National Convention is not in town. If the interest in securing public safety extends to such generic, amorphous antiterrorism claims, the substantial government interest test can be met always and everywhere; it ceases to impose any meaningful limit on the ability of government to close traditional public forums to speech activity. Nor would it take much, if any, creativity to close vast swaths of the urban landscape—bus stops, subways, sidewalks proximate to government buildings or corporate headquarters—to use for protest. Judge Krieger is undoubtedly correct to posit that "one cannot obstruct a street if no one has access to it," but this is an argument that proves far too much.[169]

As with other courts considering challenges of this sort, the *ACLU* court rejected the argument that there is any cognizable First Amendment interest in communicating directly with the delegates, party leaders, or government officials attending the DNC. Judge Krieger emphasized that "on this point, it is important to remember that 'the First Amendment does not guarantee the right to communicate one's views at all times and places or in any manner that may be desired.'"[170]

The ACLU's proposed parade route challenges fared no better, and required considerably less analytical effort on the court's part.[171] The court applied the *Ward* factors and concluded that "given the minimal burdens on speech reflected in the parade-related denials, the parties have ample alternative channels in which they can adequately communicate their messages."[172]

Judge Krieger's opinion adds little (if anything) to the preexisting doctrinal framework, although its recitation and application of decisions like *Bl(a)ck Tea Society* and *Citizens for Peace in Space* has the effect of ossifying both these decisions and their results. With each case denying access to areas proximate to government and political party meeting venues, the next decision sustaining such restrictions becomes that much easier to reach. Perhaps Judge Krieger's biggest contribution (if one may call it that) is her use of the theoretical risk of suicide bombers as a basis for closing public streets and sidewalks to protest. If the United Kingdom, during the times of "the Troubles" with the IRA, had adopted this reasoning, London could effectively have been closed to all protest activity. The irony, of course, is that workers and pedestrians in the no-protest zone present no more, and no less, security risk than would-be protestors, and yet enjoy unfettered access to these same streets and sidewalks during the pendency of the DNC. The notion that these restrictions on speech do not constitute content discrimination or, even more appropriately, overt viewpoint discrimination, requires willful judicial blindness of the very first order.

2. *The Coalition to March on the RNC and Stop the War v. City of St. Paul*[173]

The Coalition to March on the RNC and Stop the War (Coalition) was "an association of groups and individuals interested in parading within sight and sound of the Xcel Energy Center, the site of the RNC, and expressing their opposition to the war in Iraq."[174] St. Paul granted the Coalition a parade permit on May 14, 2008, but the permit modified the march's day and time, as well as its route. The Coalition wished to march on September 1, 2008, the first day of the Republican National Convention, and to parade during the convention along three sides of the Xcel Center, with an estimated group of thirty thousand to fifty thousand people.[175] The city's permit allowed the march to take place on the first day of the RNC, but required it to begin and end before the convention convened. The approved route took the march within eighty-four feet of one of two main entrances to the Xcel Center, and past two of three media work spaces, coming within forty feet of one and sixty feet of the other.[176] It bears noting the Coalition did not seek any other access to the immediate vicinity of the Xcel Center; it litigated solely over the right to stage a mass protest march during the pendency of the 2008 RNC that would, quite literally, lay siege to the meeting venue by encircling it, on three of four sides, with literally tens of thousands of antiwar protestors.

Dissatisfied with the modified parade permit, the Coalition brought suit in federal district court, seeking an injunction requiring St. Paul to authorize a march during the RNC, and using the Coalition's preferred route. On July 8, 2008, the district court visited the various venues in question and heard oral argument on July 9, 2008. Judge Joan Ericksen issued her decision, denying the requested injunction, on July 16, 2008.

In a bit of understatement, Judge Ericksen began her analysis by noting that "the Democratic and Republican parties' quadrennial conventions have proven to be fertile ground in the recent past for legal challenges based on the First Amendment."[177] She also noted, accurately, that "[c]ompared to the access afforded marchers to the sites of recent national conventions of the Democratic and Republican parties, the Coalition appears to have unprecedented access to the convention site."[178] This access did not occur by accident; the city of St. Paul consciously sought to create reasonable opportunities for an expression of diverse viewpoints about issues of the day in areas physically proximate to the Xcel Center. As the *Report of the Republican National Convention Safety Planning and Implementation Review Commission* puts it, "[F]rom the beginning, Saint Paul intended the [2008] RNC to be a 'different' convention.'"[179] "City leaders were intent on hosting a convention that mirrored the values and principles of St. Paul: free expression of ideas, community policing and an open and welcoming approach."[180]

The city's intended message was that "Saint Paul was open for business and welcomed peaceful protest—the city was prepared to handle violence but anticipated a convention conducted the 'Saint Paul way.'"[181] It was, perhaps, a naive vision: "At a public forum, [Assistant Police Chief Matt] Bostrom explained the city's vision and told those who intended to protest that they would not be greeted by police in heavy riot gear. As Bostrom explained, protesters would see police on bicycles with smiles on their faces, and those wishing to express their views would be provided with a free speech area and a stage."[182] Unfortunately, "[a]t the same time that the City was promoting its vision, law enforcement was gathering intelligence that suggested the RNC may attract hundreds, if not thousands, of violent activists" and that "Saint Paul and surrounding areas were facing an attack by violent anarchists."[183]

As it turned out, the intelligence reports suggesting a threat of attempted anarchist disruptions proved to be accurate; the 2008 RNC turned St. Paul into a pitched urban battlefield from September 1, 2008, to September 4, 2008.[184] Even so, the city deserves substantial credit for at least attempting to maintain a reasonable balance between the right to protest and the interests of the RNC delegates, party leaders, and elected officials in staging a successful meeting. But, hindsight is 20/20. At the time of her decision, Judge Ericksen could not have known with certainty that the security threat in St. Paul was quite real and not simply imagined.

In her *Ward* analysis, Judge Ericksen easily concluded that "[t]he concentration of high-ranking government officials and a substantial number of people presents daunting security challenges."[185] In St. Paul, "many groups have endorsed a call to shut down the RNC by blockading the convention site, immobilizing the delegates' transportation, and blocking bridges that connect St. Paul and Minneapolis."[186] "Threats to the convention that the Secret Service must consider include terrorist attacks, lone gunmen, fire, chemical or biological attacks, detonation of explosive devices, and suicide bombers."[187] In the face of these risks, some less speculative than others, "the Coalition seeks to encircle the arena, marching on every route that directly abuts the convention site."[188]

Although the ability to protest in a way that reaches the delegates, party leaders, and government officials should constitute a cognizable constitutional interest (whether under the Free Speech and Assembly Clauses, or rather through a synergistic exercise of expressive freedoms protected by those clauses as well as the Petition Clause), no reasonable person would endorse the proposition that fifty thousand to one hundred thousand protestors should be permitted to encircle a meeting venue while the meeting is ongoing. Indeed, I cannot fathom that St. Paul would permit such a march, simply on fire and medical safety grounds, were the Xcel Center hosting a Lady Gaga or Tom Jones concert. Simply put, the Coalition made a facially unreasonable request to effectively lay siege to the 2008 RNC, while the delegates, party leaders, and government officials (including perhaps the president and vice president) were in attendance.

In light of the outrageous nature of the Coalition's request, it was not particularly difficult for Judge Eriksen to reject it under *Ward*. "By preventing encirclement of the convention site, the denial of the Coalition's application minimizes the potential for a blockade" and also "preserves a secure zone around the convention site that mitigates the threat posed by a variety of weapons, that provides a secure space in case an evacuation of the arena is necessary, that provides for the delegates' safe and orderly arrival at and entrance into the arena, and that allows emergency vehicles to access the arena."[189] Indeed, the interest in providing fire and medical assistance personnel access to the arena, by itself, would have been a sufficient basis for rejecting the Coalition's requested "encirclement" of the Xcel Center.

The court also found that the approved parade route met the narrow tailoring and ample alternative channels of communication prongs of *Ward*.[190] On the latter point, it bears notice that "despite the massive security and logistical concerns inherent to the convention, the permit's route brings the Coalition within sight and sound of the convention site."[191] "At its closest point, the permit's route passes within approximately 84 feet of one of the primary entrances to the arena."[192] As noted before, the route also passed within forty and sixty feet of two of the three main media centers established for the RNC.

St. Paul also created a "public viewing area" within site and sound of the main entrances to the Xcel Center. The area was immediately adjacent to two of the three media centers and would be open from 7:00 A.M. to 11:00 P.M. each day of the meeting. "The City expects to place a stage with audio equipment in the public viewing area and to make the stage available for one-hour periods on a lottery basis."[193] Judge Ericksen correctly noted that "the public viewing area described by Defendants appears to compare favorably to those employed during recent political conventions."[194] And, adopting an analytical move deployed in both *Bl(a)ck Tea Society* and *Citizens for Peace in Space*, the court noted that the Coalition's members could use other venues in the Twin Cities area during the pendency of the RNC to propagate their antiwar message.[195]

The location of the designated protest zone in St. Paul merits some discussion. At the 2004 (Boston and New York) and 2000 (Los Angeles and Philadelphia) national presidential nominating conventions, the designated protest area sites were located at great distances from the meeting venue and main venue entrances—usually distances of hundreds of yards, and often separated by fencing, razor wire, and mesh screens from sight of any passerby. Because of their distant locations, journalists would have had to exit and reenter the secured zone in order to visit the designated protest zones; this factor, standing alone, provided a strong disincentive for media personnel who might otherwise have considered visiting the designated protest areas and reporting on the protests. Unlike the nominating convention organizers in Denver, Boston,

Los Angeles, New York City, and Philadelphia, the St. Paul organizers intentionally facilitated press access to the main designated protest venue. Although, because of the lottery system, there would be no guarantee that the Coalition would be able to use the stage during the meeting, the very existence of the stage in such a location reflected St. Paul's good faith in balancing security imperatives with meaningful opportunities to register dissent.

Regarding the time of the march, the Coalition objected that if it did not march while the RNC was in session, it would lack assured access to the delegates. The court acknowledged the truth of this assertion but noted that "[t]he Coalition, however, has no constitutional right to access the delegates."[196] Delegates already at the Xcel Center "will be able to see the parade" and "the Coalition, like the appellants in *Bl(a)ck Tea Society*, appears to have 'grossly underestimate[d] the nature of modern communications.'"[197] More seriously, Judge Ericksen emphasized that "[h]ere, the Coalition's parade will take place on the opening day of the RNC, on the very afternoon of a day when the President of the United States might attend the convention."[198]

Thus, the district court found that all four prongs of *Ward* had been met on the facts presented, holding that St. Paul's "denial of the Coalition's application and issuance of the permit were content neutral, were narrowly tailored to serve significant government interests, and left open ample alternatives for communication of the Coalition's message."[199] Given the extraordinary nature of the Coalition's request—essentially the ability to surround the RNC while the delegates were in session, with a crowd of fifty thousand to one hundred thousand demonstrators—this result should not be particularly surprising (or upsetting).

E. A (Limited) Ray of Hope: *Amnesty International, USA v. Battle*

In *Amnesty International, USA v. Battle*,[200] the U.S. Court of Appeals for the Eleventh Circuit, in an opinion by Judge Phyllis Kravitch, squarely rejected a post hoc security justification for prohibiting the public from attending a protest organized by Amnesty International. The highly unusual facts of the case, however, make it unlikely to serve as a conflicting authority in relation to *Bl(a)ck Tea Society, Menotti*, and *Citizens for Peace in Space*.

Amnesty International planned to hold a public demonstration rally at the Torch of Friendship, a monument and plaza park in downtown Miami, Florida, near the location of a meeting of the Free Trade Association (FTA); the event was to take place on November 20, 2003, to coincide with the FTA's meeting.[201] Significantly, Amnesty International had sought and obtained a permit for the rally from the Miami Police Department. Unlike Boston, Colorado Springs,

Denver, Seattle, and St. Paul, Miami failed to adopt a comprehensive security plan prior to the FTA meeting that declared most (or all) of downtown Miami to be a "protest free zone."

On the day of the rally, about a dozen Amnesty International demonstrators gathered at the Torch of Friendship, part of Bayfront Park in downtown Miami, and were shocked when Miami-Dade County police officers soon started creating a "police cordon 50 to 75 yards from the Torch of Friendship," and also began preventing anyone from entering or leaving the area.[202] This police cordon essentially marooned the Amnesty International anti-FTA demonstrators around the Torch of Friendship.

Police turned away anyone attempting to reach the demonstration, and members of the public "could not see or hear the people speaking at Amnesty's demonstration because the police cordon kept them at too great a distance."[203] Considering the rally useless without the ability to communicate with the general public, Amnesty International members then tried to exit the police cordon to speak with the bystanders and distribute literature. The police did not allow this either.[204] Needless to say, this presented the classic "if a tree falls in the forest" question in its starkest possible terms; the local police effectively prevented anyone from attending, seeing, or hearing Amnesty International's anti-FTA protest rally in Bayfront Park.

Amnesty International subsequently sued the Miami-Dade County Police Department for preventing the public from attending the demonstration or Amnesty members from interacting with the crowd that had gathered. The district court, however, granted Miami's motion to dismiss the case, and the appeal to the Eleventh Circuit arose in the context of the district court's grant of the motion to dismiss.[205]

Writing for the panel, Judge Kravitch reversed the district court. In so doing, the court found that the Miami police had in fact violated Amnesty International's First Amendment rights to free speech, assembly, and association.[206] Although the court agreed with Miami's assertion that "a police presence was objectively reasonable" in light of "the high profile Free Trade Association meeting" and the large number of people in the vicinity of Bayfront Park, the court could "see nothing indicating that this extreme action [using a massive police force to prohibit any interaction between the Amnesty International protestors and the general public] constituted a 'reasonable time, manner, and location restriction.'"[207] The court would "not assume from the mere presence of a large number of people in the area that a level of danger existed that justified the complete deprivation of Amnesty's right to pass out literature."[208] On the rather stark facts at issue in *Battle*, the question presented "essentially, is whether the police may restrict the right to conduct a peaceful protest rally so completely that they prevent the rally from being seen or heard."[209] One would hope that to even ask this question would be to answer it in the negative; however, the Eleventh Circuit undertook a sustained analysis of precedents restricting protests, including extended consideration of *Citizens for Peace in Space.*

Judge Kravitch distinguished these cases, noting that, for example, in the Colorado Springs case, the Tenth Circuit sustained the restrictions on demonstrating "only after assuring itself that the plaintiffs were not completely deprived of an audience for their message."[210] In the case at bar, however, "Amnesty was completely prevented from communicating its message to anyone because no one was allowed into the Torch of Friendship area to attend the rally, and no Amnesty speaker was allowed out to reach them through any other means, not even leafletting."[211] Judge Kravitch observed that "[t]his action is no different than if the City of Miami had given Amnesty a permit to hold a meeting in an auditorium and then barred the doors and windows such that no audience could enter and no sound could escape the building."[212] On these facts, the court had little trouble finding that the city's unusual approach to advancing safety concerns failed to leave open ample alternative channels of communication.[213]

The key to the case, however, was that Miami had issued a permit for the rally in Bayfront Park in the first place.[214] In other words, rather than challenging a ban (i.e., a "protest free zone") on parades or rallies near the FTA meetings, Amnesty International was complaining that a demonstration directly authorized by the city was rendered useless by the local police. Having granted a permit (perhaps by inadvertence or accident), the city had ceded the availability of the Torch of Friendship area of Bayfront Park as a suitable venue for a protest rally during the FTA meetings in November 2003. The city, having issued a permit for this use of the park, then attempted to suppress the rally itself. Had the police department consulted with the city's lawyers, however, one feels sure that the permit would never have issued in the first place, on the basis of "security concerns." Nevertheless, *Battle* is a significant case because it provides something of a smoking gun regarding the real motives of municipal officials when faced with a potentially large, embarrassing public protest near an important international meeting, like the November 2003 FTA meeting in Miami.

Judge Kravitch's opinion also merits both attention and praise because she so forthrightly rejects Miami's post hoc effort to play the security card as a justification for its (literally) Gestapo tactics in preventing the Amnesty International anti-FTA rally from being attended, seen, or heard. "We recognize that police may properly limit the exercise of free speech where necessary for the safety and protection of protestors and the community."[215] However, "[t]he alleged action in this case was not constitutionally permissible without a greater justification than has been given."[216]

Judge Kravitch emphasized that the city had "not provided sufficient detail for us to analyze this asserted significant government interest and to judge whether the action taken was narrowly tailored to serve this interest. A 'potential' for violence hardly justifies placing a cordon 50 to 75 yards—a significant distance—away from Amnesty's protest and preventing any and all communication from passing through the cordon."[217] She was careful to emphasize that the court was not requiring the city to use the least restrictive or intrusive means in advancing its security concerns, but rather that "the extreme nature of the police cordon in this case calls into question Defendants' assertion that their actions were absolutely necessary."[218]

Again, however, one must keep in mind the limited nature of *Battle* as a counterweight to the clear emerging trend in the lower federal courts to sanction remarkably broad restrictions on speech in traditional public forums when such protest activity could prove embarrassing to the city. As noted earlier, Miami voluntarily issued a permit for the Amnesty International rally, which constitutes a major material difference from the most common facts in such cases, which invariably involve a city government *denying* a request for a parade or rally permit (usually incident to a temporary protest free zone that entirely surrounds the immediate environs of a significant national or international political event). Miami simply ceded this ground, literally, in *Battle*.

Second, the Miami police effectively and intentionally prevented *all* communication between the Amnesty International protestors and anyone else; the cordon had the effect of preventing *any* communications between the rally participants and the public. As it happens, most city governments are at least somewhat more subtle in their efforts at censorship, instead using a designated protest zone well away from the political event, but nevertheless totally open to the public and media.

Miami would have been on firmer constitutional ground if it had closed Bayfront Park to any protest during the FTA meeting and offered to let Amnesty International use a designated protest site somewhere else (say, ten miles away at a public park near the international airport). This approach would not have had the effect of preventing the protestors from communicating their message, if, by some combination of chance and luck, passersby happened to be near the designated protest zone.

Nevertheless, *Battle* is one of the very few cases that rejects a government invocation of "security" as insufficiently proven to satisfy *Ward*. In this way, it suggests some cause for hope that federal judges might not invariably and reflexively defer to abstract and generalized claims that security concerns require a blanket ban on speech whenever a high-profile political event takes place in a major U.S. city.

IV. A MEANINGFUL COMMITMENT TO DEMOCRATIC DELIBERATION REQUIRES SOME CONSIDERATION OF A WOULD-BE SPEAKER'S ACCESS TO AN INTENDED AUDIENCE

The cumulative effects of the doctrines against content discrimination, viewpoint discrimination, and prior restraints have led the Supreme Court to reject, categorically, the notion that speech critical of the government could be punished because it has the effect of undermining public confidence in either government or those holding office under the government. An essential premise of *New York Times Co. v. Sullivan*[219] was the notion that public criticism of government officials could not be discouraged by direct proscriptions against seditious libel or by proxies for such proscriptions (such as the creative use of the common law of defamation by private tort plaintiffs).[220] Similarly, *Hustler v. Falwell* extends the reasoning of *New York Times Co.* to encompass speech designed, literally, to "assassinate" the character of public figures (including public officials).[221] Even speech containing factual errors enjoys constitutional protection so that, in Justice Brennan's words, "debate on public issues [may] be uninhibited, robust, and wide open."[222] Finally, *Phelps* extends the logic of these decisions to confer broad constitutional protection on incredibly offensive speech, namely, targeted protests at the funerals of military personnel who died in combat.[223] As Chief Justice Roberts so eloquently explains in *Phelps*, "As a Nation we have chosen . . . to protect even hurtful speech on public issues to ensure that we do not stifle public debate."[224]

The motivating theory behind such a sweeping protection of speech, including the protection of falsehoods if not made with malice aforethought (i.e., with either actual knowledge of falsity or with reckless indifference to the truth or falsity of the speech) and also speech designed to inflict maximum emotional harm, reflects the notion that democratic self-government simply is not possible without an open and unregulated marketplace of political ideas. This theory seems entirely plausible; after all, how can elections be meaningful if the citizenry cannot openly debate the merits and shortcomings of candidates and the policies the candidates support or oppose? The legitimacy of the electoral process would seem to require a commitment to the freedom of speech even in the complete absence of a constitutional textual guarantee safeguarding the right.[225]

It is not enough, however, simply to protect speech but not the ability to disseminate speech to an intended audience. The right to inveigh against the heavens in an empty field is meaningless because it cannot contribute to the formation of collective public opinion; citizens must be able to both access and engage government officials—and each other—if deliberative democracy is to function properly.

Professor Owen M. Fiss has written persuasively on the problem of the shrinking space available to average citizens to engage in speech activity.[226] Professor Fiss argues that a normatively attractive free speech doctrine must not only protect the content of speech but also address the question of the adequacy of channels of communication. If average citizens no longer possess an effective means of communicating with each other, then freedom of speech cannot contribute to the creation of democratic consensus. And, Fiss warns, government increasingly attempts to close off access to common spaces in the name of aesthetics, of maintaining order, and of ensuring that public property is available for its primary intended uses.[227]

To this list one should add a new and important addition: security. Increasingly, security serves as the justification for the marginalization of those seeking to use public space to communicate a message with fellow citizens. Moreover, because judges come from a common culture, watch the same news programming, and read the same newspapers, they are no less susceptible to mass hysteria and panic than other citizens.[228]

As the cases discussed in the previous section demonstrate,[229] time and again judges have simply credited security-based arguments that enjoyed broad social currency as justifications for restrictions on speech, rather than pressing government to prove the truth of those assertions.[230] Security, even more than aesthetics, traffic flow, or quiet enjoyment of a park represents a clear and present danger to any meaningful access to public space for individual and collective speech activity. It is far too easy to equate dissent with disloyalty and to label the dissenter a potential terrorist or purveyor of violence. Once one successfully defines political dissent as a marker for political violence, the government's interest in regulating, if not entirely suppressing, dissent becomes compelling.

The problem with this logic is that political dissent is *not* a marker for political violence. Most dissenters are peaceful, and those who are not can be punished for committing criminal acts. Nevertheless, when a federal judge must weigh a claimed threat to human life and safety against the theoretical right to protest on public property, it is not difficult to predict the outcome of the balancing exercise.

When a government official invokes security—whether of a public official, like the vice president, or a group, such as delegates to a NATO meeting—any appreciable risk of harm seems too great to tolerate. In a way, although never formally embraced by the Supreme Court, the Judge Learned Hand formula—which holds that speech claims must be assessed by considering the gravity of the harm the government alleges the speech will (or might) produce discounted by the probability of the harm actually coming about[231]—describes how judges actually approach free speech cases when local law enforcement or the Secret Service seeks to prohibit protest near meetings featuring incumbent government officials. The boldest alternative vision, Justice Holmes's argument that even speech "fraught with death" must be protected absent a high probability of the bad result actually occurring, such that "an immediate check is required to save the country,"[232] tends to go out the window.

In this way, the realities of the post-9/11 mindset disrupt preexisting theoretical commitments to the marketplace of ideas. Moreover, the question is almost never the eradication of the idea from the marketplace but rather denying it expression only in a specific place, and only at a particular time. In this way, giving credence to unproven and untested security concerns could easily seem to constitute but a modest incursion on the Free Speech and Free Assembly Clauses. In consequence, judges accept government decisions to close entirely large swaths of public space in order to ensure that there is no "trouble," perhaps comforted that even if the speech does not occur at the would-be speakers' preferred time and place, there is no serious question of the speech being absolutely disallowed from the marketplace of ideas.

V. CONCLUSION: EXISTING FIRST AMENDMENT FREE SPEECH AND ASSEMBLY JURISPRUDENCE CONSISTENTLY UNDERPROTECTS DISSENT AND DISSENTERS USING PUBLIC SPACES FOR PEACEFUL PROTEST ACTIVITY

This chapter has considered how the generic First Amendment rules that delimit government regulation of speech apply in general terms and also with respect to speech on government property. The outcome of this endeavor should be surprising: despite being superficially restrictive of any government efforts to censor speech, the rules against content and viewpoint discrimination quite often do not serve as a meaningful brake on attempted censorship, because the government adopts regulations that are, at least facially, content and viewpoint neutral. Even if the genesis of the restrictions relates to a particular planned protest by, for example, persons opposed to the war in Iraq, the regulations on their face close the space to *all* would-be protestors. This nullifies any potential objection based on the per se invalidity of content- and viewpoint-based speech regulations.

Similarly, the rule against prior restraints simply does not apply to content neutral, reasonable time, place, and manner restrictions. Temporary regulations, enacted in the name of security, provide a powerful and effective means for local, state, and federal government officials seeking to restrict protest at times and places that are potentially effective at communicating a message to a mass audience via the media, but also potentially annoying to the government itself and its officers.

Nor does the *Ward* doctrine requiring careful federal court scrutiny of regulations limiting the time, place, and manner of speech on public property do much good. So long as the government proffers a plausible rationale for its regulation, the "significant government interest" prong of *Ward* will be met. The "narrow tailoring" requirement, as applied, is weak and can be easily met if any public demonstration would present even a merely theoretical risk to the security of the meeting. Finally, the "ample alternative channels of communication" prong means little more than that government must permit would-be protestors to protest somewhere else, at some other time, and also allow alternative means of communication, such as Internet posts, distributing handbills and leaflets at some other time and place, and perhaps writing a letter to the editor of a local newspaper or magazine. Simply put, *Ward* places very little, if any, value, on the ability of a would-be speaker to target a particular means of communication at a specific audience, at least if the use of government property will be necessary to facilitate the speech activity.

The problem runs deep, for it is doubtful that academic admonitions to apply the various generic and time, place, and manner rules more aggressively[233] will make much headway against the reflexive deference that judges provide government when government plays the security card. Tinkering with the existing doctrinal structure is unlikely to lead to any real improvement in access to public space to protest specific policies or officials and to petition for changes in the government's policies. Instead, the solution requires the creation of an entirely new doctrinal fix; one that makes it much more difficult for a judge to fold immediately after the government plays the security card. As explained in subsequent chapters, the Petition Clause might provide the textual, theoretical, and doctrinal basis for protecting a right to protest in a fashion that secures meaningful access to an intended audience, at least when that audience is composed of government officials and political party leaders, thereby facilitating a broader engagement of the issues animating the protest within the body politic.[234]

Security as a Cellophane Wrapper: Deconstructing the Government's Security Rationale for Marginalizing Public Dissent and Dissenters

I. INTRODUCTION

Does the government's invocation of security as a justification for restrictions on core political speech possess significant merit? Or is it an obvious and unpersuasive makeweight to justify ham-handed efforts to suppress dissenting voices? Government officials may take reasonable steps to secure venues, such as convention halls and public arenas, used for mass political gatherings against the risk of disruption or even political violence.[1] It also seems reasonable to posit the legitimacy of the creation of security perimeters around the venues used for major domestic political events and international governmental meetings. If government may search all passengers seeking to enter the secure zone of an airport, by parity of logic government may take similar steps to prevent the presence of guns or explosives in or even near the venues used for contemporary political theater.

Although politicians and party officials probably have a right to prescreen audiences and to banish viewpoints that they dislike from the actual venues in which political leaders speak or conduct rallies by selecting a friendly audience,[2] the interest in avoiding hecklers and potential disruptions to the event does not extend beyond the venue itself. The Supreme Court has been willing to accept limits on protest activities to advance concerns based on privacy[3] and aesthetics;[4] surely the rights to free speech, free assembly, and free association must encompass some ability to pick and choose one's political fellow travelers.[5] Free speech, assembly, and association principles would be inhibited, not enhanced, if the federal courts required incumbent government officials and the political parties to make major events free-for-alls in which the organizers could not effectively control the message (or messages) being advanced.[6]

The limits on peaceful protest activities adopted in places like Boston, Colorado Springs, Denver, Miami, and Seattle, however, go well beyond the scope that legitimate concerns about security or message control justify. Permitting a person to carry a "No Cutting and Running" sign proximate to a venue where the president will speak but not permitting the same person to carry an "End the War Now!" sign cannot be justified in terms of either security or message control within the event itself. Moreover, the Secret Service's position that persons openly opposed to the president's policies present more of a security risk than those persons purporting to support the president's policies makes absolutely no sense at all; if someone wished to harm the president, it seems highly likely that such a person would not take any steps to attract attention to herself. A person picketing a presidential event invites precisely the kind of intense public scrutiny that a Lee Harvey Oswald or a John Wilkes Booth would certainly seek to avoid.

Antiprotest policies generally appear to be rather obvious forms of naked content—if not viewpoint—discrimination. Yet, as chapter 2 demonstrates, the federal courts consistently have held that "protest free zones" constitute content neutral policies, because the rules governing demonstrations and protests formally apply to all would-be speakers. And, again, the overriding concern with security, coupled with the ability of the would-be protestors to engage in expressive activity somewhere else, sometime else, or both, inevitably seems sufficient to justify the enactment of temporary protest bans.[7] But, what is really going on here? Is security the actual motive for these policies, even when enacted and enforced in the absence of any evidence of a particularized security threat?

For example, the George W. Bush administration's *Presidential Advance Manual* presumptively treated any and all potential demonstrators as constituting a security threat.[8] A reasonable observer might ask whether the security argument is genuine or instead a mere placeholder for something else, for example, a desire by the government and its officials to avoid potentially embarrassing public criticism in a highly visible forum (often with the television cameras rolling).[9]

The present chapter identifies, explains, and critiques the growing trend of the return of a junior varsity version of seditious libel. Once again, governments at all levels—local, state, and federal—are invoking security concerns as part of a concerted effort to marginalize, if not silence, political dissent. Moreover, in the post-9/11 world, security is, contrary to the First Circuit's protestations,[10] a "talismanic" governmental interest. Federal judges will naturally fear rejecting speech restrictions grounded on "security" concerns because doing so will require them to take responsibility for the consequences if the government's suppositions prove to be true.[11] And it bears noting that the events at the 2008 Republican National Convention, in St. Paul, Minnesota, demonstrate that sometimes security concerns are, in fact, grounded on solid intelligence rather than subterfuge and speculation.[12]

This chapter considers the surprising alacrity with which reviewing courts have accepted draconian speech restrictions applicable to traditional public forums and justified in the name of security. Simply put, why have the lower federal courts essentially refused to press the government for persuasive justifications for speech bans proximate to incumbent government officials? Perhaps, below the surface, federal judges find the kind of direct, confrontational tactics that the would-be demonstrator plaintiffs seek to pursue distasteful and insulting to the dignity interests of the officials in question, who at some level represent the state itself. Thus, in a powerful sense, protest of events like nominating conventions and presidential appearances represents an attack on the dignity of the state itself. It is not so implausible to imagine a legal regime that seeks to protect national symbols and figures from disparagement.[13]

Realistically, even if protestors do not present a risk to the life, health, or safety of government officials, they can be and often are badly behaved and inclined to act outrageously in order to garner media attention for their various causes.[14] Also fueling potential judicial skepticism is a sneaking suspicion that the goal of protests proximate to government officials has less to do with meaningful communication with the officials than with securing national, and perhaps international, media attention by using the officials as mere foils.[15] These concerns might lead a federal judge to be less inclined to press government to ensure effective access by protestors to government officials attending events in public venues. In sum, if the effort to engage the public officials directly is merely pretextual and the would-be protestors' real objective is opening and engaging a more general public debate within the body politic through the mass media, perhaps requiring protestors to voice their views at a more convenient time and place does not constitute an undue burden on the Free Speech and Assembly Clauses.[16]

Out of an abundance of caution and because there is always something to be said for considering seriously and carefully the merits of the other side of an argument, this chapter considers the plausibility of the security rationale for banning speech physically proximate to government officials, both in general and as a de facto proxy for the protection of the government's dignity. The chapter also considers the history of the seditious libel doctrine and its arguable relationship to the modern trend of adopting draconian speech regulations that banish speech in the name of obtaining security.

II. SECURITY CONCERNS DO NOT GENERALLY JUSTIFY PROPHYLACTIC RULES BANNING OR BANISHING SPEECH

If security or public safety concerns routinely justified speech restrictions in myriad contexts, it would not be surprising that federal courts would credit such concerns in the context of events like the quadrennial presidential nominating conventions or presidential appearances. However, the Supreme Court's general approach requires local and state governments to shoulder risks in order to facilitate speech—risks associated with angry crowds offended by a speaker's intemperate language, risks associated with highly unpopular groups seeking to stage parades and rallies, and risks associated with speech that vulnerable minorities genuinely find threatening.

A. Security Concerns Would Never Be Sufficient to Justify Similar Speech Restrictions in Other Contexts Involving Material Risks to Public Order and Safety

In cases like *Forsyth County*,[17] the Supreme Court has refused to allow local government to invoke security concerns to silence speech by racist and anti-Semitic protestors.[18] Instead, the court consistently has held that the problem of the "heckler's veto"[19] requires government to shoulder extraordinary burdens to facilitate speech activity by unpopular protestors.[20] In other words, when the object of protest is not a carefully orchestrated photo opportunity for incumbent government officeholders, the courts have generally required government to undertake all reasonable efforts to facilitate speech activity, even when genuine, nonpretextual concerns exist about a hostile community reaction to the protestors.[21]

Moreover, concerns about unfavorable press coverage of the community or other Chamber of Commerce concerns do not serve as counterweights to the would-be demonstrators' constitutional right to engage in protest activity.[22] This robustly speechcentric approach constitutes part of the project against viewpoint and content discrimination: any less protective regime would facilitate the invocation of security concerns as a kind of cellophane wrapper[23] for viewpoint and content discrimination. Local governments must accept substantial risks to peace and public order that inevitably attend mass public marches by the Ku Klux Klan, the American Nazi Party, or similar organizations.[24]

This rule extends beyond the context of parade permitting or protecting unpopular speakers in traditional public forums. Thus, in cases like *Hess*, the Supreme Court largely has disallowed preemptive government efforts to avoid social unrest by silencing speakers. In *Hess*, a demonstrator vowed that he and his comrades would "take back the fucking streets" even as the local police and sheriff's department were attempting to restore order to the streets of Bloomington, Indiana.[25] The Supreme Court reversed a criminal conviction on these facts because local law enforcement failed to show a high probability (an "imminent threat") of other demonstrators acting on Hess's admonition to retake the streets for unlawful protest purposes.[26] In other words, local police had to assume a nontrivial risk of public disorder and disruption in order to facilitate a wide margin of appreciation for the freedom of expression.

In the context of a large, unauthorized protest of the Vietnam War on and around the main campus of Indiana University, the question of security was more than merely speculative; the risk of violent disorder was both real and palpable. Nevertheless, the First Amendment required the citizens of Bloomington to incur the risk of disruption as the price of free speech. Under the logic of the modern designated speech zone cases, the city of Bloomington should simply have established a designated free speech zone on the edge of town, built cages or pens to hold the protestors, and arrested anyone who attempted to use a street or sidewalk proximate to Indiana University's main entrance for political demonstrations against the Vietnam War. The business of the community could have gone on undisturbed by the noise, chaos, and tumult of gnarly student protestors.

Along similar lines, the Supreme Court held as protected the violent threats issued to help enforce a boycott of local merchants in Port Gibson, Mississippi.[27] In order to induce local citizens to cease patronizing the stores, which enforced racially discriminatory policies, picket organizers threatened that "if we catch any of you going in any of them racist stores, we're gonna break your damn neck."[28] In addition, "[t]he names of persons who violated the boycott were . . . read at meetings of the Claiborne County NAACP, and they were branded as traitors to the Black cause, called demeaning names, and socially ostracized for merely trading with whites."[29]

Even though the free speech value of threats of violence is not particularly self-evident,[30] the Supreme Court reversed the convictions because "[m]ere advocacy of the use of force or violence does not remove speech from the protection of the First Amendment."[31] Both the merchants and would-be customers had to endure threats of violence as the price of protecting hyperbolic, emotionally charged expression directly related to a matter of public concern.

Nevertheless, the interest in freedom of speech, freedom of assembly, and freedom of association trumped both genuine security concerns and an independent interest in maintaining peace and tranquillity within the community.

Again, speech of the sort at issue in *Claiborne Hardware* presents more than
a merely hypothetical threat to peace and good order—yet the speech nevertheless enjoys broad protection, and the community must assume the risk of disorder as the price of securing an "uninhibited, robust, and wide-open" public
discourse.[32] Could the local sheriff have won *Claiborne Hardware Company*
simply by establishing a designated picket zone, removed a mile or two from
the white-owned store entrances, citing a concern for potential violence as a
basis for closing the area to all protests? In other words, would the federal courts
have accepted a limitation on the physical proximity of the pickets to the stores
in the name of maintaining the peace? Surely the facts of *Claiborne Hardware*
presented a more realistic threat of imminent potential violence than the hypothetical and wholly unproven security concerns at issue in *Bl(a)ck Tea Society*,
yet Claiborne County, Mississippi, was without constitutional power to either
restrict or punish the speech after the fact in order to promote civic peace in
the future.

Finally, even when the risk to security and good order is plainly real and
pressing, the Supreme Court has required local governments to take extraordinary steps to protect unpopular speakers from being denied access to public
space for expressive activity. Thus, in *Forsyth County v. Nationalist Movement*,
the Supreme Court prohibited the adoption of scaled fees for permits to protest
on local streets and sidewalks, even if public antipathy toward the speakers
would clearly require the expenditure of significant and unbudgeted public
monies to pay for extra police protection.[33] Why? Because to sustain differential
fees for parades or pickets, based on public hostility to a speaker or group, has
the effect of punishing unpopular viewpoints. Would Forsyth County, Georgia,
have fared better in the Supreme Court if, rather than charging a differential
permit fee for the racist group's protest march, it had instead closed the downtown area to all protest activity, invoking security concerns and risk of WTO-
style riots associated with the Nationalist Movement's presence, established a
designated protest zone, and required the march and rally to take place in some
other, less inconvenient area (where fewer bystanders might see the protest,
hear the racist messages, and take umbrage)?

That said, given the choice of paying a differential permitting fee (and
being allowed to march through the center of town) and being charged no fee
for a permit, but at the price of being required to remain in a cage or pen
located some distance from the town square, most demonstrators would gladly

pay the fee in exchange for more meaningful access to the target audience. Designated protest zones are far more effective at squelching and marginalizing speech than the adoption of differential, cost-based permitting schemes. Yet, the lower federal courts have routinely sustained them, on the theory that federal judges are ill equipped to second-guess the necessity of security requirements.[34]

The Supreme Court has also required local law enforcement agencies to accept a serious risk of public disturbance rather than silence unpopular speakers. For example, in *Terminiello v. City of Chicago*,[35] a public speaker's comments appeared likely to cause an altercation, if not a full-blown riot. Terminiello, speaking at a meeting of the Christian Veterans of America, in an auditorium located in Chicago, Illinois, "vigorously, if not viciously, criticized various political and racial groups whose activities he described as inimical to the nation's welfare."[36] The audience inside the auditorium numbered about eight hundred persons, and "[o]utside of the auditorium, a crowd of about one thousand persons gathered to protest against the meeting."[37] Notwithstanding a "cordon of police officers" who were "assigned to the meeting to maintain order," several disturbances had already occurred, and "[t]he crowd outside was angry and turbulent."[38]

So, we have a large meeting with a controversial speaker, and a crowd of demonstrators protesting the meeting, just outside the venue itself, with the police tasked with maintaining the peace in an atmosphere in which violence (or at least "disturbances") had already broken out. Using the logic of the protest cases involving the national nominating conventions, surely Chicago's police department could have declared the Christian Veterans of America meeting site a "protest free zone" and required those who disagreed with the organization's aims and goals to repair to a "designated protest zone," at some great remove from the auditorium where Terminiello was to speak. Justice Douglas, writing for the majority, took a very different view.

Douglas began by noting that "a function of free speech in our society is to invite dispute."[39] Free speech "is often provocative and challenging" and "may indeed best serve its high purpose when it induces a condition of unrest, creates dissatisfaction with conditions as they are, or even stirs people to anger."[40] Accordingly, the Supreme Court overturned Terminiello's conviction for a breach of the peace.[41]

Justice Jackson, in dissent, took a view more consistent with the approach of the contemporary decisions of the courts of appeals involving protests near major political gatherings. Jackson argued that the conviction should stand because the local court "was not dealing with a theory" but rather dealing "with a riot and with a speech that provoked a hostile mob and incited a friendly one, and threatened violence between the two."[42]

After providing an extensive transcript of the racist and religiously bigoted remarks made at the rally and by Terminiello,[43] Justice Jackson argued that "[t]he present mastery of the streets by either radical or revolutionary mob movements is not the opposing minority" but instead "the authority of local governments which represent the free choice of democratic and law-abiding elements of all shades of opinion."[44] For Justice Jackson, then, the city of Chicago had good cause to require Terminiello to cease speaking, on pain of arrest and conviction of breach of the peace: "I do not think that the Constitution of the United States denies to the states and the municipalities power to solve that problem [of public disorder] in the light of local conditions, at least so long as danger to public order is not invoked in bad faith, as a cover for censorship or suppression."[45]

Technically, the majority reversed Terminiello's conviction based on a flawed jury instruction that read the Illinois breach of peace statute in a way that "permitted conviction of petitioner if his speech stirred people to anger, invited a public dispute, or brought about a condition of unrest."[46] The Supreme Court held that "[a] conviction resting on any of those grounds may not stand."[47] Strictly speaking, then, *Terminiello* does not squarely address the question of a duty on the part of a local police department to protect an unpopular speaker, even at the risk of public disorder. Other cases, however, do speak more directly to this issue and hold that government has, if not an absolute duty to protect an unpopular speaker from a heckler's veto, then a very substantial duty to make all reasonable efforts to facilitate the speech.[48]

It is true that in *Feiner v. New York*[49] the Supreme Court sustained a breach of the peace conviction based on a speaker's refusal to cease speaking on a public sidewalk after an angry crowd had gathered.[50] However, since the early 1950s, the Supreme Court has usually limited *Feiner* to its facts, finding that the risk of a breach of peace was not sufficient to justify a police order requiring speakers to cease and desist.[51]

Thus, the general rule under the First Amendment is that "[p]articipants in an orderly demonstration in a public place are not chargeable with the danger, unprovoked except by the fact of the constitutionally protected demonstration itself, that their critics might react with disorder or violence."[52] Moreover, "the possibility of disorder by others cannot justify exclusion of persons from a place if they otherwise have a constitutional right . . . to be present."[53] And, even in the context of a public disturbance, the Supreme Court has disallowed convictions for breach of the peace based on speech absent a very strong showing of an imminent risk of harm.[54] Thus, rather than applying a hair trigger in circumstances where police claim that "there might be trouble," police instead have a duty "to protect . . . lawful gathering so that the speakers may exercise their constitutional rights."[55] Accordingly, Justice Black's dissenting position in *Feiner*, rather than Chief Justice Vinson's majority opinion, has come to better reflect the contemporary state of the law.[56]

This approach also comports with the rule adopted in *Schneider v. State*,[57] in which the Supreme Court invalidated municipal bans on leafleting on public streets and sidewalks as an antilitter measure. Rather than getting at the problem by banning leafleting, the justices reasoned, government has a duty to punish those who litter. "There are obvious methods of preventing littering. Amongst these is the punishment of those who actually throw papers on the streets."[58] By a parity of reasoning, the state has a duty to punish those who engage in public disorder, not those who wish to speak peacefully on a public street or sidewalk, or in a public park.

In all of these cases, a very strong burden of justification rests on the government to show that it has no other means available to it to secure its interest in public order, short of silencing an otherwise lawful speaker. We see a commitment to a kind of strict judicial scrutiny that demands the use of least restrictive means when addressing the problematic secondary effects of free expression in public places. When unpopular speakers take to the parks or streets, there is a very real risk of public disorder, perhaps including even serious damage to property, health, or, in extreme cases, even life.[59] The point is that the Free Speech and Free Assembly Clauses, as the Supreme Court has authoritatively interpreted and applied them, require average citizens, and communities, to shoulder substantial risks, including security risks, in order to facilitate free expression.

B. Imagining a First Amendment Universe in Which Genuine Perceived Threats to Safety or Security May Generally Serve to Justify Restrictions on Speech

We could imagine an alternative free speech regime that, rather than selectively crediting risks to security, takes such risks very seriously across the board. For example, incorporating more thoroughly the Judge Learned Hand theory of free speech could potentially justify the use of speech free zones and protest pens in the name of security; Judge Hand's approach would progressively reduce the protection afforded free speech as the nature of the perceived risk associated with the speech increases.[60] Under the Hand formula, for example, speech that advocates the deployment of a dirty nuclear bomb in a major U.S. city would be regulable (or even proscribable) on a much lower showing of risk than speech advocating the flat tax. Why? Because the social cost of a nuclear bomb being exploded in a major population center is sufficiently grave to warrant extraordinary vigilance on the part of the government.

Thus, under the Hand formula, one might imagine a regime in which government may regulate speech based on its content with a much freer hand than the *Brandenburg* formulation currently allows.[61] Moreover, the Hand formula does not isolate risks associated with incumbent government officials or political party meetings; any credible risk would justify a restriction on speech or publishing. The theory is quite democratic in justifying proactive government censorship to protect the community from serious harms that speech might bring about.

On the other hand, would the Hand formula approach help to justify or explain the growing use of protest free zones? Only if evidence existed on the record that the particular would-be demonstrators at bar were likely to cause serious criminal conduct through their advocacy—evidence utterly absent in virtually all of the recent protest ban cases. In fact, in none of the reported cases did the government have *any* credible evidence that the particular groups seeking to protest proximate to event venues intended to engage in any illegal conduct whatsoever themselves. Moreover, the physical spaces at issue were not closed to all persons, for all purposes, but rather were off-limits solely to demonstrators. Given this fact, it would be difficult, if not impossible, credibly to argue that the presence of would-be speakers themselves, rather than their particular speech, constituted the threat of harm. A would-be Starbucks customer seeking a late afternoon latté occupies as much space on a street or sidewalk, and is potentially as capable of making mischief, as a protestor carrying an antiwar sign.

With the notable exception of St. Paul, Minnesota (which in any event had adopted the mildest restrictions on protest near the nominating convention site in recent history), the security concerns offered in defense of the government's security rationale were no more choate than those proffered by the Nixon administration in the *Pentagon Papers* case.[62] To the extent evidence existed, it related almost exclusively to the riots at the 1999 WTO meeting in Seattle, and to more generalized concerns about security in the wake of the 9/11 attacks in New York City and Washington, D.C. Even under the Hand formula this would not suffice to justify banning speech from an otherwise appropriate public forum, like a sidewalk, street, or public park.

To put the matter in perspective, if persons seeking to advocate political assassination as a legitimate means of changing the national leadership wished to protest proximate to a presidential event, the Hand formula would justify either banning the protest entirely or relocating it to a venue very far removed from the president. Even though the Hand formula would permit government to adopt a hair trigger to suppress certain kinds of advocacy, the cases to date simply do not present facts involving efforts to advocate grossly antisocial criminal acts. Instead, the cases uniformly involve persons sincerely opposed to the policies supported by those appearing before or attending a major government or political event. Judge Hand never suggested that government could ban speech to avoid political embarrassment.

Moreover, even if one views the question through the prism of the Hand formula, the politician-regarding use of the time, place, and manner doctrine to limit (or squelch) embarrassing dissenting speech cannot be reconciled with the Supreme Court's refusal to permit legislation aimed at protecting minorities from threats or targeted insults.[63] For example, in *Brandenburg*, the participants in the Klan rally in suburban Cincinnati, Ohio, called for a race war.[64] Under the Hand formula, advocacy of a pogrom should constitute the kind of extraordinary threat that would justify the use of state power to suppress the speech. Indeed, it is far from clear precisely why advocacy of violence directed on the basis of race, sex, religion, or sexual orientation should enjoy serious free speech protection under any purposive theory of freedom of speech.[65]

In fact, many democracies quite committed to respecting the freedom of speech have concluded that the social cost of targeted insults based on race, gender, religion, or sexual orientation is simply too high to be tolerated. The German approach to freedom of expression, for example, would not tolerate targeted racial threats, on the theory that such threats deny equal dignity to those victimized by them.[66] Canada too has defined free speech rights to exclude the right to incite others to racial or religious hatred, on the theory that government could reasonably seek to advance equality and multiculturalism at the expense of speech, at least in this limited context.[67] It is not at all difficult to imagine a world in which perceived threats to the security or dignity of vulnerable groups of citizens justify restrictions on speech. Moreover, in societies that maintain such rules, reviewing courts often seem inclined to accept their necessity based on fairly generalized evidence that hate speech constitutes a serious social problem and that speech codes constitute a justifiable and effective response to this problem.[68]

The interest at issue is plainly security—the sense of safety and well-being enjoyed by minorities within a particular polity. To say that when Nazis march in Skokie, Illinois, Holocaust survivors do not fear, with justification, for their security is simply nonsensical. Whenever groups openly espousing racist, sexist, homophobic, or religiously bigoted messages appear in large numbers within a community, both the perception of safety and the reality of safety suffer for it.[69] Yet, federal courts routinely tell minorities (however defined) that their interest in being free from a perceived threat must yield to the imperatives of the First Amendment.[70] *Brandenburg* says that security concerns do not justify censorship absent an imminent threat of unlawful behavior.[71]

In other words, viewed from a broader theoretical or global perspective, the result in *Brandenburg* is far from being self-evidently correct. One could easily imagine a regime in which public calls for the extermination of racial minorities might lead to criminal sanctions, on the theory that no matter how remote the risk, the potential social harm of the speech far outweighs whatever meager contribution it might make to the marketplace of ideas. Similarly, a serious commitment to political and social equality, or cultural pluralism, might also preclude endorsement of the *Brandenburg* approach. *Brandenburg* essentially tells minorities of all stripes that because of the crucial relationship of free expression to the project of democratic self-government, members of minority groups must accept the fear and worry that accompany public dissemination of these sentiments.

Of course *Brandenburg* presents a perfectly plausible theory of free speech. If government censorship of speech represents the gravest possible threat to the ability of democratic self-government to function (if not thrive), then nearly absolute protection of political speech would be a logical response to the threat. Nor should one doubt that a censorial government, armed with the power to selectively silence speech, would deploy that power in ways that directly and indirectly advance the interests of those holding power. One need look no further than the example of the Sedition Act of 1798,[72] which the Adams administration and the Federalist Party used to silence, in a systematic way, the opposition press, in an ultimately unavailing effort to hold the reins of federal power.[73]

The problem is understanding why politicians may be protected from offensive or intentionally insulting speech, under the rubric of "security," when average citizens simply do not enjoy any comparable protection. Indeed, the *Cohen/ Gooding* line of cases effectively eviscerated a preexisting doctrine of "fighting words," which, based on security concerns, sustained limits on offensive speech activity in public.[74] If politicians have a legitimate interest in personal security that causes collateral damage to speech activity, the question that immediately presents itself should be why minority groups don't have a similar interest in being free from threatening speech. And, more generally, why society should have to tolerate speech that might "cause trouble"—don't all citizens have an interest in security that would be furthered by sustaining reasonable civility norms whenever the problem of a captive audience presents itself?

Perhaps Skokie should have simply designated its downtown a "protest free zone" with respect to major protest parades and offered the would-be Nazi protestors (and all other would-be protestors) the use of a designated speech zone on the edge of town. Why should the Holocaust survivors of Skokie accept a level of threat that an incumbent federal official or national nominating convention delegate does not?

Moreover, the security rationale seems potentially remarkably broad in its scope in the age of would-be human suicide bombers with explosives in their shoes or underwear. If the possibility of a human suicide bomber justifies closing a great swath of downtown Denver to protestors or demonstrators during the 2008 Democratic National Convention,[75] why could a city not cite the generic risk of such violence in the post-9/11, "war on terror" world to prohibit protest proximate to government buildings or major commercial districts? Surely the risk of a human suicide bomber does not cease to exist when the politicians and convention delegates leave town. Moreover, mass demonstrations and protests are seldom good for business; economic self-interest and a desire to avoid adverse publicity make it increasingly likely that the security rationale currently used in limited circumstances involving very high-profile events will be deployed more regularly, and more creatively, to banish protest activities from city centers even in the absence of a major political event or presidential appearance.

One way of solving the dilemma would be to restore *Beauharnais*[76] and *Chaplinsky*.[77] In other words, the inconsistency could be resolved by crediting more generally plausible safety concerns. Rather than leveling politicians and party leaders down to the level of African Americans and Jews in Hamilton County, Ohio (site of the Klan rally at issue in *Brandenburg*) or Holocaust survivors in Skokie, Illinois (site of the planned Nazi march in *Collin*), we could level average citizens up by embracing a free speech doctrine that more resembles the Hand formula (or that incorporates German dignitarian concerns or Canadian equalitarian concerns).

Such an approach should be rejected, however, because it would eviscerate the viewpoint and content neutrality project. *Beauharnais* and *Chaplinsky* fell into desuetude precisely because the justices correctly feared that permitting safety justifications to sustain broad-based content bans on speech would inevitably lead to targeted enforcement, giving rise to serious viewpoint discrimination problems. Thus, when Dr. Ben Marble from Gulfport, Mississippi, tells Vice President Cheney to "go fuck yourself" in a fit of pique post Hurricane Katrina, a prosecution might well result, but when the vice president deploys identical language against a member of the U.S. Senate, a prosecution would never ensue.[78] And this pattern of highly selective enforcement exists in places, like Canada, that maintain content-based limits on speech in order to promote other constitutional values (in Canada's case, equality and multiculturalism).[79]

The answer, then, would not be to level everyone up to the level of the president or party bigwigs attending the national nominating convention (we could call this the "censorship for all" approach). Reversing the Warren Court's precedents establishing a strong bulwark against viewpoint and content discrimination would not lead to normatively better results—quite the opposite. The better approach would be to apply the time, place, and manner doctrine in a fashion that advances, rather than eviscerates, the Warren Court's project of debarring government efforts to silence speech based on either its viewpoint or its content. Yet, for the reasons previously discussed, the lower federal courts have been rather reluctant to take this course of action, especially when government cloaks its censorial objectives in the language of "security."[80]

The other potential effect of generalizing the validity of the security argument premised on a human suicide bomber would be the death of the traditional public forum. If streets and sidewalks near official government buildings, banks, corporate headquarters, subway stations, bus stops, and other centers of economic, political, and social life within an urban community could be closed to protest as a prophylactic measure against terrorism, little public space would be left for expressive activity. This might make the streets and sidewalks marginally safer, but only at a severe price, in terms of democratic deliberation.

If public space ceases to be presumptively available for speech and assembly, the community's deliberative process will be worse for it. Mass protest, in public, communicates a message which a blog entry or tweet does not, for manifold reasons.[81] At its most elementary, the act of citizens coming together, in public, to protest as a group has a communicative effect simply not present in a printed pamphlet, letter to the editor, or Internet posting. The security rationale, however, poses a very stark question that merits more sustained and critical attention than it has received to date in the federal courts: Should we be willing to sacrifice the traditional modalities of democratic deliberation as necessary, but perhaps regrettable, casualties of a potentially endless war on terrorism?

C. What Values Does the Lenient Application of the Time, Place, and Manner Doctrine Actually Advance?

If the legitimate security concerns of the government could be met by quite obvious, more narrowly tailored, and self-evidently content neutral means— such as limits on the size of demonstrations or fixed protests and the use of careful screening of demonstrators protesting in areas proximate to meeting venues—what is really driving the efforts of local governments to ban or marginalize dissenting speech proximate to major political gatherings? At least arguably, the real purpose of these restrictions is to protect the dignity and sensibilities of the public officials attending the meetings.[82]

When the president or a national political party goes to the time and trouble to mount a major event, it seems unsportsmanlike to attempt to spoil the press coverage by attempting to disseminate a conflicting message, using the very cameras and reporters generated by virtue of the president's or the delegates' presence. From the perspective of the organizers, a protest proximate to a presidential appearance or a national presidential nominating convention is a kind of attempted public relations larceny. It is not at all surprising that persons planning such events would seek to monopolize all media coverage and would work diligently to avoid having the media presence used against the interests of the organizers to promote the opposition's message and viewpoints.

Security provides a trump card that organizers can deploy to minimize, if not eliminate, the possibility of media coverage of a staged political theater event being redirected against those putting on the show. In fact, the George W. Bush administration's *Presidential Advance Manual*, while not advocating a complete ban on protest activity incident to presidential appearances, squarely insists that the president must not be within eyesight of the demonstrators.[83] This blanket ban on protest activity within the eyesight of the president plainly has little to do with security and much to do with preventing the potential dissemination of viewpoints inconsistent with those of the president.

Moreover, if there are plausible security reasons for disallowing behavior that seems tacky and distasteful in the first place, why not permit the government to regulate demonstrations to the point of irrelevance? Doing so permits the organizers to harvest the positive public relations that their efforts have brought to fruition. Security, properly defined, means protection from a viable threat— here, the threat is one not of violence or physical harm but rather of political or ideological harm.

Frankly, if the efforts of Boston and Denver to facilitate dissent are the best local governments can do, consistent with the imperatives of "security,"[84] the federal courts should seriously consider endorsing even *broader* restrictions on protest near meeting venues that would obviate the need for designated protest zones altogether. Given their almost utter uselessness as a means of communication with the delegates, party leaders, and government officials, the media, and the general public, why not save everyone the time and trouble and simply abolish these free speech Potemkin villages?

The creation of useless designated protest zones in places like Boston, Colorado Springs, and Denver constitutes a silly game of cat and mouse, in which the object of the game is to render effective protest proximate to the meeting venue as close to impossible as can be managed—without quite crossing the line of a flat ban against the expression of dissent (which might itself generate negative media attention).[85] Government wants to neuter protest while, at the same time, proclaiming its deep-seated commitment to honoring the First Amendment's imperatives. Flat and total speech bans would at least be more intellectually honest than the tattered fig leaves that most designated protest zones represent.

The dignity of the public officials, which one could view as coextensive with the dignity of the state itself, demands that official events, whether dedications, rallies of the partisan faithful, or retreats to vacation homes, do not become a kind of bizarre political circus. If the ability of the government to disseminate a message without the threat of immediate and vociferous contradiction counts as a security interest, then the recent use of no-protest zones, cages, and barbed wire makes a great deal of sense. "Security" means the ability of those in power to speak directly to the citizenry without the immediate threat of contradiction. And neither the Free Speech Clause nor the Free Assembly Clause, at least according to the U.S. Courts of Appeals for the First, Ninth, and Tenth Circuits, protect any right of proximate protest to those holding political power. Instead, ordinary Americans must rely on less certain means to share their views with both public officials and the larger political community, such as Internet postings and letters to the editor.

The Adams administration sought the enactment of the Sedition Act of 1798[86] not on grounds that it would be politically useful to imprison the publishers of opposition Jeffersonian newspapers, but rather on the unassailable ground of national security.[87] Speech aimed at bringing the government into contempt and disrepute constitutes a palpable threat to the security of the state; the dignity of the state bears a material equivalence with the dignity of the incumbent public officials running the apparatus of the state.[88] The notion that security, dignity, and seditious libel all can and do relate to the same core concerns about protecting and keeping governmental power safely in the hands of those who currently hold it is far from merely hypothetical; rather, it constitutes a historical fact.[89]

III. THE DIGNITY OF THE STATE RECONSIDERED: A PLAUSIBLE RATIONALE FOR RESTRICTING SPEECH? A COMPARATIVE LAW APPROACH SUGGESTS YES

Could a free speech doctrine recognizing the importance of the dignity of the state represent a plausible conception of the right? Or, is any concern for the government's dignity necessarily inconsistent with a meaningful commitment to the freedom of expression? A comparative law perspective suggests that, in fact, one could posit a human rights regime committed to the protection of free expression, but equally committed to ensuring the survival of the institutions of government (if not the political survival of those currently staffing those institutions of government). The Federal Republic of Germany provides an example of just this approach.

Germany is a "militant democracy" and expressly withdraws constitutional protection from speech aimed at the "overthrow of the existing democratic order."[90] The Basic Law (*Grundgesetz*), Germany's constitution, repeatedly limits the scope of constitutionally protected free expression and political activity to exclude speech aimed at the destruction of democratic self-governance.[91] Speech seeking the overthrow of the free democratic basic order enjoys no protection under Article 5 of the Basic Law, Germany's analogue to the First Amendment, and Article 21 declares that political parties that seek to overthrow the free democratic basic order are unlawful and subject to being completely banned from participation in the electoral process. Moreover, the Federal Constitutional Court has agreed to ban two parties from participating in the democratic process (although this took place in the 1950s), and as recently at the early 1990s the federal government has sought to ban extreme right-wing parties from contesting local, state, and federal elections.[92] For Germany, then, a commitment to "militant democracy" is not merely a theoretical matter.

To be sure, this protection of the state itself does not rest on dignitarian concerns. The Federal Constitutional Court, in point of contrast, has repeatedly emphasized that the state itself does not possess a constitutionally cognizable interest in dignity (unlike all human beings, including persons holding government office).[93] Even so, the state has a duty and responsibility to ensure that public support for the institutions of government does not fall to a level that would create a risk to the survival of those institutions.

Accordingly, although the Basic Law's free speech guarantee privileges defacing a German flag or mocking the national anthem with a parody, a point exists at which calling the symbols of the nation into scorn or contempt might run up against the Basic Law's commitment to preserving the project of democratic self-government. When and if expressive activity reaches that point, the Federal Constitutional Court will withdraw constitutional protection from the speech in order to safeguard the institutions of democratic self-government.[94] As one commentator puts it, "To formulate this idea differently, the German flag case presupposes that the state can protect itself against seditious libel."[95]

This notion of militant democracy has little salience in the pages of *U.S. Reports*. On the contrary, many aspects of contemporary U.S. free speech doctrine expressly reject this notion of militant democracy, proudly proclaiming that the First Amendment protects even speech advocating violent proletarian revolution, unless there is a clear and present danger of the advocacy bringing the harm about in an imminent fashion outside the political process.[96] Thus, current free speech law in the United States does not take seriously the notion that speech may be censored in order to safeguard the viability of the democratic state.[97] This makes reliance on the dignity of the state, at least as the idea has developed in Germany, an implausible basis for defending the use of speech bans proximate to national political leaders and party gatherings in the contemporary United States.

Consistent with this approach, in *Boos v. Barry*[98] the U.S. Supreme Court considered, and squarely rejected, the argument for a ban on picketing within five hundred feet of a foreign embassy using signs that would tend to bring the foreign government into "public odium" or "public disrepute."[99] Writing for the majority, Justice O'Connor credited the notion that the District of Columbia government possessed a significant interest "in protecting the dignity of foreign diplomatic personnel."[100] The Court nevertheless rejected this interest as a sufficient justification for a restriction of such sweep and breadth on peaceful protest activity in a classic public forum: "We are not persuaded that the differences between foreign officials and American citizens require us to deviate" from generic U.S. free speech principles, which require extending constitutional protection to "insulting, and even outrageous speech," including "outrageous" speech intentionally designed to inflict maximum emotional harm.[101] Moreover, "the fact that an interest [in human dignity] is recognized in international law does not automatically render that interest 'compelling' for purposes of First Amendment analysis."[102]

Even assuming, for the sake of argument, that the dignitarian interest that the District of Columbia local government sought to advance was, in fact, sufficiently "compelling" to support a content-based speech ban, the Court held "that the display clause of § 22–1115 is inconsistent with the First Amendment."[103] Thus, the U.S. Supreme Court squarely rejected a speech ban as a permissible means of securing an interest in dignity, at least when the dignity interest at issue related to a representative of a foreign government. German constitutional law generally places a much higher value on securing human dignity.

To be sure, the German conception of constitutionally protected dignity is not all-encompassing. For example, it does not purport to insulate government leaders from public criticism of their policies—the dignity of the state does not require that citizens be sheep. Rather, the doctrine would justify speech restrictions that have as their purpose not a change or reform in a particular government policy or program but rather the destruction of the government and its institutions. Even the protection of human dignity, the paramount right that the Basic Law protects, does not protect politicians from public disagreement with their policies and platforms. Instead, it justifies restrictions on political speech aimed not at criticizing policies but rather at dehumanizing and degrading the government officials as human beings.[104]

Thus, although one could imagine a free speech jurisprudence that takes seriously both the need to limit speech to protect the survival of the government and also to ensure a modicum of respect for the intrinsic value and dignity of all persons (including elected officials), the German approach would not justify the results in the national convention, presidential appearance, and international meeting cases. The cases limiting protest do so in order to fence out fair criticism of government and party policy, not protests aimed at facilitating a coup d'état or denying the humanity of incumbent politicians. The U.S. restrictions have much more in common with free speech protections in contemporary China and Russia than with those in Germany—that is to say, the attempts to silence or marginalize speech have more to do with suppressing legitimate dissent than with upholding more transcendent human rights values or preserving the institutions necessary to secure human rights for all.

IV. PROTECTING THE DIGNITY OF POLITICIANS AND THE LIMITED RETURN OF SEDITIOUS LIBEL

If protecting the institutions of government or securing everyone's equal share in humanity cannot justify the draconian restrictions placed on demonstrators seeking to oppose government or party policies, and if the Hand formula is equally unavailing as a theoretical justification for these tactics, what (if any) theoretical construction of free expression undergirds the recent lower court cases sustaining the forced use of free speech cages and pens? Is there any basis, beyond a naked effort to suppress disagreeable viewpoints, that justifies the use of time, place, and manner restrictions to banish dissent from the environs surrounding an incumbent government official's appearance at a rally, meeting, or convention? In fact there is: the doctrine of seditious libel.

Succinctly put, "[s]editious libel is the crime of criticizing the government,"[105] a crime that has its origins in the crime of treason. In the early seventeenth century, the British monarchy grappled with the fact that the treason laws, which were intended to deter armed rebellion, were "too cumbersome" to be used against dissenting speech.[106] Therefore, to deal with dangerous and troublesome critics, the Stuarts came to rely upon the crime of seditious libel, "which prohibited the publishing of scandalous or discordant opinions about the crown, its policies, or its officers."[107] The Crown punished seditious libelers by whipping, branding, and mutilation.[108]

In the eighteenth century, as Parliament replaced the monarchy in matters of the state, criminal prosecutions for seditious libel continued in order to force public compliance with its agenda.[109] Seditious libel soon became the government's primary means of regulating the press, replacing the controversial and cumbersome licensing scheme.[110] As a result, it is estimated that hundreds were convicted of seditious libel in seventeenth- and eighteenth-century England.[111]

Chief Justice Holt declared the state of the law in the case of John Tutchin, who was prosecuted for seditious libel when he accused government officials of bribery and corruption: "To say that corrupt officers are appointed to administer affairs, is certainly a reflection on the government. If people should not be called to account for possessing the people with an ill opinion of the government, no government can subsist. For it is very necessary for all governments that the people should have a good opinion of it."[112] Thus, speech against the government was punishable even though true, so long as it tended to undermine government authority.[113] As Blackstone said, "It is immaterial with respect to the essence of a libel, whether the matter of it be true or false; since the provocation, and not the falsity, is the thing to be punished criminally."[114]

Although seditious libel prosecutions were commonplace in Britain, in colonial America there were relatively few.[115] Some estimate there were fewer than a dozen.[116] In those few instances in which the law of seditious libel was enforced, it was done so primarily by the provincial legislatures, then by executive officers, and lastly by the common law courts.[117] The first prosecution for seditious libel was in 1690 in Pennsylvania,[118] and the most famous of these prosecutions was that of John Zenger in 1735.[119] But both of these cases and many like them resulted in acquittals when juries refused to return guilty verdicts.[120]

Court trials for seditious libel ceased to be a serious threat to colonial publishers after Zenger was acquitted.[121] In fact, it seems that there was only one successful prosecution before the *Zenger* case, and none after it.[122]

But as revolution neared, politicians grew more fearful, and the Continental Congress urged the states to enact laws "to prevent people from being 'deceived and drawn into erroneous opinion.'"[123] By 1778, every state had passed such legislation. During the revolution, penalties in the states ranged from heavy fines, to imprisonment, to death for the simple statement of opinions denying the independent authority of the American states and asserting the authority of the British sovereign.[124]

In the early years of the new republic, the crisis with France and the vocal domestic political opposition convinced the Federalists to pass the Sedition Act in 1798.[125] The act basically codified the common law crime of seditious libel;[126] however, the act, at least on paper, differed from the common law in a few ways. First, it limited the maximum penalty to two years' imprisonment and a $2,000 fine, which significantly reduced the consequences of a conviction.[127] In addition, it allowed the accused to submit proof of the truth of her statements and gave the jury the power to determine whether the accused had acted with malicious intent; under the common law rule, truth was no defense.[128]

These efforts to make the statutory version of seditious libel less draconian than its common law counterpart fell flat. The federal courts effectively nullified these provisions by making prosecution under the Sedition Act the full equivalent of prosecutions under the common law for seditious libel by disregarding sentencing limits and nullifying the statutory truth defense through judicial construction of the statute.[129] Thus, the truth did not operate as an effective defense,[130] judges instructed juries on the defendant's intent,[131] and judges presumed the defendant's intent from the "bad tendency" of her words.[132]

For example, in the trial of Thomas Cooper, a prominent Democratic-Republican Party supporter, the judge ruled that Cooper's attempt to prove the truth of his publication proved his bad intent by showing that "he intended to dare and defy the Government, and to provoke them. . . . For he justifies the publication, and declares it to be formed in truth."[133] Thus, "it was the tendency of the words to find fault with elected officials which was penalized and not the intent to cause violence."[134]

Consequently, under the Sedition Act, individuals "were punished if the tendency of their words was to undermine public confidence in the elected officials and thus to render it less likely that they might be re-elected."[135] The courts, as a result, effectively nullified the provisions of the act that the Federalists claimed set it apart from the common law crime of seditious libel.[136] The act therefore operated, like seditious libel before it, to silence criticism of the government.[137]

In two years, the Federalists indicted fourteen individuals under the Sedition Act and ultimately procured ten convictions.[138] All of these indictments were pursued to silence speech critical of the Adams administration.[139]

The House debates make clear beyond peradventure that Federalist Party supporters of the Sedition Act believed "that the political opinion of the opposition party constituted seditious libel, subject to prosecution" under the act.[140] As Pennsylvania Representative Albert Gallatin stated:

This bill and its supporters suppose, in fact, that whoever dislikes the measures of Administration [*sic*] and of a temporary majority in Congress, and shall, either by speaking or writing, express his disapprobation and his want of confidence in the men now in power, is seditious, is an enemy, not of Administration, but of the Constitution, and is liable to punishment. That principle . . . was subversive of the principles of the Constitution itself. If you put the press under any restraint in respect to the measures of members of Government; if you thus deprive the people of the means of obtaining information of their conduct, you in fact render their right of electing nugatory; and this bill must be considered only as a weapon used by a party now in power, in order to perpetuate their authority and preserve their present places.[141]

Consistent with this legislative history, Federalists first used the Sedition Act to attack Republican Representative Matthew Lyon of Vermont, a known critic of the Adams administration and the Federalist Party in general. Shortly after the act was passed, Lyon was convicted on the basis of two letters published during his congressional reelection campaign.[142] In the letters, Lyon criticized Adams's "'continual grasp for power' and his 'unbounded thirst for ridiculous pomp, foolish adulation, and selfish avarice.'"[143]

As the election of 1800 neared, the Sedition Act prosecutions intensified. President Adams's secretary of state, Timothy Pickering, systematically orchestrated prosecutions of the leading Republican (pro-Jefferson) newspapers in preparation for the election.[144] Pickering targeted the "big five" in the opposition press: the Philadelphia *Aurora*, the Boston *Chronicle*, the New York *Argus*, the Richmond *Examiner*, and the Baltimore *American*.[145] In the summer of 1799, Pickering sent directives to district attorneys in Baltimore, New York, and Richmond, "instructing them to scrutinize the Republican papers issued in their cities and to prosecute them for any seditious libels against the President or any federal official."[146]

Pickering deliberately sent these directives early in the summer so that the district attorneys would have sufficient time to bring indictments at either the fall or the spring term of the circuit court. In addition, with President Adams's express approval, he took personal control over the proceedings against William Duane, editor of Philadelphia's *Aurora*.[147]

As a result of Pickering's scheme, indictments were brought against four of the big five[148] newspapers for criticizing the Adams administration.[149] Three of the most prominent Republican editors were forced to stop publishing, two permanently. This was no small feat; the Republican newspapers prior to the Sedition Act were already outnumbered by their Federalist counterparts.

Professor David Anderson has noted that out of 101 newspapers in existence in the United States at the time, only twelve possessed Republican editorial sympathies, and that "[t]he Republican newspapers already were greatly outnumbered by their Federalist rivals" at the time Congress enacted the Sedition Act.[150]

Furthermore, the big five newspapers' influence was not limited solely to their subscribers; at that time, smaller newspapers for the most part simply reprinted materials from the larger papers.[151] Thus, as Professor Anderson notes, "[s]ilencing them would have effectively cut off press criticism at its sources."[152] In sum, the Adams administration came dangerously close to wiping out the opposition press in America just in time for the national election of 1800.[153]

The Sedition Act, although a sordid chapter in the history of U.S. free speech law, was hardly an isolated incident. The Espionage Act of 1917,[154] as amended in 1918, contained "sections that oddly echoed the idiom of seditious libel: 'language intended to bring the form of government of the United States . . . or the Constitution . . . or the flag . . . or the uniform of the Army or Navy into contempt, scorn, contumely, or disrepute.'"[155]

Professors Judith Koffler and Bennett Gershman argue that prosecution under the Espionage Act constituted prosecution for seditious libel because those prosecuted under the act "had, by written or spoken word, defamed the government. Holding the administration up to hatred, contempt, and ridicule, they . . . had attacked official judgment as corrupt and mercenary; they had accused the government of deception," and for this they were convicted of a crime.[156] Professor David Jenkins also asserts that the Espionage Act, like the Sedition Act of 1798, constituted seditious libel because it "specifically applied to press activity that defamed the federal government."[157] Moreover, the Supreme Court expressed its acceptance of seditious libel in the series of cases that arose from prosecutions under the Espionage Act.[158]

World War I did not mark the last time the federal government attempted to adopt a law that essentially tracked the common law crime of seditious libel. At least arguably, the Smith Act of 1940[159] constituted seditious libel because it "made it a crime to help organize any group of persons 'who teach, advocate, or encourage the overthrow or destruction of any government in the United States by force or violence,' and also proscribed the advocacy of these doctrines."[160] Koffler and Gershman persuasively argue that the Supreme Court's decision in *Dennis v. United States*,[161] upholding the Smith Act, strengthened and reaffirmed the tradition of seditious libel in this country.[162]

From the creation of the doctrine of seditious libel in Great Britain, to its importation into colonial legal systems, to its subsequent adoption and ratification by the federal government as a means of promoting national security in times of perceived domestic and international stress, governments ostensibly committed to protecting the freedom of speech have consistently attempted to limit speech critical of the government in the name of national security. The rationale for the doctrine of seditious libel rests on the notion that government must be protected from criticism that has the effect of undermining its popular support and, ultimately, its effectiveness.

Government efforts in Boston, Colorado Springs, Denver, Seattle, and St. Paul[163] may not seem as vulgar or outrageous as those of the Adams administration (although the matter is debatable), but the *motivation*—avoidance of public embarrassment—is little different. Nor are the effects of the restrictions on the marketplace of ideas. Democracy suffers whenever government succeeds in banishing its critics from public view, regardless of the precise means deployed to achieve this purpose.

V. CONCLUSION

The chapter has considered the viability of security as a basis for restricting freedom of speech. As a doctrinal matter, the government's interest in peace, order, and security cannot be advanced by regulating or prohibiting speech until less drastic means have been tried and proven ineffective; government must first punish litterbugs before it seeks to ban leafleting on public streets and sidewalks.[164] Just as "public convenience in respect of cleanliness of the streets does not justify an exertion of the police power which invades the free communication of information and opinion secured by the Constitution,"[165] abstract and generalized concerns about security cannot serve to justify banning protest from the streets and sidewalks when a national or international meeting takes place, or when the president or vice president visits town. Just as the first and best remedy for litter "is the punishment of those who actually throw papers on the streets,"[166] so too the appropriate response to disorderly or disruptive conduct is to punish such conduct when and if it occurs, not to banish all speech activity as a prophylactic measure against its mere possibility.

To be sure, alternative theories of the freedom of speech exist under which a comprehensive concern for social costs might justify the creation of substantial limits on freedom of expression. The Learned Hand formula, for example, would sanction restrictions on speech that, by its very existence, enhances the risk of serious harm to the community. Thus, calls for the violent overthrow of the government, no matter how unlikely to bring about that result, might be regulated or even proscribed on the theory that the potential harm is so grave that society simply cannot shoulder *any* risk to accommodate the speech.

Here again, however, the theory does not fit the facts in Boston, Colorado Springs, Denver, and St. Paul. The proposed speech in those cities did not involve calls for unlawful action of any sort, much less the violent overthrow of the government. The speech activity *itself* was the *perceived threat of harm*, not the *content of the message*.

Finally, one might posit a theory of free speech in which the dignity of the government constitutes a valid basis for regulating, or prohibiting, speech because the survival and success of the government is a necessary condition for society to enjoy all the civil rights and liberties that government secures to the people. Germany maintains such a view of free speech, incident to its commitment to maintaining "militant democracy"; free speech cannot be tolerated to the extent that it might bring about the destruction of the institutions that make the exercise of free speech possible in the first place. This theory also provided the theoretical foundation for the doctrine of seditious libel in the United Kingdom and, later, in the United States.

Yet, even in Germany, the standard for establishing that speech critical of the government lies outside the protection of the Basic Law is quite demanding—indeed, speech that mocks national symbols of unity, such as the national flag and anthem, fall far below the threshold required to justify a ban on such speech. For the dignity of the state to serve as a basis for proscribing speech in Germany, the government must prove that the speech at issue realistically undermines popular support of the nation's governing institutions to such a degree that it constitutes a threat to the free democratic basic order. The use of protest-free zones and designated protest zones in places like Boston, Colorado Springs, Denver, Seattle, and St. Paul do not seem to be justifiable responses to such a threat in the United States.

If security is to serve as a basis for restricting speech, one would hope that the federal courts would treat security in a consistent fashion. If average citizens must assume risk in order to facilitate free speech, so too should government and its officers. And, if the dignity of the state constitutes a sufficient interest to justify speech regulations, the dignity of average citizens should count for no less. Yet, this is simply not how existing First Amendment doctrine approaches the question of social cost and speech.

At the end of the day, the government's interest in security, which, as with seditious libel, seems eerily related to its dignity interests (if not inseparable from them), is the only security interest that seems to justify prior restraints against speech at particular times and places deemed "unsafe" by the government itself. In light of these contemporary realities, a pressing question that needs to be asked and answered comes into clear focus: How best can we meet the challenge that today's new iteration of seditious libel presents to full, free, and open public discourse? At least arguably, the answer potentially lies in what, at least at present, represents a relatively unexplored and undertheorized constitutional corner: the Petition Clause.

4

The Right of Petition in Historical Perspective and Across Three Societies

I. INTRODUCTION

If the Petition Clause is to be reclaimed, what precisely would the federal courts and the American people be reclaiming? Petitioning has a long and deep history in Anglo-American law, and dates back to Magna Carta itself. But the history of petitioning is complicated by the absence of a doctrine of separation of powers in both Great Britain and the colonial and revolutionary-era United States, and the commonplace use of petitioning in both Great Britain and the British North American colonies as a means of seeking redress for private complaints—rather than changes in public policy.

Given the relative obscurity of the Petition Clause to most contemporary legal scholars, judges, and practitioners, a brief review of its origins is in order.[1] Whereas the rights of speech, press, and assembly cannot be said to have fully emerged until the late eighteenth or early nineteenth century, the near-absolute right of all British subjects to petition the king was codified in the English Bill of Rights of 1689.[2] In fact, the other First Amendment rights of speech, press, and assembly are, in many respects, the progeny of the right to petition.[3] Yet the incorporation of petitioning into the English Bill of Rights was merely the culmination, rather than the origination, of the right to petition for a redress of grievances.

To be clear, in suggesting the need to attend to the right of petition's history and significance in times past, I am not arguing for an originalist interpretation of the Petition Clause today. Like the Free Speech Clause, the Petition Clause should be interpreted and applied dynamically or purposively—the federal courts should identify the core purpose, or purposes, of the Petition Clause and then use the clause to advance and secure them. However, given the general desuetude into which the Petition Clause has fallen in the contemporary United States, a consideration of its historical origins and past meaning should be useful, perhaps even essential, to identifying and securing its proper place in contemporary constitutional law.

As the discussion that follows will show, the Petition Clause represents James Madison's appreciation of a preexisting tradition of meaningful access to the government—whether local, state, or federal. Petitioning in the United States, and at the federal level of government, significantly predated adoption of the Petition Clause. Petitioning constituted a core element of democratic theory and practice in the founding era; government, and its officers, had a duty to be accessible not only to voters but to all persons living within the polity—male or female, white or black, free or slave. In addition to providing access, petitioning served as a central focal point for democratic engagement; by the first half of the nineteenth century, systemic petitioning activities engaged not only the govern-ment and its elected officials but also the media and the public at large. Thus, the history of petitioning in the United States and the United Kingdom shows that, at its core, the concept of petitioning secures a right of meaningful *access* to the government and serves as a means of *democratic engagement* more broadly within the polity.[4]

The present chapter considers petitioning in three societies: the United Kingdom, the United States, and New Zealand. The story in the United Kingdom and the United States is largely the same: after a brief, and fairly recent, period of flourishing, classic petitioning[5] as an effective means of seek-ing changes in public policies had withered, if not died, by the 1830s. However, the standard narrative omits an important caveat: systemic, or hybrid, petition-ing activities actually grew in both number and in participation from 1840 through the close of the nineteenth century.

Although Congress and Parliament both ceased to consider and respond to petitions routinely by the 1840s, hybrid forms of petitioning that used the circu-lation of a mass public petition as the focus for a more general organizational, political, and media campaign flourished. This hybrid, or systemic, form of petitioning had as its objective moving general public opinion as much, if not more, than securing immediate legislative gains, and it used public demonstra-tions, rallies, parades, and door-to-door canvassing as central components of the petitioning exercise. In systemic petitioning, the presentation of a formal peti-tion to a legislative body was almost incidental to the larger, public effort to organize supporters, mobilize public support and media attention, and move public opinion in favor of some specific reform objective. Most accounts of petitioning, in both the United Kingdom and the United States, fail to distinguish adequately between classic petitioning and this new, radically democratized systemic petitioning.

The story in New Zealand, however, is quite different. To this day, New Zealand maintains an active classic petitioning culture in which average citizens use the petition process to initiate meaningful legislative review of existing policies, and, crucially, the national legislature takes seriously its duty to respond to citizen petitions on the merits. New Zealand provides an instructive exemplar of the possibility of an active petitioning culture in the twenty-first century, and it provides an important counterexample to those who might otherwise argue that petitioning represents little more than an outdated mode of political expression. Even so, the petitioning culture that exists in contemporary New Zealand might be difficult to transplant to an environment in which citizens do not expect incumbent legislators to consider and respond to unsolicited petitions from the general public.

II. ONE THOUSAND YEARS OF PETITIONING: THE RIGHT TO PETITION FOR REDRESS OF GRIEVANCES IN THE UNITED KINGDOM

The right of petition originated in the United Kingdom, and to this day it is possible for British citizens to petition the House of Commons. Quite literally, a bag hangs on the back of the Speaker's chair for the express purpose of members submitting petitions from constituents to the House for its consideration. The modern-day right of petition, however, bears very little relationship to petition at its inception or during its golden age.

Petition began as a kind of judicial action, effectively a kind of lawsuit prosecuted directly before the Crown. Over time, however, petitions seeking individual justice migrated to the courts, and petitions seeking changes in public policies became more commonplace. From 1779 to 1836, the age of classic petitioning, petitions seeking legislative change were commonplace, and Parliament acted under an obligation to receive, debate, consider, and answer all such petitions.

As mass systemic petitioning campaigns seeking expansion of voting rights and other electoral reforms came to dominate Parliament's floor in the 1830s, the House of Commons adopted new parliamentary procedures aimed at rendering petitions largely ineffectual as a direct means of facilitating legislative change. Ironically, however, these "reforms" came in response to a radical democratization of petitioning; increasingly, citizens used the petitioning process as much to organize and rally general public support as to achieve legislative results. Classic petitioning gave way to systemic forms of petitioning that annexed mass meetings, parades, and demonstrations to the circulation and presentation of petitions to Parliament. Even though Parliament itself responded by ceasing to debate or consider petitions, the golden age of petitioning in the United Kingdom arguably took place from 1839 to 1914, when systemic petitioning was a regular and quite common means of direct political action, and literally millions of average citizens signed, circulated, and demonstrated in favor of and against specific petitions.

After 1914, petitioning in the United Kingdom fell into general desuetude, and reached a point of obscurity so great that, in 1944, the parliamentary committee charged with receiving and considering petitions no longer possessed any sense of its proper role or function. Today, petitioning constitutes an empty legal formalism, and neither classic nor systemic petitioning has much political or cultural salience in the United Kingdom. Nevertheless, the story of petitioning in the United Kingdom provides an important gloss on the right; in particular, it seems clear that "petitioning" has always been a dynamic legal concept that, over time, has evolved and changed with great regularity. The history of petitioning in the United Kingdom also demonstrates that during the petitioning era of 1779–1914, petitions and petitioning served both as a means for ordinary people to gain access to the government and its officials and as a way of engaging the political community. Moreover, petitioning served as an important and effective means of placing concerns on the national agenda, well after the practice ceased to be a reliable means of securing the enactment of legislation.

A. The English Origins of the Right to Petition

The English origins of the right to petition are ancient, dating as far back as the tenth century, when petitions to the king were not of right and were limited to redress of property disputes that had not been resolved to the parties' satisfaction by lesser tribunals.[6] It was not until 1215, when the barons exacted Magna Carta from King John, that petitioning began to take significance as a means of asserting political power against the state.[7] In exchange for the barons' allegiance—and their agreement to finance the government—the king agreed to the following: "[I]f we or our justiciar, or our bailiffs, or any of our servants shall have done wrong in any way toward any one, or shall have transgressed any of the articles of peace or security; and the wrong shall have been shown to four barons of the aforesaid twenty-five barons, let those four barons come to us . . . laying before us the transgression, and let them ask that we cause that transgression to be corrected without delay."[8] Magna Carta thus secured to the barons, and, indirectly, the people, the right to petition the king for redress of their grievances.

Over time various segments of society, including knights and burgesses, were also granted audiences by the Crown as the royal government's financial needs increased. "The petitions, addressed to the king or to the king and his council . . . furnished abundant work to the permanent council, and the special parliaments were probably the solemn occasions on which they were presented and discussed."[9] Like those of the barons, the petitions these representatives presented on behalf of individuals and their communities were granted in exchange for commitments to make payments to the Crown. As England transitioned from feudalism toward a centralized bureaucracy, coupled with the emergence of Parliament as a governing institution independent of the Crown, the status and frequency of petitioning blossomed.[10]

By the reign of Edward III, which spanned fifty years from 1327 to 1377, petitioning was a well-accepted means of seeking legal redress from the Crown. As Professor William Stubbs notes: "It was under Edward III that it became a regular form at the opening of parliament for the chancellor to declare the king's willingness to hear the petitions of his people: all who had grievances were to bring them to the foot of the throne that the king with the advice of his council or of the lords might redress them; but the machinery for receiving and considering such petitions as came from private individuals or separate communities was perfected, as we have seen, by Edward I."[11] Edward I earlier had established a system for sorting petitions and delegating resolution of some to the courts "to which the matter in question properly belonged, so that only important questions should be brought before the king and council, especially as were matters of grace and favour which could not be answered without reference to the king."[12]

As Parliament began to gain independence from the Crown in the late fourteenth and early fifteenth centuries, petitions began to be directed to Parliament in addition to or instead of the king.[13] While the rising legislative power was beginning to supplant royal prerogative, "'[c]ommon and frequent petitioning . . . took the place of prolonged discontent and abrupt presentation of a complex cahier of grievances at the point of the sword.' Under Edward III, it became established practice at the opening of every session of parliament . . . to declare the king's willingness to consider petitions of the people."[14]

One must also keep in mind that, at this juncture in English constitutional history, a working separation of executive, legislative, and judicial powers simply did not exist. Thus, for certain matters, the Crown served as the highest executive officer, the legislature, and the judicial tribunal of last resort. Many of the petitions submitted for consideration in this period would today take the form of lawsuits in the British courts. In this sense, then, these early petitions are substantively quite different from those filed in the late eighteenth century, which sought legislative action from Parliament involving generalized public policy concerns, such as abolition of the slave trade or reforms in the electoral system,[15] rather than some form of individual justice.

Moreover, Parliament itself generally petitioned the Crown to establish a particular law; it did not purport to make laws in its own name. Only later, and not until after Charles I gave his consent to the Petition of Right in 1628,[16] did Parliament consistently enact bills on its own authority and seek after the fact an increasingly pro forma royal assent to the bill's contents.[17] In fact, "[n]early the whole of legislation of the fourteenth century is based upon petitions of Parliament."[18] Accordingly, one must recognize that petitions in this period encompassed not just what we would understand as petitions in the modern era but also lawsuits and general legislation.[19] As Professor William Anson explains, "What are called public petitions, that is, petitions complaining of public griev-ances, and asking for some change in the general law, or some legislation to meet new circumstances, are not common before the seventeenth century."[20]

Although petitioning became commonplace and took on great political sig-nificance between the fourteenth and sixteenth centuries, it was a "right" only to the extent that the king and Parliament found it expedient. Petitioners could be, and routinely were, punished for their petitions.[21] Nevertheless, petitioning flourished because the government did find it expedient, and by 1571, Parliament found it necessary and useful to establish a Committee of Grievances to receive and review petitions.[22]

Not only were petitions an effective and efficient source of information, they also constituted a means by which each branch of government, particularly the Commons, could assert and expand its power against the others. Over time, this self-interest in receiving petitions evolved into a governmental sense of obliga-tion to receive and consider all petitions, and the citizenry came to expect no less. By the close of the sixteenth century, petitioning had grown into a "right," albeit still not an absolute one, held by all of the king's subjects.[23]

By the seventeenth century, petitioning in England had reached "enormous popularity," and it was during that era that "public petitions, that is, petitions complaining of public grievances, and asking for some change in the general law, or some legislation to meet new circumstances, [became] common."[24] Even more important, it was during the seventeenth century that petitioning became an absolute—or near-absolute—right.[25] In fact, it was the outcry over an attempt to punish a petitioning group of clergy for seditious libel that "led directly to the Glorious Revolution of 1688 and to the Bill of Rights that fully confirmed the right of petition as an element of the British constitution."[26]

In 1669, the House of Commons enacted a statutory declaration providing that "it is the inherent right of every commoner in England to prepare and present Petitions to the House of Commons in case of grievance, and the House of Commons to receive the same."[27] This declaration also provided that "it is an undoubted right and privilege of the Commons to judge and determine concerning the nature and matter of such petitions, how far they are fit or unfit to be received."[28] Parliament's declaration of 1669 establishes a right to petition, but not a right to a remedy, or even a response; instead, the House of Commons reserved for itself discretion to decide how—and even whether—to proceed after submission of a petition.[29]

By the early 1700s, petitioning had come to be viewed as the birthright of the English subject. As one commentator explains, petitions represented "the one method by which the unfranchised could take part in politics."[30] This growth in the importance and frequency of petitioning corresponds to the clearer demarcation of Parliament's legislative power. By the seventeenth century, "Parliament had come to be regarded as a political and legislative body rather than as the highest court of justice."[31]

On the other hand, the great parliamentary historian Erskine May dates modern petitioning on matters of public policy only to 1779. He writes that "[i]t was not until 1779, that an extensive organisation to promote measures of economical and parliamentary reform, called into activity a general system of petitioning,—commencing with the freeholders of Yorkshire, and extending to many of the most important counties and cities in the kingdom."[32] Even so, May also notes that "the number of petitions [at this time] was comparatively small" and that these petitions "bore little proportion to the vast accumulations of later times."[33]

Professor Peter Fraser concurs, explaining that well into the eighteenth century only the gentry could lawfully convene a public meeting and that the legal prohibitions against public assemblies "operated as an effective check on all political petitioning far into the eighteenth century."[34] Thus, "while there were innumerable private petitions to Parliament . . . in the century before 1779, one has to search hard to find anything resembling political petitioning, and when one does there is always some special justification."[35]

This dispute might well relate to the *nature* of the petitioning activity at issue. May and Fraser are writing about large-scale, mass petitioning, annexed to a popular political campaign within the general public and the print media to achieve some kind of political, economic, or social reform. This kind of collective political activity, for the reasons set forth by Professor Fraser, could not come into existence until large-scale public meetings—assemblies—were permitted under the law. Fraser reports that this did not occur until the late eighteenth and early nineteenth centuries.[36]

The ability of an individual or small group to petition, without a mass public campaign in support of the effort, came into existence earlier, by the late seventeenth century. Even so, however, if a petition offended either the Crown or Parliament, punishment for petitioning remained fairly commonplace; the fate of the Kentish petitioners, in 1701, is illustrative.[37]

The Kentish petition of 1701, which sought government funding for a standing army and military supplies to prepare the nation for a possible war with France, provoked "fury" among the Tory Party's members, who controlled the House of Commons. "They voted the petition was scandalous, insolent, and seditious, tending to destroy the constitution of Parliament, to subvert the established government; and ordered that Mr. Colepepper, who had been most forward in presenting it, and all others who had been concerned in it, should be taken into the custody of the serjeant [*sic*], whereupon five were imprisoned until the end of the session."[38] So much for the 1669 declaration that "it is an inherent right of every commoner of England to prepare and present petitions to the House of Commons."[39] The Kentish petitioners invoked the 1669 declaration by asserting that their petition came within the scope of existing legal regulations: "We are humbly of opinion, that it is our right to petition this Honourable House according to the Statute of 13 Car. 2 [1661]."[40]

Daniel Defoe, a prominent political commentator at the time (as well as an author and journalist), strongly condemned Parliament's actions in a public pamphlet, arguing that "[t]he imprisoning of these five Gentlemen had neither Reason, Law, Pretence, nor Policy in it";[41] he described imprisoning the petitioners as "the most Preposterous thing in nature" and "Nonsense in itself."[42] Defoe denounced the House's action as fundamentally inconsistent with the political liberties of an English subject.[43]

In any event, what Professor Robert Luce denominates as "systematic petitions," which involved "the modern system of agitation by petition,"[44] did not arise in the United Kingdom until the 1780s. By way of contrast, "[t]he American history of petitions begins at most with the coming of the colonists,"[45] and systemic petitioning was commonplace in Britain's North American colonies long before it became commonplace in the United Kingdom itself.[46]

Ironically, perhaps, the American Revolution helped to more firmly establish a petitioning culture in the United Kingdom. Fraser suggests that "[a]fter the revolt of the American colonies and the unfortunate course of the war had aroused strong opposition to Lord North's ministry, men 'of the first consideration and property' lent themselves to the Yorkshire petition for economical reform and to Wyvill's [a contemporary member of the House of Commons] petitioning movement."[47]

Subsequent major petitioning efforts in the 1780s included petitions to enfranchise more citizens and for abolition of the slave trade.[48] Quakers were the principal sponsors of the abolition petitions, and their activity increased over time. "In 1787 and 1788, a greater number of petitions were presented for this benevolent object, than had ever been addressed to Parliament, upon any other political question."[49] Professor Fraser suggests that "[s]ome of the greatest agitations were dominated by religious organizations, and these did not fail, but achieved a series of triumphs, from the abolition of the slave trade to the repeal of the Test and Corporation Acts and Catholic Emancipation."[50]

The abolition petitions were numerous and heavily subscribed, and they enjoyed support from politically influential individuals. In consequence, Parliament found itself constrained to respond on the merits to the abolitionists. "The question of the slave trade was immediately considered by the government, by the Privy Council, and by Parliament; and remedial measures were passed, which ultimately led to its prohibition."[51] Although Prime Minister William Pitt (the Younger) and King George III were not opposed to establishing limits on the slave trade, up to and including its ultimate abolition, "[t]he king and Mr. Pitt appear, from the first, to have regarded with disfavour this agitation for the abolition of the slave trade, by means of addresses and petitions, as being likely to establish a precedent for forcing the adoption of other measures, likely less unobjectionable."[52]

May reports that during the reign of George III, petitioning for legislation altering public policies remained relatively infrequent. "As yet, it was sought to express the sentiments of influential classes only; and a few select petitions from the principal counties and cities, —drawn with great ability, and signed by leading men, —characterised this period of the history of petitions."[53] Thus, systemic petitioning, involving mass signature-gathering efforts and public demonstrations and parades in support of a petition, were simply unknown, even at the start of the nineteenth century.

By the 1810s, members of the middle class, lacking the vote, had started to embrace petitioning as a means of making their voices heard in the political process. "In 1816, for instance, they successfully defeated the government's proposal to retain the wartime income tax," using petitions to the House of Commons as the primary means of waging their campaign.[54]

The prominence of petitioning as a form of mass political action changed radically by the 1820s, as the volume of petitions increased substantially and petitioning became a more thoroughly democratic endeavor.[55] "Petitioning" also came to
include not merely the formal submission of a petition to Parliament but also mass
meetings and protests, organizational efforts, and the use of the print media to rally
general public support in favor of a particular cause.[56] Whether denominated as
"systematic" petitioning (Luce's term),[57] systemic petitioning (my preferred term),
or hybrid petitioning, it represented something new under the sun: a form of wide-
open participatory democratic politics available to virtually anyone, including
men who lacked the right to vote, women, and conceivably even noncitizens.

As petitioning became more thoroughly democratized and popular,
Parliament found it increasingly more difficult to ignore (let alone punish) petitions and petitioners. Fraser observes that "[b]efore 1779 Parliament hardly ever
received, and never debated, petitions from the public upon state affairs" but
that "[b]y 1829 things had changed so much that both Houses did little else."[58]
This increase in the volume of both petitions and petitioners reflected "a
new and more widespread political awareness in the country," as well as a
recognition by those organizing mass petition campaigns that petitioning now
constituted "a new technique of parliamentary agitation."[59]

For example, opponents of slavery submitted almost twenty thousand petitions seeking abolition of slavery from 1824 to 1833, when Parliament enacted
the Emancipation Act, and "in 1833 alone, nearly seven thousand were laid
before the House of Commons."[60] Other popular subjects of petitions in the
1820s and 1830s included repeal of the Corporation and Test Acts, in favor of the
rights of evangelical Protestants and Roman Catholics to refuse financial support for the Church of England.[61] At its best, this new petitioning culture "served
to make the unreformed House of Commons more responsive to popular
demands than is usually allowed."[62]

B. Parliament's Efforts to "Reform" Petitioning from 1832 to 1842

The radical growth in the number of petitions presented to Parliament
required more and more legislative time. However, "[w]hatever the business
appointed for consideration, the claims of petitioners to a prior hearing, were
paramount."[63] According to May, "[a]lthough the right to petition 'was a great
privilege' of long standing, 'its continuance became incompatible with good
government.'"[64] The House of Commons restricted the right to debate petitions
over time and with ever-greater force and effect.

Before 1832, it was possible to speak from the floor up to four times on a petition, which permitted a handful of "radical" members of Parliament to hold the

floor for extended periods of time. "The procedure which had grown up by custom prescribed four regular motions as to each separate petition: (1) that the petition be brought up; (2) that it be received; (3) that it do lie upon the table; and (4) that it be printed: and on each motion debates might take place."[65] Radical members of Parliament, seeking to advance electoral reform and expanded suffrage, used petitions as a primary means of drawing attention to their cause, much to the consternation of the Tories.

In 1832, Sir Robert Peel moved the creation of select committee to "frame new regulations to govern the presentation of petitions."[66] Peel's proposal met with support from both major parties, the Tories and the Whigs, and Peel was appointed to chair the committee. The committee recommended, among other things, reducing the opportunity to speak on a petition from four to one, creating a special committee to consider petitions, and limiting the presentation of petitions to certain defined time periods.[67] The House of Commons decided to limit floor time available for the presentation and debate of petitions, and limited opportunities for speaking on petitions from four to two.[68] Under the reforms adopted by the House of Commons, a member could speak only on whether the petition would lie upon the table and on whether it should be printed, "the introduction and presentation of a petition being allowed to take place as a matter of course without question or discussion."[69]

The volume of petitions continued unabated, however, and the leaders both of the Tories and and of the Whigs came to resent the temporal demands for floor time associated with the presentation and debate of petitions. Exponential growth in the number of petitions largely negated the time saving benefits of ending debate on their introduction and presentation to the House. The statistics are telling: "In the five years ending 1790, there were 880 petitions, in the five years ending 1805 there were 1,026. The period 1811–1815 produced 4,498, 1828–1832 no less than 23,283. Then in the period 1843–1847 there was the unprecedented number of 81,985. . . . These figures show the flood of petitions that burst upon the last parliament of privilege and the first Liberal middle-class parliament in the days of the Reform movement, the Anti-Corn-Law agitation, and Chartism."[70] Thus, even as Parliament began attempting to limit the legislative time and attention devoted to considering petitions, citizens were petitioning in ever-greater numbers about myriad matters of public policy.

In 1836, four years later, "a rule grew up, to be enforced by the Speaker, which effectively prevented any debate arising out of the presentation of a petition, although a Member might put down a motion, arising out of it, for the next day (and might possibly get a chance to move it)."[71] Thus, as of 1836, the House of Commons attempted once again to reduce, if not eliminate, the significant floor time used for discussion and debate of petitions. Redlich reports, however, that this effort "had no appreciable result."[72] Instead, in order to regain control of the use of floor time, "the radical expedient of entirely forbidding debates upon petitions was adopted in 1839."[73]

Robert Wallace and H. G. Ward, radical members of Parliament, attempted to challenge limits on the presentation and debate of petitions in 1839 but failed to rally the House to support their position. Instead, the "gag" rule against debate on petitions emerged from the debate more entrenched than when it commenced. From this point forward, "[d]eference to the immemorial right of presenting petitions was a thing of the past."[74] In 1842, Wallace again challenged the gag rule, but his motion to restore the right to debate petitions failed by a margin of 50–237; subsequently, the House of Commons codified the settlement of 1839 into a standing rule.[75] "Once the 'gag' was a Standing Order of the house there would be no possibility of a minority party effecting its removal (only a minority party would want to)."[76]

C. The Golden Age of British Petitioning, 1839–1914

It was not abolitionists (as in the United States) who motivated Parliament to abandon its tradition of receiving, debating, and responding on the merits to petitions, but rather "radical" democrats known as Chartists. Chartists supported "the People's Charter," a statement of principles adopted in May 1838 by the London Working Men's Association (LWMA). "The six points of the charter were annual parliaments [meaning annual elections for the House of Commons], universal male suffrage, equal electoral districts, the removal of property qualification for membership of parliament, secret ballot, and payment of members [of Parliament]."[77] One of the leaders of the LWMA, William Lovett, "wanted to include the enfranchisement of women, but his friends thought that the suggestion would not be taken seriously."[78] Professor Robin Handley notes that "[t]his widely supported working-class movement made clear that politics was no longer the exclusive preserve of the ruling class."[79]

Supporters of the People's Charter adopted mass petition drives as a means of generating political support for their cause. Although neither of the major political parties supported any of the Charter's goals, a handful of "radical" supporters of the Chartist cause succeeded in getting elected to the House of Commons.

Because Chartist sympathizers in the House were so few in number, they had no realistic prospect of passing legislation advancing their agenda, or even of successfully introducing legislation for general debate on the floor. What they could do, however, was present petitions from constituents and use these petitions to force debate on the Charter principles, including universal male suffrage. "Simultaneous petitions were the only way which, at that particular date, great publicity could be given to a drastic plan of reform without any serious risk of prosecution."[80] Moreover, leaders of the mainstream political parties had to tread lightly in restraining mass petitions: "Neither Pitt nor Eldon had cared to lay impious hands on this palladium of the constitution."[81]

One should bear in mind that the United Kingdom lacked universal suffrage until 1928;[82] moreover, voting rights were not widely held in the early nineteenth century. "Before 1832, the right to vote in general elections in the United Kingdom was based largely on property qualifications and extended to only five percent of the adult population."[83] Parliament enacted a major electoral reform bill in 1832[84] that greatly expanded voting rights but fell far short of establishing universal male suffrage. This effort followed mass organization and petitioning beginning the 1816, sponsored by organizations such as the London Hampden Club.[85]

The problem, from the perspective of advocates of the unenfranchised working class, was that these reforms did not go nearly far enough. Accordingly, the Chartist movement sought to build on the success of the earlier petitioning and mass organization efforts that led to enactment of the electoral reform bill of 1832. As Handley explains, "although the Electoral Reform Act of 1832 extended the franchise, the right to vote was still preserved as an incident of the ownership of property, thereby denying the vote to the greater part of the population, and the absence of a secret ballot left room for pressure, victimisation and corruption."[86]

In turn, this rise in mass organization and petitioning "provoked a procedural revolution [in the House of Commons] aimed at dramatically restricting the scope for MPs to occupy the time of the House with petitions."[87] Professor Paul Pickering notes, however, that "the cumulative changes to the rules did not stem the flow of petitions."[88]

Pickering posits that "notwithstanding the changes to the rules, petitioning remained an integral part of the system of political representation."[89] Because most British citizens lacked the right to vote, even after the 1832 Reform Bill, petitioning remained the only viable means of political participation and expression open to these millions of persons; that petitioning no longer enjoyed the support of Parliament as a means of advancing legislation did not affect or alter this underlying reality. As Pickering explains, "[S]igning the [Chartist] National Petition was a public act of accession, an overtly political action that was open to the scrutiny of friend and foe alike."[90] Indeed, taking a page from the Chartist playbook, women suffragists adopted petitioning as a primary means of organization and advocacy as well, and for the same general reasons.[91]

Petitioning constituted a form of political participation open to anyone, not just those who had the right to vote. As early as 1829, the House of Commons affirmed that women, who lacked the right to vote, were still entitled to sign and present petitions.[92] "As well as signing, women also made an invaluable contribution to the political process as collectors of signatures"; in fact, "[m]any of the best Chartist signature collectors were women."[93]

The Chartist supporters mounted three national petitioning campaigns, in 1839, 1842, and 1848.[94] Each of these petitions featured more than one million signatures: the 1839 mass petition had 1.2 million signatures, the 1842 mass petition had 3.3 million signatures, and the 1848 mass petition had two million signatures.[95]

May minimizes the effects of the ban on debate arising from the presentation of petitions: "Nor has the just influence of petitions been diminished by this change; for while the House restrained desultory and intrusive discussion, it devised other means for giving publicity, and extended circulation to the opinions of petitioners."[96] May further claims that the petitioner's "voice is still heard and respected in the consideration of every public measure; but it is not longer suffered to impede the toilsome work of legislation."[97] This overstates considerably the efficacy of petitions as a means of achieving legislative reform after the House of Commons institutionalized the gag rule in 1842.

Nevertheless, because petitioning remained open to those who lacked the right to vote and constituted a valuable means of generating and maintaining political support within the population for particular causes, petitioning remained an integral part of British politics long after petitions ceased to be an effective means of securing legislation. As Pickering explains, "For the Chartists [who continued to collect and present mass petitions to Parliament after both the practical decision of 1839 to cease permitting debate on petitions and the codification of the gag rule into the standing orders of the House of Commons in 1842] petitioning was, first and foremost, part of the dramaturgy of demotic politics where its function and benefits were extra-parliamentary."[98] Petitions garnered helpful media attention, constituted a "'means of keeping the agitation before the public mind,'" and "could serve the internal needs of the movement by reinforcing a sense of collective identity."[99]

Significantly, "most Chartists were in no doubt about the likely fate of their petitions."[100] Writings in Chartist newspapers of the day indicate that the petition organizers held no illusions about the probability of the petitions succeeding in bringing about serious electoral reforms: "'The Petition was not prepared, nor was it submitted to the House under any expectation, or with the slightest hope that what was set forth therein would be, for an instant, considered.'"[101] Professor Pickering persuasively argues that the Chartists relied on petitioning as a means of political organization and expression simply because of "a lack of alternatives" that existed by virtue of "its predominantly working class member-ship."[102] Petitioning also did not require significant financial resources—just paper, ink, and would-be circulators.[103]

The potential utility of petition circulation and signature gathering helps to explain statistics that are otherwise seemingly inexplicable. Even though after 1839 the House of Commons ceased to observe any duty or obligation to respond to petitions on the merits, and the petitions themselves could not give rise to *any* floor debate, the numbers of petitions submitted for its consideration *continued to rise* after the gag rule was institutionalized in the standing orders in 1842. It 1843, for example, "the record total of 33,898 petitions was received by Parliament."[104] "In the five years ending 1877 [the total number of petitions received by Parliament] was 91,846."[105] Moreover, "upwards of 10,000 petitions a year continued to reach the House of Commons throughout the nineteenth century."[106]

The notion that only those lacking suffrage engaged in petitioning, and thus that petitioning waned because of the adoption of universal male suffrage, might help to explain its continued relevance to late nineteenth century poli-tics. For example, Professor Robert Nicholls posits that "[a]s voting and party participation became available to greater numbers of people, the petition no longer served a useful purpose."[107] It is certainly true that Parliament enacted major electoral reform bills in 1832, 1867, 1884, 1918, and 1928.[108] Moreover, by 1884, with the Third Reform Act,[109] only about 60 percent of the male popula-tion enjoyed the right to vote for members of the House of Commons—roughly 40 percent of men and all women were excluded from voting. Lord Irving observes that, "[e]ven by 1910, however, only twenty-eight percent of the total adult population enjoyed the right to vote."[110]

The 1918 Representation of the People Act[111] extended suffrage to virtually all men at least twenty-one years old and to women more than thirty years old who also met certain property qualifications. However, women were not enfran-chised in the United Kingdom on the same terms as men until Parliament enacted the Representation of the People (Equal Suffrage) Act of 1928.[112]

So, it is certainly true that universal suffrage did not exist during the period from 1840 to 1914, when petitioning as a form of civic and political engagement enjoyed its zenith in the United Kingdom. The problem, however, is that no relationship appears to exist between the enfranchisement of additional numbers of citizens and a decrease in petitioning. Parliament enacted major electoral reform bills in 1867 and 1884, and yet there are peaks in petitioning, both as to the number of petitions presented and as to the number of signatures collected on these petitions, in 1871 and 1892.[113] If petitioning really served as little more than a "next best" option to voting, the number of both petitions and petition signers should fall in a consistent manner as Parliament expanded voting rights—it does not. This theory also fails to explain why petitioning activity collapses after World War I—well before enactment of either the 1918 or the 1928 electoral reform bill. Most women still could not vote after the 1918 bill; if petitioning served as a substitute for voting, one would expect these women to continue engaging in petitioning activity until at least 1928.[114]

A better explanation, it seems to me, is that petitioning Parliament was simply something that engaged and active citizens did in the nineteenth-century United Kingdom. Over time, however, petitioning fell out of vogue as a means of political engagement. Obviously, Parliament's gag rule, adopted in 1836 and made a permanent standing order of the House of Commons in 1842, did not change the contemporary petitioning culture. But after World War I, citizens simply did not seem to view systemic petitioning as a useful civic activity.

Petitioning in the middle to late nineteenth century often involved matters of church and state and questions of public morality, including pornography, gambling, prostitution, and the regulation of alcoholic beverages.[115] Professor Nicholls notes that "[p]ublic health issues accounted for many petitions" during this period.[116] He also suggests that petitioning could help drive support for legislative action: "By the end of the century Parliament had enacted legislation to alleviate many problems complained of in petitions."[117]

Although one might infer that the petitions themselves were the causal agents for these reforms, it seems more likely that members of Parliament acted in response to perceived voter demands generally, rather than directly to petitions. In other words, petitions could have a signaling effect in the period after Parliament codified the gag rule, but the petitions themselves were not the agents of change.

The volume of petitions did fall considerably by the start of World War I. Nicholls notes that "[i]n most cases individuals and groups resorted to petitions after 1914 only when normal political channels seemed closed, or the government too internally divided to accommodate demands."[118] Similarly, Leys reports that the number of petitions submitted to Parliament "falls away erratically towards the end of the century and dwindles away almost entirely with the advent of the First Word War, only once thereafter topping 600 in any year and showing an average of only 19 in the 20 years ending in 1953."[119] Although the number of petitions declines precipitously over time, the number of signatures collected per petition rises to rival and exceed those of the Chartist efforts in the 1830s and 1840s.

Leys observes that "[i]t is hard to see how petitioning . . . could well survive Parliament's refusal to pay any further attention to petitions."[120] But, as Pickering has posited, both the volume of petitioning and the number of signatories *increased dramatically* after codification of the gag rule in 1842. Pickering's thesis—that circulating petitions and gathering signatures constituted an effective means of political organizing—makes a great deal of sense, and would explain why rational citizens engaged in an activity unlikely to yield any *direct* positive legislative results.[121] And even Leys concedes, after raising the futility argument and positing it as a reason for the ultimate decline of petitions in the United Kingdom, that "it seems reasonable to infer that the collection of signatures to petitions continued to recommend itself as being as good a way as any (and better than most) of building up and maintaining the popular support on which extra-parliamentary politics depend."[122] Nicholls concurs: "[B]efore modern political techniques developed, petitioning provided a democratic surrogate" that "preserved an element of democracy and kept open the channels of communication between citizens and government."[123]

D. PETITIONING IN THE CONTEMPORARY UNITED KINGDOM: AN EMPTY FORMALISM

Even though petitioning became infrequent in the twentieth century, petitions circulated and submitted to Parliament in the early 1950s garnered mass support, including a petition for the prohibition of atomic weapons, signed by 1.5 million people, and a petition against fee increases for services provided by the National Health Service, which was signed by more than two hundred thousand persons.[124] By providing a means of "creating and measuring a necessary condition of success, namely, bodies of organized opinion,"[125] petitions by the mid-twentieth century represented a rarely used, but not useless, means of political advocacy and organization.

From 1842 to 1974, a standing committee of the House of Commons on public petitions had jurisdiction over the receipt and publication of petitions but no power to investigate them or recommend legislative action in response to them. Thus, parliamentary consideration of the merits of petitions during this period could charitably be described as de minimis.

In 1974, the House of Commons ceased to consider petitions at all, abolishing the Committee on Public Petitions in favor of a procedure whereby, under Standing Order No. 102, the clerk of the House should "transmit all petitions to a Minister of the Crown."[126] In other words, executive branch personnel receive and, in theory, review petitions seeking legislative reforms. If a minister should decide to respond to a petition, "[a]ny observation that a Minister or Ministers may make in reply to a petition are to be laid upon the Table by the Clerk of the House and ordered to be printed."[127]

This change, abolishing even the perfunctory formal parliamentary review of petitions, probably changed little in practice. From its inception in 1842, the Committee on Public Petitions did not investigate or consider the merits of petitions but instead simply arranged for them to be published in the record. "The reports of this committee, printed at intervals during the session, pointed out, not only the subject of each petition, but the number of signatures to which addresses were affixed, and which were written on sheets headed by the prayer of the petition, the general object of every petition, and the total number of petitions and the signatures in reference to each subject."[128] The standing committee had "no power to investigate or report on the merits of any petition or to interrogate representatives of government departments or other persons as to remedial action."[129]

Strictly speaking, to this very day Parliament welcomes and receives petitions, and petitioning remains a venerable and ancient right of the British citizen. "Public petitions may pray for an alteration of the general law or the reconsideration of a general administrative decision, and they may also pray for redress of local or personal grievances."[130] The current version of the May treatise on parliamentary practice explains that "[i]n view of the great increase in the number of petitions, and the simultaneous growth in Government demands on the time of the House a series of standing orders was adopted in 1842, which, as subsequently amended, made the presentation of petitions a formal proceeding incapable, except in rare cases [involving personal grievances against a member of Parliament], of giving rise to immediate debate."[131]

Nevertheless, it is still possible to petition the House of Commons, provided that the petitioner observes certain basic requirements as to form and content.[132] Under Standing Order No. 154, petitions may be received before adjournment on Mondays, Tuesdays, Wednesdays, and Thursdays, and "[o]n Fridays, petitions are presented at the beginning of the day's sitting, immediately after prayers."[133] A petition containing an appropriate prayer may be read by the member or the clerk, and "[i]f a petition conforms to the rules or practices of the House, it is brought to the Table by the direction of the Speaker and is then placed in the bag behind the Speaker's chair,"[134] and "no debate is permitted" on petitions seeking changes in laws or public policies.[135] As an alternative to formal presentation of a petition, "[i]f he prefers, a Member may present a petition duly signed by him, at any time during the sitting of the House, by placing it in the petition bag kept at the back of the Speaker's chair."[136] Thus, submission of a petition to the House of Commons need not involve any formal action on the record.

After a petition has been tossed in the bag hanging on the back of the Speaker's chair, under Standing Order No. 156, the clerk's office will ensure that it is printed in the official record of the House of Commons; the standing order also "directs the Clerk of the House to transmit all petitions to a Minister of the Crown."[137] Presumably, a petition will be sent to a ministry with jurisdiction over the subject matter of the petition. Thus, the contemporary House of Commons does not consider petitions on the merits at all.

In sum, by the early part of the twentieth century, petitioning in the United Kingdom was little more than a legal artifact. Professor Handley reports that "[s]ince the First World War the average [number of petitions presented to the House of Commons] has been about 20 petitions a year."[138] Consistent with this very low incidence of petitioning Parliament, a hornbook on British constitutional law, published in 1937, reports that "[p]etitions, at one time an essential feature in legislative procedure, serve now merely the purpose, as a rule, of calling attention to demands of all kinds, for instance the 1933 co-operative societies' objections to paying income tax on reserves."[139]

Similarly, Professor Colin Leys, of Balliol College, Oxford, wrote in 1955 that petitioning "tends to be regarded as a now rare and invariably ineffective form of political activity, as rare and ineffective as once it was common and effectual."[140] He further observes that "[p]etitions are indeed rare nowadays (not for the first time), but they tend to be signed by enormously larger numbers of people than was the case when they were common."[141] He also notes that, "[a]s for their effectiveness as a form of political activity, it is well over a century since petitions were, or could be, effective in the sense that Parliament might answer the petitioners' prayers."[142]

An even more recent commentator in the United Kingdom, Professor Paul Pickering, writing in 2001, offers an even more dismal opinion about the relevance of petitioning in the contemporary United Kingdom: "At a time when petitioning has been reduced to an anachronism with no significant role in public affairs it is easy to overlook its importance in popular politics in the 1840s."[143] No less bleakly with respect to the modern relevance of petitions, Pickering also observes that "[a]t a time when petitions have become like so much waste paper, it is difficult to appreciate the greater value that could be placed on a signature, particularly to those who had no vote."[144]

A report prepared by Committee on Public Petitions sheds considerable light on just how little political salience petitioning retained by the 1940s.

In 1944, the Committee on Public Petitions prepared a special report to the members of the House of Commons on the nature and function of petitions. At a hearing on the subject, one member of the committee notes that "because Petitions are so seldom presented" members need to be "made acquainted with the procedure and form where they can obtain the Rules for guidance."[145] He noted that "the Public Petition Rules used to be circulated once a year to all Members [and] I do not see why that practice should not be resumed."[146] However, things go downhill considerably from here.

Another member of the committee, a Mr. Tinker, makes the following observation on the record: "Here are we, a Committee which sits on these Petitions, and not one of us, faced by an examiner, could display any knowledge (I am speaking for myself) as to what our job is; what rights have we, and what rights have the people? My object is to get this matter cleared up and known to the House of Commons. If they want any better system they will decide upon it, but I want them to know exactly what public Petitions mean. It is not known yet."[147] Another member asks "as a matter of interest" whether "the presentation of Petitions at the Bar of the House is allowed only by leave of the House, and it was chiefly used in the 18th century? — Up to the 18th century."[148] Further discussion elicits that "[t]here seems to be an idea amongst the public that they can present Petitions at the Bar? — That they can appear at the Bar and present them."[149]

Mr. Viant observes that "[s]ince 1842 really nothing comes out of a Petition. There is no Debate. It stands automatically referred to this Committee. Then certain particulars are referred to the House; but nothing ever happens again."[150] Dr. Russell Thomas responds, "I am afraid it has become rather like that, yes; and that was deliberately intended, I think, in 1842."[151]

Later in the hearing, the chair, Sir Edward Campbell, asks Sir Gilbert Campion, clerk of the House of Commons, whether one should "draw a distinction between Petitions presented in the House and those dropped in the bag [on the back of the Speaker's chair]?" and also notes that "[t]he large bulk are simply dropped into a bag behind the Speaker's Chair and nobody knows anything about them."[152] Another member, Sir Ernest Makins, then insists "[t]hey have to be in order to get into the bag, have they not?" and Chairman Campbell responds negatively, explaining that "[t]hey are dropped into the bag, like putting something into the postbag."[153]

That the committee charged with reviewing and acting on petitions does not itself understand its function and role, or the function and role of the petitions themselves, is particularly telling. By 1944, scarcely one hundred years after codification of the gag rule as a standing order, the House of Commons itself had ceased to think of petitions as constituting an integral part of its legislative duties.

The testimony of Sir Gilbert Campion, clerk of the House of Commons, confirmed that by 1944, petitioning had, by design and intention, fallen into almost total desuetude as a means of obtaining legislative reforms:

> These rules dating from 1842 which are a reaction against excessive preoc-cupation with petitions in the thirties and forties of the last century (*see* Redlich I, 76 note) are designed to exclude all debate on the presentation of petitions. Taken in conjunction with Government control of the time of the House they have resulted in making the presentation of a petition to the House a comparatively rare and practically ineffective form of proceed-ing. The sole advantage of presenting a petition formally in the House over dropping it in the petitions bag at the back of the chair is some additional publicity . . . .
>
> But in order to conclude this account of the disposal of petitions by the House it may be noted that, once they are referred to the Public Petitions Committee, they are in practice finally disposed of so far as the House itself is concerned. In time a report containing the particulars of petitions received as being in order is made to the House by the Committee, but the petitions themselves, seldom, if ever, according to present practice, become the subject of further proceedings in the House . . . .
>
> The functions of the Committee are limited to those defined in the Order of appointment, and do not extend to an inquiry into the allegations con-tained in petitions.[154]

Thus, according to the clerk's office, the Committee on Public Petitions lacked jurisdiction to consider the merits of a petition, even if the committee were inclined to take action beyond authorizing publication of the petition in the record.

In sum, although the United Kingdom maintains the form of petitioning—the petition bag still hangs on the back of the Speaker's chair in the House of Commons—the act of petitioning lacks much, if any, contemporary political salience. It may well be that "[t]he right of petitioning the Crown and Parliament for redress of grievances is acknowledged as a fundamental principle of the constitution," which "has been uninterruptedly exercised from very early times, and has had a profound effect in determining the main forms of parlia-mentary procedure."[155] Nevertheless, in the contemporary United Kingdom, neither average citizens nor incumbent politicians seem to view petitions and petitioning as a mainstream form of political action that requires the attention and respect of Parliament.

E. SYSTEMIC PETITIONING AS PETITIONING'S ZENITH IN THE UNITED KINGDOM

The standard view—that Parliament's refusal to act on (or even debate) petitions signaled their irrelevance—clearly cannot account for the exponential growth of both petitions and signatories in the period 1842–1892. Moreover, even as the United Kingdom moved closer to universal male suffrage, the volume of petitions and petitioners remained quite high, which suggests that petitioning was not merely a substitute for voting. Rather, it would appear that systemic, or hybrid, petitioning, which annexed mass public petitioning campaigns with rallies, demonstrations, marches and parades, and concentrated media and publicity campaigns, simply constituted one element of democratic politics in the United Kingdom during this period.

At the outset, it bears noting that the notion of a "golden age" of petitioning in the United Kingdom seems much overstated. As noted earlier, petitions signed by a large number of persons that seek to initiate legislative change date either to the petition of the Yorkshire freeholders in 1779 or perhaps to Quaker petitions seeking the abolition of the slave trade in the 1780s. In other words, Parliament received and responded to petitions from ordinary citizens from the 1780s until 1839, a span of about fifty years. Moreover, Parliament's willingness to receive and respond to petitions does not mean that petitioning was invariably effective in achieving legislative results. Indeed, the contrary seems to be the case: even in the golden age of petitioning, most petitions failed to garner favorable legislative action. On the other hand, a plausible case can be made that the golden age of petitioning in the United Kingdom actually took place from 1839 to 1914, when what Luce denominates as "systematic petitioning" was a commonplace form of political activity.

Unlike petitions and petitioning during the period generally described as petitioning's zenith, 1779–1839, Parliament itself did not undertake to consider, much less routinely answer, petitions from 1839–1914. Nevertheless, the social and political relevance of petitioning was far more important in this later period than in the earlier one. Even if Parliament did not rely on petitions directly as a means of advancing legislation, petitions clearly played a major role in helping to set the legislative agenda, and in some notable cases, such as expansion of the franchise to all men aged twenty-one or older, women's suffrage, and the lessening of the strictures of the United Kingdom's religious establishment, they clearly served to help drive major legislative reforms forward by bringing substantial public pressure to bear upon Parliament.

Accordingly, perhaps we should think of the potential relevance of petitioning not solely in terms of its efficacy in directly securing legislative reforms but rather in terms of its utility and effectiveness at shaping, and moving, public opinion more generally. Using this metric, petitioning's zenith in the United Kingdom came well after it ceased to be a meaningful parliamentary form of action. Thus, the golden age did not end in 1836 or 1842, but rather began in 1839 with the first of the Chartist movement's systemic petitioning campaigns for major electoral and parliamentary reform.

This analysis, however, leaves open a significant unresolved question: Why did petitioning decline after 1914 in the United Kingdom? With the advent of World War I, petitioning enters a period of decline from which it never recovers. Part of the answer probably relates to improved social science polling techniques and the concomitant ability to engage in statistically sound polling, which arise at the turn of the twentieth century and become well established by the 1920s. Part of the answer might relate to expanded voting rights, as some scholars have posited. Much credit for the demise of systemic petitioning in the United Kingdom should probably go to the rise of broadcast mass media, starting with radio and continuing with television.

If one were to combine the precision of social science polling data with mass distribution of ideas and information via radio broadcast, it would be possible to assess public opinion and to signal it to elected officials without resort to mass participatory political activity. Moreover, instead of making a case directly to both citizens and legislators alike, it would be far more efficient to make the case on broadcast radio, thereby reaching a mass audience instantly (albeit impersonally).

In the end, it is not possible to isolate with precision the exact cause of systemic petitioning's decline in the United Kingdom. Undoubtedly, multiple factors played a causal role. Whatever the root cause of petitioning ceasing to be a major part of democratic politics in the United Kingdom, however, the record clearly shows that petitioning constituted an important and regular part of civic life for decades, even when Parliament itself had ceased to have much direct interest in petitions themselves. The record also shows that petitioning evolved consistently over time, from a surrogate for a legal cause of action, to a primary means of legislating, to a form of mass democratic politics. Ultimately, this process of legal evolution led to extinction (or something very close to it) in the United Kingdom.

III. THE RIGHT TO PETITION IN THE UNITED STATES

Petitioning came to the United States with the first English colonists and flourished. This probably related to the generic functions of colonial assemblies, which lacked any formal separation of powers and functioned as much as judicial entities as they did as legislative bodies. Moreover, the evolution of petitioning as a means of legislating also took root earlier in the colonies than it did in Great Britain; the colonial assemblies in Massachusetts and Virginia were considering public petitions from residents well before the practice gained salience in the United Kingdom in the 1780s.

Notwithstanding these differences, petitioning from the 1830s and onward has an eerily similar history to the history of petitioning in the United Kingdom, with Congress curtailing its willingness to use classic petitioning as a legislative form as mass systemic petitioning campaigns promoting abolition of slavery roiled both the House and the Senate. As with Parliament, Congress chose to break with its prior tradition of receiving, considering, and answering petitions. And, as in the United Kingdom, petitioning arguably became a more important political phenomenon only *after* Congress ceased to take petitions seriously as a means of legislating. The period 1835–1919 represents the period of highest petitioning activity in the United States, whether measured by the number of petitions submitted to Congress or the importance of petitioning as a means of democratic politics.

Unlike the United Kingdom, however, a strong argument can be made that petitioning in the United States evolved a step further than its English counterpart in the late nineteenth and early twentieth century. The adoption of direct democracy, in the form of the initiative in twenty-four states and the District of Columbia, arguably constitutes the most relevant iteration of petitioning in the contemporary United States. Rather than petitioning legislative bodies, engaged citizens petition their fellow citizens in an effort to simply bypass the elected legislature through a plebiscite.

A. PETITIONING IN THE COLONIAL PERIOD

The right to petition for redress of grievances was, if anything, even more robust in the American colonies than in contemporary England.[156] As British subjects, the colonists held the right to petition the king and Parliament, and through their colonial charters and assemblies, they secured for themselves the right to petition their colonial governments.[157] As Don Smith notes, "[a] content analysis of the colonial charters shows that petition appears, either specifically or as one of the 'ancient liberties' of Englishmen, in over fifty provisions."[158]

Moreover, "[c]olonial legislatures in British North America were actually more likely than the British Parliament to permit the receipt of petitions on controversial topics such as taxation."[159]

Dean Larry Kramer suggests that petitioning was second only to voting in its importance in the colonial period and also in the early years of the federal government. "First and foremost, was the right to vote," but "[n]ext in importance, though perhaps not in effectiveness, was the right to petition, together with what became its corollary, the newly emerging right of assembly."[160] If the community disliked a law, it would petition and politic against it. "If petitioning and pamphleteering failed to elicit a repeal, more assertive forms of resistance were available, invoked in many instances only after a formal public notice had been issued and a public meeting held."[161] Kramer argues that "[t]he process of governing in the eighteenth century was necessarily a local affair, and the instruments and institutions of local government were in the hands of the community."[162]

Again, one must bear in mind that the colonial assemblies were not solely legislative bodies but also served as judicial entities; the lack of a formal separation of powers in most colonial governments explains, at least in part, the frequency of petitioning and the responsiveness of colonial assemblies to petitions. For example, in many states, a losing litigant could appeal an adverse decision from the colony's courts to the state assembly.[163] "In Rhode Island . . . it was a definite part of the judicial system that appeals should be tried by the assembly."[164] Moreover, colonial assemblies in Massachusetts, Connecticut, New Jersey, Maryland, and Virginia also heard appeals from the colonial courts.[165] It might well be that this dual function, arising from the lack of a structural separation of judicial and legislative powers in the colonial governments, made legislatures more responsive to petitions generally (including those seeking legislative, rather than judicial, action).

Even if petitions seeking quasi-judicial relief contributed to the volume of petitions filed in the colonial and prerevolutionary period, petitions seeking legislative action were also commonplace. "Throughout the colonial period a vast number of petitions from individuals and groups were presented to the various legislatures."[166] Although some of these petitions involved individual requests for payment for services rendered to the government, or for land grants, as many petitions directly sought changes in the law, including regulations of trades and professions, and alterations in the laws governing vice activities, such as the sale of alcohol or authorization for a lottery.[167] Professor Mary Patterson Clarke, a scholar of parliamentary bodies in the colonial period, explains that "[a]ll assemblies expected petitions, and many resorted to the committee as a method of dealing with them."[168]

Virginia provides an instructive example of the centrality of petitioning to the lawmaking process at that time. Professor Raymond Bailey notes that "[t]he practice [of petitioning] was transplanted to Virginia literally during the first year of settlement at Jamestown, and by 1700 petitioning had assumed an important role in the political process."[169] Petitioning in Virginia involved both the right to petition a government official and a duty on the part of the government to respond. "The burgesses consistently encouraged citizens to present their requests and grievances with petitions by guaranteeing that all would be considered, by developing efficient procedures for investigating them, and by acting vigorously whenever necessary to protect the right of petition from potential threats."[170]

In fact, during the eighteenth century, "[i]n the House of Burgesses the greater part of the work had to do with petitions presented to the assembly."[171] This was so because "[a]t that time few measures demanding constructive legislation came up in the course of a session, but there were always a thousand and one local matters under consideration."[172] The petitions related to various and sundry subjects, including "the shooting of squirrels and crows, bounties for killing wolves, holding county fairs," among dozens of other subjects, so that "a classification of subjects dealt with is almost impossible."[173] Petitioning also involved a right of access to legislators: "Petitions could be given to individual councillors before they convened or else taken directly to the capital either by the petitioner or by an agent or attorney."[174]

The colonists were not shy about exercising the right to petition. For example, between 1750 and 1800, the Virginia legislature received, on average, more than two hundred petitions per legislative session.[175] The large majority of both private and public legislation arose out of petitions.[176] Unlike the contemporary Parliament, however, the colonial legislatures not only received and debated petitions but would usually make some sort of formal response to the petitioners. Professor Bailey emphasizes that in the Virginia House of Burgesses, "[w]hen a petition was received, it was automatically read once before the house, and there was no 'gag rule' to prevent petitions concerning even the most controversial topics from being read."[177] He argues that "[t]he manner in which petitions were received and considered further indicates the importance attached to them by the house."[178]

One should also bear in mind that voting rights were not widely held in the colonial period, or even in the postrevolutionary period. Universal male suffrage was an incident of Jacksonian democracy, and even after most states adopted universal male suffrage, voting was often conditioned on poll taxes.[179] Petitioning, however, was not confined to those eligible to vote, either in the colonial period, during the Revolution, or thereafter. Thus, "[p]etitioning offered a much broader means of participating in the governing process than did voting in eighteenth century elections, for even disfranchised individuals— women, free blacks, the very poor, even an occasional slave—sent petitions to the legislature."[180]

Petitions also constituted a highly effective means of securing law reform in the colonial period. Bailey notes that "the [Virginia] legislature proved extremely responsive, as far more eighteenth century laws originated directly in response to these petitions than from any other source."[181] Again, the legislature had a duty not only to receive but also to respond to petitions from state residents (regardless of a petitioner's eligibility to vote).[182]

Thus, by the time of the American Revolution, a strong petitioning culture had grown up, not only in Virginia, but in most other states as well.[183] Professor Luce explains that "by the time trouble with the mother country began, the custom of bringing influence to bear upon legislative bodies by the use of petitions was thoroughly entrenched," and "the efficacy of the procedure . . . made it doubly dear to the American people."[184] Indeed, Bailey suggests that "petitioning served as *the most important channel of communication* between local citizens and the [Virginia] assembly."[185] In Virginia, for example, "[a] typical legislative assembly in the 1700–1750 period received well over a hundred petitions, and the average more than doubled in the latter half of the century."[186]

B. Petitioning During the Revolutionary and Framing Eras

Given the deeply embedded nature of petitioning in the colonial period, it should not be surprising that, when faced with difficulties with Great Britain, citizens of Britain's North American colonies would resort to petitioning the mother country in the hope of obtaining redress. Amid the growing discontent with British rule, the colonists repeatedly petitioned George III and Parliament for redress of their grievances.[187] In fact, before declaring independence in July 1776, the delegates at the Second Continental Congress dispatched an "Olive Branch Petition" to London a year earlier, in July 1775.

Even though armed conflict had already ensued on June 17, 1775, at Bunker Hill, on the outskirts of Boston, Massachusetts, the states were badly divided about how best to respond to the growing crisis, and were far from unanimous in their support of an immediate declaration of independence from Great Britain. Accordingly, as a compromise measure that enjoyed broad, if not unanimous, support, the delegates "drafted, adopted, signed, and dispatched in duplicate by separate vessels to England (travel by sea being the hazardous

undertaking it was in those days) the document historians now speak of generally as the 'Olive Branch.'"[188]

The Olive Branch Petition described colonial complaints about British policy in the North American colonies and sought the king's active assistance in
resolving those complaints: "We therefore beseech your Majesty, that your royal
authority and influence may be graciously interposed to procure us relief from
our afflicting fears and jealousies occasioned by the System before mentioned,
and to settle peace thro' every part of your dominions, with all humility submitting to your Majesty's wise consideration."[189] More specifically, the petition
asked that "measures be taken for preventing the further destruction of the lives
of your Majesty's subjects; and that such Statutes as more immediately distress
any of your Majesty's colonies be repealed."[190]

Richard Penn delivered a copy of the petition to Lord Dartmouth, George III's
secretary of state for the colonies, on August 14, 1775, with a request to present it
to the king, but it appears that either the petition never reached George III or the
king, having received it, chose to ignore it. Lord Dartmouth's official response to
Penn was that "[a]s His Majesty did not receive the petition on the throne, no
answer would be given."[191] The Olive Branch Petition provides powerful evidence
of the centrality of petitioning to the statesmen of the revolutionary era. It also
demonstrates that personal presentation of a petition to the king was an essential
component, at least in the United Kingdom, if one wished to receive a formal
response.

After the abject failure of the Olive Branch Petition, the Continental
Congress then took the next step and declared independence from the United
Kingdom. However, the slight was not forgotten, as one of the overarching
injustices decried in the Declaration of Independence was the British government's refusal to hear the colonists' petitions: "In every stage of these Oppressions
We have Petitioned for Redress in the most humble terms: Our repeated
Petitions have been answered only by repeated injury. A Prince, whose character is thus marked by every act which may define a Tyrant, is unfit to be the
ruler of a free people."[192] To the colonists, the right to petition for redress
of grievances (and the concomitant right to have one's petition heard) was
so fundamental that denial of the right was an act of tyranny and grounds for
revolution.[193]

Following independence, the right to petition remained fundamental.[194] Of
the nine state constitutions that contained a bill of rights adopted between 1776
and 1789, "[a]ll had some provision for petition."[195] The Pennsylvania state constitution of 1776 provided: "That the people have a right to assemble together,
to consult for their common good, to instruct their representatives, and to apply

to the legislature for redress of grievances, by address, petition or remonstrance."[196] The Vermont Constitution of 1777 has an identical clause,[197] as does the North Carolina constitution of 1776.[198] Only the constitutions of Delaware, New York, and South Carolina "failed to make provision for the protection of petition or assembly."[199]

Thus, it was surprising that the new national constitution, drafted in 1787, did not include any specific safeguard of the right to petition. George Mason, a delegate at the Federal Convention from Virginia, objected to this omission (as well as omission of a more complete Bill of Rights), but this objection failed to carry the delegates. James Mason wrote to Thomas Jefferson that "Colonel Mason left Philadelphia in an exceeding ill humour indeed" and had "returned to Virginia with a fixed disposition to prevent adoption of the plan if possible."[200] George Mason "consider[ed] the want of a Bill of Rights as a fatal objection."[201]

C. PETITIONING IN THE EARLY YEARS OF THE REPUBLIC, 1789–1835

Although the conventions in the states ratified the Constitution without a formal declaration of the rights of the people against the government,[202] such a declaration was in the forefront of national political consciousness as the first Congress took up the task of building a nation. Responding to this widely felt desire, James Madison proposed amendments to the Constitution that would eventually become the Bill of Rights, including the right of petition, to the House of Representatives on June 8, 1789.[203] The right of petition, as framed in Madison's proposal, was in a clause separate from the freedoms of speech and press and stated that "[t]he people shall not be restrained . . . from applying to the Legislature by petitions, or remonstrances, for redress of their grievances."[204]

In the few extant records of the congressional debates on the Bill of Rights, the right of petition generated little discussion, most likely because the proposition that it is the right of the people to petition their government for a redress of grievances would have been viewed at the time as self-evident, a total non-issue.[205] The primary insight into the right of petition that may be gleaned from the record comes from the controversy surrounding a proposed addition to the amendment: the right of the people to instruct their representatives, or, in other words, to bind their representatives to legislate according to the popular will of their constituencies.[206]

Arguing against such a right, Madison stated:

[W]e have asserted the right sufficiently in what we have done; if we mean nothing more than this, that the people have a right to express and communicate their sentiments and wishes, we have provided for it already. The right of freedom of speech is secured; the liberty of the press is expressly declared to be beyond the reach of the Government; the people may therefore publicly address their representatives, may privately advise them, or declare their sentiments by petition to the whole body; in all these ways they may communicate their will. If gentlemen mean to go further, and to say that the people have a right to instruct their representatives in such a sense as that the delegates are obliged to conform to those instructions, the declaration is not true.[207]

It appears that Madison's argument carried the day. The proposed right of instruction fell by the wayside, and after a select committee of the House and the Senate modified Madison's original language, petitioning was enshrined in the First Amendment as "the right . . . to petition the Government for a redress of grievances."[208]

Indeed, because of the well-established nature of petitioning in the states by the time the first Congress convened on March 4, 1789, the Petition Clause was hardly essential to secure legislative consideration of citizens' petitions. "In the Federalist era, the right to petition was relatively non-controversial—enjoying, as it did, an honored place in English constitutional law."[209]

In point of fact, the first petitions arrived in Congress well before Virginia became the eleventh state to ratify the Bill of Rights, on December 15, 1791, incorporating the First Amendment, and the Petition Clause, into the federal Constitution. Professor William diGiacomantonio argues that "[t]he number and variety of petitions to the First Congress attest to the people's expectations of their new federal government and the Constitution."[210] The first Congress, which met from March 4, 1789, to March 3, 1791, received "more than six hundred petitions,"[211] even though the federal Constitution of 1787 makes no provision, anywhere, for petitioning Congress. "The belief, inherited from the practice of the colonial assemblies, that petitions should derive from personal, not broad, ideological grievances was put aside as congressmen dutifully presented their constituents' petitions on such matters of communal welfare as the institution of slavery, the prohibition of rum, and the standardization of printings of the Holy Bible."[212]

The U.S. House of Representatives received its first petition, "from the tradesmen, manufacturers, and others of Baltimore" seeking changes in national trade policy, "ten days after the House convened" in March 1789.[213] Petitions to Congress also came from local and state governments; a good example is Georgia's 1795 petition to Congress for indemnification for the cost of settling a claim arising from the Revolutionary War.[214] By 1795, congressmen spent so much time dealing with petitions that one contemporary newspaper editorialist commented that "[t]he principal part of [Congress's] time has been taken up in reading and referring petitions."[215]

To be sure, many petitioners sought compensation from the federal government, such as payment for goods or services provided during the Revolutionary War (but still unpaid), or for benefits, such as veteran's benefits. Nevertheless, many petitions sought enactment of specific public policies, involving such matters as trade, government finance and debt, and important questions of the day, such as slavery.[216] An early debate over antislavery petitions submitted in the first session of the House of Representatives set important precedents on whether and how the House would consider petitions, and also provides a good illustration of the seriousness with which the Congress considered petitions during the Federalist era.

On February 11, 1790, Representative Thomas Fitzsimons, of Pennsylvania, took to the floor of the House of Representatives to present a petition from the Quakers of "Pennsylvania, New Jersey, Delaware, and the Western parts of Maryland and Virginia" seeking an early end to the slave trade.[217] Petitions from Quakers in New York City and Philadelphia, also seeking an early end to the slave trade, were introduced contemporaneously.[218] Fitzsimons asked the House to refer the petitions to a select committee for consideration and a report; Representative William L. Smith, of South Carolina, objected to this action, and even to receipt of the petitions by the House.[219] Professor diGiacomantonio observes that "[n]o other petitions to the First Congress unleashed the passionate rhetoric that these three did; none took up as much of Congress's time; and none produced a more thorough documentary record of the sophisticated lobbying campaign that accompanied it."[220]

The following day, February 12, 1790, yet a fourth petition seeking the abolition of the slave trade reached the floor of the House. The Pennsylvania Society for Promoting the Abolition of Slavery adopted this petition at a meeting in Philadelphia on February 3, 1790; the petition bore the signature of the society's president, Benjamin Franklin.[221] Representative Thomas Hartley, of Pennsylvania, called for a second reading of the petitions submitted the day before and moved that all of the petitions be referred to a committee for consideration and a response.[222] A general debate ensued, and in the end the House voted to receive the petitions and refer them to a special ad hoc committee for consideration and an official response.[223]

The special committee presented its response to the antislavery petitions on Tuesday, March 23, 1790.[224] Southern members of the House objected to consideration of the report, as "the discussion of the subject has already excited a spirit of dissension among the members of the House, and that every principle of policy and concern for the dignity of the House, and the peace and tranquility of the United States, concur to show the propriety of dropping the subject, and letting it sleep where it is."[225] Other members, including Hartley, argued that the subject was properly before them and should be decided. The *Annals of Congress* reports that "[t]he motion for taking up the report was warmly contested in a lengthy debate, and finally passed in the affirmative, by a majority of one."[226] No record exists of the particulars of the debate. The House voted to amend the report, accepted the amended report, and voted by a margin of twenty-nine to twenty-five to print the report in the record.[227]

The special committee's report found that the federal government lacked authority to prohibit the importation of slaves until 1808, that Congress "by a fair construction of the Constitution, are equally restrained from interfering in the emancipation of slaves" already in the United States, and that Congress lacked constitutional authority to revise state laws governing the institution of slavery.[228] Nevertheless, the committee also found that Congress could tax the importation of slaves, could regulate interstate and international commerce in human slaves in order to "make provision for the humane treatment of slaves, in all cases while on their passage to the United States, or to foreign ports so far as respects the citizens of the United States," and had the power to "prohibit foreigners from fitting out vessels in any port of the United States, for transporting persons from Africa to any foreign port."[229] The special committee also proposed that "the memorialists be informed, that in all cases to which the authority of Congress extends, they will exercise it for the humane objects of the memorialists, so far as they can be promoted on the principles of justice, humanity, and good policy."[230]

The House struck out the seventh clause of the report (thereby rejecting the suggestion that Congress would exercise its commerce powers over the slave trade), and also substantially revised the other provisions of the report to reduce the claimed authority for congressional power to enact regulations of the interstate and international slave trade.[231] Thus, despite the vehement objections of Southern members of the House, the members considered, debated, and responded on the merits to the petitions seeking abolition of the slave trade.

The House response to these petitions also set an important precedent: petitions, even on controversial topics, would be received, considered, and answered. As Professor Julie Spanbauer has written, "The right to petition consisted of a right to complain and a concomitant right to receive a response."[232] The House's consideration of the antislavery petitions of 1790 set an important example and established a general precedent that petitions would be received, considered, and answered. Moreover, Congress (with some exceptions)[233] generally honored this precedent until the mass antislavery campaigns of the 1830s. As a general matter, prior to 1830 "[t]he abolition petitions were received and referred."[234] Petitions to Congress thus facilitated democratic discourse and deliberation, and, as one commentator has suggested, "general petitioning allowed the people a means of political participation that in turn demanded government response and promoted accountability."[235]

It seems likely that Congress received and responded to petitions not out of any deeply felt sense of commitment to participatory democracy but rather because their constituents, already quite accustomed to petitioning the state and local governments and to having these governments receive and respond to petitions on the merits, expected no less of the federal legislature. "When a petition reached Congress, it was presented to the legislature as a regular part of its proceedings, typically by the petitioner's representative."[236] Moreover, "[d]uring the Federalist era, this ritual was scrupulously observed," allowing the "voice of the people" to enter the halls of Congress "both figuratively and literally."[237] One scholar of the Petition Clause argues that "down to 1834 the custom or procedure in Congress was to receive, hear and then refer petitions to appropriate committees."[238]

Congress received about three thousand petitions in the first twelve years of the federal government's existence, from 1789 to 1801, which corresponds to the time of the Washington and Adams Federalist Party administrations.[239] This level of petitioning dwarfed the volume of petitions submitted to state legislatures, even in populous states with active petitioning cultures,[240] such as Pennsylvania and Virginia, suggesting that residents of the United States viewed petitioning as a core means of communicating with the new national government. During the Federalist era, petitioning served as a primary means of securing meaningful access to the federal government and facilitated an active and lively engagement on issues of the day between petitioners and Congress, as well as within the larger body politic; petitioning constituted an important and visible form of democratic politics.

As it happens, during this period Congress would often delegate the responsibility of responding to petitions to the executive branch. "In the state legislatures such work would have gone to standing committees, but Congress seemed to feel that the head of a department would answer the purpose just as well as a [legislative] committee."[241] Professor Ralph Harlow provides representative examples of petitions the House referred to the secretaries of state, treasury, and war in the early 1790s.[242]

By 1794, however, cabinet secretaries began to resist being drafted into investigating and responding to citizen petitions. On March 3, 1794, while reporting to Congress on a number of petitions, Secretary of the Treasury Alexander Hamilton suggested that it would be "expedient to place the business of reporting on petitions in some other channel, as the pressure of his official duties, in addition to the extra business of the Treasury Department, will not permit him to pay that seasonable and prompt attention to these petitions which the parties expect, and have just claim to."[243] It bears noting that, at this point, the Jeffersonian Republicans controlled the House of Representatives and were intent on reining in the Federalist administration; it is not surprising that Hamilton, a Federalist party appointee under President Washington, would seek to fight back.[244]

As Professor David Frederick explains, "Even as the country grew through the admission of new states and the government's work became more complex, therefore, Congress handled petitions according to the customs and procedures developed in the 1790s."[245] Petitioning both state and national governments remained immensely popular until the national crisis over slavery ultimately resulted in the right to petition falling from its position as the most important of expressive freedoms and a central means of securing democratic self-government to the constitutional footnote it is today.[246]

D. The Antislavery Petitioning Crisis of 1836–1844

The system of petitioning established during the first session of Congress came under increasing stress as the volume of antislavery petitions grew exponentially in the mid-1830s. This, in turn, led both houses of Congress to consider the appropriate institutional response to mass, repetitive petitioning campaigns.

"Since the daily business of Congress began with the reading by each state of its petitions, too many petitions could bring proceedings to a standstill. Groups like the American Anti-Slavery Society emerged with national constituencies able to mobilize such petitioning drives."[247] When abolitionist groups began to assert their petitioning power in the 1830s with systemic petitioning campaigns aimed at moving popular opinion as much, if not more, than moving Congress to legislate, Congress responded with various measures that allowed it to devote as little time as possible to antislavery petitioners. As Professor Gregory Mark has explained:

> Under Article I, Section 5 of the Constitution, "Each House may determine the Rules of its Proceedings." The First Amendment, however, provides that, "Congress shall make no law . . . abridging . . . the right of the people . . . to petition the Government for a redress of grievances." Those two sections of

the Constitution came into direct conflict in the years 1836 to 1844, as the House of Representatives attempted to quell the rising number of abolition petitions its members had been receiving. The attempts to stifle the petitions became known as the gag rule or gag law. For eight years, the existence of the rule was a source of tremendous controversy in the House and the nation.[248]

Mark goes on to note that "[t]he rule was the reaction of southern congressmen who felt that the South could no longer bear the insults contained in the language and content of abolition petitions. Designed to staunch the flow of such petitions to the House, it was sweeping in its breadth."[249] Frederick adds that pro-slavery members from the South argued that "once the petitioner had transmitted the plea to the legislature, Congress itself could decide whether or not to receive it and issue a response."[250]

Of course, antislavery petitioning had proven controversial from its inception in 1790, when multiple Quaker petitions sought an early end to the international slave trade in the United States. Nor did the subject cease to elicit strong, regional reactions, with members of Congress from Southern states viewing the petitions as a direct attack on the economy of the region, to say nothing of its existing social order.

Even if the first petitions, seeking an end to the slave trade in violation of Article V's promise that no amendment could affect the importation of human chattel slaves before the year 1808,[251] were not within the jurisdiction of the Congress, subsequent antislavery petitions were framed with greater care and legal precision. In particular, abolitionists sought the prohibition of slavery within the District of Columbia, an exclusively federal enclave over which Congress enjoys express constitutional authority to regulate.[252] Even if Congress could not end slavery in the states that recognized the practice, it surely could adopt a statute for the District of Columbia that abolished slavery, or at least the slave trade itself, within this jurisdiction. Clever petitioners, led once again by the Quakers, petitioned Congress to take this step.

John Quincy Adams, son of President John Adams and a former president himself, championed the right of petition in the House of Representatives during the slavery controversy. After losing his bid for reelection to the presidency in 1828, in the midterm elections of 1830 Adams sought and was elected to a Massachusetts seat in the U.S. House of Representatives. He took office in 1831 and served in the House until his death in 1848.

In his first speech on the House floor, barely a week after assuming his seat, Adams rose to present fifteen antislavery petitions from Quakers in Pennsylvania.[253] The petitions, largely identical, asked "Congress to pass such

laws as will entirely abolish slavery and the slave trade in the District of
Columbia, over which Congress has exclusive jurisdiction."[254] Adams presented the petitions, indicated that he deemed it his duty to do so, and asked
that they be referred to the House Committee on the District of Columbia
for consideration and a response.[255] The House voted to refer the petitions, and
a week later the Committee on the District of Columbia, chaired by
Representative Philip Doddridge, a slave owner from Virginia, reported to
the House that the committee deemed it "unwise and impolitic, if not unjust
to the adjoining states [Virginia and Maryland] for Congress to interfere in a
subject of such delicacy and importance as is the relation between master and
slave."[256]

Adams had no objection to this response, inasmuch as he himself did not
support the petition: "In regard to the abolition of slavery here [in the District
of Columbia], the petitioners probably supposed that their view would receive
some support and countenance from me. But I deem it my duty to declare that
the proposition does not meet my approbation; and should it become a subject
of discussion in the House, I shall oppose the wishes of the petitioners."[257] For
Adams, then, presenting the petitions for consideration by a committee of the
House constituted nothing more than honoring a duty to facilitate the House
hearing and responding to the concerns of the petitioners, rather than subjective agreement with their cause.

As antislavery petitioning grew, as part and parcel of the national campaign
for abolition of slavery, Congress became less and less inclined to receive,
consider, and respond to the repetitive petitions. The American Anti-Slavery
Society, organized in the early 1830s, like the Chartists in the United Kingdom
in the 1830s and 1840s, used petitioning as a primary means of advancing their
cause.[258] Things came to a head in 1836, when both the House and the Senate
voted to refuse to receive and consider petitions seeking abolition of slavery in
the District of Columbia.

The Senate battle over the right of petition featured efforts by Senator John
C. Calhoun, of South Carolina, to convince his Senate colleagues to refuse
receipt of antislavery petitions, or, in the alternative, to receive such petitions
but immediately table them without any formal consideration or debate, much
less a formal institutional response. His principal adversary was Senator Henry
Clay, of Kentucky, who consistently argued that the Senate had an affirmative
and absolute duty to receive, consider, and answer all petitions.

On February 12, 1836, Calhoun moved that an antislavery petition seeking
the abolition of slavery in the District of Columbia "not be received" by the
body.[259] In support of his position, Calhoun argued that he was bound "to shut

the doors of the Senate against the admission of the wicked and fanatical agita-
tors" and asked rhetorically, "When the incendiaries present themselves here,
in violation of the constitution, with petitions in the highest degree calumnious
of the people of the South, holding them up as despots, dealers in human flesh,
and pirates, was it for me, representing one of the Southern States, to be silent
on such an occasion, and to endorse such slanders on my constituents, by
receiving them?"[260] Calhoun claimed that "[r]ather than receive such a petition
against South Carolina, against those whom I represent, I would have my head
dissevered from my body."[261]

Calhoun failed to carry the day in February, but the battle was inconclusive
and resumed again a few weeks later, in March. This second debate on the
propriety of receiving and considering antislavery petitions was both long
and extensive,[262] and although Calhoun failed to convince his colleagues to
refuse to receive antislavery petitions, it was clear that referral to the Committee
on the District of Columbia was merely pro forma. Senator James Buchanan,
of Pennsylvania, argued that "the sacred right of petition and the cause for
abolitionists must rise or must fall together, and the consequences might be
fatal."[263] He categorically rejected the notion that the Senate could properly
refuse to receive a petition that related to a matter over which it possessed legislative competence. The debate proceeded from Wednesday, March 2, through
Wednesday, March 9, with various members staking out positions on whether
or not the Senate could refuse to receive antislavery petitions.[264] Calhoun generally held his powder during this extended debate and did not engage his colleagues.

Calhoun retook the floor on March 9, 1836, and insisted that the Senate
refuse to receive, much less consider on the merits, antislavery petitions related
to the District of Columbia.[265] He argued that receipt of the petitions would be
"useless," asking his colleagues: "[W]hy should these petitions be received?
Why receive, when we have made up our mind not to act? Why idly waste our
time and lower our dignity in the useless ceremony of receiving to reject, as is
proposed, should the petitions be received? Why finally receive what all
acknowledge to be highly dangerous and mischievous?"[266] He asserted that
"[o]f all the rights belonging to a deliberative body, I know of none more universal, or more indispensable to a proper performance of its functions, than the
right to determine at its discretion what it shall receive, over what it shall extend
its jurisdiction, and to what it shall direct its deliberations and actions."[267] He
urged that all such petitions be "immediately tabled without discussion or referral to committee."[268] This would, of course, constitute a breach of the longstand-
ing practice of receiving, considering, and responding to petitions, whether

submitted by voters or not. Calhoun argued that abusive, repetitive petitioning required Congress to take corrective measures against it.

Senator Henry Clay, of Kentucky, then rose in opposition to Calhoun's motion, stating that "he would vote to acceptance of any anti-slavery petition if it was not insulting and was addressed to the deliberative body having authority to act on the prayer."[269] Clay's position was that "the right of petition carried with it the right of being heard on any subject that the body addressed had the power to act on."[270] Clay reasoned that because Congress enjoyed plenary legislative power over the District of Columbia, the petitions should be received, considered, and answered; Clay carried the day, as "Calhoun's motion to bar the petitions was defeated 36–10."[271] The committee reported against granting the petition on March 11, 1836, and the Senate adopted this recommendation by a vote of 34–6, with Clay voting with the majority.[272]

Clay won the battle but lost the larger war; from this point onward, the Senate permitted the presentation of antislavery petitions related to the District of Columbia but allowed "Southern senators the privilege of immediately tabling them without discussion."[273] Thus, the Senate ceased to refer the antislavery petitions to a committee for consideration and also ceased to answer the petitions. Clay objected to this practice, on the theory that "the act of receiving a petition necessarily implied deliberation and that the simple act of reception, followed by instant rejection amounted to a substantial denial of the petition right."[274] Clay's views, however, lacked the support of a majority; the Senate continued its practice of tabling without any referral or consideration antislavery petitions from 1836 to 1840.[275]

Clay continued to insist that all petitions should be received, referred, and answered, but a majority of the Senate thought otherwise, at least with respect to petitions seeking abolition of slavery in the District of Columbia. He also continued to press the Senate to consider antislavery petitions on the merits into the early 1850s, but up to the outbreak of the Civil War, the Senate maintained its settled practice of immediately tabling all such petitions.[276]

The story of antislavery petitioning in the House of Representatives involves more drama and a more contentious fight between those in favor of maintaining and observing the traditional right of petition and those who felt that the House should be free to ignore repetitious, "abusive" petitioning.[277] Professor Robert Ludlum argues that the first instance of a gag rule in the House of Representatives arose on December 16, 1835, when the House summarily voted to table an antislavery petition offered by Representative John Fairfield, of Maine.[278] The session became increasingly entangled in a fierce debate over both the slavery question and the propriety of refusing to refer and answer antislavery petitions. Supporters of slavery sought to have the petitions summarily tabled and ignored; members from Northern states, even if not sympathetic to an immediate end to slavery in the District of Columbia, argued that Congress had a duty to receive, consider, and answer all petitions.

To be sure, other national questions generated mass petition campaigns in the 1830s. "The National Bank, the tariff, the campaign to stop the Sunday mail, and the Cherokee problem in Georgia 'had all produced their inundations.'"[279] The key difference was that in these other cases, "after the success or failure of a bill, the flood receded. Not so with abolition."[280] The volume of antislavery petitions was very high by any objective measure. Within a year and half of the American Anti-Slavery League undertaking its systemic petition campaign, Congress received 130,200 petitions seeking the abolition of slavery in the District of Columbia, 182,400 against the annexation of Texas, 32,000 for the repeal of the gag rule, 21,200 for legislation prohibiting slavery in the territories, 23,160 seeking the abolition of the interstate slave trade, and 22,160 opposing the admission of any new slave states into the Union.[281] The House tabled all of these petitions under the gag rule.

Finally, on May 18, 1836, the House adopted a select committee report that provided that "all petitions, memorials, resolutions, propositions, or papers, relating in any way, or to any extent whatever, to the subject of slavery, or the abolition of slavery, shall, without being either printed or referred, be laid upon the table, and that no further action whatever shall be had on them."[282] The proposal carried in the House by a 117–68 vote in the affirmative. The House adopted the same resolution for the next session of Congress in 1837 by a margin of 129–69.[283] The most adamant defenders of slavery wanted to establish a rule against the body even *receiving* antislavery petitions.

During this great debate on the meaning of the Petition Clause in the U.S. House of Representatives, Representative John Quincy Adams never accepted or recognized the legitimacy of the gag rule and became its fiercest, and most tireless, opponent. The gag rule notwithstanding, Adams continued to present petitions involving slavery, and also raised the question indirectly, in one instance by cleverly inquiring, on a point of order to the Speaker, whether a petition might be submitted to the House from women or from slaves.[284] The annexation of Texas also presented an indirect means of raising the slavery question.[285]

Adams consistently took the view that the gag rule was "a violation of the Constitution of the United States . . . of the rights of my constituents, and of the people of the United States to petition, and of my right to freedom of speech, as a member of this House."[286] Hundreds of antislavery petitions, signed by thousands of people, continued to flood into the House, with most directed to Representative Adams.

From 1836 to 1844, the gag rule remained in place. In 1840, the House made the gag rule a standing order of the House, so that it would automatically remain in place from year to year, and from session to session, unless amended or repealed in a subsequent vote.[287] The rule provided that "no petition, memorial, resolution, or other paper praying the abolition of slavery in the District of Columbia, or any State or Territory, or the slave trade between the States or Territories of the United States in which it now exists, shall be received by this House, or entertained in any way whatever."[288] This codification of the gag rule into the standing orders of the House went well beyond the previous rules, adopted from session to session by resolution, in that it expressly prohibited even *receipt* of antislavery petitions.

Adams, undeterred, noted that "[t]here are ways enough to get at the subject" and initiated debates both directly and also via petitions seeking repeal of this standing rule, which arguably did not themselves come within the rule itself.[289] Vast amounts of legislative time were devoted to this question. Ludlum reports that "[t]he issue of the 'gag-rule' prevented the organization of the House for more than two weeks at a special session convening on May 31, 1841."[290]

Over time, support for the gag rule waned, and Adams's efforts to secure repeal came closer and closer to success. The House voted 106–102 against repeal of the gag rule in 1842. In 1843, Adams sought to remove the gag rule from the standing orders of the House, and lost the question by a margin of 91–95. Finally, on December 3, 1844, the first day of the session in 1844, the House voted 108–80 in favor of a motion from Adams to repeal the gag rule.[291] "Thus quietly, without debate or turbulence, was repealed the rule which for ten years had caused so much excitement, so many recriminations, such long debates, such heated argument, and such dire threats."[292]

Professor Frederick notes that after repeal of the gag rule, the House began accepting and referring to appropriate committees petitions related to slavery. Indeed, a week after the House abolished the gag rule, "antislavery petitions were received and referred to the Committee for the District of Columbia, where they continued to 'sleep the sleep of death.'"[293] He suggests that "[t]he end of the gag rule brought neither an exhaustive discussion of slavery in the District of Columbia nor a full restoration of the right of petition as it had been practiced from 1789 to 1836."[294] Remarkably, throughout the gag rule controversy, Congress's infringement on the right to petition was never challenged in the Supreme Court.[295]

E. Petitioning in the Post–Gag Rule Era, 1844–1919: The Unrecognized and Underappreciated Golden Age of Petitioning in the United States

Professor Mark argues that, due to the antislavery gag rule, petitioning evolved from an activity with independent legal and political significance, indeed a primary means of empowering We the People to directly influence the government, into simply another form of indirect political propagandizing, constituting little more than a historical footnote.[296] Mark suggests that without support from the judicial branch during the great debate over antislavery petitions, and with outright hostility from the legislative branch, petitioning fell into a broad and irreversible decline as an important and popular form of democratic politics. As one commentator has suggested, "The eradication of the government's duty to respond to petitions signalled the erosion of the guarantee that general petitions would advance the interest of government accountability through citizen participation."[297] Today, even lawyers and judges steeped in First Amendment jurisprudence would be hard pressed to identify and describe the historic right of petition.

But, this story—that the gag rule against antislavery petitions destroyed the underlying right[298]—does not bear up to close scrutiny. The fact of the matter is that even after the gag rule episode of 1836–1844 in the House of Representatives, people continued to submit formal petitions to the Congress. Petitions addressed such subjects as the rights of Native Americans, women's suffrage, polygamy, and the regulation of alcohol.

To be sure, the gag rule did have a significant effect: after 1836, neither the House nor the Senate consistently and invariably respected the rule that a petitioner had a right to receive some sort of formal response from the legislature. Thus, the duty to respond to a petition *did* fall into desuetude after 1836; either house of Congress could respond or not to any given petition, as it thought best. This marked a significant departure from the classic model of petitioning the Congress observed from 1789 to 1836, under which both houses had a duty both to receive and to respond to petitions. But, it goes much too far to claim that petitioning was "a right little exercised in the aftermath of the gag rule" or that "the practice of the petition right as a means of communicating grievances to government in the eighteenth century had long since been abandoned" by the twentieth century.[299]

As in the United Kingdom, petitioning remained the most readily available avenue of political activity open to persons who lacked voting rights, such as women until ratification of the Nineteenth Amendment in 1920. Advocates of women's suffrage actively used petitioning to advance organizational goals, to achieve publicity, and to demonstrate widespread political support for their cause.[300] The first such petition, submitted by Senator Gratz Brown, a Democrat from Missouri, to Congress in 1866, was the product of a campaign organized by Susan B. Anthony and Elizabeth Cady Stanton, seeking to "prohibit the several States from disenfranchising any of their citizens on the ground of sex."[301] More than ten thousand people signed this petition. Professor Susan Zaeske explains that "[t]he decision to employ petitioning as a major means of persuasion was based on suffrage leaders' years of experience in the antislavery and temperance movements in which they had gained organizational skills and had become accustomed to public activism."[302]

Mass petitioning clearly served as a major point of organizational focus and as a means of demonstrating widespread political support for universal voting rights. For example, the pro–women's suffrage petition of 1910 had more than four hundred thousand signatures.[303] The petition of July 13, 1913, bore two hundred thousand names, whereas the petition of May 19, 1915, contained five hundred thousand names.[304] "The last great suffrage parade, held in New York City on October 27, 1917, featured some 2,500 women waving placards that enumerated the signatures of more than 1 million women to a suffrage petition."[305]

Congress passed the Nineteenth Amendment on June 5, 1919, sending it to the state legislatures for their consideration, and the amendment secured ratification by the requisite three-quarters of the state legislatures on August 26, 1920. Zaeske argues that "[t]he fact that petitioning played a major role in suffragists' strategy to win the vote confirmed the advice that [Elizabeth Cady] Stanton had given almost forty-five years earlier" that "'it is possible to roll up such a mammoth petition, borne into Congress on the shoulders of stalwart men, that we can no longer be neglected or forgotten.'"[306]

Mass parades and multiple petitions with hundreds of thousands of signatures suggest that, by the early twentieth century, mass systemic petitioning in support of a major law reform effort remained a vital, accepted, and *effective* part of the contemporary political culture. Thus, the standard narrative that petitioning simply died out after the 1840s vastly overstates the effect of the gag rule on the contemporary petitioning culture.

Moreover, it was not just suffragists who used petitioning as a means of organizing and seeking to build mass political support for a law reform effort. "After 1863 and well into the twentieth century, millions of women petitioned Congress on issues such as granting pensions to Civil War nurses, aiding freedwomen and -men, outlawing lynching, controlling the sale of alcohol, attacking and defending Mormon polygamy, and demanding suffrage for women."[307]

Professor Zaeske describes an 1898 petition seeking that the House of Representatives refuse to seat Brigham H. Roberts, of Utah, which garnered the support of "7 million signatures from both women and men."[308] As it happens, the petition worked: "the House voted by a great majority to exclude Roberts."[309]

Mass systemic petitioning also helped secure legislative support for the Eighteenth Amendment, which established a national system of prohibition on the sale of alcohol "for beverage purposes."[310] Smith reports that "[t]he petitioning campaign most reminiscent of the abolitionist movement was that of the Anti-Saloon League (1893) and its allies against the sale of liquor and beer."[311] Although this conclusion is highly contestable—the women's suffrage movement seems to bear a closer resemblance to the antislavery petition movement—Smith is surely correct to argue that petitioning was a crucial component of the national campaign that led to Prohibition.

Don Smith, in his unpublished dissertation, provides many other examples of mass petitioning campaigns in the period from 1880 to 1920. For example, supporters of new federal laws regulating the anticompetitive trusts commonly used petitions as a principal means of advancing their cause, which contributed to the enactment of the Sherman Act[312] in 1890 and the Clayton Act[313] in 1914. Smith reports that "[p]etitions against the trusts were probably most numerous during the year 1889" and that "most anti-trust petitions were received from the agricultural states, including Texas."[314]

Petitions also supported the creation of the federal income tax, through ratification of the Sixteenth Amendment in 1913. The income tax was a core tenet of the progressive movement, and it generated hundreds of petitions to Congress.[315] "On one day alone, June 2, 1894, the Senate received six petitions" favoring a federal income tax, and "the index to the Congressional Record, 53rd Congress, 2nd session, lists some 175 petitions concerning the income tax."[316]

Jacob J. Coxey, president of the Commonweal of Christ, attempted to lead a mass gathering of petitioners to Congress on May 1, 1894, in support of a petition for a massive public works stimulus program to combat the lingering effects of the financial panic of 1893.[317] "Coxey proposed simply to gather a vast army of men and make the trip [to the Capitol, in Washington, D.C.], carrying along with him a huge petition, as big as a hogshead, which would be filled with the signatures of people."[318] Coxey dubbed his protest "petition in boots."[319]

Alas, the project did not meet with ultimate success. Arthur Marchand reports that "[t]he march of the army came to an ignominious halt on May 1 [, 1894], when its leaders were arrested and held for 'lawlessly entering the capitol grounds, walking on the grass, breaking shrubbery, and displaying a banner which had for its purpose the bringing into public notice of a certain organization known as the

U.S. Coxey Good Roads Association.'"[320] Nevertheless, Coxey's petition and protest have been credited as "the first march on Washington," and they "provided a template for the many marches to come."[321]

Other major national petitioning efforts involved the rights of Native Americans, the creation of internal improvements, and immigration policies.[322] The frequency and visibility of petitioners make it quite clear that the national petitioning culture did not abruptly end with the adoption of the gag rule in 1836 or after its repeal in 1844.

Suggesting that mass petitioning "ended" after World War I also constitutes an overstatement. For instance, "[t]he march of the veterans on Washington in 1932 offers another example of the unsuccessful attempt to present petitions in force."[323] About a thousand veterans came to Washington, D.C., on May 29, 1932, for the purpose of petitioning Congress to immediately redeem for cash certain "adjusted compensation certificates," in an effort that came to be known as the "Bonus March."[324] "Other groups of veterans began arriving [in Washington, D.C.,] from all parts of the country and by June the 'Bonus Expeditionary Force' had grown to an estimated 17,000."[325]

After arriving, the veterans camped "near the edge of the city on the Anacostia Flats, but many others made their homes in shacks and unused government buildings near the Capitol."[326] The House passed legislation on June 15, 1932, to pay $2.4 billion to honor the soldiers' bonus certificates, but the legislation failed to secure passage in the Senate. Instead of cashing the bonus certificates, Congress appropriated a significantly smaller amount to provide stipends to assist the veterans in returning home, and "[m]ost of the ex-servicemen departed."[327] About two thousand veterans refused to leave, and local Washington, D.C., police evicted them using force.

The August 28, 1963, March on Washington for Jobs and Freedom, organized by a coalition of labor and civil rights organizations, including the Southern Christian Leadership Conference (SCLC), the National Association for the Advancement of Colored People (NAACP), the Urban League, the Congress of Racial Equality (CORE), the Student Nonviolent Coordinating Committee (SNCC), and the Brotherhood of Sleeping Car Porters, constitutes an even more modern example of mass systemic petitioning.[328] More than two hundred thousand participants met for a mass rally on the national mall, at which the Rev. Dr. Martin Luther King Jr., delivered his iconic "I Have a Dream" speech.[329] The purpose of both the march and the subsequent rally was to press Congress and the Kennedy administration for enactment of comprehensive federal legislation securing voting rights and basic civil rights for all citizens of the United States, regardless of their race.[330]

John Lewis, then a leader of the Student Non-Violent Coordinating Committee, and now a member of Congress from Georgia, gave a speech at the rally that plainly reflects the petitioning character of the event:

> We come here today with a great sense of misgiving. It is true that we support the administration's Civil Rights Bill. We support it with great reservation, however. Unless title three is put in this bill, there's nothing to protect the young children and old women who must face police dogs and fire hoses in the South while they engage in peaceful demonstration.
>
> In its present form this bill will not protect the citizens of Danville, Virginia, who must live in constant fear of a police state. It will not protect the hundreds and thousands of people that have been arrested on trumped charges. What about the three young men, SNCC's field secretary in Americus, Georgia, who face the death penalty for engaging in peaceful protest?
>
> As it stands now, the voting section of this bill will not help the thousands of people who want to vote. It will not help the citizens of Mississippi, of Alabama and Georgia who are unqualified to vote for lack of sixth grade education. One man, one vote is the African cry. It is ours too. It must be ours.
>
> We must have legislation that will protect the Mississippi sharecroppers, who have been forced to leave their homes because they dared to exercise their right to register to vote. We need a bill that will provide for the homeless and starving people of this nation. We need a bill that will ensure the equality of a maid who earns five dollars a week in the home of a family whose total income is 100,000 dollars a year. We must have a good FEPC [Fair Employment Practices Commission] bill.[331]

In other words, the purpose of this mass march and rally was to petition the federal government to enact comprehensive and effective civil rights legislation. Indeed, leaders of the march were late to the official start of the march, from the Washington Memorial to the Lincoln Memorial, because the march's leaders were meeting with congressional leaders that morning; in fact, the march started early and departed the staging area without the leaders, including Dr. King.[332] After the march and rally, the march's leaders met with President John F. Kennedy in the Cabinet Room of the White House and lobbied him personally for the swift enactment of comprehensive voting and civil rights legislation.[333]

The March on Washington for Jobs and Freedom plainly deserves significant credit for helping to secure passage of both the Civil Rights Act of 1964 and the Voting Rights Act of 1965 (which the Selma-to-Montgomery March of 1965 also helped to facilitate). Indeed, the march and rally were carried live on national broadcast television, and were probably the first civil rights events that many white Americans had ever witnessed live.[334] Historian Taylor Branch notes that the March on Washington "was the first—and essentially the last—mass meeting ever to reach the national airwaves"[335] during the civil rights era.

In sum, the claim that "petitioning ceased" or "died" after the early part of the twentieth century grossly overstates the case. Nevertheless, it is true that by the 1920s, petitioning largely had ceased to be a common means of political organization and expression on a national level.

A more accurate assessment of the historical record suggests that classic petitioning, in which the members of Congress served as a petitioner's principal audience, and in which a petition served primarily as a legislative vehicle, became much reduced after the gag rule controversy. But the cause for this change was the change in public petitioning behavior; as classic petitioning began to give way toward mass systemic petitioning, in which a petition served as a means of rallying public opinion in favor of a particular cause, Congress responded by declining to play its prescribed role in the drama. In other words, the gag rule itself was a response to a new, radically democratic form of petitioning activity. And after the gag rule, this new form of petitioning, systemic petitioning, constituted an important and highly visible component of democratic politics in the United States.

In addition to addressing a different primary audience (the general public rather than members of Congress), systemic petitioners did not anticipate direct legislative change as a result of their petitioning activity. Neither the abolitionists nor the women's suffragist systemic petitioners, just like the Chartist petitioners in the United Kingdom, harbored any serious hope that Congress would act favorably on their petitions in the short term. Instead, the systemic petition campaigns served as a means of organizing, demonstrating, engaging the media's attention, and slowly but surely moving public opinion toward support for their causes. In the case of women's suffrage, this effort spanned almost sixty years, from 1866 to 1919. Yet, even if systemic petitioning reflected a new way of exercising the right, one cannot plausibly claim that petitioning ceased to have cultural or political salience after Congress ceased to routinely receive, consider, and respond to citizen petitions.

Finally, in at least one isolated context, Congress continued to receive and respond, diligently, to petitions well after the adoption and repeal of the antislavery petition gag rule of 1836–1844. In the early years of the Republic, a practice arose of petitioning Congress to establish new post offices and postal routes.[336] As early as 1793, a group of South Carolinians, seeking postal services in the "extreme western corner of the state," petitioned Congress as follows: "We recommend that a post be established to our district and county towns"; in 1794, Congress granted the request.[337] Congress received literally thousands of petitions seeking either the creation of post offices or new postal routes from 1793 to 1884, when it transferred responsibility for such decisions directly to the Post Office Department.[338]

Professors Richard John and Christopher Young argue that the example of successful postal petitioning after the antislavery gag rule episode of 1836–1842 disproves the claims, advanced by many Petition Clause scholars, that petitioning did not survive the gag rule,[339] or that petitioning was left a mere remnant, an exclusive feature of "fringe politics."[340] John and Young persuasively argue that "the petition process remained a valued instrument for influencing other, less controversial, kinds of legislation, such as the designation of new post routes."[341] Indeed, "[f]or the period between the 1830s and the 1910s, the papers of the House and Senate contain hundreds of thousands of petitions on an extraordinary range of topics."[342]

I find myself in broad agreement with John and Young's suggestion that "[h]ad the gag rule truly destroyed the effectiveness of the petition process—as several legal scholars have contended—it is hard to understand why Congress would have continued to debate the issues that petitioners raised, or, for that matter, why Americans would have persisted for so long in organizing large scale petition campaigns."[343] Petitioning simply did not cease to have political or social relevance, even after Congress ceased to consider and answer all petitions.

Moreover, the mass systemic form of petitioning pioneered in the United States by the American Anti-Slavery Society in the mid-1830s, like the mass petitioning campaigns of the Chartists in the United Kingdom during the same period,[344] transformed petitioning from a relatively obscure, but highly effective, legislative practice, into a highly visible public ritual, a key feature of democratic politics at a time when voting rights were not widely distributed or enjoyed. Petitioning morphed from a parliamentary practice into a form of mass participatory politics. The results of these hybrid petition campaigns, which annexed canvassing, public demonstrations, parades, and rallies, along with sophisticated media campaigns, to the traditional act of submitting a petition to Congress, fundamentally changed what it meant to "petition." Although the classic form of petitioning observed during the Federalist era certainly should inform our contemporary understanding of the right, so too should the highly visible forms of systemic, or hybrid, petitioning practiced by advocates of women's suffrage, Prohibition, antitrust laws, and the federal income tax.

Thus, a strong case can be made that the golden age of petitioning really took place only *after* the antislavery gag rule controversy had led Congress to cease participating reliably in the classic form of petitioning that had preceded it. In fact, it was the development of systemic, or hybrid, petitioning that incented Congress to abandon the classic model of receiving, considering, and answering all petitions. The transformation of petitioning into a mass public event, involving the exercise of multiple forms of expressive freedom (not merely the right of petition but also freedom of speech, assembly, association, and press), aimed as much, if not more, at the general public as at the members of Congress, arguably enhanced and improved the democratic relevance of the practice.

In many respects, the standard narrative has missed the key point, which is that average people seized upon systemic petitioning as a practical means of democratic engagement in the service of law reform. We the People's own redefinition of the right of petition provoked Congress into adopting parliamentary "reforms," not the reverse. The fundamental *nature* of petitioning did not change either—petitioning still served as an important means of securing access to the federal government and its officers, and also facilitated a process of democratic engagement within the general citizenry. Systemic petitioning campaigns put greater relative emphasis on facilitating debate and discourse within the general public than within the halls of Congress, but toward the same basic end that classic petitioning served: securing law reform through peaceful democratic means.

F. The Continuing Legal Evolution of the Right of Petition: Initiative and Referendum

The history of the right of petition both in the United Kingdom and the United States demonstrates a pattern of dynamism and change over time. In the United Kingdom, this evolution over time has led to the extinction of petition as either a means of securing legislative reform or as an important expressive freedom in the contemporary United Kingdom. The form remains, to be sure, but the substance, in the form of either classic or systemic petitioning, simply does not.

In the United States, both classic and systemic petitioning have fallen into desuetude. Moreover, the contemporary Congress, unlike its counterpart in the United Kingdom, Parliament, does not even maintain a petition bag on the back of the Speaker's chair. The question to be asked and answered is whether petitioning simply died in the United States, not even leaving an empty legal formalism (as in the United Kingdom). The answer, I think, is that petitioning evolved in the United States in a way it did not, and has not, in the United Kingdom.

It is true that Congress "has long since abandoned the custom of formally acknowledging"[345] receipt of petitions, much less responding to them individually on the merits. It is also true that after the gag rule, Congress no longer observed its prior practice of not only receiving petitions but also invariably discussing and responding to their merits. In this sense, then, Professor Andrews is quite correct to argue that "Congressional *processing of petitions* forever changed after abolitionists, beginning in the 1830s, inundated Congress with petitions urging it to end slavery in the District of Columbia."[346]

Processing of petitions did change; not all petitions served as vehicles for legislative debate, much less for legislation or constitutional amendments. But some petitions, reflecting causes that enjoyed mass political support, such as those advocating women's suffrage, Prohibition, income taxes, and antitrust laws, did help to drive the legislative process, indeed, even the constitutional amendment process, forward, well after the antislavery gag rule had come and gone.

Moreover, as John and Young's work demonstrates, in some limited contexts, such as establishing post offices and postal routes, Congress continued to receive, debate, and respond to unsolicited petitions filed by average citizens. Accordingly, their revisionist conclusion—that "[p]etitioning remained an important, and often surprisingly effective, form of collective action until the era of the First World War, when it was supplanted—and largely superceded—by more systematic techniques for registering public sentiment, such as public opinion polls and social scientific surveys"[347]—seems spot on. Advancing a similar, but distinct, argument, Marchand argues that expanded voting rights, coupled with modern communications technologies, made petitioning obsolete.[348]

John and Young are quite correct to suggest that after the women's suffrage movement, petitioning, at least at the federal level, ceases to have major victories (the civil rights movement excepted); it also ceases to be a regular means of conveying public sentiment to Congress. I am not certain, however, that petitioning lost its relevance after World War I solely because of advances in polling and social science sampling methods or the advent of mass communications technologies. I think another possible explanation for the decline of petitions to Congress relates to the success of the progressive movement in advocating for the initiative and referendum at the state level. In other words, it might be that petitioning ceased to have much political or social relevance not because of better, more reliable public opinion survey devices and techniques but rather because engaged citizens elected to seek law reform at the state level, via initiative, rather than engage in a petition process where the prospects of securing any meaningful reform would be far from certain.

Starting with South Dakota, in 1898, the citizens initiative became a central feature of democratic politics in many states, particularly in the West. If the circulation of petitions could be used simply to bypass a legislature thought to be at best indifferent to a particular cause, and at worst hostile to it, why would rational citizens petition the legislature rather than bypass it via a plebiscite? The political history of the initiative also seems to support this theory of a legal evolution in petitioning, with both supporters and opponents of the initiative describing it as a form of petitioning.

Writing in 1912, Professor Ellis Oberholtzer asks: "For what is the system of petition for the passage of a law but the initiative?"[349] He acknowledges that "[i]t is true that the dearly bought right of the people to petition their kings and governors for a redress of grievances, of which we still see many surviving forms even in free states, is not the initiative."[350] This is so because a petition "is merely an appeal to a legislature, the members of which will afterward do quite as they please regarding this matter when the time comes for definite action on their part."[351]

Oberholtzer argues, however, that the use of initiative petitions "has long been with us in some New England towns," through which "a certain number of citizens may unite in a petition in favor of some local policy—the laying out of a new road, the vacating of a street or the enclosure of domestic animals, is the initiative in one of its true forms."[352] Thus, Oberholtzer posits that the citizens' initiative simply represents a logical form of legal evolution,[353] from a system in which citizens may ask the legislature for a change in policy, to a system in which citizens may put changes in policy up for a direct popular vote, free and clear of the legislature's permission.

Another, more contemporary, commentator agrees with this theory: "While the advent of the modern initiative and referendum is generally attributed to a constitutional amendment in the State of South Dakota, variants of the petition were operative in New England towns from the early 1600's and the Swiss Cantons of the early 1800's."[354]

Professor Joseph Zimmerman also concurs, arguing that "voters in Massachusetts towns were empowered by the General Court (provincial legislature) on December 22, 1715, to require the selectmen (plural executive) to include in the warrant (calling a town meeting) any article accompanied by a petition signed by ten or more voters."[355] To this day, in fact, "voters in all New England towns with open town meetings possess this power of initiative."[356]

Moreover, the emergence of the initiative as a key component of the Progressive movement's law reform program coincided with the decline of systemic petitioning in the United States. "The origin of the legislative initiative generally has been attributed to Swiss cantons in the nineteenth century and an 1898 South Dakota constitutional amendment."[357] Cantons in Switzerland adopted the referendum in the 1830s,[358] but the initiative came into being much later, in 1891.[359] The initiative came to the United States, seven years later, when South Dakota "became the first state to amend its constitution to give its citizens the option of the initiative and the referendum."[360] A deep economic depression and a general concern that representative government was not working effectively "convinced voters to secure the tools that would enable them to do the job themselves."[361]

Utah adopted a constitutional amendment authorizing the initiative and referendum on November 6, 1900, but the state legislature failed to adopt the necessary implementing legislation until 1917.[362] Thus, although Utah voters next adopted a state constitutional amendment authorizing initiatives, Oregon was the second state both to enact an amendment authorizing initiatives and to adopt procedures for direct legislation making the amendment operative.

"Oregonians, like South Dakotans, were also undergoing a crisis in political confidence" at the end of the nineteenth century.[363] Progressive political leaders first suggested direct legislation by initiative in 1892, and a decade later, "[b]y the time of the election in 1902, the initiative and referendum had gained strong support throughout the state."[364] The question of whether to authorize citizen-initiated referenda was placed on the November ballot and carried by a landslide margin of 62,024 to 5,668.[365]

Montana (1906), Arizona (1910), and Colorado (1910) followed the lead of South Dakota and Oregon.[366] At present, "[t]he constitutions of twenty-three states and the *Utah Code* contain provisions authorizing state voters to use one or more types of initiatives."[367]

The connection between the initiative and the petition seems relatively clear; the initiative represents a logical legal evolution from a process in which voters petition a legislature for a change in the law to a system in which voters, by signing a petition, may bypass the legislature and establish a law or constitutional amendment by a direct vote of the people themselves. As Senator Mark Hatfield, of Oregon, explained, "[T]he initiative is an actualization of the citizens' first amendment right 'to petition the Government for redress of grievances.'"[368] In other words, the initiative represents the modern-day equivalent of the pre–World War I systemic, or hybrid, petition to a legislative body.

Senator Hatfield's arguments in support of a constitutional amendment to create a federal initiative power mirror the arguments offered in support of petitions. For example, he notes that "[t]he initiative procedure is one means to provide direct access to our governmental decisionmaking process through a legal and democratic method."[369] This "democratic feedback" to incumbent government officials conveys "the people's feeling on different issues and generally produces a more responsive body of elected officials."[370] In addition, the initiative facilitates democratic discourse and deliberation by "provid[ing] a prompt public discussion of important issues which may otherwise go unaddressed."[371] Just as petitions to the national legislature once helped to focus attention on issues of concern to petitioners, supporters of a federal initiative would likewise use the device to facilitate a national debate on issues that Congress might prefer to ignore (for example, the growing national debt, unsustainable annual budget deficits, or term limits for members of Congress). Thus, the initiative, like systemic petitioning in the nineteenth and early twentieth centuries, secures access to the government for the purpose of seeking law reform and facilitates broad-based collective engagement on controversial issues of the day, ranging from limits on property taxes, to physician-assisted suicide, to the question of same-sex marriage.

Similarly, Professor Luce suggests that "[i]nitiative might not go beyond what would in effect be a mass petition to the Legislature," establishing yet another theoretical linkage between traditional petitions and the modern initiative process.[372] The nomenclature of the machinery of the initiative, and even the referendum, also directly invokes the tradition of petitioning: a group seeking either to propose a new law through initiative or seeking to strike down a statute enacted by a legislature must submit signed petitions for this purpose, with a requisite number of registered voters required to subscribe before the state government will call for a vote on the question.[373] In other words, one "petitions" for the holding of the initiative or referendum.

Another scholar of the Petition Clause, John P. Nields, writing in 1924, describes petitioning as a "bulwark of representative government" and distinguishes it favorably from "direct legislation in the form of initiative referendum, [which] has been tried out in the West on the theory that the people could not depend upon their legislatures, but must initiate legislation or revise legislation that might be regarded as harmful."[374] In Nields's view, "[t]he machinery of the initiative and referendum has proved cumbersome and ill-adapted to this country."[375] However, he suggests instead that "an *informal* referendum evoking or communicating popular opinion has no binding force upon the representative," and elected officials are "entitled to be advised of the opinion of [their] constituents and of the people generally."[376] Once again, one finds a writer at the time of the rise of the initiative clearly linking petitioning and the initiative, although in this instance clearly favoring the more traditional right of petition, rather than the initiative, as a means of facilitating democratic deliberation and effective self-government.

It is only natural that proponents of legal change with the option of securing law reform at the state level, via an initiative, would elect this course rather than petitioning either Congress or their state legislature. A petition "is merely a request, addressed to the authorities in power, by a number of more or less irresponsible persons."[377] In the case of a petition, Professor William McCrackan argues, "authorities may, or may not, take it into consideration" whereas the citizens' initiative "is a demand, made upon the government by a body of voters, to discuss a certain project, and to return it to the people for final acceptance or rejection."[378]

McCrackan commends the Swiss system of initiative, adopted in 1891 at the federal level, because "the introduction into practical politics of any question which attracts public notice, can be accomplished in a simple and direct manner. While in this country we are confronted by the almost insurmountable difficulties connected with the election of representatives pledged to lay reform bills before the House, or are obliged to content ourselves with harmless petitions."[379] For McCrackan, then, initiative constitutes a superior form of collective democratic deliberation, precisely because, unlike a petition, it permits direct lawmaking action by the people themselves.[380] Initiative is related to, but quite distinct from, the more traditional right of petition.

"Initiative . . . is an active creative force; it supplies the progressive element in the process of legislation."[381] The initiative, in tandem with the power of referendum, "produce[s] a steady see-saw of legislation, a continued to-and-fro movement, which carries certain expressions of the public will directly from the people to the legislature, and back again to the people for their verdict."[382] In this way, the initiative also serves to discharge the informational function posited by Professor Woolsey for more traditional forms of petitioning.[383]

One should bear in mind that national constitutions authorizing citizen-initiated referendums are relatively rare; few nations around the world trust their citizens with this democratic form of lawmaking power. In this regard, Professor John Parkinson observes that the initiative power "attracts a lot of interest from democratic theorists and campaigners alike in many countries, but it is much more rare in practice, with only Italy, New Zealand, and Switzerland using the device nationally."[384] He notes that "[o]ther notable examples occur at the sub-national level: of the fifty states in the USA, twenty-four use some form of [initiative], with California's attracting most of the academic attention."[385] In sum, the number of polities that permit this form of direct democracy is relatively rare, and even in the three nations that feature national initiatives, the outcome of plebiscites is binding only in Italy and Switzerland, as New Zealand's citizen-initiated referenda are merely advisory to the national parliament.[386]

G. Contemporary Petitioning and Federal Administrative Agencies

Finally, it bears noting that there is at least one context at the federal level in which petitioning retains legal significance: the Administrative Procedure Act of 1946 (APA) contains a provision, Section 555(e), that requires a federal agency subject to the APA to respond to petitions for rulemaking.[387] The provision does not require a federal agency to grant relief sought in a petition, but it does require the agency to receive and respond to the petition, which includes a duty to "explain the grounds for denial" if the agency denies relief.

The federal courts generally grant federal agencies very broad discretion to establish institutional priorities; accordingly, it is exceedingly rare for a reviewing court to reverse an agency's decision to deny relief on a petition. Nevertheless, it can and does happen. For example, the Supreme Court's major decision on the Environmental Protection Agency's authority to regulate greenhouse gases arose in the context of the agency's denial of a petition for rulemaking.[388] The Supreme Court explained that "[r]efusals to promulgate rules are . . . susceptible to judicial review, though such review is 'extremely limited' and 'highly deferential.'"[389] The EPA had a duty to provide a reasonable basis for its decision not to issue rules, and "inaction must conform to the authorizing statute."[390] Justice Stevens explained that "[u]nder the clear terms of the Clean Air Act, EPA can avoid taking further action only if it determines that greenhouse gases do not contribute to climate change or if it provides some reasonable explanation as to why it cannot or will not exercise its discretion to determine whether they do."[391]

Petitions seeking agency action certainly constitute a modern example of the older, classic form of petitioning once common in the states and Congress. And because petitioners have a right to seek judicial review of denial of these petitions, federal agencies generally take seriously their obligations to receive and respond to them under the APA. Even so, however, petitioning under the APA is not the equivalent of petitioning the Congress; for example, an agency charged with enforcing a statute would be bound to enforce the statute on the terms Congress established—it could not grant relief to a petitioner that conflicted with the plain language of its organic act. That said, in thinking about the relevance of petitioning to the contemporary federal government, the ability of adversely affected persons and entities to petition agencies for discretionary changes in rules or policies certainly bears consideration.

IV. A MODERN PETITIONING CULTURE: THE EXAMPLE OF NEW ZEALAND

Given that neither the contemporary U.S. Congress nor the U.K. Parliament takes petitions seriously as a means of driving law reform, one might conclude that petitioning is simply a relic of an earlier time and place. Certainly, scholarly commentary on petitioning in the United States and the United Kingdom seems to adopt an elegiac tone, discussing petitioning as a form of political engagement in highly nostalgic terms and treating petitions and petitioning as a kind of sociolegal anthropological artifact. For example, Professor Mark warns: "On the one hand, we should be extremely careful about legal anachronism. Petitioning was a vital element in a political and constitutional culture that is not coming back. Attempts to revivify it—to make its unmediated politics the hallmark of the constitutional order—would be fraught with both theoretical and practical difficulties. On the other hand, we should be equally careful about our constitutional teleology, both as a matter of doctrine and interpretation. Corseting the current understanding of petition and assembly in seventeenth and eighteenth century formalisms would mock our own politics."[392] In commenting on the current status of petitioning as an expressive freedom in the United States, Mark notes that "[t]o say that the right is today moribund is grossly to understate the case."[393]

Mark's thesis is that as voting rights became more universally distributed in the United States, the need to resort to petitioning diminished. "With an extended franchise, accompanied by a greater degree of actual representation, came a decreased need to make one's views known to unrepresentative representatives."[394] As he puts it, "The vote became the master."[395]

Another scholar of the Petition Clause, Stephen Higginson, warns that "[t]o explore the consequences of reinstituting the colonial process of lawmaking and representation through popular petitions would be to reargue the Federalist-Antifederalist debate, in a twentieth century context. That is too ambitious."[396]

Commentators on the British history of petitioning also tend to assume that, in an age of universal suffrage, petitioning represents a relic of a less enlightened time. Nicholls describes petitioning as a "surrogate" for democracy and suggests that "[a]s voting and party participation became available to greater numbers of people, the petition no longer served a useful purpose."[397] "Uniquely suited to the nineteenth century, petitioning as a means of obtaining legislative redress outlived its usefulness."[398]

The logical conclusion to be drawn, it would seem, is that petitioning is a feature of despotic or, less pejoratively, imperfectly democratic systems of government. This view of petitioning has deep roots in the literature. Professor Lieber, for example, observes that "[w]here the government is founded on the parental principle, or where the despot appears as an earthly Providence, the petition of individuals plays, naturally, an important part so long as it does not become either dangerous or troublesome, or unwelcome to the officers near the person of the monarch."[399] Another commentator, Theodore Woolsey, in a similar vein notes that the right of petition "is needed especially under arbitrary governments, where those who seek for redress have not representatives to intercede for them."[400] And contemporary China, where the government has recently attempted to discourage or abolish the use of petitioning, provides a useful case in point.[401]

To be clear, Lieber plainly thinks that it would be wrong to assume petitioning has relevance only in autocratic societies. He observes that "[a]n American statesman of great mark has spoken lightly of the right of petition in a country in which citizens are so fully represented as with us; *but this is an error*."[402] Petitioning is "a sacred right" that "in difficult times shows itself in its full magnitude, frequently serves as a safety valve, if judiciously treated by the recipients, and may give to the representatives or other bodies most valuable information."[403] Even so, Lieber is skeptical of the utility of petitioning in practice because the right is "so far abused [in the United States] as to deprive the petition of weight and importance."[404]

Woolsey, like Lieber, posits a meaningful role for petitioning in democratic polities and believes petition has a positive role to play in facilitating democratic self-government. The right of petition "is needed in constitutional representative governments, because opinions may change, new wants arise, and the representative may act on the base principle that he represents a party only."[405] In light of the need for public officials to legislate with knowledge of the citizenry's policy preferences, "[a]ll the people in all countries, citizens and foreigners, ought thus to have free access not only to courts but to legislatures and magistrates, either in reference to public affairs or to such as affect their own industry and calling."[406] Thus, Woolsey astutely—and correctly—posits an active and useful role for petitioning in a democratic society.

But a question arises as a counterweight to Woolsey's arguments in favor of the relevance of petitioning in a democratic society: Is it at all realistic to expect a modern national legislature to receive *and consider seriously* unsolicited petitions from ordinary citizens? Given the advances in social science and polling, most legislators, in most places, undoubtedly think that they already know what their constituents think (or ought to think). Woolsey himself argues that "[p]etitions have less weight in this country [the United States] than in some others . . . because the representatives think in all important measures that they understand the opinions of their districts better than the petitioners do" and acknowledges that "[t]here are in fact so many other ways of knowing what public opinion is, that this way has not the relative importance which it once had in affecting legislation."[407] If these observations held true in 1878, what hope is there of a national legislature taking citizen petitions seriously in 2012?

Another explanation for the demise of legislative responses to petitions involves the growth and size of the federal government. One commentator posits that it would be "impractical for the post–New Deal era" for the government to have a general obligation to respond to petitions; this is so because "the government has assumed responsibility for so many aspects of our global society and, in the process, has become so complex that it is unrealistic to expect members of Congress or the President even to read or listen to all citizen petitions, much less respond to them."[408] As a consequence of these developments, "the more traditional forms of general petitions—letters to government officials—are no longer as effective in ensuring government accountability as they were when the governmental duty to respond was feasible."[409]

This argument seems to proceed from the notion that petitioning could be a useful feedback device but no longer is so, due to the growth and complexity of modern governing institutions and the time demands associated with holding public office. The claim, if true, would explain the demise of petitioning in the United States and also in the United Kingdom. But this begs the central question: *Is* the claim *true?* Is it simply unthinkable that a modern national government's elected officials would have the time and energy to respond to random suggestions and requests submitted by ordinary citizens?

As it happens, there is at least one national legislature in a democratic polity that takes seriously its responsibility to receive and respond to citizen petitions: the New Zealand House of Representatives. For whatever reasons, New Zealand's unicameral national legislature has managed to maintain its commitment to an active petitioning culture and maintains procedures and practices that mirror those of the early Congress and the U.K. Parliament prior to 1836. In considering whether a modern petitioning culture is viable in the twenty-first century, New Zealand provides an instructive example.

A. A Brief Overview of New Zealand, Its Constitution, and Its Governing Institutions

Some basic information about New Zealand and its government might be helpful before considering the specific phenomenon of petitioning in New Zealand. New Zealand, located in the South Pacific, is composed of two large islands, North and South Island, and a number of smaller islands. The current population is about 4.2 million persons, and the main ethnic groups are descendants of the English settlers and the native Polynesian Maoris. New Zealand became a British territory in 1840, by operation of the Treaty of Waitangi.[410] Queen Elizabeth II serves as head of state.[411] The prime minister serves as head of government.

New Zealand, like the United Kingdom, lacks a written constitution.[412] Instead, a statute, the Constitution Act 1986, provides the basic framework for government.[413] In addition to the Constitution Act 1986, major statutory enactments of a constitutional nature include the New Zealand Bill of Rights Act 1990 and the Electoral Act 1993.

Certain U.K. statutory enactments also have the force and effect of law in contemporary New Zealand, under the terms of the Imperial Laws Application Act 1988. The Imperial Laws Application Act 1988 simply codified preexisting law and practice, dating back to the English Laws Act 1958, in which "the New Zealand Parliament affirmed the full inheritance of British law from 1840."[414] Professor Philip Joseph notes, however, that "[i]conic English constitutional statutes were presumed to apply through inheritance from 1840" and included "the Magna Carta and its confirmations under the Statutes of Westminster, the Petition of Right 1627, and the Bill of Rights 1688."[415]

New Zealand features a parliamentary form of government in which the heads of all executive departments must also be current members of the House of Representatives.[416] New Zealand once had an appointed upper house, the Legislative Council, but this chamber was abolished in 1950.[417] The House consists of 120 members, selected through a "mixed member proportional" system of allocating seats to the two major parties; sixty-seven members achieve office by winning election in a local district and the national election results determine allocation of the remaining fifty-three seats.

New Zealand's courts, like those of the United Kingdom, lack the power of judicial review.[418] As Professor Joseph, the leading New Zealand constitutionalist, puts the matter, "The judges recognised Parliament's law-making power and accepted the principle of unquestioning obedience to statute."[419] Accordingly, it is not possible to seek and obtain judicial invalidation of a statute. Indeed, the Bill of Rights Act 1990 expressly provides that "[n]o court shall, in relation to any enactment (whether passed or made before or after the commencement of this Bill of Rights),—(a) Hold any provision of the enactment to be impliedly repealed or revoked, or to be in any way invalid or ineffective; or (b) Decline to apply any provision of the enactment—by reason only that the provision is inconsistent with any provision of this Bill of Rights."[420] The act does admonish judges to reconcile the Bill of Rights Act with ambiguous statutes whenever doing so is possible.[421]

At the time of New Zealand's entry into the British Empire, in 1840, petitioning constituted a familiar and heavily used means of political advocacy, for this was the era of the massive Chartist petitions to Parliament seeking universal male suffrage, annual parliamentary elections, the secret ballot, and compensation for members of the House of Commons.[422] Thus, as David McGee, author of the principal treatise on parliamentary practice in New Zealand, observes, "From its first meeting in 1854, the House, continuing an ancient right exercised in England, has admitted petitions seeking redress for an almost unlimited number of real or supposed wrongs done to petitioners, advocating amendments to the law or changes in government policy, or seeking public inquiries into some unsatisfactory situation."[423] Thus, New Zealand incorporated petitioning the national parliament as part of its received British legal heritage.

B. The Right of Petition in New Zealand

Petitioning the House permits an ordinary New Zealander "to express his or her opinion on a subject of some concern and address it in a public fashion to the country's legislators."[424] As Professor Raymond Mulholland states the matter, "Any person is entitled to petition Parliament upon any matter."[425] To be sure, "[t]he act of petitioning may or may not have any practical consequences but it does ensure that the petitioner's concerns are heard and given some consideration by those in authority."[426]

This notion of actual consideration, however, separates contemporary New Zealand from both the United Kingdom and the United States, where it is virtually unthinkable that incumbent legislators would seriously consider matters presented to them in the form of an unsolicited petition from members of the public. What seems to set New Zealand apart is that the House of Representatives, for whatever reason, deems it politically expedient to consider petitions seriously and to respond to them on the merits.

1. A Historical Overview of Petitioning in New Zealand

Early New Zealand political science texts reflect that petitioning constituted a well-established part of the local political culture by the end of the nineteenth century. For example, writing in 1904, Frank Parsons reports that "[w]hen the people of any locality would like to have more land for settlement, they petition the Government to resume some large estate in the neighborhood."[427] Petitions for post offices, roads, and railroads also seem to have been commonplace.[428] Moreover, petitions involving railroad policy were widely subscribed: "As far back as 1887, it is said, petitions for it [a progressive rail tariff system] were signed by over 20,000 persons, and also by local bodies throughout the Colony."[429]

The availability of petitioning also helped to blunt efforts to secure initiative powers for the New Zealand citizenry. A member of the Legislative Council, the now-abolished upper house of the national legislature, opposed to creating the initiative argued that "[t]he people can petition Parliament, if they want a referendum, or legislation."[430] In fact, "[i]t was owing to the petitions in favor of Woman Suffrage [*sic*] that a number of this Council saw there was a general desire on the part of the women to have the franchise, and they accordingly voted for the measure."[431]

Indeed, the question of women's voting rights appears to have been a case study in the successful use of the petition to drive public policy in New Zealand. Parliament began receiving mass systemic petitions seeking voting rights for women in the 1880s.[432] In 1887, the government introduced the first bill proposing to grant women voting rights.[433] After a change in government following elections in 1887, the bill failed. When the Progressive Party returned to power in the elections of 1891, the House of Representatives passed a women's suffrage bill, but the Legislative Council, controlled by the opposition, defeated the measure. A second attempt in 1892 again passed the House but not the Legislative Council in a form acceptable to the House.[434]

In 1893, supporters of voting rights for women submitted a petition signed by more than thirty thousand women.[435] Another petition advocating women's suffrage contained more than twenty thousand signatures.[436] Moreover, legislators saw the absence of petitions opposing voting rights for women as significant. "I would point out to the Council this fact: that no petitions are being presented this year either to this branch of the Legislature or to the other, opposing the granting of the franchise to women and signed by women."[437] Finally, in 1893, Parliament enacted legislation granting voting rights to women at least twenty-one years of age (well before the United States, which did so in 1920 via a constitutional amendment, and the United Kingdom, which extended voting rights to women on the same terms as men via statute in 1928).[438] Petitioning clearly constituted a key component of the public campaign to secure universal suffrage without regard to sex in New Zealand.

McGee reports that, as in the United Kingdom and the United States, petitioning in New Zealand flourished in the mid-to-late nineteenth century, and then declined precipitously in the early twentieth century. "The number of petitions to the House increased throughout the nineteenth century to a peak in 1906" and "declined consistently from then until the mid-1980s, at which point petitions presented to the House rose significantly."[439] This is not to say that petitioning ever ceased. For example, an important petition seeking recognition and respect for Maori language rights was presented to Parliament on September 14, 1972, and led to major changes in official policy.[440]

Another significant petition submitted to Parliament on May 26, 1970, asking Parliament to "Save [Lake] Manapouri" garnered 264,907 signatures, and was "at that time the largest petition seen" in New Zealand.[441] "Almost 10 percent of New Zealand's population signed the petition, which demanded that the Government reconsider its decision to raise the level of Lake Manapouri."[442] This petition received a great deal of media attention, and the House of Representatives created a special committee to consider it, which held public hearings on the question.[443]

Thus, it appears that the arc of petitioning in New Zealand as a means of grassroots political activity largely followed the same pattern that existed in the United Kingdom and the United States, but with two significant differences: the national legislature never ceased to receive and respond to petitions on the merits, and New Zealand citizens reclaimed the right of petition in the 1980s as a means of bringing their concerns to the national legislature.

The growth in the net numbers of petitions in the late twentieth century might have something to do with the approach used by petition proponents. In years past, petition circulators would attempt to obtain as many signatures as possible on a single petition. In the modern era, however, "[r]ather than promoting one petition with a large number of signatures appended to it to demonstrate its degree of support, those responsible for organising petitions often encourage the submission of many separate petitions on the same subject with only a few signatures on each one."[444] This development means that "it is misleading to draw conclusions about the interest shown in presenting petitions to the House merely by comparing the number of petitions presented over time."[445]

2. The Contemporary Petitioning Process in New Zealand's Parliament

New Zealand's Parliament has adopted both substantive and procedural rules that seem to demonstrate a meaningful commitment to taking petitions seriously. On the substantive side of the ledger, McGee notes that "[s]o important is the right of the citizen to petition the House considered to be that where Parliament creates legal remedies it often makes clear in the relevant legislation that these remedies are not intended to qualify the ability to petition the House or to restrict the jurisdiction of any committee set up to consider such a petition."[446] Similarly, "a body set up outside the House to provide an avenue of redress may be expressly excluded from taking account of the citizen's right to petition the House in deciding whether to exercise its own powers in respect of the matter."[447] Even so, however, "[a] petition on a matter for which the petitioner has not exhausted legal remedies is not permitted."[448] In addition, the House will not consider petitions that fall within the jurisdiction of a national Office of the Ombudsmen, which is led by an official called the chief ombudsman: "Petitions from persons who have not sought the Ombudsman's assistance where the subject matter of the petition is within the competence of the Ombudsman, are not in order."[449]

The reason for the first of these two restrictions on petitioning seems to be self-evident: the House of Representatives does not want to supplant the common law courts in matters affecting property, contract, or tort. Permitting petitions seeking relief against private parties would essentially turn the House into a common law court.

The second restriction relates to the nature and purpose of the ombudsman. The House created the officer in 1962. "His prime function is to hear complaints, brought by ordinary citizens, against the administrative decisions of government departments and individual officers."[450] The ombudsman "will not generally deal with matters which are within the prerogative of the Courts."[451] Matters routinely handled by this office include disputes over government benefits, government employment, and adverse regulatory decisions.[452]

To initiate consideration of a petition, the petitioning group must secure a member of the House willing to present the petition to the body; members routinely present petitions for constituents, but this does not indicate a member's personal support for its contents. As David Bagnall, of the Office of the Clerk, explains, "Members take the presentation of petitions seriously, and it is not uncommon for members to present petitions even when they disagree with the requests set out in them."[453] Usually a constituent will ask the local member for his district to present a petition, although no rule requires this. The member then submits the petition to the Office of the Clerk.

In turn, the Office of the Clerk refers petitions suitable for consideration by the House to one of the standing committees of the House.[454] Unlike in the contemporary United Kingdom, where the clerk's office redirects petitions to various executive ministries, or even the United Kingdom prior to 1974, where a special committee on petitions arranged for the printing of petitions in the record (and nothing more), standing committees of the House regularly exercise jurisdiction over unsolicited citizen petitions.

The House clerk's office will refer a petition "to the most appropriate select committee for consideration and report."[455] From 1962 to 1985, a special Petitions Committee existed, but the House abolished this committee in 1985 in favor of having regular committees of jurisdiction review and respond to petitions.[456] Contemporary practice requires the clerk to "allocate a petition to the committee whose terms of reference relate most closely to the issue raised by the petition, without regard to whether it is politically appropriate or expedient for that committee to consider it."[457]

A standing committee of the House in receipt of a petition has a duty to conduct an inquiry into it. "The committee is required to deal with the petition and report it back to the House," although "the extent of the consideration to be given to it is entirely over to the committee."[458] Standard practice requires the committee to contact the government department with responsibility over the matter, seeking its views, as well as the principal petitioner, to ascertain whether "he or she wishes to tender any written evidence in support of the petition or, if the petition already full sets out the grounds itself, if there are any written comments the petitioner wishes to add."[459] In other words, the House expects the committee to create a written record of submissions regarding the merits of the petition.

The committee usually will schedule a hearing for the petition, at which proponents and opponents might be afforded an opportunity to present oral testimony. Petitioners also may respond to submissions of the relevant government department. In some instances, a hearing may adduce evidence from a wider group of witnesses, or even seek general public comment on the question. For example, "[i]n 1970 the public was specifically invited to submit evidence to the select committee considering the petition opposing the raising of the level of Lake Manapouri."[460] Committees also have invited public comment and participation in proceedings considering petitions involving post office closures, liquor advertising rules, and tobacco advertising.

Committees operate under a rule that requires them to report to the House on petitions referred to them.[461] "There is no prescribed form to which a report on a petition must conform."[462] Although it is permissible for a committee to report in a pro forma fashion that it deems a petition to lack merit, or had insufficient time and resources to consider the petition's merits, "this is not the norm."[463] A committee reviewing a petition will submit its report to the Office of the Clerk, which will then distribute it to the members of the House. The clerk of the House will also advise "the petitioner or the principal petitioner, if more than one, of the nature of the committee's report."[464]

Although the House usually will not debate a report on a petition, a standing order of the House requires the incumbent government (the executive branch) "to report to the House on what action, if any, it had taken to implement recommendations made to it on petitions."[465] Under the current rules, the government must respond to a petition report within ninety days after the select committee files it with the Office of the Clerk.[466] The current practice is for the relevant minister to communicate the government's response to the petition and the committee report directly to the petitioner and also to present it to the House.[467]

To be clear, petitions do not routinely lead to the introduction or enactment of legislation in New Zealand. McGee reports, however, that "[i]n exceptional cases, a favourable recommendation from a committee on a petition can be the catalyst for the Government to agree to law changes or the paying of compensation to the petitioner."[468] Mr. Bagnall concurs that legislation is seldom the direct result of a petition, but he notes that "[d]uring the preparation of its response to a report on a petition, the Government may consider whether any legislative initiatives are desirable in light of the report."[469] Thus, although petitions do not directly serve as the vehicles of legislative change, they can and do precipitate it.

Citizens also file petitions supporting or opposing pending legislation. "Many petitions are motivated through support or opposition to legislation that has already been introduced in the House."[470] Mr. Bagnall explains that "[s]uch petitions are generally considered as evidence on the bills to which they relate" and can lead to the principal petitioner being invited to testify during committee proceedings on the bill itself.[471]

Mr. Bagnall cautions that "[t]he 'success' of a petition would not necessarily be measured in terms of its implementation in legislation."[472] This is because "[i]n many cases, petitioners are pleased to receive a public hearing."[473] This corresponds to the research of Professor Tom Tyler, who has found that most people will accept an adverse decision more readily if they believe that they have received a fair hearing in a fair process.[474]

Thus, even in New Zealand, where classic petitioning still exists, petitioners seem to use petitions and petitioning not only to seek access to their elected representatives but also as a means of engaging the larger community about a specific question or concern. A public hearing, held by a standing committee of Parliament, is very likely to garner media attention that, in turn, precipitates a broader level of engagement within the community regarding the issue in question. Petitioning thus serves as a means of access to the government and as a way of engaging the government directly over policy concerns, but it also engages the larger political community in an open and public process of democratic deliberation.

C. Potential Lessons from New Zealand's Example of a Contemporary Petitioning Culture: The Possibilities and Limitations of Classic Petitioning in the Modern Era

New Zealand presents a remarkable case, and one might well be skeptical that incumbent legislators actually receive, consider, and respond on the merits to whatever petitions their constituents submit for review. This is, perhaps, a reaction that reflects an assumption that New Zealand's legislators are little different from their U.S. (or U.K.) counterparts. But this assumption does not appear to be valid. Several reasons help to explain why this is so.

First, and perhaps most important, the volume of petitions submitted in New Zealand since 1985, when petitioning came back into vogue, has not been unduly burdensome. Mr. Bagnall, of the Office of the Clerk, explains that "[t]he volume of petitions is not an issue, and in fact has been decreasing in recent years—as at today [October 2, 2009,] only 39 petitions have been lodged since the start of the current parliamentary term last December [December 2008]."[475] Mr. Bagnall adds: "During the previous parliamentary term (2005–2008) there were 190 petitions lodged. From 2002–2005 there were 183 petitions, down from 241 in the 1999–2002 term."[476] Thus, the national legislature generally receives more than fifty and fewer than a hundred petitions a year. Some of these, as McGee notes, could be duplicates circulated and submitted individually, but subject to consolidated committee review and the basis of a single committee report and response.

Simply put, the volume of petitioning in New Zealand is not so great as to overbear the ability of the standing committees to respond to petitions on the merits, and on a timely basis. This is a clear point of distinction with petitioning in the United States and the United Kingdom by the 1840s, when petitions numbered in the tens of thousands per year. A petitioning culture survives in New Zealand, at least in part, because the temporal demands petitioners place on the incumbent members of the House is not unreasonable or overtaxing.

There also does not seem to be much of an issue with repetitive, ceaseless petitioning. New Zealand petitioners appear to be satisfied when their petitions have been considered and answered, at least for the current session of the House. Contemporary New Zealand does not seem to have any problems with "abusive" repetitive petitioning (which also supports the inference that "classic" petitioning, rather than systemic petitioning, remains the norm). Moreover, even if it did, the House would probably simply extend and expand its already extant practice of consolidated proceedings on duplicative petitions.

A civic culture that embraces petitioning might also have something to do with the seriousness with which the contemporary New Zealand House of Representatives takes petitions. Bagnall explains that "petitioning is part of New Zealand's local political culture" and "Members take the presentation of petitions seriously."[477] Indeed, "Parliamentary petitions are only one form of petition—petitions addressed to other public authorities (such as the Governor-General, the Prime Minister or other Ministers, Mayors and local authorities) are not unusual."[478]

Again, a certain amount of skepticism seems warranted: Is it really plausible for the members of a modern national legislature and their staff to spend significant time and energy responding to the random requests of constituents? Is this form of grassroots democracy still viable in the present day and age?

To test this hypothesis, I first examined the subject matter and support of recent petitions filed in New Zealand's House of Representatives during 2009 and 2010. The subject matters are amazingly wide and varied, including requests for greater support for the national parks, a request that "the House recognise 'Aotearoa' as a name of this country (New Zealand), and declare and record this," requests for new roads, changes in public assistance and public welfare programs, creation and expansion of passenger rail services, opposition to commercial whaling, and seeking a ban "on the sale of fireworks for private use and allow them for use for public displays only."[479] Petitions sometimes have as few as a dozen or more signatories, but others garner more than fifty thousand signatures.[480] The wide variety of topics, from local issues such as rail service and road construction, to international issues, like whaling, suggest that contemporary petitioning in New Zealand cannot be easily characterized or pigeonholed. It appears that advocates in a variety of areas of law reform view petitioning as a useful means of promoting their causes, including identifying, organizing, and mobilizing their supporters.

In terms of responses, the quality and depth of the committee reports vary, depending on the subject matter at issue. The report responding to four petitions seeking reductions in budget cuts for adult and community education services, for example, simply states that the Ministry of Education "did not consider the proposals to reverse all the expenditure cuts for ACE either feasible or appropriate in the current fiscal environment."[481] The report then canvasses minority report views by the Labour and Green Party members of the committee, who express greater sympathy for the petitioners' request.[482] The formal recommendation of the committee in response to the four petitions was that "the House take note of its report."[483]

Even though this constitutes a rather pro forma response to the petitions, it is difficult to imagine the U.S. Senate Health, Education, Labor and Pensions Committee bestirring itself to respond formally to a petition for increased federal funding for adult educational services; the fact that the New Zealand House of Representatives standing Education and Science Committee responded at all seems significant.

But not all of the committee reports are pro forma. The report considering the petition of Juliet Pratt and 1,341 others, seeking "that the House urge the Government to stop the use of mercury amalgam in dental treatment," is illustrative.[484] Representative Sue Kedgley submitted the petition on behalf of Pratt and the other petitioners on March 2, 2009, and the clerk referred the petition to the Health Committee for consideration and a response. The Health Committee held hearings on the petition on May 6 and May 13, 2009, and filed its report to the full House on September 14, 2009.[485]

This committee report surveys available public health information regarding the safety of using mercury dental amalgam, including submissions from the Ministry of Health, the New Zealand Dental Association, and Dr. Michael Beasley, "a medical toxicologist at the National Poisons Centre, University of Otago."[486] It considers the regulation of the use of mercury dental amalgam fillings in other nations, including those with bans (Sweden, Norway, Finland, Denmark), those with advisories against use in some circumstances (Australia, Canada, Germany, and the United Kingdom), and those with no warnings or restrictions (United States).

After a review of the submissions and available medical and scientific evidence, the report concludes that "the majority of us do not consider that the petitioner's case has been proven," because "[t]he advice we received does not convince the majority of us that dental amalgam causes significant health effects, and we do not agree that it should be banned or its use phased out as the petitioner requests."[487] The committee's formal recommendation was "that the Ministry of Health continue to review the scientific evidence on amalgam . . . and on viable alternative filling materials."[488]

Thus, Ms. Pratt and the other petitioners failed to secure legislation banning the use of mercury amalgam fillings and providing for such fillings to be replaced in persons thought to be at risk from them. Even so, however, the

House conducted an extensive investigation into the question, prepared a substantial report on the available evidence, and did support further consideration of the question as new evidence becomes available. The Health Committee did not engage in a pro forma or merely symbolic review of the petition. Presumably, if the evidence against mercury amalgam fillings had been more clear-cut, the committee might have recommended legislation imposing a ban, replacement of the fillings for persons thought to be at risk, or perhaps both.

Even if one discounts the New Zealand example of an active petitioning culture because of its relatively small national population of just more than four million, it is highly unlikely that a state legislature in a state with a roughly comparable population (e.g., Alabama, Kentucky, Louisiana, or South Carolina, all of which have populations of about 4.5 million persons) would agree to investigate citizens' substantive concerns essentially on demand through a public petition process. Moreover, as Mr. Bagnall notes, the House is not the only government institution in New Zealand that takes petitioning seriously and responds on the merits to public petitions.[489]

Moreover, it bears noting that in New Zealand petitions receive *institutional* responses that carry the imprimatur of both a standing committee of the House and the House itself as a body. This seems significantly different from the commonplace U.S. practice of an incumbent member of Congress responding to a constituent's letter or e-mail. A letter from a single legislator is simply not an institutional response from the collective body. Nor does it reflect collective consideration of the problem or concern. New Zealand legislators, like their U.S. counterparts, routinely respond to constituents' correspondence as well; petitioning constitutes a means of putting specific issues before the House itself for formal consideration and a written response; in a nontrivial way, petitioning gives ordinary people the ability to help set the House's agenda. No comparable form of access exists in the U.S. Congress or, so far as I can find, any state legislature. In the United States, unlike New Zealand, citizens may attempt to bypass a state legislature through the use of a binding initiative or referendum, but they cannot directly engage the legislature itself.

The official House of Representatives website[490] also reflects the salience of petitioning in contemporary New Zealand—from its home page, the site features multiple links for "petitions," including one on "getting involved" that leads a visitor both to pending petitions and to comprehensive, online instructions on how petition the House.[491] Petitions also appear on the "parliamentary business" webpage, along with pending legislation, official reports, and the rules of the House.[492] In other words, the House itself encourages petitioning and signals that it takes seriously the public's submissions by giving significant publicity to the public petitions currently pending before the House.

E. Reconsidering the Possibility of a Modern Petitioning Culture

New Zealand's example suggests, contrary to the assumption of many scholars of petitioning in the nineteenth century United Kingdom and United States, that petitioning need not constitute an antiquated and infeasible form of collective political action. The problem for extending the model, however, is that petitioning works in New Zealand precisely because it constitutes an integral existing part of the contemporary political culture. Both citizens and incumbent government officials understand that petitions are not to be ignored; in other words, a legislator would incur greater political risk by ignoring a petition in New Zealand precisely because of a settled expectation that petitions must be received, considered, and answered.

By way of contrast, in a contemporary political culture that lacks both citizens who will petition and government officials who will consider and respond to petitions on the merits (i.e., the United States), it would be difficult to resurrect the practice without significant changes in the attitudes of both citizens and politicians. Even if citizens were to petition Congress or their state legislature, it is highly unlikely that such petitions would receive any formal consideration; indeed, the rules of the body, unlike those of New Zealand's House, do not provide for such consideration, much less require it. There also is not much political upside for an incumbent legislator in permitting citizens to set his committee's public policy agenda. As McGee notes, New Zealand's legislators recognize that considering petitions entails taking political risks; committees of jurisdiction must receive and consider public petitions "without regard to whether it is politically appropriate or expedient for that committee to consider it."[493]

Thus, New Zealand's example implies limits as well as possibilities. Classic petitioning need not constitute a kind of political fossil, as it does in the United States, or an empty formalism, as it does in the United Kingdom. But, for classic petitioning to exist, two conditions must exist concurrently: citizens must use petitioning as a means of collective political action and incumbent government officials must fear the consequences of ignoring petitions more than they resent the time and bother associated with considering and responding to them. In contemporary New Zealand, both conditions exist and, accordingly, classic petitioning maintains its cultural and political salience.

To revive classic petitioning in the United States, however, would be very difficult precisely because neither condition currently exists. Because Congress is not likely to take an unsolicited petition seriously, citizens have little incentive to engage in classic petitioning activities; at the same time, because most citizens do not petition, Congress feels no compunctions about ignoring the fringe groups that do attempt to engage in classic petitioning. The problem is very much one of the "which came first, the chicken or the egg?" variety.

In the end, then, a political culture that embraces classic petitioning is not at all inconsistent with the modern demands of government. Instead, the traditional right of petition requires both voters and elected officials holding a shared commitment to petitioning as a central component of democratic politics within the community. In New Zealand, petitioning constitutes a widely recognized and well-used tool of civic engagement and democratic deliberation, whereas in the United States and the United Kingdom it does not.

V. CONCLUSION: PETITIONING AND THE PROJECT OF DEMOCRATIC SELF-GOVERNMENT

Consideration of the right of petition in three societies shows that the concept of petitioning was and is dynamic, not static, in the United Kingdom and the United States. At its inception in the United Kingdom, petitioning initially constitutes a kind of quasi-judicial action that, over time, transforms into a parliamentary form of proceeding that can and does generate legislative reforms, and changes yet again into a form of mass organizing and protest. We see petitioning develop and change from a means of directly engaging the legislature to a broader means of engaging the body politic. In both the United Kingdom and the United States, the conveyance of universal suffrage, modern social science polling techniques, and the ability to shape public opinion through the broadcast media all worked to undermine the perceived utility of systemic, or hybrid, petitioning, so that by the end of World War I, systemic petitioning no longer played a major role in the democratic life of either nation on a regular basis (if at all).

In the United States, a plausible case can be made that petitioning evolved yet again with the emergence of the initiative after South Dakota's adoption of the device in 1898. Twenty-four states and the District of Columbia now provide for citizen-sponsored initiatives that bypass the state legislature entirely. In the modern United States, petitioning survives, but it exists at the state level and seeks not legislative action but action through a plebiscite. Although the legal genealogy seems reasonably clear, the initiative plainly differs in important ways from both classic and systemic petitioning.

Thus, in the United States, petitioning activity moved from an exclusively legislative focus (classic petitioning, in the colonial, revolutionary, and Federalist eras), to an indirect focus on the legislature through efforts to move and shape public opinion (systemic petitioning from 1835 to 1919), and finally into a process with an *exclusive* focus on general public opinion, as expressed at the polls in a vote (citizens initiative). Through the initiative process, the United States maintains a functioning petitioning culture.

The dynamic history of petitioning in the United States also provides strong support for considering the right not solely in static, originalist terms but rather in functional or purposive terms that recognize that petitioning activity does not begin, or end, with laying a scroll at the foot of the king's throne. The core of petitioning involves a right of access to the government and its officials, paired with a duty on the part of government to engage the issues brought to its attention via petitions. Petitions also have served to facilitate broader discussion and engagement within the body politic; indeed, systemic petitioning seeks to move general public opinion as much, if not more, than it seeks to log roll votes within a legislative chamber.

Finally, New Zealand's example demonstrates the feasibility of a classic petitioning culture in the twenty-first century. At a time when many citizens in the United States are skeptical of government's responsiveness to their concerns and also, perhaps paradoxically, highly disengaged from civic life (at least if one takes overall voting rates as a proxy for civic engagement), New Zealand provides a welcome counterexample of a culture in which the representatives and the represented maintain an active and effective ongoing dialogue in real time. In New Zealand, via the petition process, the sentiment that "there ought to be a law" can, and sometimes does, become a concrete reality.

If one credits the claims of the social scientists, like Tom Tyler, who argue that process values are important to the perceived fairness of adverse outcomes,[494] there is much to recommend the New Zealand approach. By providing a direct and reasonably effective means of bringing concerns directly to the attention of the national government, New Zealand's citizens have the ability to seek and obtain a fair hearing from their elected representatives on myriad subjects deemed important not by the government or its officers but rather by average people living ordinary lives.

The legal and the more general culture are essential to the survival of classic petitioning in New Zealand, and the existence of a petitioning culture there does not say much, if anything, useful about the possibility of an active petitioning culture here in the United States. With that caveat, I nevertheless believe that New Zealand's example serves to refute the notion that petitioning is exclusively a relic of a bygone political age; clearly, it is possible to maintain a system of traditional petitioning if both citizens and elected officials find it mutually beneficial to do so. Moreover, the initiative process in the United States, at the state level, provides another example of a modern instantiation of the ancient right, as does, in a more limited way, the ability of citizens to petition federal administrative agencies under the APA.

History shows that petitioning can encompass many forms of collective democratic action. There is no reason that petitioning in the 2010s must reflect the values or objectives of petitioning in the 1810s or the 1910s, any more than the concept of protected "speech" has remained static and unchanging over time. At its essence, petitioning involves collective democratic action by the people to obtain legal and social change—whether through the voluntary action of a legislative body or by bypassing the normal legislative authority completely. Petitioning partakes of elements of speech, assembly, association, and press, but it has at its core the notion of legal change through "bottom up," rather than "top down," democratic and lawful processes.

Accordingly, reclaiming the Petition Clause, in the most general terms, would imply nothing more than a commitment to maintain open channels of communication between the governors and the governed with respect to questions of public policy and governance, and among and between the citizens themselves. The key concepts are *access* and *engagement*—the ability to interact in a meaningful way with one's elected representatives and the ability to engage them, as well as one's fellow citizens, in a process of democratic discourse about the content and direction of public policies.

The precise doctrinal scope of these commitments of civic engagement and dialogue, as with the freedom of speech and assembly, would have to be worked out over time and across various factual contexts. The history of petitioning, however, lends strong support to the judicial protection of a right to access and engage government officials, as well as one's fellow citizens, regarding issues of the day; perhaps most crucially, it encompasses a right to an audience, at least insofar as the subject matter directly relates to the project of democratic self-government.[495]

5

The Jurisprudential Contours of the Petition Clause: An Examination of the Potential Doctrinal Shape and Scope of a Reclaimed Petition Clause

I. INTRODUCTION: RECLAIMING THE PETITION CLAUSE

In his seminal article on the paradigm shift in First Amendment doctrine wrought by *New York Times Co. v. Sullivan*,[1] Professor Harry Kalven eloquently expressed his regard for the civil rights movement that precipitated the case, writing that "[w]hatever the irritations and crises of 'the long hot summer,' the protest has maintained the dignity of political action, of an elaborate petition for redress of grievances."[2] Kalven's reference to a "petition for redress of grievances," however, was more than mere poeticism; it was also an invocation of the oft-forgotten Petition Clause of the First Amendment: "Congress shall make no law . . . abridging the freedom of speech, or of the press; or *the right of the people peaceably to assemble, and to petition the Government for a redress of grievances.*"[3]

This most neglected of First Amendment freedoms is little more than a footnote in modern Supreme Court jurisprudence.[4] Yet the right to petition for redress of grievances predates both the derivative rights of speech and assembly; it once held an importance that equaled, if not exceeded them, and retained that status for well over a hundred years after giving birth to the secondary freedoms of speech and press.[5]

Although made during the height of the civil rights era, almost a half-century ago, Professor Kalven's assessment of political protest activity of a petitioning cast remains as relevant now as ever. The ability to access and engage government, in a meaningful way, remains central to the success of the project of democratic self-government. For government to address successfully the wants and desires of We the People, it must listen and engage popular concerns on a timely basis.

Moreover, concerns about risks to public safety and security also remain pressing today,[6] so that Kalven's admonition that "[t]he central meaning of the [First] Amendment is that seditious libel cannot be made the subject of government sanction"[7] continues to have relevance as we think about the potential social cost associated with the exercise of expressive freedoms. Despite the lower federal courts' willingness of late to underappreciate this "central meaning," permitting the government interest in security to all but entirely displace the *Ward* time, place, and manner doctrine,[8] Kalven's recognition that a political protest is a "petition for redress of grievances" hints at a novel solution to this unwelcome return of seditious libel in the guise of abstract and unproven government security concerns.

As the preceding chapters have shown, at its core the Petition Clause stands for the proposition that government, and those who work for it, must be accessible and responsive to the people. Governance in a representative democracy is supposed to be a collaborative enterprise in which those holding government power engage and respond to the citizenry, not only at election time, but also while engaged in the day-to-day task of governing. Moreover, this is not merely a theoretical commitment; classic forms of petitioning, of the sort practiced in the United States from the inception of the federal government in 1789 to 1836, in the United Kingdom from 1779 to 1839, and in New Zealand even today,[9] involve the power of ordinary, average people to put items on the government's agenda for consideration and response—regardless of whether or not those holding public office wish to consider, much less address, those precise issues. This power also helped to drive broader political engagement within the community, facilitating a process of democratic deliberation across all strata of society. The question that remains to be addressed is: How could a renewed commitment to the Petition Clause be operationalized doctrinally? In other words, how could the right of access and engagement, both quite central to the Petition Clause, work in the contemporary United States?

The doctrines associated with petitioning in earlier times might provide at least some initial guideposts for developing a contemporary Petition Clause jurisprudence. For example, for hundreds of years before the Petition Clause fell into desuetude through a combination of disuse by the public and Supreme Court doctrinal neglect, one of the foremost common law principles associated with the right of petition was that petitioners enjoyed absolute immunity from prosecutions for seditious libel based on the contents of their petitions.[10] Moreover, the history of the Petition Clause, including the history of its colonial and English antecedents, strongly suggests that the right to petition the government for redress of grievances contemplates a right to do so in close proximity to the government officials to whom the petition is addressed. In other words, the Petition Clause of the First Amendment, properly construed and applied, should guarantee would-be petitioners a right, exclusive of their speech and assembly freedoms, to seek redress of their grievances within both sight and hearing of those capable of giving redress.[11]

At a minimum, then, petitioning involves some sort of access to the government and its officers, coupled with a presumption against punishment for those who seek to exercise this right of access. A Petition Clause restored to doctrinal significance should reflect both these principles.

To be sure, access cannot be absolute, any more than the right to speak or assemble is absolute or unqualified. Reasonable limits to this right of proximity, as the history of petitioning amply demonstrates, would be consistent with the underlying right.[12] Both public safety and privacy remain legitimate concerns; thus, petitioning activity could be restricted to public forums proximate to places of official business. Petitioners do not have a right, for example, to encamp at Senator John McCain's private residence;[13] the sidewalks outside the Senate office buildings or the Republican National Convention, however, can and do present a different, and easier, question. With respect to official government buildings and also the venues in which government or political party business will be conducted, the presumption should be in favor of access, although government officials should have some discretion to determine how access will occur.

Moreover, consistent with Professor Alexander Meiklejohn's admonition, one should readily concede that the right of petition does not imply a right to disrupt a political event, meeting, or convention.[14] The right of petition does not imply a right to "bum rush"[15] the door or to confront public officials at any time, or any place, of a would-be petitioner's choosing. As Meiklejohn so eloquently explains:

> When self-governing men demand freedom of speech they are not saying that every individual has an unalienable right to speak whenever, wherever, however he chooses. They do not declare that any man may talk as he pleases, when he pleases, about what he pleases, about whom he pleases, to whom he pleases. The common sense of any reasonable society would deny the existence of that unqualified right. No one, for example, may, without consent of nurse or doctor, rise up in a sickroom to argue for his principles or his candidate. In the sickroom, the question is is not "before the house." The discussion is, therefore, "out of order." . . . Anyone who would thus irresponsibly interrupt the activities of a lecture, a hospital, a concert hall, a church, a machine shop, a classroom, a football field, or a home, does not

thereby exhibit his freedom. Rather he shows himself to be a boor, a public nuisance, who must be abated, by force if necessary.[16]

Thus, consistent with Meiklejohn's observations, the right of access secured under the aegis of the Petition Clause must be meaningful, but this does not mean that it must be infinite.

Furthermore, the claim that the Petition Clause contemplates a right to be seen and heard is itself limited—I do not argue, as have some scholars, that the Petition Clause imposes on government officials an absolute and judicially cognizable obligation to consider and respond to petitions for redress of grievances on the merits.[17] Even in the era of classic petitioning in the United States and the United Kingdom, legislative bodies can and did choose not only to decline relief but also to cite the press of other business as precluding sustained consideration of the subject matter raised in a petition. Similarly, in contemporary New Zealand, the lack of time and the press of other legislative business can and sometimes does constitute Parliament's official response to a petition (although this is not the usual response).[18]

Yet even with these limitations, the Petition Clause should secure a baseline right of access to a particular intended audience, access that the other First Amendment expressive freedom guarantees have thus far failed to provide.[19] By treating regulations that would remove protestors from the sight or hearing of government officials as presumptively invalid absent a substantial justification supported by the record, the government loses the benefit of a presumption in favor of limiting, or even completely closing off, access to the government's agents for the purpose of hybrid petitioning activity.[20] At a minimum, when petitioning speech[21] is at issue, the federal courts should require the government to justify its interest in security with more than mere speculation and to carry out that interest with the means that are least restrictive to petitioning protestors' right to be seen and heard, and thereby to enjoy access to the government officials with responsibility for the public policies that relate to the protest activity.

This chapter also considers the Supreme Court's unfortunate and highly circumscribed jurisprudence of the Petition Clause, which to date has largely failed to give the clause much, if any, independent legal significance.[22] With the exception of a generic exemption from antitrust liability for media campaigns and more direct forms of lobbying aimed at securing favorable legislation that might have anticompetitive effects, the Petition Clause has little, if any, independent doctrinal significance. The Supreme Court has, for almost all intents and purposes, simply subsumed and merged the Petition Clause into the rights of speech, assembly, and association.

In the 1960s, however, a handful of federal judges were bold enough to suggest that the Petition Clause can and should do independent work in political protest cases.[23] With the reemergence of vaguely stated security concerns as a basis for limiting, and often prohibiting, access to government officials by ordinary people in the context of hybrid petitioning,[24] the Petition Clause must be reclaimed as a source of substantive constitutional civil liberties. Through a Petition Clause–based right of proximity to government officials, the overbroad invocation of unproven and abstract security concerns may be overcome, and the doctrine of seditious libel can be returned to its rightful place in the dustbin of legal history.[25]

II. THE SUPREME COURT'S GENERAL NEGLECT OF THE PETITION CLAUSE

Before addressing how contemporary Petition Clause jurisprudence could best advance the underlying values of the Clause (access and engagement), one should first consider the existing doctrine of petitioning (such as it is). It was not until 1867 that the Supreme Court first addressed the right to petition; even then, the Court did so only in the context of an interstate right to travel.[26] After some early signs that the Justices would give the Petition Clause independent significance,[27] the Court declared in 1945 that "[i]t was not by accident or coincidence that the rights to freedom in speech and press were coupled in a single guaranty with the rights of the people peaceably to assemble and petition for redress of grievances. All these, though not identical, are inseparable. They are cognate rights."[28]

Since that time, the Court has focused far more on the petition right's inseparability from the other expressive freedom guarantees rather than on its distinct identity,[29] giving independent effect to the Petition Clause in only one limited context that is discussed below.[30] As the Supreme Court has explained the matter, "[t]he right to petition is cut from the same cloth as the other guarantees of [the First Amendment], and is an assurance of a particular freedom of expression."[31] For the most part, the insignificance of the Petition Clause in Supreme Court jurisprudence is due simply to inattention—the Court believes that it can resolve its cases on other First Amendment grounds, so it does so.[32]

However, in *McDonald v. Smith*,[33] the Supreme Court's most important modern Petition Clause precedent, the Court went beyond merely ignoring the Petition Clause and instead struck an affirmative blow by grossly misstating the history of petitioning in order to hold that there is no immunity from civil libel for statements made in petitions.[34] In doing so, the Court made explicit its long practice of treating the protection afforded by the Petition Clause as coequal and coextensive with that of the other First Amendment expressive freedoms, and therefore having no independent legal significance for most intents and purposes. According to the *McDonald* Court, not only is the right to petition "cut from the same cloth as the other guarantees of [the First] Amendment,"[35] "there is no sound basis for granting greater constitutional protection to statements made in a petition to the President than other First Amendment expressions."[36]

As the preceding discussion of the history of the right of petition in chapter 4 should make abundantly clear,[37] the latter statement is simply false, particularly as applied to libel actions.[38] The Court was correct that "[t]o accept petitioner's claim of absolute immunity would elevate the Petition Clause to special First Amendment status."[39] What the Court failed to recognize was that through its history, the Petition Clause virtually demands special First Amendment status. True enough, "[t]he Petition Clause . . . was inspired by the same ideals of liberty and democracy that gave us the freedoms to speak, publish, and assemble."[40] It is equally true, however, that the freedoms to speak, publish, and assemble—freedoms of relatively recent vintage—were inspired by the ideals of the Petition Clause. The right of petition antedates the rights of speech and assembly, both of which derive from the right of petition. To fail to give the Petition Clause independent meaning and effect is, quite simply, to ignore history. It also violates the notion that a court, when interpreting a legal text, should attempt to give legal effect to all provisions of the text.[41]

The Supreme Court's most recent Petition Clause decision, *Borough of Duryea v. Guarnieri*,[42] decided in 2011, simply extends the Court's preexisting practice of denying the clause any independent meaning. In *Guarnieri*, the Supreme Court considered and decided a relatively narrow question: Does the Petition Clause confer any special protection on a government employee against employment retaliation for using a union grievance procedure? The Supreme Court's decision in *Guarnieri* did not alter its preexisting neglectful approach to Petition Clause claims.

The *Guarnieri* Court squarely held that job-related petitioning speech by government employees does not enjoy any special First Amendment protection under the Petition Clause and directed the lower federal courts simply to apply more generic rules, arising under the Free Speech Clause, to such cases.[43] Writing for the majority, Justice Anthony Kennedy explained that a government employee's petitioning speech must relate to a matter of public concern to fall within the protection of the First Amendment—whether under the rubric of the Petition Clause or the Free Speech Clause—because "[p]etitions, no less than speech, can interfere with the efficient and effective operation of government."[44]

Although the *Guarnieri* Court considered creating a Petition Clause–specific standard for claims involving grievances by public employees against their government employers for job-related complaints, it rejected this approach because "[a] different rule for each First Amendment claim would require employers to separate petitions from other speech in order to afford them different treatment; and that, in turn, would add to the complexity and expense of compliance with the Constitution."[45] Accordingly, the Petition Clause protects a government employee's "right to participate as a citizen, through petitioning, in the democratic process," but does not encompass "a right to transform everyday employment disputes into matters for constitutional litigation in the federal courts."[46]

To be sure, unlike the *McDonald* Court, the *Guarnieri* Court broadly hinted that, in a different context, a Petition Clause–specific jurisprudence might apply.[47] Moreover, Justice Kennedy expressly limited the scope of the decision to the context of a government employee complaining about a workplace matter solely of private interest: "Although retaliation by a government employer for a public employee's exercise of the right of access to the courts may implicate the protections of the Petition Clause, this case provides no necessity to consider the correct application of the Petition Clause beyond that context."[48] Even so, and dicta aside, the opinion's holding and reasoning plainly represent a continuation of the preexisting "cut from the same cloth" approach to interpreting and applying the Petition Clause.[49]

The Supreme Court's unwillingness to give independent meaning and effect to the Petition Clause is also inconsistent with the Court's treatment of other amendments, and even other provisions of the First Amendment. By its terms, the First Amendment protects the following freedoms: the freedom from religious establishments, the freedom of religious exercise, the freedom of speech, the freedom of the press, the freedom of assembly, and the freedom to petition the government.[50] Of these freedoms, the Supreme Court denies independent doctrinal significance to only the freedom to petition.[51] Incredibly, even the nontextual freedom of association is given far greater meaning by the Court than the right of petition.[52]

Looking to other amendments, the inconsistency of the Supreme Court's treatment of the Petition Clause is further underscored. For example, the clauses of the Fifth Amendment relating to grand jury indictment, double jeopardy, self-incrimination, due process, and takings are each given independent significance.[53] The Court also gives independent significance to each of the Sixth Amendment rights to a speedy trial, to an impartial jury, to be informed of the nature and cause of the accusation, to confront witnesses, to compulsory process for obtaining favorable witnesses, and to the assistance of counsel.[54]

The Supreme Court's inconsistency is not, however, limited only to history and its treatment of other amendments. Its general reluctance to give independent significance to the Petition Clause is also inconsistent with the Court's own application of the clause in the (apparently unique) context of antitrust cases. In antitrust cases alone, the Court has given independent meaning to the Petition Clause in the form of the *Noerr-Pennington* doctrine, and in so doing has displayed a highly dynamic and purposive, as opposed to originalist, understanding of the precise contours of the concept of "petitioning" activity.

Arising out of *Eastern Railroad Presidents Conference v. Noerr Motor Freight, Inc.*[55] and *United Mine Workers of America v. Pennington,*[56] the *Noerr-Pennington* doctrine relies on the Petition Clause to give absolute immunity from suit under federal antitrust laws for actions such as advertising and lobbying that are intended to influence legislation, even if the actions are in furtherance of an anticompetitive scheme that is itself illegal under antitrust laws.[57]

Noerr involved a mass media campaign waged by railroads in Pennsylvania to help secure enactment of legislation in the state legislature that would impede the ability of trucking companies to compete with the railroads for freight business. "The gist of the conspiracy alleged was that the railroads had engaged [in] a publicity campaign against the truckers designed to foster the adoption and retention of laws and law enforcement practices destructive of the trucking business, to create an atmosphere of distaste for the truckers among the general public, and to impair the relationships existing between the truckers and their customers."[58] Thus, the railroad "petitioning" activity was not of the classic sort involving one-on-one lobbying of a member of a legislative body or an executive branch official, but was rather indirect and aimed at moving public opinion, in a general sort of way, in favor of railroads and against trucking companies. The Pennsylvania Motor Truck Association filed an antitrust complaint against the twenty-four railroads that were underwriting the media blitz, as well as "an association of the presidents of those railroads known as the Eastern Railroads Presidents Conference, and a public relations firm, Carl Bynoir & Associates, Inc." which was responsible for the media campaign's design and execution.[59]

Writing for the majority, Justice Hugo Black squarely reversed the district court and U.S. Court of Appeals for the Third Circuit, which both had ruled in favor of the trucking companies' antitrust claims and against the defendants, reasoning that "[t]o hold that the knowing infliction of [reputational injury to a particular industry] renders the campaign illegal would thus be tantamount to outlawing all such campaigns,"[60] an outcome that would be inconsistent with the Petition Clause. Even though the specific activity at issue was a "publicity campaign,"[61] it "does not follow, however, that the use of the technique [of criticizing competitors publicly] in a publicity campaign designed to influence governmental action constitutes a violation of the Sherman Act."[62] This is so because "[t]he right of petition is one of the freedoms protected by the Bill of Rights, and we cannot, of course, lightly impute to Congress an intent to invade these freedoms."[63]

Justice Black also offered a purposive gloss on the Petition Clause, linking the clause to the ability to access and engage the government on matters of concern:

> In a representative democracy such as this, these branches of government act on behalf of the people and, to a very large extent, the whole concept of representation depends upon the ability of the people to make their wishes known to their representatives. To hold that the government retains the power to act in this representative capacity and yet hold, at the same time, that the people cannot freely inform the government of their wishes would impute to the Sherman Act a purpose to regulate, not business activity, but political activity, a purpose which would have no basis whatever in the legislative history of the Act. Secondly, and of at least equal significance, such a construction of the Sherman Act would raise important constitutional questions.[64]

The import of Justice Black's language is clear: the Petition Clause secures a right of access to the government and its officers, and a reading of the Sherman Act that rendered such activity unlawful would stand on very thin constitutional ground.

For better or worse, however, Justice Black's opinion does not link a mass media campaign—or other forms of indirect petitioning—to the traditional exercise of the right, which involved direct communication between a group of petitioners, on the one hand, and a legislator or an executive branch official, on the other.[65] It is certainly true that this sort of indirect petitioning seems rather far removed from the historical paradigm of petitioning, which involved, quite literally, laying a petition at the foot of the throne.[66]

Nevertheless, Justice Black's theory of indirect petitioning seems doctrinally sound, particularly at a time when both Congress and the state legislatures no longer participate in classic forms of petitioning.[67] If the Petition Clause secures a right of access to the government, and the government no longer provides any official legislative proceeding in which to bring forward concerns, it seems entirely foreseeable that other, less traditional forms of petitioning, such as mass media campaigns, are likely to flourish. Moreover, *Noerr's* grant of Petition Clause immunity appears consistent with the larger history of petitioning; certainly speech directed toward government officials for the purpose of influencing public policy seems to constitute a kind of petitioning activity.

The main difference between a mass media "publicity campaign" and more traditional forms of petitioning would appear to be that the *Noerr* railroad defendants sought to move and influence general public opinion as much, if not more, than legislative opinion. In this respect, it resembles systemic petitioning more than classic petitioning.[68] However, there is no particularly compelling reason to limit "petitioning" solely to speech aimed *exclusively* at government officials. Indeed, many of the most important and successful examples of petitioning campaigns, such as the effort to secure women's suffrage, involved systemic, or hybrid, forms of petitioning. If Justice Black simply means that a petitioner may seek to reach a larger target audience that includes the government, but also the body politic, his analysis and the underlying argument appear reasonably persuasive.

Yet, at the end of the day, the policies against anticompetitive activities underlying the federal antitrust laws are an invention of the twentieth century and played no part in the development of the right to petition. In contrast, the *McDonald* Court faced an opportunity to apply the Petition Clause to libel, an issue that has been at the heart of petitioning for hundreds of years,[69] and turned a blind eye, holding that "[t]he Petition Clause . . . was inspired by the same ideals of liberty and democracy that gave us the freedoms to speak, publish, and assemble" and does not have any independent force and effect.[70] As Chief Justice Burger explained in rejecting an independent Petition Clause based theory of libel law, "These First Amendment rights are inseparable . . . and there is no sound basis for granting greater constitutional protection to statements made in a petition to the President than other First Amendment expressions."[71] Thus, the Supreme Court's willingness to apply the Petition Clause broadly and purposively in the limited context of antitrust suits serves only to make its unwillingness to apply it generically, and in more traditional contexts, all the more perplexing.

III. TOWARD AN INDEPENDENT JURISPRUDENCE OF THE PETITION CLAUSE: ENHANCED PROTECTION FOR "PETITIONING" PROTEST ACTIVITY PROXIMATE TO GOVERNMENT OFFICIALS

As the preceding materials demonstrate, the Supreme Court, except in the narrow area of antitrust law, has not developed a separate and distinct Petition Clause jurisprudence. The creation of such a body of law would require careful attention to several discrete problems.

First, what precisely constitutes "petitioning"? Is any and all political speech also "petitioning" speech, by virtue of its relationship to the project of self-government, and the possibility that it might influence a public official's thinking about a problem of public policy? Alternatively, perhaps only a smaller subset of political speech should be classified as possessing the requisite "petitioning" characteristics to bring it within the special protection of the clause. Next, how should the federal courts frame a general test for analyzing Petition Clause claims? Should a strict scrutiny regime apply, or would a less demanding standard of review adequately safeguard the right of petition and also better accommodate the government's legitimate security concerns? Third and finally, how might the common law privileges associated with the right of petition historically inform a new, contemporary Petition Clause jurisprudence? In this section, each of these considerations will be considered and addressed.

Although establishing a complete doctrinal methodology for any and every conceivable Petition Clause claim lies beyond the scope of this chapter, some clear guiding principles do come into relatively clear focus upon careful analysis. Petitioning should be defined broadly and purposively, like the freedom of speech, because this approach will better advance the core purposes of the clause. Although strict scrutiny might not be the appropriate baseline standard of review for all Petition Clause claims, a presumption should exist in favor of access to public officials for the purpose of engaging in hybrid petitioning activities in spaces that otherwise constitute traditional public forums. Moreover, the burden should squarely rest on the government to rebut this presumption in specific circumstances, and based on record evidence. Finally, the common law privileges of immunity from seditious libel and access to officers of the government for the purpose of petitioning lend significant historical and doctrinal support to these conclusions.

A. DEFINING "PETITIONING" ACTIVITY

Although he stated the matter in particularly eloquent terms, Professor Harry Kalven was not alone in recognizing that a political protest can be "an elaborate petition for redress of grievances."[72] During the 1960s, the Supreme Court itself also acknowledged that civil rights protests constituted petitions for a redress of grievances (though its majority opinions uniformly avoided developing an independent theory of the Petition Clause, relying instead on the other First Amendment freedoms for its decisions).[73] Even *McDonald* reiterated this theme, with Justice Brennan stating in a concurrence that the Petition Clause "includes such activities as peaceful protest demonstrations."[74]

This broad view of the nature of petitions and petitioning is not entirely inconsistent with historical practice. In England, "[a] petition was not just any form of communication addressed to the King, his officers, or Parliament. Rather, it was a communication which, to be protected, had to take a certain form and embody certain components."[75] The colonies, however, were not always so formal. For example, the Body of Liberties adopted by the Massachusetts Bay Colony Assembly in 1641 allowed "[e]very man whether Inhabitant or fforreiner, free or not free shall have libertie to come to any publique Court, Councell, or Towne meeting, and either by speech or writing . . . to present any necessary motion, complaint, [or] petition."[76] Thus, the Massachusetts colony appears to have allowed petitions to be presented both orally and in writing.

At the outset, however, it seems reasonably clear that not all speech constitutes petitioning speech. "Petitioning speech" is not all speech, or even all political speech; it is only speech which has as its object changing some policy or practice of the government, and which is aimed at a government official, or group of officials, with some responsibility for the policy or practice in question. As Professor Carol Andrews explains:

> But the right to petition is a right *in addition* to the right of free speech. It is different from the general right of free speech in two material respects. First, the right to petition guarantees the right to speak to a particular body of persons, those comprising the government. This targeted speech serves values not achieved by general speech. It gives citizens a better chance at having their voices heard by the very public servants who are making the decisions in government. People do not have to wait or hope that their views will be channeled by the press or others to the government. This not only gives citizens a sense of participation in government, but it also helps to keep the government better informed.[77]

Thus, Andrews suggests that "petitioning" speech can and must be distinguished from speech, even political speech, more generally. This seems essential if the right of petition is to have independent doctrinal significance from the freedoms of speech, assembly, and association; if all speech is "petitioning" speech, then the rights really do not relate to distinguishable forms of expressive activity.

There is also the question of the form, or format, of a petition. Certainly, notwithstanding counterexamples in some of the states, an originalist view of a "petition" would limit the scope of the concept to presenting a physical document, signed by supporters, to a government official, such as a state legislator.[78] As Professors Gary Lawson and Guy Seidman state the matter: "The right to petition served, and in many ways continues to serve, an important function in the development of modern government, but that function exhausts the meaning of the Petitions [*sic*] Clause. Put simply, the constitutional right to petition the government for a redress of grievances is precisely—for want of a better phrase—the right to petition the government for a redress of grievances."[79] Notwithstanding the obvious circularity of this definition, it tends to beg the question of what precisely constitutes, or reasonably could constitute, a "petition."

Lawson and Seidman argue that the Petition Clause imposes no duty on the part of any government official to respond to a petition;[80] however, from an originalist perspective, this seems to depart from the actual practice of legislative bodies from the inception of British colonies in North America through the Federalist era.[81] As classic petitioning gave way to systemic petitioning, legislatures declined to play their part in the political Kabuki theater that supporters of abolition and women's suffrage sought to foment; if petitioners were unserious about seeking direct legislative change, and instead used petitions and petition gathering as a basic means of general political organization and agitation, then the legislature should, and did, feel free to largely ignore the petitions themselves.

However, if one looks at what average citizens considered "petitioning" from the 1830s to the early twentieth century, the activity simply is not limited to the act of circulating a petition for signatures and presenting a physical document to a legislator or executive branch official. Petitions were part of a larger program of expressive activity that included marches, demonstrations, and mass meetings and conventions.[82] The petition itself served as an important focal point for these other, related activities, but petitioning itself was very much a hybrid activity that married multiple forms of expressive freedom into a single whole.

To be clear, this does not mean that expressive freedoms are entirely fungible and redundant; instead, it would be more accurate to suggest that the exercise of the right of petition was often conjoined with the exercise of other forms of expressive freedom, including speech, assembly, and association. Thus, this hybrid activity involved petitioning, annexed to speech, assembly, and association, with the goal of engaging the government, through public protest, and also the media, with an eye toward initiating a wider discussion of a particular subject or concern within the general political community.

Accordingly, the purpose of systemic, or hybrid, petitioning is not simply engaging the government but also initiating a wider consideration of a policy question within the broader political community. It would be unfair to suggest that the government's officers are mere foils for the protestors, but the ability of the media to report on the fact of dissent is an essential component of systemic, or hybrid, petitioning activity. If protest occurs at a time and place far removed from both government officials and the media, the dissent cannot precipitate the wider engagement that lies at the core of the Petition Clause.

B. The General Contours and Objectives of a Distinctive Petition Clause Jurisprudence

If one accepts as persuasive the proposition that political protests have a legitimate claim to Petition Clause protection as legitimate forms of "petitioning" activity, the next question involves the precise nature and scope of that protection. As the history of the Petition Clause demonstrates, fundamental to the right to petition are two constituent rights: the right to immunity from prosecution for seditious libel and the right to be heard. When considered in the light of history, these two rights work together to provide political protestors with a right of access to those government officials to whom their petitions are addressed, as well as a concomitant duty on the part of those officials to consider the petition and engage the petitioners regarding their concerns.

At least arguably, the Petition Clause exists to facilitate democratic deliberation that originates from the bottom up, rather than the top down. Elected officials can use the bully pulpit of public office to raise issues and focus sustained attention on questions and issues that they believe to be of public importance.[83] Petitioning serves as a means of facilitating bottom-up agitation for consideration of issues or problems that, in the opinion of the petitioners, government is not addressing adequately.

First, a doctrinal presumption should exist in favor of access to government officials for the purpose of hybrid petitioning, at least from the vantage point of traditional public forums. At the same time, however, government officials should have some discretion to structure how this access will occur. For example, if Congress were to embrace the New Zealand model of classic petitioning, courts might well take this into account when determining if a particular time, place, and manner restriction unduly burdens the right of petition. Assuming that Congress does not wish to permit ordinary citizens to help set its agenda through petitions, as the New Zealand House of Representatives does, then courts should be more vigilant in ensuring access in other contexts.

Security concerns in the context of a system in which effective alternative means of access and engagement exist would present a much harder question than unproven security concerns in the absence of such a system. On the other hand, when the public street or sidewalk is the only means of ensuring communication with a member of Congress, courts should be very reticent to permit government to close this avenue of petitioning based on vague assertions that "there could be trouble."

Moving in the opposite direction, it seems doubtful that the federal courts would attempt to mandate a return to classic petitioning of the Congress or the president. In other words, notwithstanding the original understanding of the Petition Clause, as practiced during the Federalist era, the contemporary federal courts would not attempt to force Congress or the president to consider petitions on the merits. Indeed, the question would likely prove to be nonjusticiable on political question grounds.[84] In sum, very little reason exists to believe that the Supreme Court would attempt to force the restoration of classic petitioning in the contemporary United States.

Access to the media also should play some part in the analysis. One of the reasons protestors seek to decamp near major political and government meetings is the presence of a dedicated media corps, dispatched to cover the event. The history of petitioning shows that petitioners often sought to engage the media, as a means of generating a wider public awareness of the petitioners' cause within the general citizenry, as much as, if not more than, incumbent government officials. The examples of "hopeless" Chartist and women's suffrage petitions provide illustrative examples.[85] It seems possible that, even if Congress were to revive classic petitioning, at least some petitioners would choose to engage in systemic, rather than classic, forms of petitioning. And were a group of petitioners to make this choice, should the federal courts permit government to foreclose systemic petitioning because of the availability of classic petitioning?

My preliminary thought is that petitioners should probably receive some consideration for their preferred means of petitioning, even—and counterfactually—if classic petitioning were otherwise open and available to them. The

American Anti-Slavery Association could have engaged solely in classic petitioning, rather than systemic petitioning, but deemed the latter potentially
more effective at moving public opinion than the former. If a group of petitioners prefers to engage in street theater, courts should afford this choice at least
some margin of appreciation. Generally speaking, the fact that a group can
speak at a different time and place does not justify the government in suppressing speech based on the possibility of a hostile reaction; the same reasoning
would seem to support the conclusion that would-be systemic petitioners
should have at least some ability to choose how to exercise their right of access
to the government and its officials.

In the most general terms, then, federal courts should start from a presumption that favors the ability of ordinary citizens to engage their elected representatives, government officers, and party leaders who control the process of
electing candidates to public office.[86] In other words, when the speech at issue
constitutes petitioning speech, there *is* a constitutional interest in reaching a
particular audience. The idea would be consistent with Alexander Meiklejohn's
initial theory of free speech (which he later broadened),[87] which held that "free
speech" was nothing more, or less, than "self-government."[88] Consistent with
this view, Meiklejohn argued that First Amendment rights should be limited to
expressive activity that relates to self-governance and public policy.[89] To be
clear, the notion *is not* that speech unrelated to governance and governing is
not entitled to full First Amendment protection as "speech"; the question in a
given case would be whether the content of the speech brings it within the
ambit of "petitioning."

Nonpetitioning speech, consistent with existing doctrinal rules, would not
secure a right to a preferred audience of government officials. This result makes
sense; if one seeks to promote a furniture sale at a local Macy's department store
or a production of the *Mikado* at the local little theater, a nexus between the
speech and an incumbent government official, related to a policy over which
the official bears some modicum of responsibility, simply does not exist. In such
cases, an interest in limiting access to public space to facilitate security concerns might be more readily accepted than in cases in which the speech relates
to a matter over which the official has some measure of responsibility.

Finally, the right to an intended audience should not otherwise affect existing free speech and free assembly doctrine; the marginal addition of a petitioning character to speech activity, however, should secure a higher burden of
justification on the government for denying access to a preferred audience.[90]
In this context, for example, "ample alternative channels of communication"
would mean alternative means of reaching the intended audience, and not

merely the theoretical ability to disseminate a message in general within the marketplace of ideas.

C. THE RIGHT TO IMMUNITY FROM PROSECUTION FOR SEDITIOUS LIBEL

One of the most central common law doctrines associated with the right of petition relates to immunity from prosecution for seditious libel. In other words, even during the era when prosecution for seditious libel was seen as a justifiable government policy, the government nevertheless had to shoulder perceived risks to its security and popular support in order to accommodate petitions and petitioners.

In 1688, the right to petition faced perhaps its greatest challenge up to that point. That year, King James II, a Roman Catholic, issued a Declaration of Indulgence that many perceived as the first step in the reestablishment of Catholicism as the state religion of England.[91] As head of the Protestant Church of England, James ordered that his declaration be read from all church pulpits.[92] The archbishop of Canterbury and six other bishops petitioned the king, setting forth the reasons why they could not comply with the order and asking to be excused.[93] "The seven bishops were arrested and prosecuted for seditious libel, the allegedly libelous statement being the petition they had presented to the King."[94] Rather than defend against the charge on its merits, the bishops asserted, in effect, that they were immune from seditious libel prosecution for statements made in a petition.[95]

At the famous *Trial of the Seven Bishops*, the defendants were acquitted, much to the joy of the populace.[96] Nevertheless, the public outrage that the Crown would even attempt such a prosecution "led directly to the Glorious Revolution of 1688 and to the Bill of Rights that fully confirmed the right of petition as an element of the British constitution."[97] In response to the *Trial of the Seven Bishops*, the English Bill of Rights stated that "it is the right of the subjects to petition the King, and all committments [sic] and prosecutions for such petitioning are illegal."[98] Moreover, the government was nearly as good as its word—the Bill of Rights was enacted in 1689, and the last recorded prosecution for seditious libel based on the contents of a petition occurred in 1702.[99]

This absolute immunity crossed the Atlantic into the American colonies, where, with few exceptions, it persisted through the passage of the First Amendment and beyond.[100] For example, there were seventeen prosecutions under the Sedition Act of 1798, but none resulted from a petition for redress of grievances.[101] A New York assemblyman, Jedediah Peck, was, however, indicted for "a vehemently worded petition to Congress advocating repeal of the Alien and Sedition laws"—one of many such petitions—but the case was dropped "due to pressure from popular demonstrations in Peck's favor."[102]

Of course, *New York Times Co. v. Sullivan*[103] ostensibly closed the book on seditious libel prosecution for any First Amendment activity.[104] Yet, as demonstrated by cases such as *Bl(a)ck Tea Society*[105] and *Citizens for Peace in Space*,[106] the government interest in security has given new life to the doctrine of seditious libel as applied to political protest activity.[107] But if a watered-down form of seditious libel is returning through the courts' willingness to allow protestors to be involuntarily shoved out of seeing and hearing of government officials on pain of arrest and criminal prosecution, then the absolute immunity from seditious libel afforded to petitioning suggests that there must also be a return to the Petition Clause privilege that secures a right of meaningful access to government officials without threat of punishment.

The use of security to silence or marginalize dissent is hardly new. And yet, even in Great Britain, a nation lacking a written constitution, much less an entrenched bill of rights enforced through independent courts vested with the power of judicial review, the national commitment to petitioning led British judges to create a common law privilege that safeguarded petitioning from attack on the theory that a petition constituted a risk to the security or stability of the state. Moreover, Parliament, although possessed of the power to overrule this common law privilege, declined to exercise this power, essentially ceding the matter to the judiciary. If security was not a talisman justifying the proscription of petitions and the punishment of petitioners in eighteenth century England, it certainly should not play such a role in the twenty-first century United States.

D. The Right to Be Heard

Common law practices with respect to the right of petition also strongly support the proposition that petition secures a meaningful right of access to the government and its officers and agents. The evidence is clear that as a matter of history, petitioners have a right to have their petitions be received and heard by the government.[108] To be given effect in the context of political protests, this right to be heard must include a right of proximity to the government officials to whom a petition is addressed. To the extent that petitioning protestors are being moved out of the sight and hearing of government officials,[109] these protestors are being denied their Petition Clause right to have their petitions actually heard by those capable of acting on them.

Furthermore, the history of the Petition Clause strongly suggests that the right to petition has always contemplated a coordinate right of proximity: "It was under Edward III that it became a regular form at the opening of parliament for the chancellor to declare the king's willingness to hear the petitions of his people: all who had grievances were to bring them to the foot of the throne that the king with the advice of his council or of his lords might redress them."[110] That "all who had grievances" were to bring their petitions "to the foot of the throne" clearly establishes that the right of petition, at least as a historical matter, encompassed a right to in-person presentation. Moreover, this "up close and personal" aspect of petitioning recurs throughout the history of the right. In short, petitioners have a historical right to present their petitions in the physical presence of the government officials to whom they are addressed.

For example, in the Tumultuous Petition Act of 1661, designed to prevent the near-riots that had sometimes accompanied the presentation of petitions by limiting the number of persons who could present a petition to ten, Parliament was careful to note that "this Act . . . shall not be construed to extend to debar or hinder any person or persons not exceeding the number of ten aforesaid to present any publique or private grievance or complaint to any member or members of Parliament . . . or to the Kings Majesty for any remedy to bee thereupon had."[111] The language and intent of the Act clearly contemplate in-person presentation, else why a need to specify "any member or members of Parliament," much less to limit the number of presenters at all?

The *Trial of the Seven Bishops* case also makes the case for in-person presentation of petitions. In summarizing the testimony of a witness, "my lord president," the Lord Chief Justice explained the presentation of the seven bishops' petition as follows:

> [The court] staid till my lord president came, who told us how the bishops came to him to his office at Whitehall, and after they had told him their design, that they had a mind to petition the king, they asked him the method they were to take for it, and desired him to help them to the speech of the king: and he tells them he will acquaint the king with their desire, which he does; and the king giving leave, he comes down and tells the bishops, that they might go and speak with the king when they would; and, says he, I have given direction that the door shall be opened for you as soon as you come. . . . [W]hen they came back, they went up into the chamber and there a petition was delivered to the king."[112]

Further evidence for a right of in-person presentation may be found in the "necessity of frequent sessions of parliament for providing subjects with an opportunity to present their petitions,"[113] and in the fact that "[w]hen petitions were presented to the [king's] council, the council would examine the petitioners."[114] Moreover, in-person presentation carried over into the colonies, where "[p]etitioners directly presented written petitions . . . to the court, legislative body, council, or governor."[115]

This is not to suggest that in-person presentation need rise to the level of a personal audience with a government official.[116] Rather, in the context of political protest activity, the right to present petitions in the physical presence of the government officials to whom they are addressed amounts simply to a right of physical proximity such that the officials can see and hear the protestors' petitions; thus, it implies a right of meaningful access, not a right of unilateral, or unlimited, access.

Moreover, "access" does not mean that the Petition Clause, properly interpreted and applied, requires that high-ranking government officials accept unreasonable risks to their health or safety. As a general proposition, the federal courts are correct to give considerable weight to the government's strong interest in security, and the Petition Clause should not impede or prevent the attainment of these pressing government interests, at least when the record establishes that the concerns are genuine and not mere pretext. Indeed, its history strongly supports the notion that the Petition Clause should accommodate reasonable concessions to security.[117] "During 1641–42, petitions were often delivered by riotous assemblies, some plainly for the purpose of trying to coerce or intimidate parliament and other officers of the government."[118] Faced with such circumstances, sometimes resulting in bloodshed, Parliament on more than one occasion restricted both the numbers of persons who could sign petitions and the number who could present them.[119]

Moreover, the text of the Petition Clause itself can be read to protect only "the right of the people peaceably . . . to petition the Government for redress of grievances."[120] And there is nothing to suggest that the right of in-person presentation of petitions has ever extended beyond places of official government business.

Accepting that each of these limitations applies to hybrid petitioning, the limitations on protest activity sustained in cases such as *Citizens for Peace in Space*[121] are nevertheless clear violations of protestors' rights under the Petition Clause of the First Amendment.[122] None of the historical limitations on the right to petition countenances the total ban on proximity that was upheld in each of these cases; only reasonable limits on the number of petitioners is consistent with historical practice.

Moreover, advances in security technology, such as metal detectors, X-ray machines, computer-assisted background security checks, and bomb-sniffing dogs, should in most cases allow for more than ten petitioners to safely exercise their rights of proximity to government officials. It strains credulity to posit that local and federal law enforcement agencies, in concert with the organizers of mass political events, like the presidential nominating conventions, have the technological and staffing ability to screen quite literally tens of thousands of delegates, guests, support staff and technicians, and press reporters, and to do so on a daily basis for the better part of a week, but lack *any* residual capacity to screen even a single would-be protestor seeking to engage in peaceful petitioning activity within the event venue's security perimeter. These facts strongly suggest that something other than an inability to screen any would-be petitioners explains the government's position.

The nature of political protests as opposed to more traditional petitioning also counsels in favor of expanding rather than contracting the number of protestors, in that protests, with their banners, slogans, signs, and chants, require a lesser degree of proximity—again, sight and sound are the fundamental requirements of access.[123] And perhaps most important, the use of speculative predictions of possible violence as a basis for eliminating proximity is also inconsistent with the history of the Petition Clause. Past incidents of violence did not cause the seventeenth century Parliament to adopt complete prophylactic bans on the in-person presentation of petitions, and neither should these concerns do so for the present-day federal courts.

It bears noting, moreover, that in the one doctrinal area where the Supreme Court has given the Petition Clause independent effect, the *Noerr-Pennington* doctrine, the justices had no problem embracing the concept of "indirect" petitioning via billboards, print advertisements, and broadcast commercials.[124] It is more than a little ironic that, under contemporary doctrine, the Petition Clause affords no meaningful right of access to government or political party officers, in direct contravention of historical practice, but does protect indirect petitioning through mass media publicity campaigns, which, as a matter of history, would not have been considered "petitions" at all. In any event, if the Petition Clause reaches indirect forms of petitioning, it certainly should extend to the older, more well-established forms of the right involving more direct communications between citizens and their government.

IV. POTENTIAL OBJECTIONS AND RESPONSES TO A REVIVED RIGHT OF PETITION

Several potential objections, possessing various degrees of merit, exist to the analysis set forth in the immediately preceding section. Perhaps most obviously, could federal courts simply hold that any form of access, no matter how ineffectual, satisfies the imperatives of the Petition Clause? For example, if a government official's willingness to receive unsolicited e-mails discharges a government official's Petition Clause duties, reclaiming the Clause would change very little regarding meaningful citizen access to the government. Alternatively, could government officials avoid embarrassing public confrontations by reviving classic forms of petitioning, of the sort practiced in the Federalist era? Were Congress or a state legislature so inclined, could these bodies preempt constitutional protection for hybrid petitioning activities by reviving petition in its traditional format?

Another potential objection relates to the content-based nature of the proposed new jurisprudence. A speaker's ability use particular government property for protest would depend entirely on the content of the speech. One could object that this violates the long-standing rule against content based restrictions on speech.

Finally, one might question the concept of "hybrid" petitioning and also the limits associated with the precise location of hybrid petitioning activity. More specifically, assuming that hybrid petitioning really is a form of petition cognizable under the Petition Clause, is it possible to "petition" at places other than the seat of government? For example, can a protest outside a municipal sports stadium or convention center realistically constitute "petitioning" activity, if that term is to have any meaningful limits? These questions all raise important issues about the practical and theoretical viability of the proposal, and merit a sustained consideration and response.

A. Limiting Petitioning to Remote and Impersonal Forms of Access, Such as E-mails or Letters

The most obvious way for the federal courts to limit the potential effect of the Petition Clause would be simply to hold that the availability of electronic forms of communication, such as e-mail, constitute sufficient "access" to satisfy the Petition Clause. Consistent with this approach, a reviewing court, at least in theory, could cynically find that ineffectual means of access, such as websites with "feedback" e-mail options, satisfy the Petition Clause. A federal court could certainly so hold, and this approach could halt any sustained effort to reclaim the Petition Clause in its tracks. To be sure, there is a plausible argument that a government official's willingness to receive e-mail satisfies the dictates of the Petition Clause.

The history of petitioning, however, suggests that the right of access must be meaningful; classic petitioning involved presentation, consideration, and a formal institutional response by the legislative body as a whole. Simply permitting members of the public to send unanswered emails would not seem a sufficient alternative means of communication, precisely because the sender cannot know what, if any, consideration either the member or the body as a whole afforded the petition. By way of contrast, the New Zealand approach to petitioning, involving hearings (whether with only a written record or with oral testimony as well), a response to the petition from the relevant executive branch entity at the committee's request, a formal committee report and recommendation to the House, and House action on the report, clearly requires both committees of jurisdiction and the House itself to devote substantial time and energy to considering the merits of a petition.[125] An e-mail submission system, coupled with an autobot response algorithm, would not seem to constitute a material equivalent.

Perhaps the best potential response to this objection would be to invoke the historical precedents involving in person communication with incumbent government officers. The ability to e-mail an elected official simply does not ensure communication with that official, any more than would dispatching a petition by messenger or post in the eighteenth century. Even though it was possible to present a petition through an intermediary, historically the right of petition also included the right to present the petition to a government officer personally and directly. Just as a would-be petitioner could elect to present a petition in person, rather than rely on a lawyer, courier, or postal worker to do so, a twenty-first century petitioner should not be limited to submitting a petition via e-mail.

A strong policy reason exists for this rule as well: if a petition is not delivered in person, there is always some risk that a government official might claim, truthfully or otherwise, that she did not receive it. Recall, for example, that King George III declined to answer the Olive Branch Petition because, his secretary of state explained, His Majesty did not receive the petition on the throne.[126] Given the absence of any formal institutional consideration of petitions, save in federal administrative agencies subject to the APA,[127] there is no way, other than by direct, in-person communication, to ensure that a specific policy request actually reaches a government official with authority to act on the petition, such as a member of Congress or an executive branch official. The potential accountability function of the Petition Clause would be significantly enhanced if the right of petition included a right to communicate directly with government officials who enjoy responsibility for the public policy at issue.

Finally, the availability of one means of petitioning the government should not imply the absence of other means of engaging in petitioning activity that would-be petitioners might prefer to use. For example, government may not ban the distribution of leaflets or pamphlets on city streets, sidewalks, or parks simply because a would-be pamphleteer could instead speak in real time to persons using a park or sidewalk or, alternatively, waive a sign at motorists in passing automobile traffic.[128] So too, then, the availability of one means of petitioning, in an impersonal—and likely ineffective—fashion through e-mail, would not justify denying constitutional protection to other alternative means of petitioning, such as through peaceful protests that seek to communicate a message directly to government officials responsible for the policy at issue.

As a general proposition, the government may not dictate precisely how a citizen will exercise her expressive freedoms. This proposition holds true with respect to the rights of speech, press, assembly, and association; it also should hold true with respect to the right of petition. Accordingly, half-hearted government efforts to preempt a reclaimed Petition Clause through devices like dedicated websites with feedback features should not be effective at precluding judicial protection of other forms of petitioning activity.[129]

B. Potential Preemption of Hybrid Petitioning Through a Renewal of Classic Petitioning Opportunities

Suppose, faced with the prospect of an emerging jurisprudence of the Petition Clause emanating from the federal courts, incumbent government officials decided to create dedicated opportunities for officially sanctioned petitioning activities—for example, if the House of Representatives revised its rules and established clear and effective procedures for petitioning the House, with consideration of petitions on the merits by committees of jurisdiction, and with a formal institutional reply to the petitioners. In light of such enhanced, and meaningful, access to Congress, would street protests aimed at Speaker John Boehner or Majority Leader Harry Reid still be entitled to any special consideration as "petitioning speech"?

This presents a harder question. Properly understood, the Petition Clause secures a right of access and duty to engage the merits of a petition. If Congress and executive branch officers were to create alternative means of access and engagement, much as the APA does with respect to federal executive agencies, the need for resort to street theater would be much reduced. Indeed, if the Supreme Court simply exported the "ample alternative channels" prong of *Ward* into the access analysis required by the Petition Clause, it might well be that the creation of an effective alternative petitioning system would satisfy the access and engagement mandates.

Even so, however, the ability to disseminate a message in one way does not generally prohibit a would-be speaker from exercising her First Amendment rights in some different way. Thus, the availability of the Internet as a potential forum for speech would not justify a city government in banning leafleting in city parks or on sidewalks. So too the ability to leaflet would not justify a ban on demonstrations or parades within the city. The availability of a revived form of classic petitioning would certainly be relevant to considering the merits of a claim that the government has unconstitutionally restricted petitioning speech in a traditional public forum, but it should not necessarily preclude such claims automatically. Whether to engage in classic petitioning or in a form of systemic petitioning should be a question left to would-be petitioners to decide.

C. The Proposed Use of a New Category of "Petitioning Speech" Violates the Norm Against Content-Based Speech Regulations

Turning to the next potential objection, the content-based nature of the proposed approach, it is certainly true that, in practical terms, recognition of petitioning speech would lead to variations in the right to use public property for speech activity, based solely on the content of the speech. Some might object to this outcome on the grounds that all First Amendment doctrines must be content neutral.

The easy, and obvious, response to this objection is that contemporary First Amendment law is simply rife with content-based distinctions. Rules regarding, for example, commercial speech and noncommercial speech rest entirely on the content of the expression at issue.[130] So too rules on sexually explicit speech.[131] To create a new category of speech based on its content, petitioning speech, would simply follow the current doctrinal practice of the federal courts.

Moreover, petitioning speech would be distinguished from other kinds of speech not only based on its content but also based on its intended audience. To be petitioning speech, the speech would have to relate to a matter of public policy or governance; speech unrelated to these subjects could not constitute petitioning speech. In addition, the would-be petitioners would have to seek to communicate their concerns about government policy to someone with authority or responsibility over those policies. One could not petition a federal member of Congress over the renaming of a state university, for example, or petition a state governor over nuclear arms proliferation. To constitute "petitioning speech," the speech would have to relate to matter within the portfolio of the intended audience.

These limitations would thus limit the potential universe of petitioning speech even more — not even generic "political speech" would necessarily also constitute "petitioning speech" in a given context. As the scope of petitioning speech becomes more narrow, the net amount of risk that must be assumed to accommodate it correspondingly falls. A clear potential benefit of narrowing the scope of petitioning speech would be to reduce the burden on the government required to accommodate it. Only when speech relates to a matter of public policy within the portfolio of a particular government official could the right to access a preferred audience for the purpose of petitioning come into play. This means, in practice, that security concerns could be used to limit quite a lot of political protest unrelated to a political or government event.

Moreover, this result can be defended on entirely plausible grounds: if protestors merely wish to use the president or a member of Congress as a background device or prop, their interest in interacting with the official, in confronting the official, seems highly attenuated and unworthy of serious First Amendment protection. Demanding that Senator Diane Feinstein "Free Lindsay Lohan Now!" cannot be petitioning speech precisely because Senator Feinstein has absolutely no responsibility for the prosecution of California state criminal offenses, for state sentencing policy, or for state parole decisions. To picket Senator Feinstein on behalf of Lindsay Lohan would be to attempt to use Senator Feinstein as a mere decoration or prop.

By way of contrast, however, a protest of federal sentencing policy regarding federal court sentencing policy for crack versus powder cocaine offenses would present a quite different question. Senator Feinstein sits on the Senate Judiciary Committee and, as a member of the Senate, bears responsibility for the scope and content of federal criminal law, including sentences and sentencing policies. Communicating concerns about federal sentencing policy to Senator Feinstein constitutes a form of petitioning, whereas protesting for the early release of Lindsay Lohan from the California state penal system simply does not.

D. Hybrid Petitioning Is Not Really "Petitioning" for Purposes of the Petition Clause

The use of hybrid forms of petitioning might serve as a basis for objection. Classic petitioning involved a legislative procedure in which a petition served as a vehicle for legislative consideration of a problem deemed important by a petitioner. Even if a petitioner might present a petition in person to a member of Congress, classic forms of petitioning did not involve mass street protests. Is it possible to characterize mass marches and demonstrations as "petitions," given the more limited historical understanding of a "petition"?

Several responses exist to this potential objection. The first, and most obvious, is that the Supreme Court itself has declared that "indirect" forms of petitioning, such as mass media campaigns using television and radio advertisements, billboards, and newspaper advertisements, aimed at lobbying Congress or a state legislature, constitute "petitioning" activity. If the purchase of a half-minute television or radio spot can be petitioning, surely a street protest can serve this purpose when it aims to communicate a concern directly to a government official with some measure of responsibility for the matter at issue.

The second response relies on the Supreme Court's consideration of protests by civil rights era protestors in the 1960s. For example, in *Edwards v. South Carolina*,[132] the Supreme Court overturned breach of the peace convictions against nonviolent protestors seeking to petition the South Carolina state government to respect the civil rights of its African American citizens.[133] The fact that the petition took the form of a march and mass demonstration on the state capitol grounds did not affect its status as petitioning activity.

Moreover, the preeminent First Amendment scholar Harry Kalven directly invoked the petitioning character of the protest as a basis for affording the protestors greater access to the capitol grounds:

> [T]his is orderly protest to the public and to the state legislature. They have selected a public place where, as citizens, they have a right to enter; they have picked a time when the legislature is in session; they make no threatening gestures, and are co-operative about not blocking traffic; they have the ironic wit to sing the "Star Spangled Banner" after the ultimatum of the police. And above all, they are young, and their statement of purpose is touching in its confidence in the democratic processes, including the one they were using—"to let them know we were dissatisfied and that we would like for the laws which prohibited Negro privileges in this State to be removed."[134]

Professor Kalven further characterizes this protest as "in the form of a petition for a redress of grievances."[135]

Members of the Supreme Court too, albeit sometimes in dissent, have drawn the connection between targeted protests of state government officials and the right of petition.[136] In other words, some political speech, assembly, and association partakes of a petitioning quality, such that the expressive conduct at issue should be viewed as the hybrid exercise not only of speech, assembly, and association rights but also of the right of petition. When expressive activity seeks to communicate grievances to the government, in order that they might be considered and redressed, should this element of the speech affect its constitutional status? Arguably, in light of the Petition Clause, it should.[137]

Although, like many others, I object to the appearance of content-based (if not viewpoint-based) speech bans proximate to major political events, presidential appearances, and international government meetings,[138] the fact remains that the Supreme Court's existing free speech, assembly, and association doctrines do not take into account the ability to access and engage a particular potential audience. Moreover, to the extent that the concept of an audience has salience, it tends to be a negative consideration, as in the notion of an unwilling or captive audience, that wishes to avoid involuntary exposure to particular speech or speakers. Although it might be possible to emphasize the importance of a particular location or space for speech, it seems to me that the better course of action is to theorize a right to an audience as an incident of the Petition Clause. At least with respect to government officials and political party leaders who control the process of election through the nomination stage of the electoral process, the Petition Clause represents the most logical place to locate a right of access, and a right to engage, a particular preferred audience.

Moreover, because the audience in question—government officials (whether elected or appointed) and party leaders—voluntarily assumed their positions, their status as a kind of potential captive audience may be justified as a necessary cost of holding government power in a democratic polity. One could extend the argument, to encompass public figures, in the same way that the Supreme Court has extended the rationale of *New York Times Co. v. Sullivan*,[139] but I need not defend such an extension in order to justify a right of access to those who act for the government and to those who control the path to elected government office at the local, state, and federal levels.

A private citizen may have a privacy interest in avoiding unwanted speech, including, for example, residential pickets,[140] but this interest should not extend to government officials, at least insofar as the unwanted speech relates to their official duties and responsibilities and occurs in locations routinely used for the conduct of governmental and political affairs. If an elected official does not wish to provide access to a potentially infinite universe of citizens, and would prefer not to engage people who disagree with her on various and sundry questions of the day, the appropriate remedy is to resign from office, not to banish those who seek to inform their government of questions and concerns related to government policy from one's sight or hearing.

E. "Petitioning" Can Only Occur at the Official Seat of Government

Yet another potential objection: Can petitioning occur other than at the seat of government? One might argue that, in its classic form, petitioning involved official communications at the seat of government, whether at the English court in the fourteenth century or at the federal Capitol building in the 1790s. How can it be said that a protest or picket in a city where the president happens to giving a speech constitutes "petitioning"?

Once again, the objection can be met and overcome. It is certainly true that, as a historical matter, the seat of government constituted the locus of classic petitioning activity. Even so, however, not all petitions were necessarily conveyed at the seat of government. For example, in colonial Virginia, a petition could be presented to a burgess by a constituent at a local town hall meeting convened by the member of the state legislature.[141] It was not at all essential that the petition be taken to the state capitol building in Richmond by the petitioner, rather than by the petitioner's local member of the legislature.

Moreover, the locus of the royal court also changed, and literally moved with the king. If one wishes to be truly originalist, then petitioning is appropriate wherever the king happens to be holding court. By parity of logic, it should be possible to petition whenever, and wherever, it is possible to interact with an incumbent government official who is engaged in official or political party business. Certainly, waiving a sign supporting or opposing a particular government policy on a street or sidewalk as a government official's motorcade speeds by seems as good as way as any to secure access to the official and to engage the official on the precise question at issue.

Finally, the Supreme Court's *Noerr-Pennington* jurisprudence on indirect forms of petitioning also has relevance in this context. If a television advertisement or a billboard outside the capital city may constitute "petitioning," it seems easy and obvious that protests directed at incumbent government officers may also constitute petitioning, even if outside the immediate environs of the capitol building.

V. CONCLUSION

The lower federal courts' application of the *Ward* time, place, and manner test to define the metes and bounds of access to public property for protest activity has failed to protect core petitioning speech adequately, in circumstances where it is quite clear that the speech activity seeks to bring grievances directly to the attention of those holding governmental power.[142] Since the events of 9/11, the U.S. courts of appeals have sustained ever broader, ever more draconian limits on public protest activity proximate to government officials and the political party leaders who control the means of selection to elected office.[143] Although I agree with the scholarly commentary that decries the lax application of the narrow tailoring and alternative channels of communication requirements of the *Ward* time, place, and manner test, it is abundantly clear that these admonitions are not likely to reform judicial decision making in this area. Simply put, when government officials invoke security concerns as the basis for restricting, or proscribing, speech activity, federal judges are not inclined to enforce the time, place, and manner test strictly in order to safeguard the rights of protestors.[144]

The heart of the problem lies in the fact that, under the traditional time, place, and manner test, a would-be speaker enjoys no right of access to an intended audience. In this respect, the U.S. Court of Appeals for the First Circuit was correct in observing that "there is no constitutional requirement that demonstrators be granted that sort of particularized access" to an intended audience.[145] Moreover, this result holds true even if the group seeks to reach an intended audience by engaging in protest activity in a traditional public forum, such a public sidewalk or street, that would otherwise be open and available for speech activity both before and after the intended audience leaves the area. Thus, resolution of the conflict requires a balancing of the state's interest in shielding the intended audience from the speech activity (in the name of security) against the interest of would-be demonstrators in communicating a message directly to a particular audience, at least when that audience consists of the government itself.

The traditional *Ward* time, place, and manner test works reasonably well as a means of analyzing government-imposed limits on access to particular public spaces for speech activity, as opposed to more routine uses, such as for pedestrian and vehicular traffic. It does not, however, take into account at all the interest of a group of speakers in communicating directly with a particular audience. Accordingly, the First Circuit was correct to hold that access to a specific audience, as opposed to access to a particular kind of public space, is simply not a part of the time, place, or manner analysis.[146] Attempting to rehabilitate the existing time, place, and manner test to incorporate greater consideration of whether a speaker can reach her intended audience, although presenting a potential solution, seems unlikely to meet with substantial success. Rather than reforming the traditional test, the test must be displaced entirely and transcended.

The Petition Clause presents a logical textual source of a right of access to incumbent government and political party officials for expressive activity that advocates changes in existing government policy (to seek "a redress of grievances" in the actual language of the clause). Hybrid petitioning should not lose its petitioning characteristics solely because the petitioners elect to annex speech, assembly, and association rights to advance their cause in conjunction with petitioning speech. The historical roots of the right of petition include a right to present petitions in person and also to petition collectively. Although it is true that the right of petition fell into a state of desuetude in the United States by the mid-twentieth century, this fact provides no good reason, or substantive support, for failing to reanimate the Petition Clause in the twenty-first century. On the contrary, the importance of the right in times past suggests that the right of petition's obscurity today constitutes something of an anomaly.

The framers viewed the right of petition as of no less importance to securing democratic accountability than suffrage itself. Voting secured democratic accountability at regular intervals, whereas the right of petition secured democratic accountability after and between those elections. If the people cannot communicate directly with those elected to public office, how can it be expected that those holding office will be accountable to the people who elected them?[147]

Finally, the Petition Clause presents a near-perfect antidote to the invocation of security as a means of protecting incumbent politicians from seeing or hearing dissent. In historical terms, the right of petition not only guaranteed a right of access to government officials but also enjoyed an exemption from the doctrine of seditious libel. Even during times when public opposition to the government's policies could be prosecuted as a crime, such as during the first Adams administration under the Sedition Act of 1798, the right of petition remained a lawful means of expressing dissenting views directly to the government. In other words, at a time when security concerns justified generalized criminal bans on speech activity thought to present a risk to national security, the right to petition provided a legally protected means of direct communication with government officials.

The Petition Clause can and should provide a qualified right of access to seek a redress of grievances on a public street or sidewalk within the personal hearing and seeing of incumbent government and political party officials. This is not to say that government has no interest in ensuring the personal security of the president, other government officers, or political party leaders. The Petition Clause, properly construed, does not guarantee an absolute and unqualified right of access to government officials; instead, the federal courts should read the Petition Clause to create a general duty on the government's part to facilitate meaningful access to government and political party officials, at least in public places that are otherwise open to expressive activity.

In order to operationalize this restored right of petitioning, federal courts should require that any and all restrictions on protest activity proximate to government officials should be justified by actual—as opposed to merely hypothetical—risks, and that the government should be required to use the least restrictive means possible to address those security concerns.[148] Thus, the Petition Clause should support a right to communicate a message directly to the relevant government officials in a meaningful way, at a meaningful time, and in a fashion that reasonably ensures that the message could be received by its intended audience.

If government officials and political party leaders were to move toward reviving petitioning in its classic form, however, courts could reasonably take this more formal, and regularized, access into account when determining whether restrictions on hybrid petitioning are necessary or justified. The availability of classic forms of petitioning, however, would not necessarily obviate the need for careful judicial scrutiny of restrictions on hybrid forms of petitioning peacefully conducted in traditional public forums. Again, as a general proposition, the government may not dictate precisely how, where, and when citizens choose to exercise expressive freedoms. Thus, the fact that an individual might be free to operate a newspaper or an Internet site would not be a basis for a municipal government closing the streets and sidewalks to leafleting because the government would prefer the use of one channel of communication rather than another.[149]

In sum, the First Amendment can and should secure an interest in communicating with a particular audience when that audience consists of the government itself and those who exercise authority in its name. Effective and vibrant democratic deliberation requires that the represented have meaningful access to their representatives, that the governed have access to those who govern. Moreover, this ability to access and engage one's government lies at the very core of the Petition Clause. In the words of Justice Jackson:

> The First Amendment forbids Congress to abridge the right of the people "to petition the Government for a redress of grievances." If this right is to have an interpretation consistent with that given to other First Amendment rights, it confers a large immunity upon activities of persons, organizations, groups and classes to obtain what they think is due them from government. Of course, their conflicting claims and propaganda are confusing, annoying and at times, no doubt, deceiving and corrupting. But we may not forget that our constitutional system is to allow the greatest freedom of access to Congress, so that people may press for their selfish interests, with Congress acting as arbiter of their demands and conflicts.[150]

The Selma-to-Montgomery March as an Exemplar of Hybrid Petitioning

At times history and fate meet at a single time in a single place to shape a turning point in man's unending search for freedom. So it was at Lexington and Concord. So it was a century ago at Appomattox. So it was last week in Selma, Alabama.

— *President Lyndon B. Johnson, March 15, 1965*

The iconic Selma-to-Montgomery march, of March 21 to 25, 1965, provides an example of precisely how advocates of legal change can and do exercise their expressive freedoms conjunctively, and for the need for the federal courts to consider the implications of petitioning in the context of speech, assembly, and association. Almost fifty years ago, five days in March helped to begin a new era for the South, and for the nation.

From March 21 to March 25, 1965, thousands of civil rights protesters marched down U.S. Highway 80 from Selma to Montgomery, Alabama, to call attention to the state's systematic disenfranchisement of African American citizens. Then as now, Highway 80 was a main regional corridor, connecting Selma and Montgomery with points east and west, symbolically linking Alabama's denial of the right to vote with similar abuses throughout the South. The Selma march represents a high-water mark for the vindication of expressive freedoms, notably including the right of petition, and the democratic values these rights embody. In the words of the Rev. Martin Luther King Jr., "Selma, Alabama became a shining moment in the conscience of man."[1]

The social significance of the Selma march is well documented.[2] By focusing national attention on the disenfranchisement of Southern blacks, it prompted Congress to pass one of the most sweeping civil rights laws in history: the Voting Rights Act of 1965.[3] The Voting Rights Act, in turn, led to a dramatic rise in

African American citizens' participation in democratic government, forever altering the shape of politics throughout the South and throughout the nation.[4] Yet the opinion that made the march possible, written by then District Judge Frank M. Johnson Jr.,[5] has faded from our collective memory with time. In some ways, however, Judge Johnson's opinion in *Williams v. Wallace*[6] is every bit as remarkable as the Selma march itself. As we approach the fiftieth anniversary of the march, it is fitting and proper to look back at the events that took place in Selma in the spring of 1965, and to reconsider their relevance to our present.

This chapter argues that the Selma march should be—although it plainly is not—as well regarded for its contribution to the development of First Amendment law as to the development of our national morality. Judge Johnson's opinion in *Williams* rests on two principles: first, the principle that the right to protest on public property should, at least in some circumstances, be determined in relation to the wrongs being protested and, second, that the right to petition may be exercised through petitioning speech that annexes the rights of speech, assembly, and association to the right of petition. Moreover, such "petitioning speech," particularly petitioning speech related to an effort to seek redress of a legal wrong committed by the government entity being petitioned, justifies imposing greater burdens on the community than would nonpetitioning speech, even of a political character.

When deciding whether to permit the four-day march on U.S. Highway 80, Judge Johnson observed that "it seems basic to our constitutional principles that the extent of the right to assemble, demonstrate and march peaceably along the highways and streets in an orderly manner should be commensurate with the enormity of the wrongs that are being protested and petitioned against."[7] After examining an extensive record, he concluded that the wrongs suffered by the African American citizens of central Alabama were "enormous."[8] The scope of the right to petition through a mass protest, he ruled, "should be determined accordingly."[9] In light of the state of Alabama's long-standing and systematic denial of basic civil rights to its African American citizens, Judge Johnson issued an injunction that permitted the plaintiffs to conduct a four-day march over fifty-two miles on a major highway.

The proposition that the scope of the right to engage in petitioning speech should be commensurate with the wrongs one seeks to protest seems to cut against the grain of contemporary content neutral First Amendment analysis.[10] Nevertheless, Judge Johnson was correct to recognize enhanced rights of access to public property for petitioning speech seeking a redress of grievances from the government entity being both petitioned and protested against through the same hybrid petitioning activity.

Yet Judge Johnson's "principle of proportionality"[11] in the context of petitioning speech has not received the serious consideration that it deserves. In the almost five decades following Judge Johnson's decision in *Williams v. Wallace*, his opinion has frequently been cited for the proposition that local hostility to an exercise of First Amendment rights is an insufficient basis for prohibiting the exercise of the right.[12] To be sure, *Williams* is a paradigmatic example of the proposition that a "heckler's veto"[13] cannot be permitted to silence otherwise protected expressive activity. Most courts have not been willing to apply the broader proportionality principle that Judge Johnson enunciated, however.[14] And although several law review articles in the late 1960s and early 1970s criticized the proportionality principle in passing, none of these works has included a comprehensive analysis—or a defense—of Judge Johnson's opinion.[15]

This book has argued for a renewed and expanded commitment to the project of deliberative democracy by reclaiming the Petition Clause and deploying the clause to secure a right of personal access to the government and its agents. Careful examination of Judge Johnson's *Williams* opinion will show that Judge Johnson very much appreciated the importance of the right of petition and also the centrality of hybrid forms of petitioning to securing legislative, as opposed to judicial, relief for deprivations of constitutional rights.

I. MARCHING TO FREEDOM: A BRIEF HISTORY OF THE SELMA MARCH

Perhaps the most striking (and therefore memorable) moment of the Selma march was its conclusion, when some twenty-five thousand people marched up Dexter Avenue to the Alabama state capitol, in downtown Montgomery, Alabama, to demand that the state guarantee all its citizens their civil rights.[16] The march ended with a rally on the steps of the capitol, at which Martin Luther King announced to the nation that segregation was "on its deathbed."[17] His rhetorical question "How long?" was both a call to arms and a ringing indictment of Southern society:

> I know you are asking today, "How long will it take?" I come to say to you this afternoon however difficult the moment, however frustrating the hour, it will not be long, because truth pressed to earth will rise again.
> How long? Not long, because no lie can live forever.
> How long? Not long, because you still reap what you sow.
> How long? Not long, because the arm of the moral universe is long but it bends toward justice.

How long? Not long, 'cause mine eyes have seen the glory of the coming of the Lord, trampling out the vintage where the grapes of wrath are stored. He has loosed the fateful lightning of his terrible swift sword. His truth is marching on.[18]

These images, these words, remain with us because of their scope and poignancy.

Another point, largely lost to history, was that the march and rally served as a framing device for a petition to Governor George C. Wallace. Following the conclusion of the public rally on the steps of the state capitol building, the Southern Christian Leadership Conference's (SCLC) plans for the event included having a delegation of twenty persons "enter the Capitol Building, proceed to the Governor's office, seek an audience with the Governor and present a petition."[19]

The SCLC's petition read: "We have come not only five days and 50 miles, but we have come from three centuries of suffering and hardship. We have come to you, the governor of Alabama, to declare that we must have our freedom NOW. We must have the right to vote; we must have equal protection of the law and an end to police brutality."[20] However, the effort to deliver the petition immediately following the rally did not meet with success. Around 5:40 P.M. on March 25, 1965, following the conclusion of the rally (which Governor Wallace watched through his partially opened office window blinds),[21] a delegation of twenty SCLC representatives approached the state capitol building, led by the Rev. Joseph E. Lowery, of Birmingham.[22] This group was composed of eighteen African American and two Caucasian residents of Alabama.[23]

The group was initially blocked from entering the capitol grounds by Major W. L. Allen, of the Alabama Highway Patrol; Governor Wallace's office, however, instructed Allen to permit the group to enter the capitol grounds and building. The Rev. Mr. Lowery and the delegation then entered the capitol building with signed copies of the petition, but were met about ten feet inside the door by Cecil C. Jackson Jr., Governor Wallace's executive secretary.[24]

Jackson told Lowery and the delegation, "'[T]he Capitol is closed today'" and noted, "'The Governor has designated me to receive your petition.'"[25] Lowery replied, "We are very sorry that he cannot see us," while "clasping copies of the petition to his chest." He then asked Jackson, "Please advise the Governor that as citizens of this state we have legitimate grievances to present to him. Please advise the Governor that we will return at another time."[26] Jackson responded, "That would be appropriate." Roy Reed, the *New York Times* reporter who covered this event, notes that "[t]he petitions never left

Mr. Lowrey's hands."[27] On Wednesday, March 31, 1965, about a week after the march's conclusion, Governor Wallace met with a delegation of sixteen SCLC representatives in his official capitol office and received—in person—a signed copy of the petition.[28]

Thus, the Selma march and rally led up to an effort to meet, in person and face to face, with Governor Wallace. The Selma march, then, represents a modern example of systemic petitioning,[29] in which petitioners seek to exercise expressive freedoms conjunctively for the purpose of engaging not only the government but also the general body politic about the object of the petition.

The Selma-to-Montgomery march, however, was not simply the product of inspiring leadership and the commitment of the civil rights community to progressive change. It was also the result of thoughtful judicial intervention. Any analysis of the march's significance must therefore include some consideration of the federal judiciary's role in securing for the marchers the right both to protest and to petition. And in order to appreciate that role, one must first understand the context in which the march arose, and the precise facts on which Judge Johnson relied in reaching his *Williams* decision.

In King's words, "The Civil Rights Act of 1964 gave Negroes some part of their rightful dignity, but without the vote it was dignity without strength."[30] In 1965, the disenfranchisement of the black citizens of Alabama was nearly complete. Although 15,115 black persons of voting age resided in Dallas County, the central Alabama county of which Selma is the principal city, only 335 (representing 2.2 percent of all black citizens) were registered to vote.[31] In contrast, 9,542 of the 14,400 white residents of Dallas County were registered.[32] This appalling pattern repeated itself throughout other counties in central Alabama's "black belt."[33] In some areas, dead white Alabama residents apparently enjoyed greater access to the ballot than live black ones. In Wilcox County, for example, not one of the 6,085 black residents was registered to vote, but 2,959 of only 2,647 white residents were registered.[34]

The reason for this pattern was simple: the State of Alabama maintained a systematic program to prevent its black citizens from voting, relying on such devices as discriminatory application of qualifying tests, discriminatory enforcement of registration rules, poll taxes, and outright racial gerrymandering.[35] "Throughout the state . . . all types of conniving methods were used to prevent Negroes from becoming registered voters and there were some counties without a single Negro registered to vote despite the fact that the Negro constituted a majority of the population."[36] By 1965, this state of affairs had become intolerable to the black citizens of Alabama. The time for change had come.

The horrors of Birmingham in 1963, when Police Commissioner Bull Connor used dogs and fire hoses to terrorize protesters who were engaging in a peaceful protest seeking basic civil rights, played no small part in the passage of the Civil Rights Act of 1964.[37] King and his SCLC colleagues believed a similar mass demonstration would be necessary to secure the voting rights of Southern blacks. In late December 1964, leaders of the SCLC, including King, decided that it was time to implement a new phase of the "Alabama Project," a series of demonstrations designed to wrest the right to vote from reactionary Southern state governments.[38] On New Year's Day in 1965, Jim Bevel of the SCLC met with the Dallas County Voters League to discuss renewed efforts to roll back Jim Crow.[39]

Selma's sheriff, Jim Clark, enjoyed a statewide reputation for "vicious and violent behavior" toward civil rights protesters.[40] The organizers of the Alabama Project chose Selma as the focal point of the voting rights campaign because the volatile Sheriff Clark was likely to react badly to their demands for suffrage.[41] They hoped that publicity generated by the SCLC's nonviolent protests would arouse the conscience of the nation and lead to federal legislation securing the right of all citizens to vote without regard to race.

King and his staff held an organizational meeting on January 2, 1965, at the Brown Chapel African Methodist Episcopal Church.[42] At the meeting, King set forth the goals of the Alabama Project and emphasized his determination to force the nation to take action to end the disenfranchisement of African American citizens.[43] He returned to Selma on January 14 for a second organizational rally.[44] At this meeting, he outlined the SCLC's plan for escalating the confrontation with the state authorities, and urged the local citizens to support the coming mass actions.[45]

In January and February, the black citizens of Selma repeatedly marched on the county courthouse, demanding the right to register to vote.[46] Sheriff Clark responded with mass arrests, beatings, and forced marches.[47] The protests reached a climax on Sunday, March 7. On that day, about 650 protesters left the Brown Chapel, intent on marching from Selma to Montgomery to demand a redress of their grievances from the state government.[48] Proceeding in an orderly and peaceful manner through Selma, the marchers crossed the Edmund Pettus Bridge and continued to march east on U.S. Highway 80 toward Montgomery. Sheriff Clark and Colonel Al Lingo, head of the Alabama Highway Patrol, met the marchers with about seventy state troopers, a detachment of Dallas County deputy sheriffs, and a group of neovigilante "possemen" nominally under the control of Sheriff Clark.[49]

Major John Cloud of the State Highway Patrol ordered the marchers to disperse within two minutes. After only a single minute expired, however, the "lawmen" moved against the protesters.[50] Using tactics "similar to those recommended for use by the United States Army to quell armed rioters in occupied countries," the state troopers attacked the marchers with clubs, tear gas, nausea gas, and canisters of smoke.[51] More than six dozen people were injured in the melee, some seriously.[52]

The public's response to the events of March 7 was "little less than seismic."[53] As had happened after the Birmingham protests in 1963, the brutality of the Alabama authorities provoked national and international revulsion. The SCLC immediately began a national campaign to draw attention to the events in Selma, issuing a public call urging leaders of the civil rights community to come to Selma for a second attempt to march from Selma to Montgomery.[54] King wrote that "no American is without responsibility" for the events in Selma and that "clergy of all faiths" should come to Selma to make their voices heard.[55] Thousands responded to this call to action.[56] The second march was to take place on Tuesday, March 9, 1965.

In light of the March 7 attack at the bridge, the leaders of the protest movement decided to seek federal court protection for the planned march.[57] The protest organizers filed a class-action lawsuit on March 8, 1965, in the federal district court for the Middle District of Alabama, on which Frank M. Johnson Jr. served as chief judge, seeking an order permitting a peaceful protest march from Selma to Montgomery.[58] Hosea Williams, a young SCLC activist from Savannah, Georgia, who had proved his ability by organizing demonstrations in St. Augustine, Florida, in 1963, served as the lead plaintiff.[59] The protest organizers hoped to obtain an immediate injunction from the court on an ex parte basis allowing them to proceed with the march. The court, however, rejected this request.[60] Instead, Judge Johnson entered a temporary restraining order that barred the plaintiffs from marching until the court could conduct a full hearing on the merits of their complaint.[61] The hearing was scheduled for March 11.

Prior to the hearing, another confrontation took place. Because of the high visibility of the events of March 7, King was under intense pressure to proceed with the march, notwithstanding the district court's restraining order.[62] On the night of Monday, March 8, King wrestled with the question of whether to violate the restraining order by going forward with the march.[63] Late that evening, he apparently decided that the march would proceed. On the following morning, March 9, civil rights activists gathered at the Brown Chapel, in Selma, for a mass rally.[64]

Following the rally, King led a procession of civil rights demonstrators through downtown Selma toward the Edmund Pettus Bridge. Before the marchers crossed the bridge, U.S. Marshal H. Stanley Fountain halted them and read

Judge Johnson's restraining order to the demonstrators, but he made no attempt to stop the march from proceeding.[65] King then led the marchers across the bridge.

On the eastern side of the bridge, they were met by Sheriff Clark, his deputies, and Alabama state troopers. Once again, Major Cloud ordered the crowd to disperse.[66] He and the other law enforcement officers then withdrew, leaving the road open to King.[67] Their accommodating stance was reportedly the result of direct orders from Governor Wallace.[68] Wallace may have hoped to place King in a catch-22. If King led the marchers down Highway 80 toward Montgomery, he would violate the court's restraining order, exposing himself and the other SCLC leaders to contempt charges. On the other hand, if King failed to proceed with the march, his credibility within the movement might be damaged.

King did not proceed with the march. Instead, he turned around and led the would-be marchers back across the bridge to the Brown Chapel.[69] The reasons for King's decision to turn back are not entirely clear. It is perhaps best understood as an example of his overall commitment to the rule of law, at least insofar as particular laws were "just."[70] One of King's advisers, Bernard Segal, later commented that if King had "suited his deed to his word" by violating the order, "his act would be no different in principle from the defiance of Governor Wallace and Governor Barnett."[71]

Hearings on the *Williams* lawsuit began two days later.[72] They lasted over four days, and established a conclusive record of systematic state-sponsored brutality against African American citizens designed to deny them the vote.[73] Judge Johnson found that Sheriff Clark and his deputies had engaged in a pattern of behavior that included mass arrests without just cause, forced marches, and the use of cattle prods and night sticks on peaceful marchers.[74] The court also found that Sheriff Clark had been assisted by Colonel Al Lingo, the head of the Alabama state troopers. The state troopers' contributions to Sheriff Clark's efforts included beating protesters and even, in at least one instance, shooting and killing a protester.[75]

The court held that the State of Alabama had undertaken a program of intimidation aimed at "preventing and discouraging Negro citizens from exercising their rights of citizenship, particularly the right to register to vote and the right to demonstrate peaceably for the purpose of protesting discriminatory practices in this area."[76] The court further observed: "The attempted march alongside U.S. Highway 80 from Selma, Alabama, to Montgomery, Alabama, on March 7, 1965, involved nothing more than a peaceful effort on the part of Negro citizens to exercise a classic constitutional right; that is, the right to

assemble peaceably and to petition one's government for the redress of grievances."[77] Based on the facts before it, the court reasoned that the protesters had
a right to march in support of their petition for a redress of grievances. The
question that it had to decide was the scope of the remedy.

II. RIGHTS AND REMEDIES: THE SELMA MARCH AS AN ILLUSTRATION OF HYBRID PETITIONING

Judge Johnson's opinion in *Williams* is notable for its restraint. He approached
the legal questions presented in *Williams* dispassionately, and his opinion demonstrates a careful and systematic adaptation and application of law to the facts
presented to the court. To be sure, the task before the court was not an easy one.
Even if the African American citizens of Selma had a right to engage in peaceful protest, it was not clear that this right was so broad as to encompass a fifty-
two-mile march along the main east-west corridor in central Alabama over four
consecutive days.[78]

Judge Johnson began his analysis of the plaintiffs' request with a few simple
observations. He noted that "[t]he law is clear that the right to petition one's
government for the redress of grievances may be exercised in large groups."[79]
Conversely, however, he recognized that government officials "have the duty
and responsibility of keeping the streets and highways open and available for
their regular uses."[80] As a result, he held that governments may place "reasonable" restrictions on speech activities "in order to assure the safety and convenience of the people in the use of public streets and highways."[81]

These principles clearly conflict to some degree. The use of a public street
for protest activities will obviously impinge on the ability of motorists and other
pedestrians to use the same street at the same time for travel. Judge Johnson
noted that such conflicts existed in this case but explained that "there is room
in our system of government for both, once the proper balance between them
is drawn."[82] The court had "the duty and responsibility . . . of drawing the 'constitutional boundary line.'"[83] The trick, of course, was to draw the proper line.

In striking the balance, Judge Johnson could have viewed the proposed activity without regard to the specific context in which it arose. Considered out of its
context, *Williams* would not have been a difficult case. Heavily trafficked highways exist principally to facilitate travel and commerce, not speech activities. As
a general matter, large groups of protesters cannot routinely be permitted to
march down such highways for four days at a stretch — in fact, the Selma March
involved closure to traffic of two of four lanes of Highway 80 over the four-lane
portions of the route. Hence, if the court had attempted to make a universal

pronouncement on the availability of highways for speech activities, it almost certainly could not have permitted the Selma march.

Current First Amendment doctrine supports this conclusion. Under the existing analytical framework, a major highway would undoubtedly be classified as a "nonpublic forum," in which speech rights are severely limited. In a nonpublic forum, the government may impose any regulations it wants so long as they are reasonable and not intended to suppress the expression of a particular point of view.[84] By contrast, in traditional public forums, places like parks and city streets, which "by long tradition or by government fiat have been devoted to assembly and debate,"[85] the government may impose only reasonable and content neutral restrictions as to the time, place, or manner of the speech activity. Content-based restrictions may be applied to traditional public forums only if the regulation directly advances a compelling state interest, is narrowly drawn, and leaves open "ample alternative channels of communication."[86]

Thus, if a court today were to confront a situation like the Selma march, it would almost certainly deny the plaintiffs the requested relief on the grounds that state restrictions on protest activities on public highways are reasonable. Although such plaintiffs would be able to protest in other spaces, they probably could not receive legal sanction for a protest on the scale the Selma marchers intended.[87] The impact of this mode of analysis is significant. It is doubtful that the Selma march would be long remembered had it taken place on a single day on a side street or seldom-used park in Selma.

The *Williams* court, however, did not ignore the context of the plaintiffs' proposed speech activity.[88] Instead, it considered the context in which the suit arose essential to determining whether the requested relief was appropriate. Judge Johnson explained: "[T]he extent of a group's constitutional right to protest peaceably and petition one's government for redress of grievances must be, if our American Constitution is to be a flexible and 'living' document, found and held to be commensurate with the enormity of the wrongs being protested and petitioned against. This is particularly true when the usual, basic and constitutionally-provided means of protesting in our American way—voting—have been deprived."[89] Applying the foregoing test to the facts of the case, the court concluded that "plaintiffs' proposed plan of march from Selma to Montgomery, Alabama, for its intended purposes, is clearly a reasonable exercise of a right guaranteed by the Constitution of the United States."[90]

Essentially, the court began its analysis with a recognition of a constitutional floor, a minimum of inconvenience that the First and Fourteenth Amendments require the general public to countenance. It did not stop there, however.

Instead, the court recognized that the constitutional floor does not necessarily define the limits of what is permissible expressive activity on public property. This allowed the court to ask two questions: (1) What is constitutionally required? and (2) What is constitutionally permitted?

In approving the marchers' plan and enjoining the state from interfering, the court observed: "[T]he plan as proposed and as allowed reaches, under the particular circumstances of this case, to the outer limits of what is constitutionally allowed. However, the wrongs and injustices inflicted upon these plaintiffs and the members of their class (part of which have been herein documented) have clearly exceeded—and continue to exceed—the outer limits of what is constitutionally permissible."[91] The court sanctioned a march large enough to disrupt the lives of thousands of people trying to go about their daily business. Protests on this scale, and in this type of venue, are an anomaly; other persons or groups could not routinely obtain official sanction for demonstrations on a similar scale. Hence the court provided the *Williams* plaintiffs with expanded speech and assembly rights that other individuals probably would not have received, and it did so precisely because of the petitioning nature of the expressive activity at issue. Moreover, the expanded access to public space for petitioning activity also clearly related to the remedial cast of the petition itself; the *Williams* petitioners sought to use petitioning speech to obtain legal redress for clear, systematic constitutional deprivations.

Several commentators have criticized *Williams* for this result, arguing that the decision appears to give greater speech rights to certain groups on the basis of an individual judge's sympathies for the policy preferences of particular speakers.[92] The danger of allowing judges to apportion speech rights based on their individual assessments of the value of particular types of speech is suggested by Justice Scalia in his partial dissent in *Madsen v. Women's Health Center*.[93] In *Madsen*, the Court upheld a thirty-six-foot "buffer zone" around abortion clinics that had been the target of numerous disruptive antiabortion protests. Within the zone, protesters were prohibited from engaging in any speech activities—even in traditional public forums like public streets and sidewalks. Justice Scalia suggested that the Court would not have sustained a similar restriction if the object of the protest had been racial equality instead of the protection of unborn fetuses.[94] He accused the majority of protecting speech rights subjectively.[95]

Justice Scalia's concern about the selective protection of speech rights is not particularly far-fetched. Any First Amendment doctrine that openly vests the judiciary with the power to favor one speaker over another deserves to be greeted with healthy skepticism.

Even those who argue that courts should take context into consideration when deciding the scope of First Amendment protections balk at the prospect of giving particular speakers enhanced First Amendment rights based on the content of their message.[96] For example, Professor Vincent Blasi has suggested that context is essential to applying the First Amendment properly, but in his model of the First Amendment, all boats rise and fall with the same tide.[97] He argues that courts should carefully consider historical context and contemporary attitudes toward dissent when determining the scope of the First Amendment's protection of social protest and speech activities. Hence, in periods when the public's tolerance of dissent is low (such as during the Red Scare years), the federal courts' efforts and determination to protect speech rights should be higher than in more stable periods.[98] But he expressly disavows any interest in having courts lift some of the boats, some of the time.[99]

The visceral aversion to context-specific applications of the First Amendment is somewhat puzzling. Contemporary First Amendment jurisprudence makes a number of fine distinctions based solely on the content of the speech at issue.[100] Perhaps the objection stems not from the idea of considering context but rather from the belief that speech rights should not be apportioned on the basis of the speaker's identity.

If this is the case, much of the criticism that commentators have leveled at *Williams* has been wide of the mark. *Williams* neither stands for nor supports the proposition that courts should bestow preferential speech rights on some individuals or groups based on the court's perception of the "justice" of the individual's or group's cause.[101] In *Williams*, the court squarely rested its holding on an analysis of the particular wrongs that the protest would call to the attention of the state, the nation, and the world, and on the "classic" petitioning character of the speech activity.[102] Indeed, Judge Johnson repeatedly emphasizes the "petitioning" aspect of the march and places significant weight on this fact.[103]

In deciding whether the state's restrictions were "reasonable," the court paid primary attention to the issue of government culpability for the unlawful acts that the plaintiffs wished to protest and the fact that the march and rally involved core petitioning speech—the speech had a compelling nexus with both the government of Alabama and also with the voters who enabled that government to act in patently unconstitutional ways.[104] Hence Judge Johnson keyed his analysis to the nature of the wrongs being protested and petitioned against, *not* the identity of the protesters.[105] The court sanctioned the parceling of speech rights based not on the perceived merit of particular speakers but rather on the importance of particular speech in the context of a mass systemic petition.

Judge Johnson's opinion in *Williams* is, if not unique, then unusual in its overt and repeated invocation of the Petition Clause in support of the injunction permitting a multiday march on the major regional highway linking Selma and Montgomery. As Judge Kermit Lipez observed near the time of the *Williams* decision: "But the case, by its very uniqueness, reveals the dramatic potency of these neglected rights of assembly and petition. The court, if it had taken a more restricted view of those rights, would have dismissed the Selma March as an outrageous intrusion on the public convenience."[106]

Thus, the court's decision to permit such extraordinary access to public property for protest activity can be justified only by recourse to the petitioning nature of the speech activity, as well as the enormity of the constitutional wrongs that the participants sought to have redressed. Presumably, other would-be speakers, who did not seek to petition the state government or who had not suffered legal wrongs that served as the basis for the protest, could not make an identical demand for access to public property with the same result.[107]

III. THE RIGHT TO ACCESS A PREFERRED AUDIENCE AS AN INCIDENT OF PETITIONING SPEECH

Notwithstanding the strength of his argument in favor of enhanced access to public property for the purpose of engaging in petitioning speech, Judge Johnson's *Williams* opinion is open to serious criticism. Perhaps the most powerful argument against the proportionality principle is that it threatens to move the courts a step closer to the creation of a First Amendment with two distinct classes: the preferential forum haves and the preferential forum have-nots. Or, alternatively, those who enjoy a right to access an audience of their choosing directly and personally, and those who do not enjoy such a right of direct and personal access.

If one believes that absolute equality of access to public forums is necessary to avoid marginalizing unpopular groups, it is inappropriate for courts to afford some groups preferred access to nonpublic forums, even when they wish to protest a serious legal wrong in the hope of obtaining, through their petitioning activity, redress for their grievances against the government. One might reasonably argue that the result in *Williams* was well and good, but that vesting judges with the power to favor some groups over others in the allocation of public space for speech activities is at best misguided and at worst quite dangerous. Although this criticism of *Williams* is not easily overcome, it can be answered.

Simply put, it is necessary to provide some groups with greater speech rights than others in certain situations if we are to secure the full benefits of the First

Amendment. To be sure, this proposition fits uncomfortably into our current jurisprudence. If one starts from the proposition that the First Amendment is designed to protect speech by persons holding minority views, then vesting the federal courts with the power to pick and choose among speakers seems inappropriate.[108] If one properly limits the scope of the proportionality principle, however, the danger of creating a speech caste system can be significantly reduced, if not entirely avoided. An important initial premise should be that petitioning speech must be heard by its intended audience to have any prayer of being effective (i.e., answered); this fact establishes an important initial boundary line for the potential scope of the *Williams* proportionality principle.

A. Values and Public Policies Underlying the First Amendment

Whether one embraces the proportionality principle will turn at least in part on how one views the raison d'être of the First Amendment's free speech, assembly, association, and petition guarantees. If these clauses are meant to foster democratic self-governance though the maintenance of a lively and robust public debate[109]—one that includes in particular discussion of government wrongdoing—it is entirely appropriate (and indeed necessary) to afford groups suffering legal wrongs at the hand of the government greater access to public forums than groups wishing to protest other matters, at least when such groups wish to exercise their right of petition to seek voluntary forms of redress of these wrongs from the government itself.

The free speech and assembly guarantees of the First Amendment provide political minority groups an outlet to express their concerns over government conduct. Moreover, the Petition Clause has even more direct relevance in this context, as it should secure a right of direct access to the government, including the ability to meaningfully engage government officials regarding public policies that abridge or deny completely well-established constitutional rights, like voting.[110] The exercise of these rights, through systemic forms of petitioning, helps to ensure that these groups can obtain a hearing not only from the government but also by the general community. In addition, the ability to engage in social protest on the public streets may reduce the likelihood that groups will undertake other, less savory measures to attract the community's attention.[111] The First Amendment thus provides disenfranchised subgroups within the community with a peaceful means of agitating for change.

Relatedly, the community can benefit from having its conscience pricked. Without speech activities by affected groups, unlawful government conduct might go unnoticed by the general public.[112] The exercise of the right of petition, in conjunction with speech, assembly, and association, can call problems to the attention of the majority, permitting them to make necessary corrections through the democratic process, rather than through the courts.

The Selma march is a perfect example of petitioning speech activities facilitating democratic reform. Six months after the march, Congress passed the Voting Rights Act of 1965,[113] which had a "spectacular" impact on minority political participation.[114] Within two months of its passage, the number of African American voters in counties subject to Justice Department monitoring programs more than doubled, and within a decade African American voters would increase their numbers from 1.5 million to 3.5 million.[115] The number of African American officeholders increased correspondingly: "By 1990, more than 4,000 blacks held elective office in the South, including a governor, five members of Congress, and more than 175 legislators, compared with less than 100 black elected officials in the region before passage of the Voting Rights Act."[116]

The march and subsequent rally on the steps of the Alabama state capitol building facilitated democratic reform in two ways. First, it alerted the immediate community to the concerns of the African American citizens of Alabama, serving as, in Judge Johnson's words, a "classic petition" for a redress of grievances.[117] In this way, it provided the white citizens of both Dallas County and the entire state of Alabama with the opportunity to initiate reform without the intervention of federal authorities. Although the white citizens of Alabama failed to respond to this historic demand for the observance of basic constitutional rights, the march nevertheless facilitated a process that could have resulted in a local resolution of the crisis. In other circumstances, one can imagine local citizens demanding reform in response to speech activity.

Second, the Selma march created tremendous pressure at the level of the national government for the enfranchisement of all citizens. The sad truth is that, more than a decade after the Supreme Court's decision in *Brown v. Board of Education*,[118] segregation was still a pervasive feature of Southern culture in 1965. Indeed, some legal scholars and historians have argued that *Brown* was never fully implemented.[119] *Brown* and its progeny provide a striking example of the potential shortcomings of judicial relief.[120] When one compares the present-day results of the Voting Rights Act to the results of *Brown*, it is obvious that legislative reform is often not only faster than judicial reform but also may be much more effective.[121] Thus, it may be logical for those suffering systematic deprivations of legal rights to engage in mass public systemic petitioning campaigns seeking legislative relief.

The public forum doctrine, however, has created a barrier to the public spaces needed for effective protest activity directed against existing legal wrongs.

The contemporary approach to free speech issues leads courts to adopt unduly narrow definitions of public forums. Once a particular location is declared a public forum, it is open season for all comers. Understandably, courts are reluctant to open up new public spaces for speech activities.[122] Instead, courts define public forums narrowly in order to ensure that public spaces are available for their principal uses, and speech activities are, if not entirely prohibited, severely restricted.[123] This approach leaves groups wishing to protest particularly egregious wrongs with insufficient public space to make their protest heard.[124]

It is doubtful that courts will reverse course and expand the public spaces that must be made available for speech activities. Given the constant danger of undue disruption of community activities, the judicial trend of limiting access to public forums cannot be avoided in a First Amendment jurisprudence that makes no accommodations for context. Unless courts can pick and choose among speakers on the basis of the petitioning character of the protest activity, the balancing of the public's need to use public roads and buildings against the use of such facilities for speech activities will invariably cut against the speech activities. Current doctrine forces courts to ask whether groups like the Ku Klux Klan should routinely be permitted to use a particular public space for speech activities. All too often, the answer is no, not only for small minorities holding extremist views, but also, by operation of the content-neutrality doctrine, for those who wish to call the attention of the community to serious government wrongdoing through petitioning speech.

The proportionality principle permits courts to make rational distinctions between proposed uses of public forums for speech activities. Rather than prohibiting all groups from parading on a community's main arteries, the proportionality principle permits most groups to be relegated to less busy corridors but holds out the possibility of using major highways and byways under sufficiently compelling circumstances.[125] The proportionality principle permits courts to match venues for speech activities with the speaker's need to speak and the community's need to hear. The principle also, and critically, takes into full account the petitioning nature of speech activity of a dissenting cast. It thus maximizes the "public debate" function of the First Amendment.[126]

By restriking the balance in favor of speech activities under limited circumstances, such as when a protest march or rally seeks to petition government authorities for redress of alleged constitutional wrongs, the proportionality principle ensures that groups with serious grievances can make their case to both the government and also to the community effectively. If a minority group's protest is invariably relegated to the forums most convenient to the general public, the community at large will not be in a position to hear the group's grievances. Moreover, if protests are banished to convenient locations far removed from the centers of government, commerce, and community life, the effectiveness of a protest as a form of petition can be fatally undermined. The content neutral approach to apportioning public space for speech activity denies disenfranchised groups adequate forums for petitioning speech, just as it denies the general community the right to hear such groups' grievances.

Moreover, to the extent that democratic self-governance both presupposes and requires the existence of an active, informed electorate,[127] the proportionality principle helps to ensure that the community is fully informed about instances of government wrongdoing, and thereby empowered to act. The proportionality principle makes it easier for the community to listen when a speaker has a legitimate complaint about the government that the community itself has installed. If a sheriff's department is routinely beating minority suspects, the community should tolerate inconvenience in order to accommodate speech activities calling this state of affairs to the body politic's attention in order to obtain remedial measures. If speech activities are limited to side streets, parks, and other traditional public forums, it is less likely that a group's message will be heard. And if the message is not heard, the problem may never be resolved peaceably.[128]

Essentially, the public forum doctrine lacks needed depth, because it fails to take context into account when apportioning public space for speech activity.[129] Although the particular facts and history of the Selma march are unique, one can imagine other situations in which a state government denies or abridges a constitutional right, even though the degree and scale of deprivation pales in comparison to the police state tactics once used in the South.

In such circumstances, the federal courts should weigh the nature of the alleged constitutional deprivation when considering whether to permit the use of normally unavailable public property for speech activity protesting the deprivation. In such cases, the would-be petitioning speakers have a heightened interest in the use of particular public property for their expressive activity and also in reaching a particular audience. Neither of these factors turns on the *viewpoint* of the speech, but both admittedly relate to the *content* of the proposed speech activity. But "petitioning" speech, by its very nature, implies a specific kind of content.

A flyer promoting public tours of a decommissioned submarine does not constitute petitioning speech, whereas a public remonstrance against the local city dock department regarding its policies on dock access and wharfage fees *would* fall within the classification.[130] Thus, not all speech, even all political speech, constitutes petitioning speech. Judge Johnson's *Williams* opinion recognized and emphasized that the community has a higher duty to facilitate and accommodate petitioning speech than it does for other kinds of speech activity.

B. Subjectivity and the Proportionality Principle

If one accepts that the principle of popular sovereignty is fundamental to democracy, the government serves as an agent of the people.[131] Popularly elected officials, like governors and sheriffs, are accountable to the citizens who elected them.[132] So too are city councils, library boards, and police departments. Public entities and officers exercise authority derived from the community, ostensibly for the benefit of the community that selected them. If an agent of the community violates the legal rights of an individual or group within the community, the community at large shares responsibility for that action. So it is that when a Bull Connor turns loose his dogs on innocent children, or a Jim Clark instructs his men to beat peaceful protesters with billy clubs, or a Daryl Gates (the highly controversial chief of the Los Angeles, California, Police Department from 1978 to 1992) permits his officers to terrorize persons suspected of committing crimes, culpability lies in part with the people who delegated that power to them.

When an agent of the people commits a wrong, the aggrieved person can go to court and seek redress on the merits of the claim. That may not be enough to resolve the problem fully, however. The injured person also may wish to call the community's attention to the wrong, in hopes that the community might take action to resolve the problem without judicial intervention. In such circumstances, the public's right not to be inconvenienced is significantly less weighty than in circumstances where the proposed speech activity does not implicate wrongdoing by the government.

A group that has suffered a legal wrong at the hands of a government institution has a greater claim on the community's collective ear than, say, a person wishing to protest the use of disposable plastic bags by local grocery stores. The community's responsibility for the actions of its government requires that the balance between the right to use the streets for speech activities and the right to use the streets for travel be struck in favor of the speech activities more often and to a greater degree when government wrongdoing is at issue.[133] By delegating power to an official who systematically violates the community's laws, the community has in some measure forfeited the right to avoid the inconvenience occasioned by speech activities on the public streets protesting such action.[134]

Williams can be viewed as an instance in which the community, through its governor, sheriff, and voting registrars, permitted the systematic violation of fundamental constitutional rights. In such circumstances, it was (and is) entirely appropriate to require the community to be inconvenienced by persons wishing to call the community's attention to its abrogation of responsibility for the actions of its elected officials through mass systemic petitioning activity. Viewed in this light, whether a speech restriction is "reasonable" will turn as much on the content of the speech as on the venue for the speech activity.[135]

Indeed, some legal wrongs committed by the government reflect a failure of executive and legislative officials to act in the face of clear legal obligations.[136] In such circumstances, the federal judiciary may have to act creatively in order to provide meaningful relief. In the context of social protest, "this is particularly true when the usual, basic, and constitutionally provided means of protesting in our American way—voting—have been deprived."[137] Thus, to the extent that the legal wrongs offered to support the invocation of the proportionality principle include an assertion that the aggrieved group has been effectively denied access to the political process by the state, the group has established a sufficient condition for the application of the proportionality principle.[138]

The proportionality principle does not sanction subjective decisions by judges based on ideological factors but rather calls upon judges, when analyzing claims to a particular public forum or to access directly and personally a particular audience of government officials, to consider the nature of the speech activity (i.e., whether it constitutes petitioning speech) and the relationship of the proposed speech activity to the community in which the speech activity will occur (i.e., whether the community itself bears some measure of responsibility for empowering those who have transgressed the rights of the petitioners).[139] When protestors seek an audience that includes incumbent government officials with responsibility for the policies and practices at issue in the petitioning protest, the reviewing court should find a substantial First Amendment interest in reaching that audience through the proposed protest activity. And, to the extent that the speech is the direct result of actions implicitly sanctioned by the community through the democratic process, the court must correspondingly discount the community's interest in reserving the forum for its normal, everyday uses. Considered in this light, *Williams* requires judges to do little more than determine whether the proposed speech activity involves a protest seeking to petition against unlawful conditions brought about by the state.

Of course, not every claim of government wrongdoing can give rise to mass protests that significantly disrupt the everyday life of the community. Not every group wishing to protest a legal wrong caused by the government may be permitted to qualify for a preferred venue for its speech activities. Courts must evaluate the strength of such requests on an individual basis, granting requests for expanded access to public spaces in some cases and rejecting them in others. But this process is really no different from the balancing of equities that courts routinely conduct in evaluating requests for preliminary injunctions.[140] Like the preliminary injunction analysis, the proportionality principle requires the development of a rational limiting principle that permits courts to sift competing claims to public space. The key issues are (1) securing access to the government officials being petitioned, and (2) the ability to use public space that permits an effective and visible appeal to the general community as well.

The *Williams* court painstakingly documented the existence of grievous legal wrongs committed by agents of the Alabama state government, with the tacit, if not overt, consent of the white citizens of the state.[141] The court granted enhanced speech rights to the plaintiffs only after the plaintiffs had established that the wrongs they sought to protest were colorable claims raising serious constitutional issues.[142] Courts should undertake application of the proportionality principle only after a similarly rigorous analysis.

C. The Problem of Judicial Discretion

Even if the proportionality principle is thus limited, its exercise raises potential problems concerning the application of judicial discretion. The decision to grant Group A but not Group B access to a particular forum requires an exercise of discretion. And for Group B to be told that it cannot use the same public space that Group A can use will, to Group B, seem arbitrary indeed.

No easy answer exists to this criticism. Clearly, implementation of the proportionality principle will mean that some groups will perceive themselves to have been unfairly disadvantaged.[143]

There are at least two partial responses, however. First, the proportionality principle deals only with the constitutional ceiling, not the constitutional floor. Thus, every individual or group will have access to traditional or designated public forums. Incorporation of the principle will not leave any individual or group without significant access to public space in which to engage in speech activities. At worst, some people may not enjoy access either to the particular audience they seek or to the exact forum that they wish to use.

Second, existing First Amendment jurisprudence already makes a number of fine distinctions based on a judge's characterization of particular speech. For example, depending on its context, a court could characterize nude dancing as mere "conduct" or alternatively as "expressive activity."[144] The degree of protection afforded the communicative element of the activity will depend almost entirely upon which characterization the court chooses. Similarly, deciding how to characterize the nature of the speech requires the exercise of discretion.[145]

Whether speech is "political," "commercial," "erotic," or "obscene" will turn, to some degree, on the sensibilities and professionalism of individual jurists.[146] Such decisions are essentially no different in character from the exercise of the discretion the proportionality principle would require. If anything, the existing distinctions are potentially more troublesome, because they may well determine whether the expressive activity at issue enjoys *any* constitutional protection under the First Amendment.[147]

When applying the proportionality principle, judges will have to use their discretion to fit particular forums to particular wrongs.[148] The task is one of "fashioning relief to fit the case."[149] Although this exercise creates the possibility of unfairness in individual cases, the benefits of providing access to the agents of the government for petitioning speech and adequate public forums for speech activity aimed at official government wrongdoing more than offset this opportunity cost.

If application of the proportionality principle is limited to petitioning speech involving colorable allegations of serious legal wrongdoing by a government official or agency, it is difficult to see how it could serve as a vehicle for permitting judges to implement their arbitrary or narrow ideological policy preferences. *Williams* certainly does not invite such behavior, nor is it necessary to construe the proportionality principle so as to provide cover for such unscrupulous conduct. In sum, the proportionality principle is not, and need not be, hopelessly subjective.

One also should note that the Petition Clause, of its own force, should secure direct, in-person access to government officials for the purpose of petitioning activity.[150] *Williams* involved a four-day march using the main regional highway, culminating in a huge rally and demonstration at the center of the state's capital city, attended by more than twenty thousand people. The proportionality principle justified imposing substantial public disruptions on the local community, in order to permit an exercise of petitioning speech commensurate with the legal, indeed constitutional, wrongs at issue. Not all petitioning speech necessarily involves government wrongdoing; much relates to constitutional, but, from the petitioners' perspective, undesirable or mistaken, government policies.

Judge Johnson's extraordinary remedy should not be taken as a general measuring stick for the rights of any person or group that wishes to petition the local, state, or federal government.[151] Access to the government of a more limited nature, associated with less potential disruption to the more regular activities of the general community, will usually be sufficient to honor the constitutional imperatives of the Petition Clause.

IV. CONCLUSION

Judge Johnson's theory that the right to protest and petition should, in limited circumstances, be commensurate with the legal wrongs being protested and petitioned against is both justifiable and necessary. The body politic should be constitutionally required to provide access to the government and general political community, by making adequate public space available for petitioning protest activities by an individual or group if the individual or group intends to protest legal wrongdoing by the government. The strict rule of content neutrality currently in vogue—which the federal courts observe when apportioning access to public forums—undoubtedly deprives some speakers of adequate public space in which to make their voices heard. The proportionality principle provides a needed remedy for the limited situations in which a protest of official wrongdoing in a generally available public forum is simply insufficient to achieve the manifold policies embodied by the First Amendment.

Although *Williams* may be novel as a matter of First Amendment law, it is not novel in a more fundamental sense. The civil rights activists in Selma had a right to vote, and they also had a right to protest and petition against the state's denial of that right. The question was not the existence of the right but the proper remedy for the violation of it. And in fashioning a remedy, Judge Johnson took into account the totality of the circumstances and determined that extraordinary wrongs called for extraordinary remedies.

Almost fifty years after the great march, it is clear that Judge Johnson decided *Williams* correctly, with respect to both the means and the ultimate result. Despite the academy's failure to recognize the power of Judge Johnson's constitutional logic, the proportionality principle is essential to ensuring that courts will be able to afford a full measure of relief to individuals or groups wishing to petition against official government wrongdoing through systemic forms of petitioning.[152]

As we approach the fiftieth anniversary of the Selma march and the *Williams* decision, it is appropriate once again to give Judge Johnson the last word:

> From the moment I issued the order permitting that march, I had been certain that I had done what was right according to the laws of this nation. As I watched those people—and some were mere children—I was absolutely convinced I had been right. I had never watched a march or demonstration before, but there was something special about the Selma-to-Montgomery march. I think the people demonstrated something about democracy: that it can never be taken for granted; they also showed that there is a way in this

system to gain human rights. They had followed the channel prescribed within the framework of the law. . . . [C]omplaints can be addressed within the system, according to the Constitution, and can be addressed without resorting to violence.[153]

7

CONCLUSION

The Petition Clause represents the most logical textual basis for securing a right of citizen access to government, whether at the local, state, or federal level. At its most basic, the clause stands for the proposition that government must be accessible—not only to voters, but to any person living within the community. This promise of access in turn secures the ability of the citizenry to engage the government regarding matters of concern—regardless of how picayune incumbent politicians might find these concerns.

The Petition Clause constitutes a kind of democratic feedback loop, through which the represented and their representatives can engage in process of democratic engagement. Moreover, this process of engagement includes not only interactions between the government and citizens but also among the members of the political community. In a sense, then, petitioning, properly conceptualized, constitutes the kind of democratic engagement that Alexander Meiklejohn identified as essential to the project of democratic self-government.[1]

When average people become disconnected from the institutions and agents of government, democracy itself is poorer for it. Yet, the aggressive use of the time, place, and manner doctrine under *Ward*[2] has permitted the government to deny in-person access to citizens seeking to communicate their views with incumbent government officials. The most recent lower federal court applications of *Ward*, such as *Bl(a)ck Tea Society*[3] and *Citizens for Peace in Space*[4] reflect a numbing indifference to the interest of citizens in personally communicating their views to government officials with responsibility to maintain—or alter—existing government policies.[5]

The root problem is, and remains, that an interest in using government property for speech activity simply does not encompass a right to a preferred audience, even when that audience consists of agents of the government. The space itself—a street, sidewalk, or public park—is not really at issue; indeed, the government has no objection to the use of these very spaces for protest activity, at times when the president, incumbent members of Congress, or senior political party leaders are not present. Thus, it is not access to public property for speech activity but rather access to the government itself that lies at the heart of the problem.[6]

The Petition Clause, as a textual source of a right to a particular audience, provides a logical basis for recognizing a limited right of access to the government. In other words, when speech activity partakes of a petitioning quality, meaning that it addresses a matter of public policy and seeks to communicate a point of view directly to a government official or political party leader with some measure of responsibility for the policy at issue, the federal courts should recognize a presumption in favor of access, thereby permitting petitioning speech within the hearing and seeing of this audience. Personal, direct access to the government should not be limited to those with the financial wherewithal to write $2,400 campaign contribution checks. And yet, if it is not possible to protest along a presidential motorcade route or outside a convention center where an incumbent U.S. senator is conducting a town hall meeting, how precisely is an average person supposed to communicate her views effectively to those exercising government power?

For elections to have meaning, the electorate has to be clearly informed of the issues and choices presented. Moreover, holding government accountable requires some ability to communicate ideas and suggestions to government, in order to permit government to act, or fail to act, on them. As one commentator has explained: "If the government has no duty to consider or respond to petitions, the right to petition contributes little to democratic decision making. Indeed, the right would guarantee no more than freedom of speech. Defining the right to petition as merely a right to come forward is similar to saying that citizens can vote but candidates with the most votes will not necessarily take office, or that plaintiffs can file lawsuits but defendants will have no duty to answer."[7] I would not, and do not, go so far as to advocate a firm requirement that public officials answer, or respond to, all petitioning speech. Surely public officials enjoy the same First Amendment right as other citizens to speak, or not, as they think best. Moreover, the ability of federal judges to enforce such a right strikes me as, at best, quite limited.[8] But I do think that public officials should be required to see or to listen, at least if the speakers seek to communicate by using a traditional public forum to communicate their message.

In a democratic polity, the government ostensibly serves as an agent of the people. Yet, increasingly, senior government officials seem to view interacting with the general public, in unscripted environments, as a politically risky venture not worth the bother. As Professor Meiklejohn warned, however: "A government of free men can properly be controlled only by itself. Who else could be trusted by us to hold our political institutions in check? Shall any single individual or any special group be allowed to take domination over the agencies of control? . . . If We, the People are to be controlled, then We, the People must do the controlling."[9] If democratic self-government is to work, then, there must be a dialogue, rather than a monologue between the governed and the governors.[10] The Petition Clause, properly understood and applied, serves both as the basis of this dialogue and as its guardian.[11]

One might object, of course, that noisy protestors outside presidential appearances and major political or international events are not seriously interested in engaging in a dialogue with government and its agents about the course and content of public policy. Instead, they seek merely to obtain media attention, in the hope of gathering greater support to their causes;[12] the proximity of protest to these venues is merely an attempt to garner unwarranted media attention by siphoning the attention of the press.[13] Under this view, such protests are not "engagement" but rather an impolite and ineffective form of naked confrontation.[14] Rather than attempt to engage the government in a thoughtful and serious way, they are a mere distraction, perhaps even something of a sideshow.

Although it is certainly true that, in classic forms of petitioning, the petition itself had to be "respectfully" worded in order to be received, little reason exists to deny petitioning speech its character as a petition simply because it is loud, raucous, or inconvenient. Moreover, the effort to precipitate a community-wide discussion of particular issues or concerns by seeking and obtaining media attention hardly seems good reason to refuse to recognize the petitioning character of the speech. From the perspective of Governor George C. Wallace, the Selma-to-Montgomery march was an impolite, and highly inconvenient, commandeering of the public highways, streets, and sidewalks in support of a cause inconsistent with his constituents' views about a properly ordered biracial society. Nevertheless, the Rev. Dr. Martin Luther King Jr. and the Southern Christian Leadership Conference were entitled to engage in their petitioning protest in an effort to change hearts and minds both in Montgomery, Alabama, and in Washington, D.C.[15]

The fact that protest is unlikely to lead to immediate changes in government policy and may attempt to do so through media attention also should not affect the protected status of communication through protest aimed directly at the government and its agents. Change comes slowly in some cases; the fact that petitioning was not immediately successful in securing either the abolition of slavery or the enfranchisement of women should not strip petitioning activity of its protected status.[16] "A petition is nonetheless a petition, though its futility may make martyrdom attractive."[17]

A purposive interpretation of the Petition Clause, as well as history, would suggest that the right of petition encompasses a right of *effective* communication; the ability to communicate in person with someone having a measure of responsibility for the issue in question. Must a petition be limited to the act of handing a piece of parchment to an incumbent legislator? Is petitioning, as Professors Gary Lawson and Guy Seidman have suggested, nothing more than the ability to send a letter or an e-mail to a member of Congress or a state executive official?[18]

If a merely theoretical ability to communicate with government and its agents satisfies the requirements of the Petition Clause, perhaps this is so. But surely Justice Douglas has the better of this argument when he asserts that "[t]he right to petition for the redress of grievances has an ancient history and is not limited to writing a letter or sending a telegram to a congressman" but rather reaches protest activity aimed at communicating directly a message of dissent to the government and its officers.[19] Moreover, as Judge Lipez has suggested, "[t]he more dramatic petition, achieved by public assembly, must also be protected."[20]

It also makes little sense to direct would-be petitioners to submit parchment papers to Congress or the state legislature when these bodies have long since ceased considering petitions as a normal legislative function. In other words, Professors Lawson and Seidman suggest the use of an originalist understanding of petitioning, even though those holding government power no longer honor an originalist duty to receive, consider, and answer citizen petitions.[21] It would be rather odd to interpret and apply the Petition Clause in a fashion that renders it largely useless as a means of accessing and engaging the government. If Congress, and the state legislatures, were to revive the classic form of petitioning recognized and practiced, for example, in contemporary New Zealand,[22] this argument might possess greater persuasive force.

Again, Meiklejohn's laser-like focus on the relation of the First Amendment to the project of democratic self-government seems relevant to the problem. Meiklejohn argued that the First Amendment did not exist merely to advance interests in personal autonomy, or the quest for truth, or some abstract interest in the existence and operation of markets for information and ideas. Instead, Meiklejohn insisted that the First Amendment existed to advance the process and the project of democratic self-government:

The First Amendment does not protect a "freedom to speak." It protects the freedom of those activities of thought and communication by which we "govern." It is concerned, not with a private right, but with a public power, a governmental responsibility.

In the specific language of the Constitution, the governing activities of the people appear only in terms of casting a ballot. But in the deeper meaning of the Constitution, voting is merely the external expression of a wide and diverse number of activities by means of which citizens attempt to meet the responsibilities of making judgments, which that freedom to govern lays upon them.[23]

Thus, democratic self-government requires some level of constant engagement between those holding government office and the people they ostensibly serve, but also among the people themselves.

Meiklejohn worried about the poor levels of civic engagement that exist in the United States, lamenting "how inadequate, to the degree of non-existence, are our public provisions for active discussions among the members of our self-governing society."[24] He argued that "[a]s we try to create and enlarge freedom, universal discussion is imperative" and suggested that "[i]n every village, in every district of every town or city, there should be established at public expense cultural centers inviting all citizens, as they may choose, to meet together for the consideration of public policy."[25]

To be sure, anarchist protestors firebombing a Starbucks café in Seattle, Washington, at the WTO meetings[26] or attempting to storm the 2008 Republican National Convention in St. Paul, Minnesota,[27] probably do not constitute the kind of "democratic engagement" that Meiklejohn has in mind. In fact, he specifically emphasizes that "I am not thinking of such lunatic-fringe activities as those in Hyde Park, in London," but thinking rather "of a self-governing body politic, whose freedom of individual expression should be cultivated, not merely because it serves to prevent outbursts of violence which would result from suppression, but for the positive purpose of bringing every citizen into active and intelligent sharing in the government of his country."[28]

Although I am sympathetic to Meiklejohn's dream of an active and engaged population of policy wonks, considering how best to improve the delivery of public services, I fear that this vision of democratic engagement might be unduly optimistic. In the real world, democratic self-government is messy. It involves intentional misrepresentation of the ideas of one's political opponents, obfuscation, and efforts at outright political deceit. Yet, warts and all, it represents the best hope of securing effective, humane governance. One should not be too quick to reject the benefits of higher levels of democratic engagement, even if the agents of this activity are not up to Meiklejohn's high standards, falling closer to the "lunatic-fringe activities of those in Hyde Park" rather than to the model of Jefferson's engaged and enlightened yeoman farmers.[29]

Moreover, as another commentator has noted, "[t]he petition clause is rooted in the idea that citizens should participate in government decisionmaking."[30] We need to recognize the truth of this observation and restore the Petition Clause, and petitioning, to its proper place as a primary means of facilitating democratic discourse and deliberation. The ability to criticize the government and its policies in ways that directly challenge, and even embarrass, those holding office under its auspices constitutes an important part of our history (particularly the history of the development of civil rights).[31] Directly confronting government officials in an effort to obtain a redress of grievances, whether to secure the abolition of slavery, the enfranchisement of women, or civil rights and voting rights for African American citizens, is an essential part of our democratic history.

The increasing use of ill-defined and unproven security justifications to limit petitioning speech proximate to incumbent government officials, however, threatens to disrupt this long-standing tradition going forward.[32] The problem of security—and the threat of efforts to achieve political change through violence rather than peaceful, and lawful, electoral means—will always be with us. Indeed, a serious commitment to the freedom of speech requires that both society as a whole and its individual members accept some level of risk to facilitate a vibrant marketplace of ideas.

In general, the Supreme Court's First Amendment jurisprudence recognizes this fact and requires communities, particularly minority communities, to shoulder risk in order to facilitate the exercise of expressive freedoms.[33] And any right of access under the Petition Clause to government officials will, necessarily, entail some measure of risk. Terrible occurrences, such as the tragic events in Tucson, Arizona, on Saturday, January 8, 2011, when Jared Lee Loughner, a violently deranged and mentally unstable constituent, attempted to assassinate U.S. Representative Gabrielle Giffords (D-AZ) at a "Congress on Your Corner" public event held at a local Safeway grocery store, demonstrate quite concretely the potential danger that can inhere in interactions between elected officials and the public they serve.[34] But we must take care not to reflexively equate dissent—or dissenters—with the threat of political violence or terrorism.

To say that security concerns can be—and often are—quite legitimate[35] is not to validate any and all invocations of security as a basis for restricting, perhaps to the point of effectively proscribing, hybrid petitioning activities that seek to use traditional public forums near the venues at which major govern-ment or political meetings are to take place. Moreover, Sirhan Sirhan, Lee Harvey Oswald, and John Wilkes Booth were most assuredly *not* demonstrators seeking to express concerns to their duly elected government, via its elected officers, through peaceful expressions of dissent on public streets and sidewalks. Rejecting all forms and instances of political violence, and seeking to prevent such acts, does not imply or require acceptance of flat bans on the most effec-tive means of communicating directly and effectively with incumbent govern-ment officials in real time and in public. The unfortunate and painful history of political violence in the United States should not serve—indeed, must not serve—as a generic license for severing the ties between elected representatives and their constituents in public spaces.

To state the matter simply, the process of democratic self-government requires that elected officials be accessible to and engage with their constituents. As Senator Chuck Schumer (D-NY) explained in the immediate aftermath of the Tucson tragedy, "If we put every senator and congressman behind a thick brick wall and make them completely safe, we wouldn't have the democracy that we have today."[36] Thus, citizen access to government officials and the process of engagement that this access facilitates are simply essential to the ability of the electorate to make meaningful and informed choices on election day. And, unfor-tunately, as former Congressman Paul E. Kanjorski has observed, "[A]ccepting the risk of political violence [is] part of the price of freedom," "there can never be freedom without risk," and "[w]e all lose an element of freedom when security considerations distance public officials from the people."[37]

The indiscriminate use of "security" as a basis for banishing those who dis-agree with incumbent government officials about matters of public policy ill serves both the First Amendment and the process of democratic deliberation.[38] Professor Harry Kalven Jr., an iconic scholar of the First Amendment, posited that "[p]olitical freedom ends when government can use its powers and its courts to silence its critics."[39] Moreover, his "point is not the tepid one that there should be leeway for criticism of the government. It is rather that defamation of the government is an impossible notion for a democracy."[40] A government that is free to invoke security as a basis for denying would-be petitioners access to its officers and agents is a government that has gone a long way toward banishing those who wish to disagree with it—who seek to criticize it in ways likely to catch the attention of the mass media, and thus the attention of the general body politic.

The forgotten right of petition should be reclaimed and deployed as a shield against efforts to brush aside those who seek to speak truth to power. The ability to communicate concerns directly with the government is no less essential to the processes of democratic self-government than the ability to criticize the government more generally.[41] Moreover, petitioning speech facilitates and helps to secure democratic accountability through elections; the ability to petition, to access the officers of government, permits citizens to demand change directly and then to reward, or punish, elected officials depending on their responsiveness (or lack of it). Indeed, the right of petition is a corollary of the right to vote; the former permits citizens to inform their elected officials of their concerns and problems, whereas the latter enables them to hold elected officials accountable for their response (or lack of one).

In the post-9/11 world, it may seem optimistic, even naive, to posit a right of access to the government and its officers on the part of ordinary people. Yet, as Professor Meiklejohn argued, it is precisely these ordinary people who are charged with keeping the government honest and within the channels of its constitutional authority. If citizens cannot access their government and its officials in a meaningful way, their ability to oversee government's operation and activities will be the poorer for it. To be sure, access entails risk, but surely it cannot be said that any and all forms of access entail undue risk, particularly when the government seems to have little trouble providing security for invited audiences at mass participation political events.[42]

In the end, I think that Judge Frank M. Johnson Jr. had it right as he weighed the merits of facilitating a mass protest march from Selma, Alabama, to the state capitol grounds in Montgomery, Alabama. The level of disruption to the community would be great, even assuming that it did not provoke social unrest or violence from a hostile community; the simple fact of the march itself would be a major disruption to those seeking to use the highway and roads in question for their usual purposes. Even so, Judge Johnson concluded that the right of petition justified imposing this cost and assuming this risk: "[T]he law in this country constitutionally guarantees that a citizen or a group of citizens may assemble and petition their government, or their governmental authorities, for redress of their grievances even by mass demonstrations as long as the exercise of these rights is peaceful. The rights may also be exercised by marching, even along public highways, as long as it is done in an orderly and peaceful manner; and these rights to assemble, demonstrate and march are not to be abridged."[43] Thus, in a democratic polity like the United States, a strong presumption should exist at all levels of government, and particularly within the federal courts, in favor of the proposition that citizens have a right to access and engage their elected government officials.

Liberty and security always coexist in a constant state of tension; achieving perfect or absolute security of the state and its officers can only come at the potential price of compromising, perhaps fatally, our collective commitment to democratic self-governance and freedom of expression. Reclaiming the Petition Clause can and should constitute an important first step in establishing an effective doctrinal and theoretical bulwark that safeguards the right of We the People to actually access and engage our government in a meaningful fashion.

NOTES

1. THE GROWING MARGINALIZATION OF DISSENT AND THE NEW SEDITIOUS LIBEL

1. Adderley v. Florida, 385 U.S. 39, 50–51 (1966) (Douglas, J., dissenting).
2. Peggy Noonan, *The Town Hall Revolt, One Year Later*, WALL ST. J., July 10–11, 2010, at A13.
3. *See* Janet Adamy & Naftali BenDavid, *Lawmakers Rethink Town Halls*, WALL. ST. J., Aug. 8–9, 2009, at A5 (noting that "after a series of contentious town-hall meetings, some Democratic lawmakers are thinking twice about holding large public gatherings" and instead "are opting for smaller meetings by phone or inviting constituents for one-on-one office hours"). To be sure, not all members of Congress responded to the raucous public meetings by canceling public events or limiting access to hand-selected audiences. *See id.* ("Rep. Lloyd Doggett (D, Texas), who was recently heckled over health care at a supermarket, said he would attend a veterans-center opening, a community-health event and a meeting with Austin public school teachers in coming days.")
4. Jeff Zeleny, *Sidestepping Displays of Rage, Democrats Forgo Town Halls*, N.Y. TIMES, June 7, 2010, at A1.
5. *See* Max Schulz, *A Town-Hall Protest in Maryland*, WALL ST. J., Aug. 8–9, 2009, at A11 ("By tradition, town-hall meetings are sedate, boring, sparsely attended affairs."); *see also* Sheryl Gay Stolberg, *Where Have You Gone, Joe the Citizen?*, N.Y. TIMES, Aug. 9, 2009, at WK1–2 (noting that "[c]itizen gatherings, of course, are as old as the republic itself, but as a form of constituent relations town hall meetings are relatively new" and tracing the history and practice of constituent meetings from the 1950s to the present).
6. *See* Noonan, *supra* note 2, at A13 ("It was a real pushback, and it was fueled by indignation."). For contemporary accounts of the rambunctious town hall meetings of summer and fall 2009, see Associated Press, *Longtime advocate slams health care protests*, PALM BEACH POST (Florida), Aug. 8, 2009, at A3 (reporting on Rep. John Dingell's displeasure with confrontational constituents at town hall meetings in his district and

noting that "[t]he boos, jeers and shouts of 'Shame on you!' at the events in a gym in Romulus, Mich., mirror what other Democrats are encountering around the country but are particularly striking because of Dingell's stature"); Paul Krugman, *The Town Hall Mob*, N.Y. TIMES, Aug. 7, 2009, at A17 (describing the angry protestors at town hall meetings, observing that "I haven't seen any evidence that the people disrupting those town halls are Florida-style rent-a-mobs," and noting that "[f]or the most part, the protesters appear to be genuinely angry"); Ian Urbina, *Beyond Beltway, Health Debate Turns Hostile*, N.Y. Times, Aug. 8, 2009, at A1, A10 ("The bitter divisions over an overhaul of the health care system have exploded at town hall meetings over the last few days as members of Congress have been shouted down, hanged in effigy and taunted by crowds.").

7. Zeleny, *supra* note 4, at A1.

8. *Id.*

9. *See id.* at A1, A11 (noting that "the opportunities for voters to openly express their displeasure, or angrily vent as video cameras roll, have been harder to come by in this election year" and observing that the dearth of unticketed constituent town hall meetings since 2009 "was no scheduling accident").

10. Another aspect of the problem involves the obvious "astroturf" nature of some of the protests at "Congress on Your Corner" events, at which organized lobbyists and leaders of the opposition party participated in the heckling. *See* Stolberg, *supra* note 5, at WK1–2. As one commentator has aptly noted, "If the pattern continues, lawmakers could grow suspicious, refusing to believe that their encounters with voters are genuine." *Id.* at WK2.

11. *See infra* chapter 2.

12. For example, the official Secret Service presidential advance manual issued during the George W. Bush administration defines "protesters" as a threat to the security of the president if within the "view of the event site or motorcade route." OFFICE OF PRESIDENTIAL ADVANCE, PRESIDENTIAL ADVANCE MANUAL 34 (2002), *available at* http://www.aclu.org/pdfs/freespeech/ presidential _advance_manual.pdf (last visited April 14, 2010) [hereinafter "PRESIDENTIAL ADVANCE MANUAL"]. It is unclear whether the Obama administration has maintained these policies or similar policies since taking office in January 2009.

13. *See* Kirk Johnson, *Cheney Deposition Is Ordered in Lawsuit by Protester*, N.Y. TIMES, Mar. 3, 2009, at A13. Steven Howards had the temerity to approach Vice President Dick Cheney while Cheney was in a public area of a Colorado ski resort; Howards told Cheney that "the administration's policies in Iraq were disgusting, or words to that effect." *Id.* Although Howards was initially permitted to walk away from the vice president, 'Secret Service agents arrested him "about 10 minutes later for what they said was the 'assault' on the vice president." *Id.* The charges were later dropped, and Mr. Howards initiated a lawsuit against the Secret Service for a violation of his civil rights.

14. PRESIDENTIAL ADVANCE MANUAL, *supra* note 12, at 34–35; *see also id.* at 34 (helpfully observing that "[t]here are several ways the advance person can prepare a site to minimize demonstrators").

15. *Id.* at 34.

16. Sadly, it appears that all presidential administrations, regardless of political party, seem prone to suppress bad news whenever possible. For example, on June 30, 2010, the Coast Guard Unified Command responding to the Deep Water Horizon oil spill disaster issued regulations that prohibited anyone, including journalists, from coming within sixty-five feet (twenty meters) of *any* Deepwater Horizon oil disaster recovery operation, including, for example, beach clean-up operations and oil-resistant booms placed in coastal waters. *See* Deepwater Horizon Incident Joint Information Center, *Coast Guard establishes 20-meter safety zone around all Deepwater Horizon protective boom operations,* June 30, 2010, *available at* http://www.deepwaterhorizonresponse. com/go/doc/2931/726955/ (last visited on July 15, 2010); *see also* Chris Kirkham, *Coast Guard puts up 65-foot cleanup buffer; News media, public can't get close,* TIMES-PICAYUNE (New Orleans), July 2, 2010, at A9. The Federal Aviation Administration also banned flights below three thousand feet proximate to the spill or recovery efforts. *Id.* On July 12, 2010, after intense public criticism, the Coast Guard revised the policy to permit "credentialed media" more liberal access to clean-up sites. *See* Deepwater Horizon Incident Joint Information Center, *Coast Guard Announces New Procedures for Media Access to Boom Safety Zones,* July 12, 2010, *available at* http://www.deepwaterhorizonresponse.com/go/doc/2931/777343/ (last visited on July 15, 2010); *see also* Chris Kirkham, *Media allowed to enter "safety zones,"* TIMES-PICAYUNE (New Orleans), July 14, 2010, at A6. While in effect, the directive had the effect of rendering it virtually impossible to photograph the effects of the spill on both wildlife and beaches along the central Gulf Coast.

17. *See* Bl(a)ck Tea Soc'y v. City of Boston, 378 F.3d 8, 13–14 (1st Cir. 2004); Citizens for Peace in Space v. City of Colorado Springs, 477 F.3d 1212, 1225 (10th Cir. 2007). As the federal district court considering limits on protests and marches proximate to the Xcel Energy Center, in St. Paul, Minnesota, during the 2008 Republican National Convention explained, the would-be protestors "ha[ve] no constitutional right to physical access to the delegates." The Coalition to March on the RNC and Stop the War v. City of St. Paul, 557 F. Supp. 2d 1014, 1031 (D. Minn. 2008).

18. McCullen v. Coakley, 571 F.3d 167, 180 (1st Cir. 2009), *cert. denied,* 130 S. Ct. 1881 (2010).

19. *Id.*

20. *Bl(a)ck Tea Soc'y,* 378 F.3d at 13–14.

21. U.S. CONST. amend. I.

22. *Id.*

23. 1 ANNALS OF CONG. 434 (Joseph Gales & William Winston Gales eds., 1834) (June 8, 1789).

24. *Id.*

25. *See* Peter Fraser, *Public Petitioning and Parliament before 1832,* 46 HISTORY 195, 200–201 (1961). Professor Fraser explains the very direct linkage between assembly and petitioning in the United Kingdom, from which the U.S. petitioning culture developed:

> In the eighteenth century the only really legitimate form of public meeting at which any alteration in church or state could be considered was a county meeting

convened by the gentry, or in London a meeting of the Common Council. Only such meetings could legally petition the King or either House of Parliament with more than twenty signatures in favour of political change... The prohibition operated as an effective check on all political petitioning well into the eighteenth century. What few cases there were—and they can be counted on one hand—afford examples of the severity with which Parliament treated any interference in its affairs.

Id. To be sure, assembly and petitioning in the colonies were much more common-place, and not subject to punishment, such that petitioning was the primary source of colonial legislation in Virginia and Massachusetts. *See* RAYMOND C. BAILEY, POPULAR INFLUENCE UPON PUBLIC POLICY: PETITIONING IN EIGHTEENTH CENTURY VIRGINIA 6, 23–31 (1979); ROBERT LUCE, LEGISLATIVE PRINCIPLES: THE HISTORY AND THEORY OF LAWMAKING BY REPRESENTATIVE GOVERNMENT 519–28 (1930). Professor Bailey reports that "far more eighteenth century laws originated directly in response to these petitions than from any other source." Bailey, *supra*, at 6.

26. WILLIAM STUBBS, 2 THE CONSTITUTIONAL HISTORY OF ENGLAND 602 (1880).
27. James E. Pfander, *Sovereign Immunity and the Right to Petition: Toward a First Amendment Right to Pursue Claims Against the Government*, 91 Nw. U.L. Rev. 899, 905 n.22 (1997); Julie M. Spanbauer, *The First Amendment Right to Petition Government for a Redress of Grievances: Cut From a Different Cloth*, 21 HASTINGS CONST. L.Q. 15, 33 38, 49 (1993). As Professor Spanbauer succinctly states the proposition, "Inherent in the right to petition was a corresponding right to a response." *Id.* at 33.
28. *See infra* chapter 3.
29. *See infra* chapter 5.
30. *See, e.g.,* United States v. Playboy Entertainment Group, 529 U.S. 803 (2000) (holding that the distribution of sexually explicit indecent programming on subscription cable channels constitutes protected speech for purposes of the First Amendment); 44 Liquormart v. Rhode Island, 517 U.S. 484 (1996) (holding that the Free Speech Clause protects competitive price advertising for alcoholic beverages); Sable Communications, Inc. v. FCC, 492 U.S. 115 (1989) (holding that the Free Speech Clause protects the commercial operation of "dial-a-porn" telephone entertainment services). *Cf.* Valentine v. Chrestensen, 316 U.S. 52 (1942) (holding that commercial advertising handbills do not enjoy any First Amendment protection as speech but rather constitute merely an aspect of commerce). The Supreme Court has declined to apply an original-ist interpretative methodology to either the scope of the Free Speech Clause or to its potential applications to communication. An originalist approach, for example, would likely exclude, categorically, commercial speech from protection. Indeed, it was not until the 1970s that the Supreme Court definitively held that commercial advertising enjoys any serious First Amendment protection at all. *See* Central Hudson Gas & Elec. Corp. v. Public Serv. Comm'n, 447 U.S. 557 (1980). Similarly, it is doubtful that James Madison would have understood the Free Speech Clause to protect the commercial purveyance of either sexually explicit cable television programming or naughty tele-phone chat lines. Nevertheless, the Supreme Court, including ostensibly textualist and

originalist justices, such as Antonin Scalia and Clarence Thomas, have interpreted the Free Speech Clause in a dynamic and purposive fashion. Accordingly, rather than asking how the framing generation would have asked and answered particular free speech problems, they instead read the Free Speech Clause as creating a broad mandate for open speech markets free and clear of direct government regulation that proscribes speech based on either its viewpoint or content. Thus, the central meaning of the Free Speech Clause is to be found not in the Sedition Act of 1798, or the writings of George Washington and John Adams, but rather by considering the role and importance of a free and open marketplace of ideas, in which private parties, rather than the government, establish the relative priority and value of different kinds of speech.

31. *See* David Jenkins, *The Sedition Act of 1798 and the Incorporation of Seditious Libel into First Amendment Jurisprudence*, 45 AM. J. LEG. HIST. 154, 170–71 (2001); *see also* James P. Martin, *When Repression Is Democratic and Constitutional: The Federalist Theory of Representation and the Sedition Act of 1798*, 66 U. CHI. L. REV. 117, 126–27, 139, 145–50, 160–61 (1999) (describing the Federalist Party's strong support of the doctrine of seditious libel and also how party members believed the doctrine to be essential to the functioning of democratic self-government). As Martin notes, the Federalist Party and its leaders "tenaciously" defended the proposition that "protecting the reputation of rulers and repressing political associations were necessary to representative government," including the related idea "that opposing and campaigning against government was undemocratic since the majority had elected the government to make policy decisions." *Id.* at 126–27.

32. Jenkins, *supra* note 31, at 178–79; Martin, *supra* note 31, at 126–27, 149–50. Martin explains that "[t]hroughout Federalist literature, the obligation to support the laws and Constitution of the country was consistently confounded with the obligation to support the current administration." *Id.* at 150.

33. James Morton Smith, *The Sedition Law, Free Speech, and the American Political Process*, 9 WM. & MARY. Q. 497, 499–500 (1952). Martin helpfully observes that "[u]nder this conception, it is clear that opposition to the policies of the government was tantamount to opposing both representative government and the Constitution itself." Martin, *supra* note 31, at 149. Moreover, "Federalist theory . . . found expression in the charge that opposition to [the] government was a traitorous attempt to defeat the will of the people." *Id.* at 139.

34. *See infra* chapter 4.

35. *See id.* at section III.C., text and accompanying notes 209–46.

36. *See* Johnson, *supra* note 13, at A12.

37. Paul E. Kanjorski, *Why Politicians Need to Stay Out in the Open*, N.Y. TIMES, Jan. 11, 2011, at A23.

38. *Id.*

39. *Id.*

40. Sam Dolnick, Katherine Q. Seelye, & Adam Nagourney, *In Giffords's District, a Long History of Tension*, N.Y. TIMES, Jan. 11, 2011, at A1; Darren Everson and Angel Gonzalez, *Sorrow Racks Tucson After Killings*, WALL ST. J., Jan. 10, 2011, at A4; Eric Lipton, Charlie Savage, & Jennifer Steinhauer, *Congress Weighs Enhanced Security*, N.Y.

TIMES, Jan. 11, 2011, at A18; Jennifer Medina, *At Victim's School, Shock, Sorrow and Nightmares*, N.Y. TIMES, Jan. 11, 2011, at A17. The six victims also included Gabriel Zimmerman, 30, Dorothy Morris, 76, Dorwin Stoddard, 76, and Phyllis Schneck, 79. *The Six Who Died*, STAR TRIB. (Minneapolis, MN), Jan. 10, 2011, at A5.

41. John R. Emshwiller, Devlin Barrett, & Charles Forelle, *Suspect Fixated on Giffords*, WALL ST. J., Jan. 10, 2011, at A1, A4; News Services, *Routine event turned deadly fast*, STAR TRIB. (Minneapolis, MN), Jan. 10, 2011, at A4. In fact, Loughner attempted to reload his weapon, a thirty-one-round semi-automatic Glock, and continue shooting, but persons attending the event successfully subdued Loughner and prevented any further injuries or deaths. *See id.*

42. Shaun McKinnon, *Collision Course Toward Morning*, ARIZ. REPUBLIC (Phoenix), Feb. 6, 2011, at A18 ("On Jan. 5, Giffords stood in the House chamber on Capitol Hill, repeating the oath of an office she had fought so hard to keep. When the Republicans staged an opening-week reading of the Constitution aloud on the House floor, Giffords joined in and proudly read the First Amendment."); *see also* Editorial, *After shooting spree in Tucson, time to tone down the vitriol*, USA TODAY, Jan. 10, 2011, at A8 ("As one of her last official acts before the shooting, Giffords, a 40-year-old centrist Democrat, read the First Amendment to the Constitution on the House floor. The parts about freedom of assembly and the right to petition the government for the redress of grievances, which she was fulfilling with her meet-and-greet for constituents outside the Safeway. And, of course, the part about freedom of speech.").

43. Jennifer Steinhauer, *Constitution Has Its Day (More or Less) in House*, N.Y. TIMES, Jan. 7, 2011, at A15 ("'I just read the First Amendment!' Representative Gabrielle Giffords, an Arizona Democrat, said gleefully as she exited the floor. 'I wanted to be here, I think it's important,' Ms. Giffords said. 'Reflecting on the Constitution in a bipartisan way is a good way to start the year.'").

44. *See* Mark Z. Barbarak, Lisa Mascaro & Robin Abcarian, *A Calm Voice in a Divided District; Giffords Had Brushes with Danger Before; Friends Say She Was Always Undaunted*, L.A. TIMES, Jan. 9, 2011, at A12 ("According to the National Journal, Giffords made 340 appearances in her district in her first term.").

45. Kanjorski, *supra* note 37, at A23.

46. *See* United Mine Workers of America v. Pennington, 381 U.S. 657 (1965); Eastern Railroad Presidents Conference v. Noerr Motor Freight, Inc., 365 U.S. 127 (1965).

47. *See* Pfander, *supra* note 27; *see also* Carol Rice Andrews, *A Right of Access to Court Under the Petition Clause of the First Amendment: Defining the Right*, 60 OHIO ST. L.J. 557 (1999).

48. *See* William C. diGiacomantonio, *Petitioners and Their Grievances: A View From the First Federal Congress, in* THE HOUSE AND SENATE IN THE 1790s: PETITIONING, LOBBYING, AND INSTITUTIONAL DEVELOPMENT 31–35 (Kenneth R. Bowling & Donald R. Kennon eds., 2002). Professor diGiacomantonio provides a comprehensive overview of the subject matter of petitions filed in Congress during the Federalist era, 1789–1801, *see id.* at 29–56.

49. *Id.* at 36–37; *see also* Jeffrey L. Pasley, *Private Access and Public Power: Gentility and Lobbying in the Early Congress, in* Bowling & Kennon, *supra* note 48, at 57, 64–66.

Pasley reports that "[b]y far the most elaborate petition and lobbying campaign in the First Congress (and probably for the rest of the 1790s as well) was that mounted against slavery by Philadelphia-area Quakers." *Id.* at 64.

50. *Id.* at 64–66.

51. *Id.* at 65. One should note, however, that "[s]triking as it was, the Quaker antislavery lobby failed." *Id.* at 66.

52. *See infra* chapter 4, section II.

53. I am indebted to former University of Oregon president and current professor of law David Frohnmeyer for calling this fact to my attention at a workshop presentation to the University of Oregon law faculty on October 21, 2009.

54. *See* Williams v. Wallace, 240 F. Supp. 100, 121 (M.D. Ala. 1965).

55. *See infra* chapter 6.

56. *Id.*

57. *See Williams,* 240 F. Supp. at 106–07.

58. *See* Owen M. Fiss, *Silence on the Street Corner,* 26 SUFFOLK U. L. REV. 1, 3–18 (1992); *see also* OWEN M. FISS, THE IRONY OF FREE SPEECH (1996); OWEN M. FISS, LIBERALISM DIVIDED: FREEDOM OF SPEECH AND THE MANY USES OF STATE POWER (1996).

59. *See* ALEXANDER MEIKLEJOHN, FREE SPEECH AND ITS RELATION TO SELF-GOVERNMENT 11–12 (1948); Alexander Meiklejohn, *The First Amendment Is an Absolute,* 1961 SUP. CT. REV. 245, 255.

60. *Compare* Rumsfeld v. Forum for Academic and Inst'l Rights, Inc., 547 U.S. 47, 68–70 (2006) (holding that the First Amendment affords protection to free association through a "right of expressive association" because the "right to speak is often exercised most effectively by combining one's voice with the voices of others" and that if "the government were free to restrict individuals' ability to join together and speak, it could essentially silence views that the First Amendment is intended to protect"); Boy Scouts of America v. Dale, 530 U.S. 640, 647–48 (2000) (reaffirming a First Amendment right to free association and holding that "this right is crucial in preventing the majority from imposing its views on groups that would rather express other, perhaps unpopular, ideas") *with* McDonald v. Smith, 472 U.S. 479, 482, 485 (1985) (holding that "[t]he right to petition is cut from the same cloth as the other guarantees of th[e First] Amendment," that the rights protected in the First Amendment "are inseparable" for purposes of defining and protecting expressive freedoms, and concluding that "there is no sound basis for granting greater constitutional protection to statements made in a petition to the President than other First Amendment expressions").

61. THEODORE D. WOOLSEY, 1 POLITICAL SCIENCE OR THE STATE: THEORETICALLY AND PRACTICALLY CONSIDERED § 92, at 270 (1878).

62. *Id.*

63. *See infra* chapter 2.

64. *See* Ward v. Rock Against Racism, 491 U.S. 781, 791 (1989).

65. *See, e.g.,* Phred Dvorak & Monica Gutschi, *Protests Rock Toronto Despite Security; After a $1 Billion Safety Effort, Police Struggle to Halt Violence Near Meetings, Arresting Nearly 600 Over the Weekend,* WALL ST. J., June 28, 2010, at A14. Both

national and local law enforcement authorities feared that anarchist protestors might attempt to disrupt the G20 summit and attempted to devise a plan that would ensure the security of the meeting. *See* Phred Dvorak, *Toronto Locks Down Its Downtown for G-20*, WALL ST. J., June 26–27, 2010, at A9. The sad truth, however, is that violence, rioting, and even looting occurred in downtown Toronto even with the massive security effort, and persons seeking to express dissent peacefully were entirely silenced. *See* Dvorak & Gutschi, *supra*, at A14. Police "detained many [peaceful] activists in mass arrests during demonstrations at a park and downtown hotel." *Id*. In fact, police arrested and detained monitors from the Canadian Civil Liberties Association, leading the organization's general counsel to opine that "the police response 'seems to have spiraled out of proportion.'" *Id*. On the other hand, local authorities did permit a large organized march more-or-less proximate to the meeting venue zone; this march "went off peacefully" and featured participants from "Greenpeace, Oxfam, and the Canadian Labour Congress." *Id*. These same conflicts between accommodating peaceful protest and avoiding violence have become endemic at virtually all major political and governmental meetings. *See, e.g.*, Patrick Healy & Colin Moynihan, *As Throngs of Protesters Hit Streets, Dozens Are Arrested After Clashes*, N.Y. TIMES, Sept. 2, 2008, at A20 (describing melees between law enforcement officers and anarchist protestors in St. Paul, Minnesota, during the 2008 Republican National Convention, but also including mass arrests of peaceful protestors and journalists not involved in unlawful conduct).

66. *See infra* chapter 3.
67. Consider that the Australian federal High Court, interpreting a constitution that does not include a written bill of rights of any kind, nevertheless inferred a right to free speech from the Australian Constitution's guarantee of a democratic form of government with meaningful free and fair elections. Lange v. Australian Broad. Corp., (1997) 189 C.L.R. 556 (Austl.); Australian Capital Tele. v. Commonwealth, (1992) 177 C.L.R. 144 (Austl.); Adrienne Stone, *Australia's Constitutional Rights and the Problem of Interpretive Disagreement*, 27 SYDNEY L. REV. 29, 34 (2005). It is simply impossible to maintain a functioning democracy without the ability of citizens to engage in free speech about the government.
68. *See infra* chapter 2.
69. *See infra* chapter 3.
70. *See infra* chapter 4.
71. *See infra* chapter 5.
72. 240 F. Supp. 100 (M.D. Ala. 1965).
73. *See infra* chapter 6.
74. *See generally* MEIKLEJOHN, FREE SPEECH, *supra* note 59, at 12–27.
75. *See Disaster; Brown Apologizes for Calling Voter "Bigoted,"* FINANCIAL TIMES, Apr. 29, 2010, at 1.
76. *PM Apologizes Over "Bigot" Gaffe*, FINANCIAL TIMES, Apr. 29, 2010, at 3.
77. *Id*.

CHAPTER 2. THE GROWING LOSS OF PUBLIC SPACE FOR COLLECTIVE EXPRESSION
OF DISSENT AND THE FAILURE OF CONTEMPORARY FIRST AMENDMENT DOCTRINE
TO ADDRESS THIS PROBLEMATIC PHENOMENON

1. Coalition to Protest the Democratic National Convention v. City of Boston, 327 F. Supp. 2d 61 (D. Mass. 2004), *aff'd sub nom.*, Bl(a)ck Tea Society v. City of Boston, 378 F.3d 8 (1st Cir. 2004).
2. *Id.* at 67.
3. *Id.* at 76. The court continued, "It is a brutish and potentially unsafe place for citizens who wish to exercise their First Amendment rights." *Id.* The court also compared the appearance of the DZ to "that of an internment camp," described the situation as "irretrievably sad," and stated that "the DZ conveys the symbolic sense of a holding pen where potentially dangerous persons are separated from others. Indeed, one cannot conceive of what other design elements could be put into a space to create more of a symbolic affront to the role of free expression." *Id.* at 74–75, 77.
4. *Id.* at 76.
5. Bl(a)ck Tea Soc'y v. City of Boston, 378 F.3d 8, 15 (1st Cir. 2004). The First Circuit did not dispute the district court's factual assessment of the shocking character of the DZ but nevertheless affirmed the district court's legal conclusion that the DZ was constitutional. *Id.; see also infra* section III.A. (discussing *Bl(a)ck Tea Society*).
6. *Bl(a)ck Tea Soc'y*, 378 F.3d 8, 13 (1st Cir. 2004).
7. *Id.* at 13–14 (noting that "[t]he appellant points out, correctly, that there is no evidence in the record that the City had information indicating that demonstrators intended to use [unlawful] tactics at the Convention" but nevertheless concluding that "[w]e do not believe a per se rule barring the government from using past experience to plan for future events is consistent with the approach adopted in the Court's time-place-manner jurisprudence").
8. *Cf.* Williams v. Wallace, 240 F. Supp. 100, 105–06, 108–09 (M.D. Ala. 1965) (issuing injunction to facilitate the famous Selma-to-Montgomery civil rights protest march, even though a march of this scale and scope would create serious security risks and disruptions for persons seeking to use the U.S. highway between Selma and Montgomery for its more usual purpose of intercity travel). For a discussion and defense of how Judge Frank M. Johnson Jr. deployed creative legal reasoning in aid of the right to petition for a redress of grievances, see chapter 6. *See also* Ronald J. Krotoszynski Jr., *Celebrating Selma: The Importance of Context in Public Forum Analysis*, 104 YALE L.J. 1411, 1420–32 (1995).
9. *Cf.* Schneider v. State, 308 U.S. 147, 162 (1939) (holding that government may not ban leafleting, even though some persons who receive leaflets choose to litter the streets with them, because permitting the government to punish the speaker for the bad behavior of others would essentially permit a hostile mob to silence core political speech with the government's active assistance).
10. Menotti v. Seattle, 409 F.3d 1113, 1131–32 (9th Cir. 2004) ("The City also had an interest in seeing that the WTO delegates had the opportunity to conduct their business at the chosen venue for the conference; a city that failed to achieve this

interest would not soon have the chance to host another important international meeting.").

11. *Cf.* OFFICE OF PRESIDENTIAL ADVANCE, PRESIDENTIAL ADVANCE MANUAL 34 (2002) (instructing those responsible for preparing a site for a presidential appearance to have the Secret Service "ask the local police department to designate a protest area where demonstrators can be placed, preferably not in view of the event site or motorcade route"), *available at* http://www.aclu.org/pdfs/freespeech/presidential_advance_manual.pdf. (last visited on Sept. 18, 2010). Another tactic for "dealing with demonstrators" advocated in the recently released (and heavily redacted) PRESIDENTIAL ADVANCE MANUAL is the formation of "rally squads"—small groups of presidential supporters who "spread favorable messages using large hand held signs, placards, or perhaps a long sheet banner." *Id.* The rally squads "should be instructed always to look for demonstrators. The rally squad's task is to use their signs and banners as shields *between the demonstrators and the main press platform.* If the demonstrators are yelling, rally squads can begin and lead supportive chants to drown out the protestors (USA!, USA!, USA!)." *Id.* (emphasis added). Elsewhere, the MANUAL instructs that "[i]f it is determined that the media will not see or hear them [demonstrators], and that they pose no potential disruption to the event, they can be ignored." *Id.* at 35.

12. *See infra* chapter 2, sections A. and B., text and accompanying notes 27–80.

13. *See infra* chapter 2, section III.

14. *See* Mary Cheh, *Demonstrations, Security Zones, and First Amendment Protection of Special Places,* 8 D.C. L. REV. 53 (2004); Thomas P. Crocker, *Displacing Dissent: The Role of "Place" in First Amendment Jurisprudence,* 75 FORDHAM L. REV. 2587 (2007); Joseph Herrold, *Capturing the Dialogue: Free Speech Zones and the "Cage" of First Amendment Rights,* 54 DRAKE L. REV. 949 (2005); Tabetha Abu El-Haj, *The Neglected Right of Assembly,* 56 UCLA L. REV. 543, 544–45, 587–88 (2009); James J. Knicely & John W. Whitehead, *The Caging of Free Speech in America,* 14 TEMP. POL. & CIV. RTS. L. REV. 455 (2004); Aaron Perrine, *The First Amendment Versus the World Trade Organization: Emergency Powers and the Battle in Seattle,* 76 WASH. L. REV. 635 (2001); Timothy Zick, *Space, Place, and Speech: The Expressive Topography,* 74 GEO. WASH. L. REV. 439 (2006); Timothy Zick, *Speech and Spacial Tactics,* 84 TEX. L. REV. 581 (2006); *see also* Michael J. Hampson, Note, *Protesting the President: Free Speech Zones and the First Amendment,* 58 RUTGERS L. REV. 245 (2005); Susan Rachel Nanes, Comment, *"The Constitutional Infringement Zone": Protest Pens and Demonstration Zones at the 2004 National Political Conventions,* 66 LA. L. REV. 189, 215–18 (2005); Joshua Rissman, *Put It on Ice: Chilling Free Speech at National Conventions,* 27 LAW & INEQUALITY 413, 416–20, 439–40 (2009); Nick Suplina, Note, *Crowd Control: The Troubling Mix of First Amendment Law, Political Demonstrations, and Terrorism,* 73 GEO. WASH. L. REV. 395, 402 (2005); Nicole C. Winnett, Note, *Don't Fence Us In: First Amendment Right to Freedom of Assembly and Speech,* 3 First Amendment L. Rev. 465 (2004).

15. Coalition to Protest the Democratic National Convention v. City of Boston, 327 F. Supp. 61, 67 (D. Mass. 2004), *aff'd sub nom.,* Bl(a)ck Tea Soc'y v. City of Boston, 378 F.3d 8 (1st Cir. 2004).

16. *See* ACLU of Colo. v. City and County of Denver, 569 F. Supp. 1142, 1181–89 (D. Colo. 2008); Coalition to March on the RNC & Stop the War v. City of St. Paul, 557 F. Supp. 1014, 1028–31 (D. Minn. 2008). For a critical analysis of the decision associated with the proposed protests at the 2008 GOP national convention in St. Paul, Minnesota, see Rissman, *supra* note 14, at 413–20, 426–27, 439–40.

17. In *Ward v. Rock Against Racism*, 491 U.S. 781 (1989), the Supreme Court held that time, place, and manner restrictions on speech are consistent with the Free Speech and Free Assembly Clauses of the First Amendment if the regulations "are justified without reference to the content of the regulated speech," "narrowly tailored to serve a significant government interest," and "leave open ample alternative channels for communication of the information." *Id.* at 791. Security of the government officials and those attending mass political meetings and conventions clearly satisfies the "significant government interest" aspect of the second prong. And, in practice, the content neutrality requirement reduces to a mere requirement that the speech ban not name any particular speakers but rather banishes all potential speakers (even though those supporting the Democratic Party are not likely to protest their own convention). The hardest part of the test for government to meet should be the "ample alternative channels of communication prong," but even this is but a speed bump: "[A]lthough the opportunity to interact directly with the body of delegates by, say, moving among them and distributing literature, would doubtless have facilitated the demonstrators' ability to reach their intended audience, there is no constitutional requirement that demonstrators be granted that sort of particularized access." *Bl(a)ck Tea Soc'y*, 378 F.3d at 14.

18. For a psychological explanation of this and similar judicial phenomena, *see generally* Christina E. Wells, *Fear and Loathing in Constitutional Decision-Making*, 2005 WIS. L. REV. 115 (explaining how the psychology of threat perception and risk assessment affect judicial decision making); *see also* Vincent Blasi, *The Pathological Perspective and the First Amendment*, 85 COLUM. L. REV. 449 (1985) (arguing that federal courts should be most vigilant in protecting speech rights in times of national emergency precisely because it is at such times that the political process is likely to overreact to perceived threats and adopt measures that have the effect of silencing public discourse at a time when full and robust public debate is most essential to wise policy making).

19. *See* U.S. CONST. amend I ("Congress shall make no law . . . abridging . . . the right of the people . . . to petition the Government for a redress of grievances.").

20. *Cf.* WILLIAM VAN ALSTYNE, THE AMERICAN FIRST AMENDMENT IN THE TWENTY-FIRST CENTURY: CASES AND MATERIALS 27–29 (4th ed. 2011). Although Professor Van Alstyne's well-regarded casebook mentions and quotes the Petition Clause in the introductory materials, it does not include even a single principal case related to the clause, such as *McDonald v. Smith*, 472 U.S. 479 (1985), the Supreme Court's last major general decision considering the scope and meaning of the Petition Clause. *Cf. id.* at xxix (omitting *McDonald* from the table of cases). In this way, the Van Alstyne casebook seems to confirm, rather than refute, the general trend of minimizing the relevance of the Petition Clause.

21. *See infra* chapter 5.

22. *See* Steven H. Shiffrin, Dissent, Injustice, and the Meanings of America 24–31, 57–67 (1999).

23. *See* Brandenburg v. Ohio, 395 U.S. 444, 447–49 (1969) (holding protected advocacy of the violent overthrow of the government and a race war unless government establishes, by clear and convincing evidence, a "clear and present danger of imminent lawlessness"); *see also* Hustler Magazine v. Falwell, 485 U.S. 46, 53 (1988) ("[I]n the world of debate about public affairs, many things done with motives that are less than admirable are protected by the First Amendment. . . [Although] such a bad motive may be deemed controlling for purposes of tort liability in other areas of the law, we think the First Amendment prohibits such a result in the area of public debate about public figures."); Perry Educ. Ass'n v. Perry Local Educators' Ass'n, 460 U.S. 37, 45 (1983) ("In places which by long tradition or by government fiat have been devoted to assembly and debate, the rights of the State to limit expressive activity are sharply circumscribed. . . In these quintessential public forums, the government may not prohibit all communicative activity."); FCC v. Pacifica Found, 438 U.S. 726, 745–46 (1978) ("If there were any reason to believe that the Commission's characterization of the Carlin monologue as offensive could be traced to its political content. . . First Amendment protection might be required."); N.Y. Times Co. v. Sullivan, 376 U.S. 254, 270 (1964) ("[We] consider this case against the background of a profound national commitment to the principle that debate on public issues should be uninhibited, robust, and wide-open, and that it may well include vehement, caustic, and sometimes unpleasantly sharp attacks on government and public officials."); De Jonge v. Oregon, 299 U.S. 353, 365 (1937) ("[I]mperative is the need to preserve inviolate the constitutional rights of free speech, free press and free assembly in order to maintain the opportunity for free political discussion. . . Therein lies the security of the Republic, the very foundation of constitutional government."); Whitney v. California, 274 U.S. 357, 375 (1927) (Brandeis, J., concurring) ("Those who won our independence . . . believed that freedom to think as you will and to speak as you think are means indispensable to the discovery and spread of political truth; . . . that public discussion is a political duty; and that this should be a fundamental principle of the American government.")

24. *Brandenburg*, 395 U.S. at 445–46.

25. *See, e.g.*, Menotti v. City of Seattle, 409 F.3d 1311, 1123–25 (9th Cir. 2005); Citizens for Peace in Space v. City of Colorado Springs, 477 F.3d 1212, 1219–21 (10th Cir. 2007); ACLU of Colo. v. City & County of Denver, 569 F. Supp. 1142, 1175–78, 1181–89 (D. Colo. 2008).

26. *See* Richard Delgado, *Words That Wound: A Tort Action for Racial Insults, Epithets, and Name Calling*, 17 Harv. C.R.-C.L. L. Rev. 133, 177–78 (1982); Charles R. Lawrence III, *If He Hollers Let Him Go: Regulating Racist Speech on Campus*, 1990 Duke L.J. 431, 452–57; Mari Matsuda, *Public Response to Racist Speech: Considering the Victim's Story*, 87 Mich. L. Rev. 2320, 2356–58 (1989).

27. *See* N.Y. Times Co. v. Sullivan, 376 U.S. 254, 270 (1964) (recognizing "a profound national commitment to the principle that debate on public issues should be uninhibited, robust, and wide-open"); *see also* Harry Kalven Jr., *The* New York Times *Case: A*

Note on "The Central Meaning of the First Amendment," 1964 SUP. CT. REV. 191, 204–06, 209–10.

28. *See* Dennis v. United States, 341 U.S. 494 (1951).

29. *See id.* at 510–11.

30. *See* William T. Mayton, *Seditious Libel and the Lost Guarantee of Freedom of Expression,* 84 COLUM. L. REV. 91, 97–98, 102–08, 123–27 (1984); *see also infra* chapter 3, section IV.

31. The bad tendencies test under *Dennis* reflected and incorporated Judge Learned Hand's formulation of free speech protection, which permitted government to regulate speech based on a sliding scale that incorporated the nature of the harm to be prevented and the probability of the harm coming to pass. *See* Dennis v. United States, 183 F. 201, 212–13 (2d Cir. 1950), *aff'd,* 341 U.S. 494 (1951). For some minor harms, such as advocacy of jay walking, the probability of the speech causing the harm would have to be very high, perhaps even reaching the point of certainty, before government could act to suppress or punish the speech. For more serious harms, like violent overthrow of the government, the probability of the harm coming to pass could be much lower, yet the government would have a legitimate claim to regulate or ban the speech. Thus, the gravity of the potential harm, as much if not more than the risk of it occurring, prefigured the ability of the government to regulate or suppress speech. *Brandenburg* rejects this approach and requires a high probability of the risk coming to fruition as a precondition of government regulation or suppression, regardless of how grave the risk happens to be. Jonathan S. Masur, *Probability Thresholds,* 92 IOWA L. REV. 1293, 1310–12 (2007); *see* Richard A. Posner, *The Learned Hand Biography and the Question of Judicial Greatness,* 104 YALE L.J. 511, 518 (1994) ("Elegant and eloquent as it is, Hand's opinion in *Dennis* was a period piece and it was not the best period for freedom of thought and expression. *Brandenburg* may have borrowed from *Masses,* but it certainly repudiated *Dennis.*"); *cf.* Martin H. Redish, *Unlawful Advocacy and Free Speech Theory: Rethinking the Lessons of the McCarthy Era,* 73 U. CIN. L. REV. 9, 61–68 (2004) (arguing that *Brandenburg* and *Dennis* are not entirely unreconcilable and that the Supreme Court plainly did not wish to overrule *Dennis* in *Brandenburg*).

32. CASS R. SUNSTEIN, DEMOCRACY AND THE PROBLEM OF FREE SPEECH 169 (1993).

33. *See generally* Hustler v. Falwell, 485 U.S. 46, 51–53 (1988) (holding protected on free speech grounds an intentionally malicious parody of a public figure because constitutionally protected criticism of public officials and public figures "inevitably, will not always be reasoned or moderate; public figures as well as public officials will be subject to vehement, caustic, and sometimes unpleasantly sharp attacks").

34. *See, e.g.,* Snyder v. Phelps, 131 S. Ct. 1207, 1220 (2011) ("Speech is powerful. It can stir people to action, move them to tears of both joy and sorrow, and—as it did here—inflict great pain."); *but cf. id.* at 1229 (Alito, J., dissenting) ("In order to have a society in which public issues can be openly and vigorously debated, it is not necessary to allow the brutalization of innocent victims like petitioner [Albert Snyder].").

35. *See* Rosenfeld v. New Jersey, 408 U.S. 901, 901 (1972); *id.* at 910–12 (Rehnquist, J., dissenting) (describing the facts at issue in the case); *see also* Gooding v. Wilson, 405 U.S. 518, 525–28 (1972).

36. *See* Justin Hooks, *Overnight Celebrity Reaps Benefits*, SUN HERALD (Biloxi, MS), March 16, 2007, at A2 (recounting Dr. Marble's famous encounter with Vice President Cheney outside Marble's wrecked post-Katrina Gulfport home on September 8, 2005); *cf.* Julian Borger, *Cheney vents F-fury at senator*, THE GUARDIAN (London), June 26, 2004, at 14 (reporting and quoting Vice President Cheney's suggestion to Senator Patrick Leahy (D-VT), offered on the floor of the United States Senate, that Leahy "go fuck yourself").

37. *See* Cohen v. California, 403 U.S. 15, 16–17 (1971).

38. Thus, the Supreme Court has overturned criminal convictions based on the use of opprobrious and profane language to law enforcement personnel. *See, e.g.,* Lewis v. New Orleans, 415 U.S. 130, 131–34 (1974); *Gooding,* 405 U.S. at 518–20, 526–28.

39. Beauharnais v. Illinois, 343 U.S. 250, 265–67 (1952).

40. Dennis v. United States, 341 U.S. 494, 510 (1951).

41. *See, e.g.,* R.A.V. v. City of St. Paul, 505 U.S. 377, 391–96 (1992); American Booksellers Ass'n, Inc.v. Hudnut, 771 F.2d 323 (7th Cir. 1985), *summarily aff'd,* 475 U.S. 1001 (1986); Collin v. Smith, 578 F.2d 1197 (7th Cir. 1978), *cert. denied sub nom.,* 439 U.S. 916 (1978).

42. New York Times Co. v. Sullivan, 376 U.S. 254, 270 (1964).

43. *See* Snyder v. Phelps, 131 S. Ct. 1207, 1218–20 (2011).

44. *See* N.Y. Times Co. v. United States, 403 U.S. 713, 714 (1971); *see also* Hague v. C.I.O., 307 U.S. 496, 515–18 (1939); Lovell v. Griffin, 303 U.S. 444, 451–53 (1938); Near v. Minnesota, 283 U.S. 697, 712–15 (1931).

45. 4 WILLIAM BLACKSTONE, COMMENTARIES *150–52.

46. *See* Thomas I. Emerson, *The Doctrine of Prior Restraint,* 20 LAW & CONTEMP. PROBS. 648 (1955); John C. Jeffries Jr., *Rethinking Prior Restraints,* 92 YALE L.J. 409 (1984); Martin H. Redish, *The Proper Role of Prior Restraint Doctrine in First Amendment Theory,* 70 VA. L. REV. 53 (1984); Christina E. Wells, *Bringing Structure to the Law of Injunctions against Expression,* 51 CASE W. RES. L. REV. 1 (2000).

47. The Supreme Court's time, place, and manner jurisprudence is discussed at length, *infra,* in section II.B. of this chapter.

48. *See infra* chapter 2, section II.B., text and accompanying notes 60–80.

49. Ward v. Rock Against Racism, 491 U.S. 781, 791 (1989) (*quoting* Clark v. Cmty. for Creative Non-Violence, 468 U.S. 288, 293 (1984)).

50. *See* Owen M. Fiss, *Silence on the Street Corner,* 26 SUFFOLK U.L. REV. 1, 3–18 (1992) (describing the evolution of the Supreme Court's test for time, place, and manner restrictions).

51. *Hill,* 530 U.S. at 765 (Kennedy, J., dissenting).

52. *See* Nanes, *supra* note 14, at 215–18; Suplina, *supra* note 14, at 402.

53. *See Ward,* 491 U.S. at 797–800 (discussing the narrow tailoring requirement). In contrast, a court considering a content-based regulation must "assume[] that certain protected speech may be regulated, and then ask[] what is the least restrictive alternative that can be used to achieve that goal." Ashcroft v. ACLU, 542 U.S. 656, 666 (2004).

54. *Ward,* 491 U.S. at 799–800 (citations omitted). In Hill v. Colorado, 530 U.S. 703 (2000), the court articulated an even less demanding view of narrow tailoring, stating

that "when a content neutral regulation does not entirely foreclose any means of communication, it may satisfy the narrow tailoring requirement even though it is not the least restrictive or least intrusive means of serving the statutory goal." *Id.* at 726.

55. *Id.* at 800 (stating that "[t]he Court of Appeals erred in failing to defer to the city's reasonable determination [of how] its interest . . . would be best served"); *see also* Turner Broad. Sys., Inc. v. FCC, 520 U.S. 180, 195–96 (1997) (discussing the "substantial deference" owed to Congress's judgments as to the existence of a harm and the best means of alleviating it).

56. *Id.* at 807 (Marshall, J., dissenting).

57. The requirement of ample alternative channels of communication is also subject to manipulation. *See, e.g., infra* sections III.A.–C. (discussing cases in the federal circuit courts applying the time, place, and manner doctrine).

58. *See* Boos v. Barry, 485 U.S. 312, 321 (1988); Turner Broadcasting System, Inc. v. FCC, 512 U.S. 622, 642 (1994) (citing Clark v. Community for Creative Non-Violence, 468 U.S. 288, 293 (1984)).

59. *See, e.g., infra* II.B.2., text and accompanying notes 62–80 (discussing the Court's neutrality inquiries in *Hill v. Colorado* and *Turner Broadcasting System, Inc. v. FCC*).

60. City of Renton v. Playtime Theatres, Inc., 475 U.S. 41, 48–49 (1986).

61. *See Ward*, 491 U.S. at 791.

62. 530 U.S. 703 (2000).

63. *Hill*, 530 U.S. at 707 n.1 (quoting COLO. REV. STAT. § 18-9-122(3) (1999)).

64. *Id.* at 719–20. Without elaboration, the Court also made a head-scratch-inducing third argument that the statute is content neutral because it is not a "regulation of speech" at all. "Rather, it is a regulation of the places where some speech may occur." *Id.* at 719. Though it would no doubt come as a surprise to the authors of the Court's previous decisions on time, place, and manner regulations, apparently such regulations are, by definition, content neutral.

65. *Id.* at 719.

66. *Id.* at 719–20.

67. *See id.* at 725–30.

68. *See, e.g.*, Hunter v. Underwood, 471 U.S. 222, 229–32 (1985); Yick Wo v. Hopkins, 118 U.S. 356, 369–74 (1886). For an excellent discussion of the concept of discriminatory intent and the difficulties associated with proving it, see Michelle Adams, *Causation and Responsibility in Tort and Affirmative Action*, 79 TEX. L. REV. 643 (2001).

69. *See* Griffin v. County Sch. Bd. of Prince Edward County, 377 U.S. 218, 221–22, 230–32 (1964) (invalidating scheme to avoid desegregation of the county public schools by simply closing them); *see also* R. C. SMITH, THEY CLOSED THEIR SCHOOLS: PRINCE EDWARD COUNTY, VIRGINIA 1951–1964 (1965). Initially, the county and state did not provide any assistance to parents to facilitate enrolling their children in private schools; however, for the second school year after the closure of the county's public primary and secondary schools, the state and county authorized grants, on a nondiscriminatory basis, of up to $225 per child, per year, to offset the cost of attending a private, nonsectarian primary school and up to $250 per year, per child, to offset the cost of attending a private, nonsectarian secondary school. *See id.* at 223–24. Prince Edward County also

offered a property tax credit of up to 25 percent for donations to private, nonsectarian primary and secondary schools operated within the county. *See id.* The closing of the public schools to avoid desegregation, however, was the primary constitutional defect in the scheme. *See id.* at 225 ("under the circumstances here, closing the Prince Edward County schools while public schools in all the other counties of Virginia were being maintained denied the petitioners and the class of Negro students they represent the equal protection of the laws guaranteed by the Fourteenth Amendment"); *id.* at 231 ("Whatever nonracial grounds might support a State's allowing a county to abandon public schools, the object must be a constitutional one, and grounds of race and opposition to desegregation do not qualify as constitutional."); *see also* Norwood v. Harrison, 413 U.S. 455, 465–66 (1973) (disallowing a "neutral" state program providing free textbooks, on a loaned basis at state expense, to primary and secondary school students attending private, racially discriminatory schools because "the Constitution does not permit the State to aid discrimination even when there is no precise causal relationship between state financial aid to a private school and the continued well-being of that school" and holding, accordingly, "[a] State may not grant the type of tangible financial aid here involved if that aid has a significant tendency to facilitate, reinforce, and support private discrimination"); *but cf.* Palmer v. Thompson, 403 U.S. 217, 224 (1971) (plurality opinion) (rejecting a claim that an impermissible motive to close the Jackson, Mississippi, municipal public swimming pools, after a local district court ordered them operated on a racially desegregated basis, could be impeached based on the city's illicit discriminatory motive because "no case in this Court has held that a legislative act may violate equal protection solely because of the motivations of the men who voted for it."). Justice Black's plurality opinion in *Palmer* simply does not reflect the settled law under the Fourteenth Amendment, which in fact *does* permit a reviewing court to apply heightened scrutiny to a facially neutral law, enacted with discriminatory purpose, when such a law produces racially discriminatory effects. *See Hunter*, 471 U.S. at 229–32.

70. Turner Broad. Sys., Inc. v. FCC, 512 U.S. 622 (1994).

71. Cable Television Consumer Protection and Competition Act of 1992, Pub. L. 102–385, 106 Stat. 1460.

72. *Turner*, 512 U.S. at 633.

73. *Id.* at 630 (citations omitted).

74. *Id.* at 674–75 (O'Connor, J., concurring in part and dissenting in part).

75. *Id.* at 644–45.

76. *Id.* at 643 (emphasis added).

77. *Id.* at 676–78 (O'Connor, J., concurring in part and dissenting in part) (quoting Cable Television Consumer Protection and Competition Act of 1992 2(a)(6), (8)(A), (10), (11)). Joining Justice O'Connor's opinion was the unusual combination of Justices Ginsburg, Scalia, and Thomas. *Id.* at 674.

78. *Id.*

79. *Id.* at 645 (citing United States v. Eichman, 496 U.S. 310, 315 (1990)).

80. *See id.* at 646–48.

81. *See Hill*, 530 U.S. at 742, 764; *see also* Ronald J. Krotoszynski Jr., *Dissent, Free Speech, and the Continuing Search for the "Central Meaning" of the First Amendment*, 98 MICH. L. REV. 1613, 1667 & n.178 (2000). The Court's pro-abortion-rights justices, however, are not alone in their willingness to subvert First Amendment values in favor of their views on abortion. In *Rust v. Sullivan*, 500 U.S. 173 (1991), for example, Justices Scalia and Kennedy, who dissented so vociferously in *Hill*, joined the majority in upholding a regulation prohibiting physicians from even mentioning the availability of abortion to women who participated in a government-sponsored family planning program. *Id.* at 176. The majority's credulity-stretching argument was, in essence, that "neither the physician nor the patient had any free speech interest in speech related to abortion in a government-sponsored family planning clinic." *See* RONALD J. KROTOSZYNSKI JR., THE FIRST AMENDMENT IN CROSS-CULTURAL PERSPECTIVE: A COMPARATIVE LEGAL ANALYSIS OF THE FREEDOM OF SPEECH 200–209 (2006) (comparing *Rust* with *Hill* and arguing that "[f]ree speech principles were simply collateral damage in [cases] perceived as part of the overall battle over the scope and meaning of *Roe v. Wade*").

82. *Hill*, 530 U.S. at 742 (Scalia, J., dissenting).

83. *See supra* section I.

84. *See* Suplina, *supra* note 14, at 395–96 (describing the "free speech zones" established at presidential appearances and at the 2004 Democratic and Republican national conventions); United States Secret Service, National Special Security Events, http://www.secretservice.gov/nsse.shtml (last visited July 31, 2008) (describing the underlying law and the process and significance of designating an event a "National Special Security Event").

85. *See* Andrew Blake, *Atlanta's Steamy Heat Cools Protests: More than 25 Groups Rally in Demonstration Area*, BOSTON GLOBE, July 20, 1988, at 12 (describing the "demonstration area" established by Atlanta's mayor, termed a "free-speech cage" by one of the protestors).

86. *See* Bl(a)ck Tea Society v. City of Boston, 379 F.3d 8, 11 (2004) (describing the enclosed free speech zone at the 2004 Democratic National Convention, which was located under elevated railroad tracks edged with "coiled razor wire").

87. *See* OFFICE OF PRESIDENTIAL ADVANCE, *supra* note 11, at 34–35 (describing White House procedures for keeping protestors away from the president and the press at presidential appearances); *see also* Hampson, *supra* note 14, at 257; Suplina, *supra* note 14, at 396.

88. *Compare* Mitchell Locin & John O'Brien, *For Convention Protests, This Time It's the Pits*, CHI. TRIB., Apr. 2, 1996, News, at 1 (1996 DNC); Nicholas Riccardi, *Convention Planners Wary of a New Style of Protest*, L.A. TIMES, June 23, 2000, at 1 (2000 DNC); Rick Klein, *Convention Plan Puts Protesters Blocks Away*, BOSTON GLOBE, Feb. 20, 2004, at A1 (2004 DNC), *with* Tony Perry, *Protestors Toe the Line for GOP Convention*, L.A. TIMES, June 23, 1996, at 3 (1996 RNC); Thomas Ginsberg, *Convention Pact Gives GOP Control Of Center City Sites*, PHILA. INQUIRER, Mar. 24, 2000, at A01 (2000 RNC); Diane Cardwell, *The Contest Of Liberties And Security*, N.Y. TIMES, July 26, 2004, at B1 (2004 RNC).

89. *See infra* sections II.A.–E. (discussing cases involving challenges to no-protest and free speech *zones*); Nanes, *supra* note 14, at 209; Suplina, *supra* note 14, at 396–97.

90. *See* Hampson, supra note 14, at 253–59 (describing numerous instances of government suppression of political dissent since 9/11); Suplina, *supra* note 14, at 396 ("[W] hen the state raises powerful antiterrorism concerns within the weak First Amendment time, place, manner framework it will almost always prevail.").

91. *See* Blair v. City of Evansville, Ind., 361 F. Supp. 2d 846, 859 (S.D. Ind. 2005) ("Defendants' creation of a large no-protest zone, and the creation of a designated protest zone 500 feet or more away from Blair's targeted audience violated Blair's First Amendment Rights."); Stauber v. City of N.Y., No. 03 Civ. 9162 (RWS), 2004 WL 1593870, at *29 (S.D.N.Y. July 16, 2004, as amended July 19, 2004) (finding that the city's use of free speech "pens" was not narrowly tailored due to the extreme limitations on entry to and exit from the pens); Serv. Employee Int'l Union v. City of L.A., 114 F. Supp. 2d 966, 975 (C.D. Cal. 2000) ("[T]he Court finds that the proposed 'secured zone' . . . is not narrowly tailored to serve that interest [in security] because it burdens more speech than is necessary. The Court further finds that defendants' proposed 'Demonstration Site' is not an adequate alternative for communication to the delegates and Democratic Party officials.").

92. *See* ACLU of Colo. v. City & County of Denver, 569 F. Supp. 2d 1142, 1173–75, 1181–89 (D. Colo. 2008); Coalition to March on the RNC & Stop the War v. City of St. Paul 557 F. Supp. 2d 1014, 1021–23, 1028–31 (D. Minn. 2008). No reported decision of either the Eighth Circuit or the Tenth Circuit considering appeals in these cases existed as of March 15, 2011.

93. Bl(a)ck Tea Soc'y v. City of Boston, 378 F.3d 8, 10 (1st Cir. 2004).

94. *See supra* section I, text and accompanying notes 1–12 (describing the district court's assessment of the DZ).

95. Coalition to Protest the Democratic National Convention v. City of Boston, 327 F. Supp. 2d 61, 76 (2004), aff'd sub nom., Bl(a)ck Tea Society v. City of Boston, 378 F.3d 8 (1st Cir. 2004).

96. *Bl(a)ck Tea Soc'y*, 378 F.3d at 10.

97. *Id.* at 12.

98. *See* Nanes, *supra* note 14, at 209 ("Although the Boston demonstration zone could theoretically have been filled by pro-Kerry demonstrators and the protest pens outside [the RNC] in New York City could have housed pro-Bush demonstrators, common sense argues this would not be the case.").

99. *Bl(a)ck Tea Soc'y*, 378 F.3d at 13. In addition, the district court's opinion makes clear that, at most, only half of the delegates would be able to even see the DZ on their way into the convention. See Coalition to Protest, 327 F. Supp. 2d at 67–68 (describing in relation to the DZ site the configuration of the bus terminal where delegates would arrive and depart).

100. *Bl(a)ck Tea Soc'y*, 378 F.3d at 13–14.

101. *Id.* at 14.

102. *Id.*

103. *Coalition to Protest*, 327 F. Supp. 2d at 76.

104. *Bl(a)ck Tea Soc'y*, 378 F.3d at 14.
105. *Id. But see infra* note 128 (discussing the Ninth Circuit's view of this approach to the ample alternative channels of communication requirement).
106. *Id.* at 15.
107. Menotti v. City of Seattle, 409 F.3d 1113 (9th Cir. 2005).
108. *See id.* at 1123 (citing a Seattle report indicating that "violent protestors were less than one percent of the total protestors").
109. *Id.* at 1120.
110. *Id.* at 1121.
111. *Id.* at 1124.
112. *Id.* at 1125.
113. *Id.* at 1159 (Paez, J., dissenting).
114. *Id.* at 1125.
115. *Id.*
116. *See id.* at 1125–28 (describing the exceptions to the order and the police implementation of it); *see also id.* at 1159 (Paez, J., dissenting) ("While the text of Order No. 3 may be content neutral, the City's policy was to apply the law selectively such that it was not narrowly tailored to serve its asserted non-speech-related interest of preserving safety and order."). Judge Paez, writing in dissent, explained the city's policy as follows: "Notably, the Order allowed anyone who did not visibly display opposition to the WTO to enter the zone, without regard to dangerousness or likelihood of violence. While the police scoured for 'No WTO' signs and buttons, there was no evidence that officers checked bags for crowbars, weapons, or bombs... Even those who should have been granted access to the zone according to the plain terms of the Order, such as people who lived or worked in the zone, were denied entry if they wore 'No WTO' stickers or carried protest signs." *Id.* at 1162 (Paez, J., dissenting).
117. *Id.* at 1117–18.
118. *Id.* at 1118.
119. *Id.* at 1129 (citing City of L.A. v. Alameda Books, Inc., 535 U.S. 425, 448 (2002) (Kennedy, J., concurring); Ctr. For Fair Pub. Policy v. Maricopa County, 336 F.3d 1153, 1164 (9th Cir. 2003)).
120. *Id.* (citing Hill v. Colorado, 530 U.S. 703, 719 (2000); Madsen v. Women's Health Ctr., Inc., 512 U.S. 753, 763 (1994)).
121. *See id.* at 1131.
122. *Id.* at 1132–33; *see also id.* at 1141 ("If the City had permitted chaos and violence to continue unabated, it would not merely lose its standing as a host city for international conferences."); *id.* at 1155 ("When a city is charged with the critically important responsibility of hosting a convention of world leaders, a setting in which the eyes of the world are on the city and our country, and our nation's reputation is at stake as well, the city must have the power to maintain civic order.").
123. *See id.* at 1168 n.8 (Paez, J., dissenting) ("I am not convinced that a city's interest in hosting such an event is 'significant' for purposes of this analysis."); *cf. id.* at 1167 n.6 (Paez, J., dissenting) ("[T]he city did not have a constitutionally significant interest in

sheltering delegates from the unpleasantness or inconvenience of a large demonstration."). As one commentator has explained:

> [T]he assumed neutrality of . . . pen and zone schemes should be questioned more thoroughly, particularly because these schemes [are] devised by authorities having a far greater interest in avoiding protest speech than in reasonably accommodating it. A large motive in luring the national political conventions, indeed, any major convention or significant event like the Olympics or the Super Bowl, is for a host city to attract the spending power of delegates and to put on a great show for those delegates and for the national media. Convention boosters recruit business communities with promises of boom days. Host city mayors become deeply involved in bidding for conventions and great effort is taken to resolve labor disputes and other such sticking points that might mar the presentation. Those representing the city, then, are motivated to keep the peace largely by keeping noisy and irate demonstrators far away from delegates and other visitors.
>
> National party personnel are equally interested in smooth sailing . . . .
>
> . . . At the 2004 conventions, the pens and zones would most likely be filled by protestors expressing views that did not fit well into the upbeat and urbane images the Boston and New York City authorities wished to project. If so, the assumed content neutrality of the pens and zones should not be so easily accepted.

See Nanes, *supra* note 14, at 208–09 (citations omitted). The government's asserted significant interest in attracting convention business also highlights a larger question—viz., whether government in a free and democratic society may ever legitimately serve as the midwife to North Korean-style political theater.

124. *See* Williams v. Wallace, 240 F. Supp, 100, 105–08 (M.D. Ala. 1965).

125. *See Menotti*, 409 F.3d at 1137 ("In light of the City's significant governmental interest in restoring and maintaining civic order to the core downtown area, Order No. 3 and the restricted zone it implemented were narrowly tailored.").

126. *Id.* at 1132–37. *But cf. id.* at 1169 (Paez, J., dissenting) ("Order No. 3 banned peaceful expressive activity without regard to the City's stated safety-related goals. . . . The majority would allow the police to search people they suspected of carrying stickers and handbills, but concludes that it 'would not have been practical' for police to search for crowbars or spray paint.").

127. *Compare id.* at 1138–41 & n.54 (arguing that, despite the no-protest zone, protestors retained the "ability to communicate directly across the street from most WTO venues), *with id.* at 1173 & n.16 (Paez, J., dissenting) (stating that Order No. 3 "confined all demonstration to outside areas where the message the protestors sought to convey may never have reached the intended audience" and disputing the majority's assertions to the contrary).

128. *Id.* at 1141–42. In a footnote, the court also acknowledged, but did not evaluate, the First Circuit's position in *Bl(a)ck Tea Society* that the ample alternative channels requirement may be satisfied by messages that, although not expressed within sight and sound of the intended hearer, may be picked up the media. *See id.* at 1139 n.49 (citing *Bl(a)ck Tea Soc'y*, 278 F.3d at 14). The dissent, however, was not satisfied by

this approach, arguing that the court "should dispel any notion that media interest in an event can be a substitute for constitutionally-required alternative avenues of communication. As the Seventh Circuit stated in *Hodgkins* [*v. Peterson*], 'there is no internet connection, no telephone call, no television coverage that can compare to attending a political rally in person.'" *Id.* at 1174 (Paez, J., dissenting) (quoting Hodgkins v. Peterson, 355 F.3d 1048, 1063 (7th Cir. 2004)).

129. *See Bl(a)ck Tea Soc'y*, 278 F.3d at 10–11 (describing the procedural history of the case).

130. *See id.* at 15 ("With the Convention looming and with few options at its disposal, we think the district court's resolution of the preliminary injunction requires was fully supportable."); *Coalition to Protest*, 327 F. Supp. 2d at 77 ("[T]he City of Boston . . . has provided protestors with an inadequate space. Unfortunately, . . . there is little time, and no practical means, available for significant modifications to the secured environment."). In his concurrence, Judge Lipez strongly emphasized timing: "Time constraints shadowed every aspect of this case. In the future, if the representatives of demonstrators ask the courts to modify security measures developed over many months of planning for an event of this magnitude, they should come to court when there is enough time for the courts to assess fully the impact that modifications will have on the security concerns advanced. . . . Adequate time means months or at least weeks to address the issues. It does not mean five days before the event begins." *Bl(a)ck Tea Soc'y*, 278 F.3d at 16 (Lipez, J., concurring).

131. Citizens for Peace in Space v. City of Colo. Springs, 477 F.3d 1212 (10th Cir. 2007).

132. *Id.* at 1217.

133. *Id.*

134. *Id.*

135. *Id.* at 1217–18.

136. *Id.* at 1218–19.

137. *Id.* at 1226.

138. *Id.* at 1217.

139. *Id.* at 1220.

140. *See id.* at 1218–19.

141. *Id.* at 1220 (emphasis added). Later in its opinion, the court reiterated this principle in perhaps even more startling language, arguing that "[w]hile an extremely important government interest does not dictate the result in time, place, and manner cases, the significance of the government interest bears an inverse relationship to the *rigor* of the narrowly tailored analysis. *Id.* at 1221 (emphasis added). The court cited no authority for its first statement, but for this latter statement it cited the narrow tailoring standard of *Board of Trustees, SUNY v. Fox*, 492 U.S. 469, 480 (1989), a commercial speech case that the Supreme Court has only applied to other commercial speech cases. *See, e.g.,* 44 Liquormart, Inc. v. Rhode Island, 517 U.S. 484 (1996).

142. *See Citizens for Peace in Space*, 477 F.3d at 1220 ("[T]he City's security plan was narrowly tailored to advance its significant security interest because the security zone . . . directly and effectively protected the conference from the threat of terrorism, explosives, and violent protests.")

143. *Id.* (quoting Ward v. Rock Against Racism, 491 U.S. 781, 799 (1989)).

144. Ward v. Rock Against Racism, 491 U.S. 781, 799 (1989).
145. *Citizens for Peace in Space,* 477 F. 3d at 1220.
146. The court did eventually address the "burden substantially more speech than neces-
     sary" statement from *Ward,* as well as other arguments that conflicted with the court's
     presumption of narrow tailoring. *See id.* at 1222–25. However, the court reached the
     "obvious conclusion" that the security zone was narrowly tailored *before* it consid-
     ered these arguments to the contrary in a portion of the opinion that the court clearly
     regarded as dicta. *Id.*
147. *Id.* at 1226.
148. *Id.* at 1220.
149. 569 F. Supp. 2d 1142 (D. Colo. 2008).
150. *Id.* at 1154.
151. *Id.* at 1156.
152. *Id.* ("The fencing and buffer zone will effectively prohibit the passage of leaflets or
     other material to the delegates."). Concerned about this lack of access and commit-
     ted to facilitating the broadest possible public discourse, Denver convention organiz-
     ers agreed to establish tables along the delegates' walkway and to place materials
     from the protestors on the tables, "such that delegates can take and peruse them" and
     "[p]ersons in the Public/Demonstration Zone can watch and encourage delegates to
     take specific leaflets." *Id.* Of course, this assumes that delegates could hear from two
     hundred feet away or, alternatively, would voluntarily elect to walk seventy yards or
     so toward the zone in order to be better informed about the pamphlets.
153. *Id.* at 1159–60.
154. *Id.* at 1156–57.
155. *Id.* at 1149.
156. *See id.* at 1161–89.
157. *See id.* at 1161–64.
158. *See id.* at 1164–71.
159. *Id.* at 1172–89.
160. *Id.* at 1174–75.
161. *Id.* at 1175.
162. *Id.* at 1175–76.
163. *Id.* at 1175.
164. *Id.*
165. *Id.* at 1176.
166. *Id.* at 1177.
167. *Id.*
168. *Id.* at 1178.
169. *Id.* at 1179.
170. *Id.* (quoting *Citizens for Peace in Space,* 477 F.3d at 1225).
171. *See id.* at 1184–89.
172. *Id.* at 1189.
173. 557 F. Supp. 2d 1014 (D. Minn. 2008).
174. *Id.* at 1016.

175. *See id.* at 1016–18.
176. *Id.* at 1018.
177. *Id.* at 1021.
178. *Id.*
179. Pub. Safety Planning and Implementation Review Comm'n, Report of the Republican National Convention Public Safety Planning and Implementation Review Commission 4 (2009).
180. *Id.*
181. *Id.* at 5.
182. *Id.* at 7.
183. *Id.* at 8.
184. *See id.* at 38–65.
185. *Coalition,* 557 F. Supp. 2d at 1025.
186. *Id.*
187. *Id.*
188. *Id.*
189. *Id.* at 1026.
190. *See id.* at 1027–29.
191. *Id.* at 1028.
192. *Id.*
193. *Id.* at 1029.
194. *Id.*
195. *See id.* at 1029–30.
196. *Id.* at 1030.
197. *Id.* at 1031.
198. *Id.*
199. *Id.*
200. 559 F.3d 1170 (11th Cir. 2009).
201. *Id.* at 1175.
202. *Id.*
203. *Id.*
204. *Id.*
205. *Id.* at 1176 ("The district court granted the motion, finding that the allegations were not detailed enough to satisfy the heightened pleading standard for § 1983 actions, especially in light of the failure to identify a specific individual who was prevented from joining the rally or a specific media reporter that was unable to cover the protest.").
206. *See id.* at 1181–85.
207. *Id.* at 1181.
208. *Id.* at 1181–82.
209. *Id.* at 1182.
210. *Id.* at 1183.
211. *Id.*
212. *Id.*

213. *See id.* at 1183–84.

214. *Id.* at 1175 ("Amnesty obtained a permit from the City of Miami Police Department to conduct this demonstration on that date at the Torch of Friendship, a monument with a surrounding plaza within Bayfront Park in Miami.").

215. *Id.* at 1183.

216. *Id.* at 1184.

217. *Id.*

218. *Id.* at 1184 n.8.

219. 376 U.S. 254 (1964).

220. New York Times Co. v. Sullivan, 376 U.S. 254, 269–71, 275–76 (1964); *see also* Kalven, *supra* note 27, at 204–10

221. Hustler v. Falwell, 485 U.S. 46, 51–53 (1988).

222. *Sullivan*, 376 U.S. at 270.

223. Snyder v. Phelps, 131 S. Ct. 1207 (2011).

224. *Id.* at 1220.

225. The Supreme Court of Australia used precisely this reasoning to find an implied right (or, more precisely, an "implied freedom") to the freedom of political speech in the Constitution of Australia. The justices concluded that the Constitution created a democratic form of government and that such government was simply not possible without significant protection for the freedom of speech. *See* Australian Capital Television Pty. Ltd. v. Commonwealth, 108 A.L.R. 577 (1992) (Austl.) (finding an implied right of free speech as an incident of Australia's commitment to democratic self-government and invalidating a ban on broadcast political advertisements under this implied right). For a critical analysis of the case, see Gerald R. Rosenburg & John M. Williams, *Do Not Go Gently into That Good Night: The First Amendment in the High Court of Australia*, 1997 SUP. CT. REV. 439.

226. OWEN M. FISS, THE IRONY OF FREE SPEECH (1996); OWEN M. FISS, LIBERALISM DIVIDED: FREEDOM OF SPEECH AND THE MANY USES OF STATE POWER (1996).

227. *See* Fiss, *supra* note 50, at 3–18; *see also* Owen M. Fiss, *Free Speech and Social Structure*, 71 IOWA L. REV. 1405, 1410–21 (1986).

228. Wells, *supra* note 18, at 201–09.

229. *See supra* chapter 2, section III.

230. *See* Blasi, *supra* note 18, at 466–76 (1985) (arguing that judges should define "the freedom of speech" narrowly but protect speech coming within that definition in near-absolute terms during times of crisis or unrest, in order to facilitate meaningful democratic discourse at times when such discourse is most crucial).

231. *See* Dennis v. United States, 183 F.2d 201, 212 (2d Cir. 1950), *aff'd*, 341 U.S. 494 (1951) ("In each case they must ask whether the gravity of the 'evil,' discounted by its improbability, justifies such invasion of free speech as is necessary to avoid the danger. We have purposely substituted 'improbability' for 'remoteness,' because that must be the right interpretation."). In *Dennis*, Judge Hand concluded that the risk of a violent overthrow of the government easily justified a proscription against advocacy of communism. *See id.* at 212–14. He explained:

The only justification which can be suggested is that in spite of their [Communists'] efforts to mask their purposes, so far as they can do so consistently with the spread of the gospel, discussion and publicity may so weaken their power that it will have ceased to be dangerous when the moment [to violently overthrow the U.S. government] may come. That may be a proper enough antidote in ordinary times and for less redoubtable combinations; but certainly it does not apply to this one. *Corruptio optimi pessima.* True, we must not forget our own faith; we must be sensitive to the dangers that lurk in any choice; but choose we must, and we shall be silly dupes if we forget that again and again in the past thirty years, just such preparations in other countries have aided to supplant existing governments, when the time was ripe. Nothing short of a revived doctrine of *laissez faire,* which would have amazed even the Manchester School at its apogee, can fail to realize that such a conspiracy creates a danger of the utmost gravity and of enough probability to justify its suppression. We hold that it is a danger "clear and present."

    Id. at 213.

232. Abrams v. United States, 250 U.S. 616, 630–31 (1925) (Holmes, J., dissenting).
233. *See, e.g.,* Cheh, *supra* note 14; Crocker, *supra* note 14; Zick, *Space, Place, and Speech, supra* note 14; Zick, *Speech and Spatial Tactics, supra* note 14.
234. *See infra* chapters 4, 5, and 6.

CHAPTER 3. SECURITY AS A CELLOPHANE WRAPPER

1. After all, threatening the life of the president could be characterized as "political speech," and no serious person would argue that a true threat ought to receive serious First Amendment protection. *See* 18 U.S.C. § 871 (2006); Watts v. United States, 394 U.S. 705, 707 (1969) ("The Nation undoubtedly has a valid, even an overwhelming, interest in protecting the safety of its Chief Executive and in allowing him to perform his duties without interference from threats of physical violence."); *see also* S. Elizabeth Wilborn Malloy & Ronald J. Krotoszynski Jr., *Recalibrating the Cost of Harm Advocacy: Getting Beyond* Brandenburg, 41 WM. & MARY L. REV. 1159, 1180–86 (2000) (noting that the Supreme Court has upheld significant limits on free speech when justified by overriding governmental objectives).
2. *See* Weise v. Casper, 593 F.3d 1163, 1168–70 (10th Cir.), *cert. denied,* 131 S. Ct. 7 (2010) ("Plaintiffs simply have not identified any First Amendment doctrine that prohibits the government from excluding them from an official speech on private property on the basis of their viewpoint."); Sistrunk v. City of Strongville, 99 F.3d 194, 196–200 (6th Cir. 1996) (sustaining exclusion of a person from a Bush/Quayle '92 rally because she wore "a political button endorsing Bill Clinton for President," even though Sistrunk possessed an otherwise valid ticket to attend the campaign event); Weise v. Casper, 2008 U.S. Dist. Lexis 90,211, at *22 (D. Colo. Nov. 6, 2008) ("President Bush had the right, at his own speech, to ensure that only his message was conveyed."). *Cf.* Sherill v. Knight, 569 F.3d 124, 129–30 (D.C. Cir. 1977) (disallowing the use of vague standards to deny access to the White House by refusing to issue a press pass and requiring the

Secret Service to "publish or otherwise make publicly known the actual standard employed in determining whether an otherwise eligible journalist will obtain a White House press pass.").

3. *See* Frisby v. Schultz, 487 U.S. 474, 486 (1988) (upholding a town ordinance that banned targeting picketing of a private residence because such picketing "inherently and offensively intrudes on residential privacy").

4. *See* Members of the City Council of the City of Los Angeles v. Taxpayers for Vincent, 466 U.S. 789, 805–11 (1984) (upholding a ban on the placement of political signs on public property, including rights of way adjacent to streets and on city-owned utility poles, based on the city's legitimate interest in promoting aesthetic interests by avoiding unsightly visual clutter).

5. *See, e.g.,* Boy Scouts of America v. Dale, 530 U.S. 640, 647–49, 656–59 (2000) (upholding free association claim that the Boy Scouts could exclude openly gay scouts and scoutmasters because imposing a state nondiscrimination policy on the Boy Scouts "would significantly burden the organization's right to oppose or disfavor homosexual conduct" and constitute an unconstitutional "severe intrusion on the Boy Scouts' rights to freedom of expressive association"); Hurley v. Irish-American Gay, Lesbian and Bisexual Group of Boston, 525 U.S. 557, 572–75 (1995) (upholding free association claim by the sponsors of St. Patrick's Day parade in Boston that inclusion of an openly gay and lesbian parade unit would constitute an unwanted forced association and compromise the free speech rights of sponsors because government lacks the power "to compel the speaker to alter the message by including one more acceptable to others").

6. *Cf. Hurley,* 525 U.S. at 572–75 ("Petitioners claim to the benefit of this principle of autonomy to control one's own speech is as sound as the South Boston parade is expressive.").

7. *See supra* chapter 2, sections III and IV.

8. OFFICE OF PRESIDENTIAL ADVANCE, PRESIDENTIAL ADVANCE MANUAL 34–35 (2002).

9. *See id.* at 33–35.

10. Bl(a)ck Tea Soc'y v. City of Boston, 378 F.3d 8, 13–14 (1st Cir. 2004) (observing that "[s]ecurity is not a talisman that the government may invoke to justify *any* burden on speech (no matter how oppressive)" but then holding that generalized security concerns justified closing the streets and sidewalks around the Fleet Center to protest activity during the 2004 Democratic National Convention and requiring would-be protestors to use a designated protest zone that resembled a concentration camp).

11. *See* Christina E. Wells, *Fear and Loathing in Constitutional Decision-making,* 2005 WIS. L. REV. 115, 159–194, 201–07.

12. PUBLIC SAFETY PLANNING AND IMPLEMENTATION REVIEW COMM'N, REPORT OF THE REPUBLICAN NATIONAL CONVENTION PUBLIC SAFETY REVIEW AND IMPLEMENTATION COMM'N 37–66 (2009) (describing in detail the four-day-long melee that took place on the streets of Minneapolis and St. Paul, Minnesota, during the 2008 RNC after violent anarchist demonstrators attempted to overrun the downtown area and the Pepsi Center grounds); *see* Patrick Healy & Colin Moynihan, *As Throngs of Protestors Hit Streets, Dozens Are Arrested After Clashes,* N.Y. TIMES, Sept. 2, 2008, at A20 (noting

that "[t]housands of protestors, many of them demonstrating against the war in Iraq, marched on Monday through the streets outside the area where the Republican National Convention is being held" and observing that "[a]lthough most of the protestors were peaceful, the police used pepper spray and long wooden sticks to subdue some").

13. *See* Douglas Frantz, *As Former Leader Faces Jail, Turks Rethink Limits on Speech*, N.Y. TIMES, July 11, 2000, at A3 (describing a prison sentence for a Turkish politician who publicly criticized government policy as anti-Islamic); Christopher Torchia, *Punk band's protest song lands members a trial date*, SEATTLE POST-INTELLIGENCER, July 16, 2007, at A4 (reporting on criminal prosecution of a band in Turkey based on a song that mocks the local SAT test because it defames the state); Mar Roman, *Spanish journal's royal cartoon stirs fuss*, SEATTLE TIMES, July 21, 2007, at A11 (reporting that "[a] judge ordered copies of a satirical magazine [*El Jueves*] confiscated . . . for publishing a cartoon of Spain's Crown Prince Felipe in an intimate bedroom scene with his wife" because the cartoon constituted "libeling the crown," a crime punishable with up to "a two-year prison sentence"); Jeffrey Simpson, *For Turkey's sake, stop snowing Orhan Pamuk*, THE GLOBE AND MAIL (Canada), Jan. 21, 2006, at A23 (reporting on Turkish criminal prosecution of Nobel Laureate author Orhan Pamuk for writing novels that violate a criminal proscription against "anti-Turkishness").

14. *See, e.g.*, Snyder v. Phelps, 131 S. Ct. 1207, 1213, 1217–18, 1220 (2011).

15. *See id.* at 1224–25 (Alito, J., dissenting).

16. *See id.* at 1222–24, 1229 (arguing that Phelps and the Westboro Baptist Church should seek out and use alternative forums for their public advocacy and questioning the selection of funeral protests as a crass effort to secure unwarranted media attention).

17. *See* Forsyth County v. Nationalist Movement, 505 U.S. 123 (1992).

18. *Id.* at 134–35.

19. *See* HARRY KALVEN JR., THE NEGRO AND THE FIRST AMENDMENT 140–41 (1965). According to Professor Owen Fiss, Kalven coined the phrase "heckler's veto," *see* Owen E. Fiss, *Free Speech and Social Structure*, 71 IOWA L. REV. 1405, 1416–17 (1986), although the concept itself arguably relates back to Justice Douglas's majority opinion in *Terminiello* and Justice Black's dissenting opinion in *Feiner*. *See* Terminiello v. Chicago, 337 U.S. 1, 4–6 (1949); Feiner v. New York, 340 U.S. 315, 326–29 (1951) (Black, J., dissenting).

20. *Forsyth County*, 505 U.S. at 134–36 (noting that a "[l]istener's reaction to speech is not a content neutral basis for regulation," collecting relevant case citations, and concluding that "[t]his Court has held time and again [that] [r]egulations which permit the government to discriminate on the basis of the content of the message cannot be tolerated under the First Amendment" (internal citations and quotations omitted)).

21. Terminiello v. City of Chicago, 337 U.S. 1, 4–5 (1949); Murdock v. Pennsylvania, 319 U.S. 105, 115–17 (1943); *see also* Fiss, *supra* note 19, at 1416–18 (noting the reasons supporting the "heckler's veto" doctrine and its well-established status in free speech jurisprudence); Geoffrey R. Stone, *Content Regulation and the First Amendment*, 25 WM. & MARY L. REV. 189, 214–16 (1983) (noting rule that government may not proscribe speech because of an audience's hostile reaction to the content).

22. *But cf.* Menotti v. City of Seattle, 409 F.3d 1113, 1132–33 (9th Cir. 2005) (suggesting that bad press might be a valid consideration in regulating potentially unruly protest activity).

23. *Cf.* United States v. Kahriger, 345 U.S. 22, 38 (1953) (Frankfurter, J., dissenting) ("when oblique use is made of the taxing power as to matters which substantively are not within the powers delegated to Congress, the Court cannot shut its eyes to what is obviously, because designedly, an attempt to control conduct which the Constitution left to the responsibility of the States, merely because Congress wrapped the legislation in the verbal cellophane of a revenue measure").

24. *See* Collin v. Smith, 578 F.2d 1197 (7th Cir.), *cert. denied*, 439 U.S. 916 (1978).

25. Hess v. Indiana, 414 U.S. 105, 106–07 (1973).

26. *Id.* at 107–08.

27. *See* NAACP v. Claiborne Hardware Co., 458 U.S. 886, 902 (1986).

28. *Id.*

29. *Id.* at 904 (internal quotations and citations omitted).

30. Interestingly, the Supreme Court of Canada has defined free speech very expansively, up to and including threats of violence. *See* Attorney General (Quebec) v. Irwin Toy Ltd., [1989] 1 S.C.R. 927, 970–71. In Canada, Section 2(b) of the Charter of Rights and Freedoms protects any human activity reasonably intended to convey a message or meaning. *See id.* Prominent Canadian legal scholars, such as Richard Moon, have questioned the wisdom of abjuring a purposive definition of protected expression. *See* Richard Moon, The Constitutional Protection of Freedom of Expression 65–75 (2000). For a general overview of free speech principles in Canada, *see* Ronald J. Krotoszynski Jr., The First Amendment in Cross-Cultural Perspective: A Comparative Legal Analysis of the Freedom of Speech 26–92 (2006).

31. *Claiborne Hardware Co.*, 458 U.S. at 927.

32. New York Times Co. v. Sullivan, 376 U.S. 254, 270 (1964).

33. 505 U.S. 123, 134–36 (1992).

34. *See supra* chapter 2, section III.

35. 337 U.S. 1 (1949)

36. *Id.* at 3. This is Justice Douglas's rather euphemistic description of the racist and religiously bigoted ravings of Father Terminiello. For a fuller, bolder account of the precise language at issue in the case, see Justice Jackson's lengthy reproduction of choice quotes from a transcript of the address, *id.* at 14–22 (Jackson, J., dissenting).

37. *Id.* at 3.

38. *Id.*

39. *Id.* at 4.

40. *Id.*

41. *Id.* at 4–5.

42. *Id.* at 13 (Jackson, J., dissenting).

43. *See id.* at 14–22.

44. *Id.* at 24.

45. *Id.* at 35.

46. *Id.* at 5.

47. *Id.*

48. *See, e.g.,* Edwards v. South Carolina, 372 U.S. 229, 236–38 (1963).

49. 340 U.S. 315 (1951).

50. *See id.* at 319–21.

51. *See, e.g.,* Cox v. Louisiana, 379 U.S. 536, 550–51 (1965) (declining to apply *Feiner* because the probability of violence was too remote, unproven, or both); *Edwards,* 372 U.S. at 236–37 (declining to apply *Feiner* because the facts presented were "a far cry" from those at issue in *Feiner,* with the *Edwards* majority finding that the realistic threat of unrest arising from the expressive conduct at issue in the case was entirely unproven and wholly conjectural).

52. Brown v. Louisiana, 383 U.S. 131, 133 n.1 (1966).

53. Wright v. Georgia, 373 U.S. 284, 293 (1963); *see* KALVEN, *supra* note 19, at 140–160.

54. *See* Hess v. Indiana, 414 U.S. 105, 105–09 (1973).

55. *Feiner,* 340 U.S. at 331 (Douglas, J., dissenting); *see* Beattie I. Butler, Note, *Muzzling Leviathan: Limiting State Powers over Speech and Expression,* 5 KAN. J.L. & PUB. POL'Y 153, 158 (1996) ("Subsequent decisions, following the dissent in *Feiner,* have criticized that decision on the grounds that the state's duty to protect the free speech rights of the speaker is greater than its duty to protect the audience from becoming unwilling listeners. Thus, in circumstances such as Feiner's, the police should first control those in the audience who threaten violence, even where the ideas presented are controversial."); Kevin Francis O'Neill, *Disentangling the Law of Public Protest,* 45 LOYOLA L. REV. 411, 491 (observing that "*Terminiello* and its progeny make clear that a speaker cannot be punished for an angry reaction to his ideas—even, per *Cantwell,* if he resorts to exaggeration or vilification in pressing his beliefs" and concluding that "the police have an affirmative duty . . . to protect the unpopular speaker").

56. *See Feiner,* 340 U.S. at 326 (Black, J., dissenting) (rejecting "the implication that the police had no obligation to protect petitioner's constitutional right to talk" and suggesting that "if, in the name of preserving public order, they can interfere with a lawful public speaker, they first must make all reasonable efforts to protect him"). Justice Black found that the police in Syracuse, New York, had utterly failed to discharge their constitutional responsibilities and observed that "[t]heir duty was to protect petitioner's right to talk, even to the extent of arresting the man who threatened to interfere." *Id.* at 327. "Instead, they shirked that duty and acted only to suppress the right to speak." *Id.*

57. 308 U.S. 147 (1939).

58. *Id.* at 162. Moreover, Justice Black endorsed and adopted this analogy in his *Feiner* dissent. *Feiner,* 340 U.S. at 327 n.9 (Black, J., dissenting).

59. In this regard, the Kent State Massacre comes almost immediately to mind. Free speech often is not free, insofar as it imposes very serious social costs on both speakers and the community to which they belong. *See* David E. Engdahl, *Soldiers, Riots, and Revolution: The Law and History of Military Troops in Civil Disorders,* 57 IOWA L. REV. 1, 1–2, 73 (1971); Krause v. Rhodes, 471 F.2d 430 (6th Cir. 1972), *rev'd sub nom.,* Scheuer v. Rhodes, 416 U.S. 232 (1974). On May 4, 1970, four students died for participating in a mass protest against the Vietnam War. Engdahl, *supra,* at 73.

60. Dennis v. United States, 183 F.2d 201, 212–13 (2d Cir. 1950) ("In each case [courts] must ask whether the gravity of the 'evil,' discounted by its improbability, justifies such invasion of free speech as is necessary to avoid the danger."), *aff'd*, 341 U.S. 494 (1951); *cf.* Masses Pub. Co. v. Patten, 244 F. 535 (S.D.N.Y.) (featuring Judge Hand propounding a different test that relies on whether the words directly and plainly advocate unlawful conduct, rather than on the probable effects of the words at issue), *rev'd*, 246 F. 24 (2d Cir. 1917); *see* WILLIAM W. VAN ALSTYNE, FIRST AMENDMENT CASES AND MATERIALS 140–42 (1st ed. 1991) (describing the operation of Judge Hand's *Dennis* test); Gerald R. Gunther, *Learned Hand and the Origins of Modern First Amendment Doctrine: Some Fragments of History*, 27 STAN. L. REV. 719 (1975) (providing a comprehensive overview of Judge Hand's First Amendment jurisprudence, including his *Dennis* sliding scale of risk approach to permitting government to proscribe or punish speech).

61. Under *Brandenburg*, regardless of the precise nature of the risk, government may regulate only if a clear and present danger of imminent lawlessness exists. See Brandenburg v. Ohio, 395 U.S. 444, 447–49 (1969); *see* Malloy & Krotoszynski, *supra* note 1, at 1192–97. Hence, under *Brandenburg*, government may not proscribe speech advocating the necessity of exploding a nuclear bomb in a population center, any more than it could proscribe speech advocating income tax avoidance, or speech advocating recoining parking meters. Government's ability to regulate speech is entirely a function of a realistic probability of speech causing the harm to be avoided, regardless of the potential gravity of the harm.

62. N.Y. Times Co. v. United States, 403 U.S. 713 (1971).

63. *See* R.A.V. v. City of St. Paul, 505 U.S. 377, 395–96 (1992).

64. Brandenburg v. Ohio, 395 U.S. 444, 445–47 (1969). Statements such as "We're not a revengent [*sic*] organization, but if our President, our Congress, our Supreme Court continues to suppress the white, Caucasian race, it's possible that there might have to be some revengence [*sic*] taken," *id.* at 446, "[p]ersonally, I believe the nigger should be returned to Africa, and the Jew returned to Israel," *id.* at 447, and "Bury the niggers!," *id.* at 446 n.1, are illustrative of the general tone and substance of the meeting, at which hooded members of the Ku Klux Klan openly brandished firearms and also burned a cross, *id.* at 445–46.

65. *See* RICHARD DELGADO & JEAN STEFANCIC, MUST WE DEFEND NAZIS? HATE SPEECH, PORNOGRAPHY, AND THE NEW FIRST AMENDMENT (1997); CATHARINE A. MACKINNON, ONLY WORDS (1993); MARI J. MATSUDA, WORDS THAT WOUND: CRITICAL RACE THEORY, ASSAULTIVE SPEECH, AND THE FIRST AMENDMENT (1993). Moreover, the notion that free speech must give way in order to secure other fundamental values, such as equality or multiculturalism, has proven persuasive in places like Canada, where the Supreme Court of Canada has sustained laws aimed at securing these interests, even at the cost of prohibiting, indeed criminalizing, speech. *See, e.g.,* R. v. Butler, [1992] 1 S.C.R. 452, 486–510; R. v. Keegstra, [1990] 3 S.C.R. 697, 714–22, 744–88; *see also* Krotoszynski, *supra* note 30, at 51–60. Under a true marketplace theory of free speech, any speech would enjoy protection on the theory that government must be barred from attempting to control access to the market. The problem, of course, is that the Supreme Court has not generally been willing to commit itself to a true

marketplace approach, permitting selective regulation of speech based on content thought to be of low value, such as obscenity or child pornography. *See, e.g.,* Osborne v. Ohio, 495 U.S. 103 (1990); New York v. Ferber, 458 U.S. 747 (1982); Miller v. California, 413 U.S. 15 (1973). In a truly unregulated marketplace, sexually explicit materials would have the right to compete for attention with President Barack Obama's position papers, and would be subject to no more regulatory burdens than core political speech. *See* Krotoszynski, *supra* note 30, at 24 ("Under a pure market based approach to the First Amendment, speech should be treated the same regardless of its content. Its success or failure would be a function of its ability to persuade.")

66. *See* Krotoszynski, *supra* note 30, at 102–118.

67. *See id.* at 51–69.

68. *Id.* at 42–45, 54–56.

69. *See* Kathleen E. Mahoney, *Hate Speech: Affirmation or Contradiction of Freedom of Expression,* 1996 U. Ill. L. Rev. 789, 797–804.

70. *See* Cohen v. San Bernardino Valley College, 92 F.3d 968, 972 (9th Cir. 1996); Sigma Chi Fraternity v. George Mason University, 993 F.2d 386 (4th Cir. 1993); Daubot v. Central Mich. Univ., 839 F. Supp. 477, 484 (E.D. Mich. 1993); UWM, Inc. v. Bd. of Regents of the Univ. of Wis., 774 F. Supp. 1163, 1173 (E.D. Wis. 1991); Doe v. Univ. of Mich., 721 F. Supp. 852 (E.D. Mich. 1989); *see also* J. Peter Byrne, *Constitutional Academic Freedom after* Grutter: *Getting Real about the "Four Freedoms" of a University,* 77 U. Colo. L. Rev. 929, 944 (2006) (noting that federal courts "unanimously struck down university speech codes directed at racial insults or sexual harassment for being overbroad and vague"); Melanie A. Moore, Note, *Free Speech on College Campuses: Protecting the First Amendment in the Marketplace of Ideas,* 96 W. Va. L. Rev. 511, 531 (1996) ("Courts analyzing university speech codes have uniformly held that the codes represent unconstitutional restrictions on free speech in violation of the First Amendment."). For an overview of the various kinds of speech codes that both public and private colleges and universities have adopted over the past several decades, see James R. Bussrian, Comment, *Anatomy of the Campus Speech Code: An Examination of Prevailing Regulations,* 36 S. Tex. L. Rev. 153, 172–89 (1996).

71. *Brandenburg,* 395 U.S. at 447–49.

72. Sedition Act, ch. 74, 1 Stat. 596–97 (July 14, 1798). However, the Federalists were no fools: the Sedition Act contained a sunset provision of March 3, 1801, a date that just happened to correspond with the end of President John Adams's term of office. *See* 1 Stat. 597, § 4 (stating that the Sedition Act would expire on March 3, 1801, literally the day before the end of President Adams's term of office expired). Thus, the law silenced critics (on pain of a criminal conviction and imprisonment) for the remainder of Adams's term but released Federalists to attack the new Democratic-Republican administration if Thomas Jefferson were to be elected to the presidency in national election of 1800.

73. *See infra* chapter 3, section IV, text and accompanying notes 125–53.

74. *See* Gooding v. Wilson, 405 U.S. 518, 523 (1972) (holding protected threats directed to police officer, including "white son of a bitch, I'll kill you"); Rosenfeld v. New Jersey, 408 U.S. 901, 901, 904 (1972) (holding protected the use of the phrase "mother fucker"

at a public school board meeting "on four occasions, to describe the teachers, the school board, the town, and his own country"); Cohen v. California, 403 U.S. 15, 22–23 (1971) (holding protected the wearing of a jacket emblazoned with "Fuck the Draft" in public).

75. *See* ACLU of Colo. v. City & County of Denver, 569 F. Supp. 2d 1142, 1176–78 (D. Colo. 2008).

76. Beauharnais v. Illinois, 343 U.S. 250 (1952).

77. Chaplinsky v. New Hampshire, 315 U.S. 568 (1942).

78. *See supra* chapter 2, section II.A.1., text and accompanying notes 32–38.

79. KROTOSZYNSKI, *supra* note 30, at 82–89 (discussing the inconsistent enforcement of hate speech regulations in Canada).

80. *See supra* chapter 2, sections III. and IV.

81. *See* Timothy Zick, *Space, Place, and Speech: The Expressive Topography*, 74 GEO. WASH. L. REV. 439, 440–42, 466–87 (2006); Timothy Zick, *Speech and Spatial Tactics*, 84 TEX. L. REV. 581, 583–87, 640–50 (2006). As Professor Zick persuasively argues, "Speakers there [at antiabortion protests outside family planning clinics] are not concerned with access to the sidewalk itself; they want access to the listeners' personal spaces in order to deliver their message." Zick, *Space, Place, and Speech, supra*, at 489. Moreover, he is quite correct to posit that "[e]ntire aspects of an expressive culture, including face-to-face proselytizing and political assembly and dissent, have been substantially diminished and devalued as a result of our failure to grasp the importance of 'place.'" *Id.* at 440.

82. *See, e.g.*, Boos v. Barry, 485 U.S.312, 320–23 (1988) ("We consider first whether the display clause serves a compelling governmental interest in protecting the dignity of foreign diplomatic personnel. Since the dignity of foreign officials will be affronted by signs critical of their governments or governmental policies, we are told, these foreign diplomats must be shielded from such insults in order to fulfill our country's obligations under international law."); *cf. id.* at 322 (noting that the well-established free speech doctrine in the United States includes legal protection for "insulting, and even outrageous, speech" notwithstanding the insulting, demeaning, or emotionally debilitating nature of the speech and observing that "[w]e are not persuaded that the differences between foreign officials and American citizens require us to deviate from these [First Amendment] principles here").

83. *See* OFFICE OF PRESIDENTIAL ADVANCE, PRESIDENTIAL ADVANCE MANUAL 34 (2002); *see also* Peter Baker, *White House Guidebook on Protestors*, SEATTLE TIMES, Aug. 23, 2007, at A11 (noting that official *Presidential Advance Manual* instructs those organizing and supervising presidential events to banish protestors to areas that are not within eyesight or earshot of the president and quoting the manual as stating that "[i]f it is determined that the media will not see or hear them [the protestors] and that they pose no potential disruption to the event, they can be ignored"). Obviously, this strongly suggests that avoiding the redeployment of media coverage, rather than genuine security concerns, has much to do with the limits on protest activity physically proximate to the president.

84. *See supra* chapter 2, sections III.A. and D.

85. Comedy Central dispatched a crew to the Denver 2008 DNC designated protest area and found it largely empty, save for a large group of skateboarders using the area to practice their moves. In other words, the site was so unsuitable for an effective protest that, in point of fact, it did not get much, if any, use.

86. An Act for the Punishment of Certain Crimes Against the United States, ch. 74, 1 Stat. 596 (July 14, 1798).

87. *See infra* chapter 3, section IV, text and accompanying notes 125–53 (discussing the enactment and Adams administration's strategic enforcement of the Sedition Act of 1798); *see also* William T. Mayton, *Seditious Libel and the Lost Guarantee of a Freedom of Expression*, 84 Colum. L. Rev. 91, 123–25 (discussing and critiquing the politically motivated adoption and subsequent enforcement of the Sedition Act of 1798 to silence the opposition Republicans).

88. Mayton, *supra* note 87, at 123–24 ("But undoubtedly this Federalist talk of internal enemies was not more than poor camouflage for a measure favoring incumbency."); *see* James P. Martin, *When Repression Is Democratic and Constitutional: The Federalist Theory of Representation and the Sedition Act of 1798*, 66 U. Chi. L. Rev. 117, 126–27 (1999) (noting that the Federalists "tenaciously . . . argued that protecting the reputation of the rulers and repressing political associations were necessary to representative government" because "the majority had elected the government to make policy decisions" and "by obstructing the government, one obstructs the majority").

89. *See infra* chapter 3, section IV.

90. *See Lüth*, 7 BverfGE 198, 208 (1958); *see also* David P. Currie, The Constitution of the Federal Republic of Germany 175 (1994); Edward J. Eberle, *Public Discourse in Contemporary Germany*, 47 Case W. Res. L. Rev. 797, 825 (1997); Krotoszynski, *supra* note 30, at 118–20, 123–30.

91. Grundgesetz [Basic Law], arts. 5(3), 8(2), 18, 20(4), 21(2) (F.R.G.) [hereinafter Basic Law]; *see also* Krotoszynski, *supra* note 30, at 96–102.

92. *See* Krotoszynski, *supra* note 30, at 124–25.

93. *See, e.g.*, *German National Anthem*, 81 BverfGE 298 (2000), *reprinted in* 2 Decisions of the Federal Constitutional Court (Part II) 450 (1992); *Flag Desecration Case*, 81 BverfGE 278 (1990), *reprinted in* 2 Decisions of the Federal Constitutional Court (Part II) 437 (1992); *see generally* Krotoszynski, *supra* note 30, at 117–18.

94. *See* Ute Krüdewagen, *Political Symbols in Two Constitutional Orders: The Flag Desecration Decisions of the United States Supreme Court and the German Federal Constitutional Court*, 19 Ariz. J. Int'l & Comp. L. 679, 707–10 (2002). Krüdewagen argues that an attack on the flag "is understood to include an attack on the symbolized—the free democratic basic order"—and "[i]n this situation, the concept of militant democracy requires the state to defend itself." *Id.* at 709.

95. *Id.*

96. *See* Brandenburg v. Ohio, 395 U.S. 444, 447–49 (1969).

97. United States v. Eichman, 496 U.S. 310, 315, 317–19 (1990); Texas v. Johnson, 491 U.S. 397, 410–14 (1989); *cf. Eichman*, 496 U.S. at 319–22 (Stevens, J., dissenting) (arguing that the federal government possesses a compelling interest in preserving the flag as a

sacred national symbol that "uniquely symbolizes . . . ideas of liberty, equality, and tolerance" that help to constitute a national identity).

98. 485 U.S. 312 (1988).

99. *See id.* at 315–16; *see also* D.C. Code § 22–1115 (1981). Michael Boos, and his companion, Bridget M. Becker, wished to display signs with slogans such as "Release Sakharov" and "Solidarity" on a public sidewalk outside the Soviet Embassy in Washington, D.C. *Boos*, 485 U.S. at 315. Another plaintiff, J. Michael Waller, wished to picket the Nicaraguan Embassy, in Washington, D.C., with a sign that said "Stop the Killing." *Id.*

100. *Id.* at 822.

101. *Id.*; *see* Hustler Magazine, Inc. v. Falwell, 485 U.S. 46, 50–51, 55–56 (1988).

102. *Boos*, 485 U.S. at 324.

103. *Id.* at 329.

104. *See* KROTOSZYNSKI, *supra* note 30, at 114–18, 136–37.

105. Judith Schenck Koffler & Bennett L. Gershman, *The New Seditious Libel*, 69 CORNELL L. REV. 816 (1984).

106. *Id.* at 819

107. *Id.*; *see also* Mayton, *supra* note 87, at 97–108; Alan J. Koshner, *The Founding Fathers and Political Speech: The First Amendment, the Press and the Sedition Act of 1798*, 6 ST. LOUIS U. PUB. L. REV. 395, 400–404 (1987).

108. Koffler & Gershman, *supra* note 105, at 820.

109. *Id.* at 822.

110. David Jenkins, *The Sedition Act of 1798 and the Incorporation of Seditious Libel into First Amendment Jurisprudence*, 45 AM. J. LEGAL HIST. 154, 160 (2001).

111. Leonard Levy, FREEDOM OF SPEECH AND PRESS IN EARLY AMERICAN HISTORY: LEGACY OF SUPPRESSION 11 (1963).

112. Koffler and Gershman, *supra* note 105, at 822.

113. Jenkins, *supra* note 110, at 162–63.

114. 4 WILLIAM BLACKSTONE, COMMENTARIES ON THE LAWS OF ENGLAND *150.

115. Levy, *supra* note 111, at 19 (estimating there were only six prosecutions); *see also* Harold L. Nelson, *Seditious Libel in Colonial America*, 3 AM. J. LEGAL HIST. 160, 165–70 (1959) (finding that there were only nine prosecutions brought against publishers during the colonial period).

116. Levy, *supra* note 111, at 18–19.

117. *Id.*

118. *Id.*; *see* David A. Anderson, *The Origins of the Free Press Clause*, 30 UCLA L. REV. 455, 510 (1983).

119. *Id.* at 510–11.

120. *Id.*

121. Koshner, *supra* note 107, at 404.

122. Nelson, *supra* note 115, at 170.

123. Levy, *supra* note 111, at 87.

124. *Id.* at 181–82.

125. Sedition Act, ch. 74, 1 Stat. 596 (July 14, 1798); *see* Jenkins, *supra* note 110, at 164.

126. Sedition Act, ch. 74, 1 Stat. at 596, § 2; *see* Jenkins, *supra* note 110, at 165.

127. Sedition Act, ch. 74, 1 Stat. at 597, § 2.

128. *Id.* at § 3; *see* Jenkins, *supra* note 110, at 165.

129. Thomas Carroll, *Freedom of Speech and of the Press in the Federalist Period: The Sedition Act*, 18 MICH. L. REV. 615, 648 (1920).

130. *Id.*

131. *Id.* at 639.

132. James M. Smith, *The Sedition Law, Free Speech, and the American Political Process*, 9 WM. & MARY QTRLY. 497, 502 (1952).

133. *Id.*

134. *Id.*

135. *Id.*

136. *Id.* at 504.

137. Carroll, *supra* note 129, at 648.

138. David Yassky, *Eras of the First Amendment*, 91 COLUM. L. REV. 1699, 1711 (1991).

139. *Id.; see also* Smith, *supra* note 132, at 504.

140. Leonard Levy, FREEDOM OF SPEECH AND PRESS IN EARLY AMERICAN HISTORY: LEGACY OF SUPPRESSION 259 (1963).

141. 8 ANNALS OF CONGRESS 2110 (Joseph Gales & William W. Seaton eds., 1851) (statement of Rep. Gallatin) (July 5, 1798); *see* Martin, *supra* note 88, at 139 ("Federalist theory also found expression in the charge that opposition to the government was a traitorous attempt to defeat the will of the people."); *id.* at 149 ("Under this conception, it is clear that opposition to the policies of the government was tantamount to opposing both representative government and the Constitution itself.").

142. Yassky, *supra* note 138, at 1711.

143. *Id.* By far the most ludicrous of the Sedition Act prosecutions was that of Luther Baldwin. Baldwin was indicted, convicted, and fined $150 for stating that the country would have benefitted if some cannon fire had lodged in President Adams's buttock. *See id.* For an account of every prosecution under the Sedition Act, *see* James M. Smith, FREEDOM'S FETTERS: THE ALIEN AND SEDITION LAWS AND AMERICAN CIVIL LIBERTIES 254 (1956). In his book, Smith also details the prosecution of the Act's state law equivalents during Adams's presidency.

144. Smith, *supra* note 132, at 504.

145. *Id.* The Boston *Chronicle* had already been prosecuted for violation of the Sedition Act in March 1799. Its bookkeeper, Abijah Adams, was convicted under the act because the *Chronicle's* editor, Thomas Adams, was too ill to stand trial. Smith, *supra* note 132, at 254.

146. *Id.* at 254, 504–05.

147. *Id.* at 504–05.

148. The Baltimore *American* was excluded from prosecution. *See id.*

149. *Id.* at 505.

150. Anderson, *supra* note 118, at 515–16 n.345.

151. *See id.* at 516 n.345. Professor Anderson notes that "the papers that were prosecuted . . . were those from which most of the lesser Republican papers copied their political material." *Id.*

152. *Id.*

153. *See id.* at 515 ("The Act came perilously close to eliminating the entire opposition press in the United States.").

154. Ch. 30, 40 Stat. 217 (1917), *repealed by* Act of June 24, 1948, ch. 645, § 21, 62 Stat. 864.

155. Harry Kalven Jr., *The* New York Times *Case: A Note on the "Central Meaning of the First Amendment,"* 1964 Sup. Ct. Rev. 191, 207.

156. Koffler & Gershman, *supra* note 105, at 832.

157. Jenkins, *supra* note 110, at 205.

158. *Id.* at 207. Contemporary scholarly commentary also supported the notion that the federal government could criminalize seditious libel. *See* Edward S. Corwin, *Freedom of Speech and Press under the First Amendment: A Resume,* 30 Yale L.J. 48 (1920); *see* Pierce v. United States, 252 U.S. 239 (1920); Schaefer v. United States, 251 U.S. 466 (1920); Frowerk v. United States, 249 U.S. 264 (1919); Debs v. United States, 249 U.S. 211 (1919); Schenck v. United States, 249 U.S. 47 (1919); *see also* Koffler & Gershman, *supra* note 105, at 831–40 (discussing and critiquing several of the principle cases arising under the Espionage Act of 1917).

159. Ch. 439, 54 Stat. 670 (1940).

160. Koffler & Gershman, *supra* note 105, at 840.

161. 341 U.S. 494 (1951).

162. Koffler & Gershman, *supra* note 105, at 840.

163. *See supra* chapter 2, section III.

164. Schneider v. State, 308 U.S. 147, 162–63 (1939).

165. *Id.* at 163.

166. *Id.* at 162.

CHAPTER 4. THE RIGHT OF PETITION IN HISTORICAL PERSPECTIVE AND
ACROSS THREE SOCIETIES

1. For in-depth histories of the Petition Clause, see generally Carol Rice Andrews, *A Right of Access to Court under the Petition Clause of the First Amendment: Defining the Right,* 60 Ohio St. L.J. 557 (1999); Gregory A. Mark, *The Vestigial Constitution: The History and Significance of the Right to Petition,* 66 Fordham L. Rev. 2153 (1998); Norman B. Smith, *"Shall Make No Law Abridging . . .": An Analysis of the Neglected, but Nearly Absolute, Right of Petition,* 54 U. Cin. L. Rev. 1153, 1190–91 (1986); Julie M. Spanbauer, *The First Amendment Right to Petition Government for a Redress of Grievances: Cut from a Different Cloth,* 21 Hastings Const. L.Q. 15 (1993); Stephen A. Higginson, Note, *A Short History of the Right to Petition Government for a Redress of Grievances,* 96 Yale L.J. 142 (1986). The history of the Petition Clause is also discussed in Gary Lawson & Guy Seidman, *Downsizing the Right to Petition,* 93 Nw. U. L. Rev. 739 (1999); James E. Pfander, *Sovereign Immunity and the Right to Petition: Toward a First Amendment Right to Pursue Judicial Claims against the Government,* 91 Nw. U. L. Rev. 899 (1997); Eric Schnapper, *"Libelous" Petitions for Redress of Grievances—Bad Historiography Makes Worse Law,* 74 Iowa L. Rev. 303 (1989);

Rebecca A. Clar, Comment, Martin v. City of Del City: *A Lost Opportunity to Restore the First Amendment Right to Petition,* 74 St. John's L. Rev. 483 (2000); James Filkins, Note, Tarpley v. Keistler: *Patronage, Petition, and the* Noerr-Pennington *Doctrine,* 50 DePaul L. Rev. 265 (2000); Kara Elizabeth Shea, Recent Development, San Filippo v. Bongiovanni: *The Public Concern Criteria and the Scope of the Modern Petition Right,* 48 Vand. L. Rev. 1697 (1995).

2. *See* Schnapper, *supra* note 1, at 318; Smith, *supra* note 1, at 1155–62, 1165–69; Spanbauer, *supra* note 1, at 34–39. Even after their codification in the First Amendment, the rights of speech, press, and assembly in both the United States and the United Kingdom still lacked the near-absolute character of the right to petition, largely due to the continuing existence of seditious libel laws. *Compare id.* (describing the means by which speech and press continued to be limited through the early nineteenth century); Smith, *supra* note 1, at 1181 ("[P]rior to the American Revolution, several of the other rights guaranteed by the Bill of Rights, including the cognate rights of speech, press, and assembly, were subjected to widespread suppression."), *with* Bill of Rights, 1 W. & M., c. 2, § 5 (1689) (Eng.), *reprinted in* 5 The Founders' Constitution 2 (Philip B. Kurland & Ralph Lerner eds., 1987) ("[I]t is the right of the subjects to petition the King, and all committments [*sic*] and prosecutions for such petitioning are illegal."); Smith, *supra* note 1, at 1165 ("In England, after 1702, there appear to have been no cases of criminal prosecution or parliamentary contempt proceedings on account of petitioning.").

3. *See* Smith, *supra* note 1, at 1168–69 (describing the role of petitioning in giving birth to the rights of expression and assembly); *id.* at 1179–80 ("Petitioning, in a sense, is the fountain of liberties, because historically it was the first popular right to be recognized. Vigorous exercise of the right to petition has been associated with forward strides in the development of speech, press, and assembly."). Highlighting the supremacy of petitioning, an English judge in 1688 interrupted the Recorder's comparison of writing a book with writing a petition to say, "Pray, good Mr. Recorder, don't compare the writing of a book to the making of a petition; for it is the birthright of the subject to petition." Trial of the Seven Bishops for Publishing a Libel, 12 How. St. Tr. 183, 415 (1688), *reprinted in* 5 The Founders' Constitution, *supra* note 2, at 191.

4. *See infra* chapter 4, sections II and III.

5. By "classic petitioning," I mean petitioning that had as its primary objective some sort of legislative remedy, involving a petition presented by a small group, with the principal intended audience of the petition being legislators rather than the general public. Classic petitioning flourished in the United Kingdom from 1779 to 1836, see *infra* chapter 4, section II.A., and in the United States from the very first meeting of Congress, in 1789, until 1836, see *infra* chapter 4, section III.C. I maintain a distinction between this "classic" form of petitioning and later, more hybrid forms of petitioning, which involved a traditional petition, but which had as their object a mass public campaign to move public opinion, in which the petition was simply a focal point for organizational and political activity. In systemic, or hybrid, petitioning, the legislature constitutes only one of several intended audiences, which include other citizens and the media. Systemic petitioning seeks ultimately to secure legislative, even

constitutional, change but does so through both direct and indirect means. Public demonstrations, rallies, and parades, as well as door-to-door mass canvassing, also make up part of systemic petitioning but did not play much, if any, role in classic petitioning. One might think of classic petitioning as primarily a legislative proceeding and systemic petitioning as a kind of political activity with legislative objectives.

6. Mark, *supra* note 1, at 2163 & nn.24, 26 ("The ability to apply for redress of grievances was, at least in its earliest stages, clearly not a tool for general grievances, much less reform, or even a mechanism for first hearing an individual's grievance, but rather was akin to an appellate mechanism from the decisions of inferior authorities.").

7. *Id.* at 2164–65.

8. Magna Carta, c. 61 (1215) (Eng.), *reprinted in* 5 THE FOUNDERS' CONSTITUTION, *supra* note 2, at 187.

9. WILLIAM STUBBS, 2 THE CONSTITUTIONAL HISTORY OF ENGLAND 285 (1880).

10. *See* 2 RUDOLPH GRIEIST, THE HISTORY OF THE ENGLISH CONSTITUTION 13 (Philip A. Ashworth trans., G. P. Putnam's Sons, 1886) ("[T]he whole of the Middle Ages is a practical refutation of the theory of an executive power *in abstracto.* The motions of the commoners and the petitions which they recommended, gain with each ensuing generation a stronger stress, which metamorphosed their right of praying into a virtual right of co-resolution."); *see also* Mark, *supra* note 1, at 2165–66; Smith, *supra* note 1, at 1155–56; Spanbauer, *supra* note 1, at 23.

11. Stubbs, *supra* note 9, at 623.

12. *Id.* at 286.

13. *See* Mark, *supra* note 1, at 2166 n.34. As Rudolph Grieist explained in his *History of the English Constitution:* "The custom of presenting private petitions immediately to the Lower House, with the desire that the House be pleased to exert its influence with the King, occurs for the first time under Henry IV. Such petitions are now directed sometimes to the King, sometimes to the King in council, sometime to the King, Lords, and Commons, sometimes to the Lords and Commons, and sometimes to the Commons alone, with the request to use their good offices with the King and the council." GRIEIST, *supra* note 10, at 14–15.

14. Smith, *supra* note 1, at 1155 (quoting J. E. A. JOLLIFFE, THE CONSTITUTIONAL HISTORY OF MEDIEVAL ENGLAND 405 (4th ed. 1961)).

15. *See infra* chapter 4, sections II.A. and B.

16. *See* Elizabeth Read Foster, *Petitions and the Petition of Right,* 14 J. OF BRIT. STUD. 21 (1974).

17. EDWARD WAVELL RIDGES, CONSTITUTIONAL LAW OF ENGLAND 183 (A. Berriedale Keith ed. 6th ed. 1937) ("The result of the Petition of Right, 1628, the Bill of Rights, 1689, and the Act of Settlement, 1701, was thus a vast curtailment of the unbridled prerogative claimed by the Stuarts under the theory of divine right.").

18. Stubbs, *supra* note 9, at 625.

19. *See id.* at 623–25.

20. WILLIAM R. ANSON, THE LAW AND CUSTOM OF THE CONSTITUTION, PART 1 at 346 (2nd ed. 1892).

21. *See* Spanbauer, *supra* note 1, at 19–20; THOMAS ERSKINE MAY, 1 THE CONSTITUTIONAL HISTORY OF ENGLAND SINCE THE ACCESSION OF GEORGE THE THIRD 1760–1860, at 436 (noting that "[n]umerous petitions of a political character, and signed by large bodies of people, were addressed to the Long Parliament" but also observing that "[t]he supporters of their [Parliament's] cause, were thanked and encouraged: its incautious opponents, if they ventured to petition, were punished as delinquents").

22. Anson, *supra* note 20, at 346 ("A Committee of Grievances, to which petitions were referred, was appointed by the House of Commons in 1571, and throughout the reigns of James I and Charles I entries appear in the Journals of the House regulating or referring to the proceedings of this Committee.").

23. Mark, *supra* note 1, at 2169–70 ("Petitioning came to be regarded as part of the Constitution, that fabric of political customs which defined English rights. . . . Petitioning became part of the regular political life of the English, not just because it was conducive to the interests of petitioners, and not just because it provided a foundation for Parliament, especially the Commons, to assert its own expanding legislative powers. It was also a mechanism that bound the English together in a web of mutual obligation and acknowledgment of certain commonalities.").

24. Anson, *supra* note 20, at 346. Prior to the seventeenth century, most petitions were private petitions; i.e., those "which asked for changes or exemptions from the law on behalf of individuals." *Id.*

25. Smith, *supra* note 1, at 1157.

26. Smith, *supra* note 1, at 1160. That prosecution has come to be known as *The Case of the Seven Bishops. See infra* chapter 5, section II.C., text and accompanying notes 83–91.

27. A. GREY, 1 DEBATES OF THE HOUSE OF COMMONS FROM THE YEAR 1667 TO THE YEAR 1694, at 209–10 (1769); *see* Anson, *supra* note 20, at 347. For a discussion of the events of 1668–1669 that led the House of Commons to adopt this declaration, see Schnapper, *supra* note 1, at 333–34, 344.

28. Grey, *supra* note 27, at 209–10; Anson, *supra* note 20, at 347; ROBERT LUCE, LEGISLATIVE PRINCIPLES: THE HISTORY AND THEORY OF LAWMAKING BY REPRESENTATIVE GOVERNMENT 516–17 (1930).

29. DON L. SMITH, DISSERTATION, THE RIGHT TO PETITION FOR REDRESS OF GRIEVANCES: CONSTITUTIONAL DEVELOPMENT AND INTERPRETATION 43 (unpublished dissertation August 1971) (manuscript on file with author) (noting that petitions did not always generate a favorable response and observing that "whenever a petition offended them [the Crown and Parliament], they simply ignored it or took years to grant settlement") [hereinafter Smith Dissertation].

30. *Id.* at 44.

31. ERSKINE MAY'S TREATISE ON THE LAW, PRIVILEGES, PROCEEDINGS AND USAGE OF PARLIAMENT 809 (Donald Limon & W.R. McKay eds. 22nd ed. 1997).

32. May, *supra* note 21, at 438.

33. *Id.*

34. Peter Fraser, *Public Petitioning and Parliament before 1832,* 46 HIST. 195, 200–201 (1961).

35. *Id.* at 201.

36. *See id.* at 199–204.

37. *See* May, *supra* note 21, at 437 (noting that "in 1701 the Commons imprisoned five of the Kentish petitioners, until the end of the session, for praying that loyal addresses of the House, might be turned into bills of supply" for King William in preparation for a possible war with France).

38. Luce, *supra* note 28, at 517.

39. Grey, *supra* note 27, at 209–10; *see* Luce, *supra* note 28, at 518.

40. *See* DANIEL DEFOE, THE HISTORY OF THE KENTISH PETITIONERS 9 (1701). For a contemporary account of the events associated with the Kentish petition, see *id.* at 1–17.

41. *Id.* at 19.

42. *Id.*

43. *See id.* at 18–22.

44. Luce, *supra* note 28, at 518.

45. *Id.* at 519.

46. *See id.* at 519–23.

47. Fraser, *supra* note 34, at 202.

48. May, *supra* note 21, at 439.

49. Fraser, *supra* note 34, at 202.

50. *Id.* at 199.

51. May, *supra* note 21, at 440.

52. *Id.*

53. *Id.*

54. *See* Fraser, *supra* note 34, at 204. Professor Lieber concurs with this assessment of the importance of petitioning to the lapse of the income tax in 1816: "He recalled the circumstances under which the old income tax was repealed, in defiance of the government of that day; through the instrumentality of nightly discussions on petitions—*a popular privilege no longer allowed in the house of commons.* . . . [Thus] the campaign which took place in 1816 could not be fought again. How was that campaign conducted? By means of petitions. For five or six weeks, from four o'clock in the afternoon until two or three o'clock in the morning, petition after petition was presented, and each petition was debated." FRANCIS LIEBER, ON CIVIL LIBERTY AND SELF-GOVERNMENT 122 n.1 (3rd ed. 1875) (emphasis in the original).

55. *See* Fraser, *supra* note 34, at 202–09.

56. *See* Paul A. Pickering, *"And Your Petitioners &c": Chartist Petitioning in Popular Politics 1838–48,* 116 ENG. HIST. REV. 368, 372–78 (2001).

57. Luce, *supra* note 28, at 518–19.

58. Fraser, *supra* note 34, at 207.

59. *Id.*

60. May, *supra* note 21, at 441.

61. *Id.* at 441–42; *see also id.* at 442 ("On a single day, in 1860, nearly four thousand petitions were presented, on the question of church rates.").

62. Fraser, *supra* note 34, at 211.

63. May, *supra* note 21, at 443.

64. *Id.* at 443.

65. JOSEF REDLICH, 1 THE PROCEDURE OF THE HOUSE OF COMMONS: A STUDY OF ITS HISTORY AND PRESENT FORM 76 (A. Ernest Steinthal trans., 1903); *see also* Fraser, *supra* note 34, at 208 n.58 ("There were four motions upon which discussion could arise: that the petition be brought up, that it be received, that it lie on the table, and the it be printed.").

66. Colin Leys, *Petitioning in the Nineteenth and Twentieth Centuries*, 3 POL. STUD. 45, 48 (Feb. 1955)

67. *See* REPORT FROM SELECT COMMITTEE ON PUBLIC PETITIONS WITH MINUTES OF EVIDENCE; 1831–32; H.C. 639 (Eng.) (July 25, 1832).

68. Leys, *supra* note 66, at 50–51.

69. Redlich, *supra* note 65, at 76.

70. *Id.* at 76 n.1 (quoting petition statistics from *Report of the Office of the Speaker on Public Petitions* 33 (1853)).

71. Leys, *supra* note 66, at 52.

72. Redlich, *supra* note 65, at 77.

73. *Id.*

74. Leys, *supra* note 66, at 52.

75. *See* REPORT FROM THE SELECT COMMITTEE ON STANDING ORDERS REVISION 1854 at 80; 1854; H.C. 371 (Eng.) (July 14, 1854) (reprinting the standing order of April 14, 1842, prohibiting all debate on public petitions and requiring that a member presenting a petition to the House "do confine himself to a statement of the Parties from whom it comes, of the number of signatures attached to it, and of the material allegations contained in it, and to the reading of the prayer of such Petition").

76. Leys, *supra* note 66, at 53.

77. LLEWELLYN WOODWARD, THE AGE OF REFORM 1815–1870, at 134–35 (2nd ed. 1962); *see* Robin Handley, *Public Order, Petitioning, and Freedom of Assembly*, 7 J. LEGAL HIST. 123, 129 (1986) ("1836 saw the birth of the Chartist movement, demanding annual elections to Parliament based on equal electoral districts, universal male suffrage, a secret ballot, the removal of property qualifications for Members of Parliament, and payment for Members.").

78. Woodward, *supra* note 77, at 134 n.1.

79. Handley, *supra* note 77, at 129.

80. H. W. CARLESS DAVIS, THE AGE OF GREY AND PEEL 173 (1929).

81. *Id.* at 174.

82. *See infra* chapter 4, section II.C., text and accompanying notes 104–14.

83. Lord Irving of Lairg, *Sovereignty in Comparative Perspective: Constitutionalism in Britain and America*, 76 N.Y.U. L. REV. 1, 12 (2001).

84. *See* Reform Act, 1832, 2 & 3 Will. 4, ch. 65 (Eng.). Nevertheless, as one British jurist recently observed, "it was not until the nineteenth century (at the earliest) that it became possible, with the passing of the Reform Acts, to articulate any sort of normative democratic justification for the sovereign power wielded by Parliament." Lord Irving of Lairg, *supra* note 83, at 9.

85. Davis, *supra* note 80, at 174–75.

86. Handley, *supra* note 77, at 129.
87. Pickering, *supra* note 56, at 372.
88. *Id.* at 373.
89. *Id.* at 374.
90. *Id.* at 375.
91. *See id.* at 387 ("From her vast experience, Eleanor Rathbone, one of the leaders of the constitutional women's suffrage movement and later MP, raised the idea of the canvass to a new level of sophistication when she calculated that one million signatures could be collected in 13 and a half weeks by 900 activists working 12 hours a week.").
92. Linda Colley, Britons: Forging the Nation, 1707–1837, at 292–95 (1994).
93. Pickering, supra note 56, at 382.
94. *Id.* at 372.
95. *Id.* at 373.
96. May, *supra* note 21, at 443–44.
97. *Id.* at 444.
98. Pickering, supra note 56, at 378.
99. *Id.*
100. *Id.* at 377.
101. *Id.* (quoting an editorial published in the *Charter*, a pro-Chartist newspaper, on July 21, 1839).
102. *Id.* at 378.
103. *See id.*
104. Leys, *supra* note 66, at 54.
105. Anson, *supra* note 20, at 348.
106. Leys, *supra* note 66, at 54.
107. Robert L. Nicholls, *Surrogate for Democracy: Nineteenth-Century British Petitioning,* 5 Maryland Historian 43, 51 (Spring 1974).
108. *See* Lord Irving of Lairg, *supra* note 83, at 11–15 (discussing and citing major electoral reform bills and their effect on enfranchising larger percentages of the British population from the Reform Act of 1832 to the Equal Suffrage Act of 1928).
109. Representation of the People Act, 1884, 48 Vict., ch. 3 (Eng.).
110. Lord Irving of Lairg, *supra* note 83, at 12.
111. Representation of the People Act, 1918, 7 & 8 Geo. 5, ch. 64 (Eng.); Parliament (Qualification of Women) Act, 1918, 8 & 9 Geo. 5, ch. 47 (Eng.).
112. Representation of the People (Equal Franchise) Act, 1928, 18 & 19 Geo. 5, c. 12 (Eng.).
113. *See* Nicholls, *supra* note 107, at 46 (providing a graph of the frequency of petitions and number of signatories from 1830 to 1920, showing spikes in 1871 and 1892).
114. The growth of reliable polling techniques might have undermined the utility of petitioning as a means of signaling elected officials about the wishes and attitudes of the body politic. The time at which petitioning seems to wane most dramatically—the early twentieth century—is also the time when reliable public polling began to emerge as a valid form of social science research. *See* Jean M. Converse, Survey Research in the United States: Roots and Emergence 1890–1960 (1987). For

example, in the Soviet Union, letter writing and letters to the editor served as a proxy for public opinion for incumbent government officials, but they no longer serve this role in the contemporary Russian Federation. *See* ELLEN MICKIEWICZ, MEDIA AND THE RUSSIAN PUBLIC 1–17 (1981). On the other hand, this explanation also seems at best partial; a more complete explanation would require careful consideration of cultural changes in the United Kingdom during and after World War I. It might be, after the horrors of the "war to end all wars," that organic community-based political activities, such as circulating petitions for presentation to Parliament, seemed at best naive and at worst useless. My own best guess is that significant cultural changes in the attitudes of U.K. citizens, perhaps brought about or exacerbated by World War I, probably account for the radical change in petitioning behavior by the 1920s.

115. Nicholls, *supra* note 107, at 47–49.

116. *Id.* at 50.

117. *Id.* at 51.

118. *Id.*

119. Leys, *supra* note 66, at 55.

120. *Id.* at 56.

121. Pickering, *supra* note 56, at 377–78.

122. Leys, *supra* note 66, at 59.

123. Nicholls, *supra* note 107, at 51.

124. Leys, *supra* note 66, at 61.

125. *Id.* at 62.

126. ERSKINE MAY'S TREATISE ON THE LAW, PRIVILEGES, PROCEEDINGS AND USAGE OF PARLIAMENT 822 (David Lidderdale ed., 19th ed. 1976) [hereinafter "Lidderdale"].

127. *Id.*

128. *Id.* at 821.

129. *Id.* at 821–22.

130. ERSKINE MAY'S TREATISE ON THE LAW, PRIVILEGES, PROCEEDINGS AND USAGE OF PARLIAMENT 932 (William McKay ed. 23rd ed. 2004).

131. *Id.*

132. *See id.* at 933–35.

133. *Id.* at 939.

134. *Id.* at 940.

135. *Id.*

136. *Id.*

137. *Id.* at 941.

138. Handley, *supra* note 77, at 153 n.88.

139. Ridges, *supra* note 17, at 80.

140. Leys, *supra* note 66, at 45.

141. *Id.* at 62.

142. *Id.*

143. Pickering, *supra* note 56, at 369.

144. *Id.* at 375.

145. SPECIAL REPORT FROM THE COMMITTEE ON PUBLIC PETITIONS 1, ¶ 1; 1943–44; H.C. 80 (Eng.) (May 24, 1944) (hearing of March 30, 1944).
146. *Id.*
147. *Id.* at 2, ¶ 6 (hearing of March 30, 1944).
148. *Id.* at 2, ¶ 11 (statement of Dr. Russell Thomas).
149. *Id.* at 3, ¶ 16 (statement of Dr. Russell Thomas).
150. *Id.* at 3, ¶ 18 (statement of Mr. Viant).
151. *Id.* at 3, ¶ 19 (statement of Dr. Russell Thomas).
152. *Id.* at 4, ¶ 34 (statement of Sir Edward Campbell).
153. *Id.* at 5, ¶ 36 (statements of Sir Ernest Makins and Sir Edward Campbell).
154. *Id.* at 7–8, appendix (Memorandum of Sir Gilbert Campion) (March 27, 1944).
155. Lidderdale, *supra* note 154, at 811.
156. *See* Mark, *supra* note 1, at 2176–77 ("Colonial experience appears not only to have replicated England's widespread use of the petition, it likely extended it in both law and practice.").
157. *See id.* at 2176–78. For example, the Body of Liberties adopted by the Massachusetts Bay Colony Assembly in 1641 promised an exceptionally broad right to petition almost fifty years before passage of the English Bill of Rights: "Every man whether Inhabitant or fforreiner, free or not free shall have libertie to come to any publique Court, Councell, or Towne meeting, and either by speech or writing to move any lawfull, seasonable, and materiall question, or to present any necessary motion, complaint, petition, Bill or information, whereof that meeting hath proper cognizance, so it [can] be done in convenient time, due order, and respective manner." *Id.* at 2177 (quoting A COPPIE OF THE LIBERTIES OF THE MASSACHUSETTS COLLONIE IN NEW ENGLAND (December 1641)), *reprinted in* 1 DOCUMENTS ON FUNDAMENTAL HUMAN RIGHTS: THE ANGLO-AMERICAN TRADITION 122, 124 (Zechariah Chafee Jr. ed. & compiler, 1963) (1951)).
158. Smith Dissertation, *supra* note 29, at 46. For a discussion of these provisions with citations, see *id.* at 37–57.
159. Richard R. John and Christopher J. Young, *Rites of Passage, in* THE HOUSE AND SENATE IN THE 1790s: PETITIONING, LOBBYING, AND INSTITUTIONAL DEVELOPMENT 103 (Kenneth R. Bowling & Donald R. Kennon eds. 2002).
160. LARRY D. KRAMER, THE PEOPLE THEMSELVES: POPULAR CONSTITUTIONALISM AND JUDICIAL REVIEW 25 (1994).
161. *Id.*
162. *Id.* at 26.
163. MARY PATTERSON CLARKE, PARLIAMENTARY PRIVILEGE IN THE AMERICAN COLONIES 30–31 (1943) ("In addition to the trying of criminal and civil cases, a number of colonial assemblies entertained petitions for the right to appeal; and in so doing, seem to have been following, to some degree at least, English precedents.").
164. *Id.* at 31.
165. *Id.* at 31–33, 35–38.
166. *Id.* at 209.
167. *Id.* at 209–10.

168. *Id.* at 210.

169. RAYMOND C. BAILEY, POPULAR INFLUENCE UPON PUBLIC POLICY: PETITIONING IN EIGHTEENTH-CENTURY VIRGINIA 7 (1979).

170. *Id.*

171. RALPH VOLNEY HARLOW, THE HISTORY OF LEGISLATIVE METHODS IN THE PERIOD BEFORE 1825, at 14 (1917).

172. *Id.*

173. *Id.* at 15.

174. Bailey, *supra* note 169, at 24. Professor Bailey also notes that "[p]rior to 1660 citizens generally presented petitions in person to the assembly or gave them to the burgesses when elections were conducted." *Id.* at 27.

175. Higginson, *supra* note 1, at 145 n.10.

176. *Id.* at 146.

177. Bailey, *supra* note 169, at 29.

178. *Id.*

179. Poll taxes were common in many states until the twentieth century. *See* Breedlove v. Suttles, 302 U.S. 277, 283–84 (1930) ("The payment of poll taxes as a prerequisite to voting is a familiar and reasonable regulation long enforced in many States and for more than a century in Georgia."); *see also* Harper v. Virginia Bd. of Elections, 383 U.S. 663, 684–85 (1966) (Harlan, J., dissenting) (discussing various historical limitations on voting rights, including property qualifications and poll taxes).

180. Bailey, *supra* note 169, at 6.

181. *Id.*

182. David C. Frederick, *John Quincy Adams, Slavery, and the Disappearance of the Right of Petition*, 9 LAW & HIST. REV. 113, 115 & 143 n.9 (1991). As Professor Frederick correctly observes, the right of petition "served as a vehicle for the political participation of the disenfranchised, a point highlighted when southerners attempted to block petitions from slaves." *Id.* at 115.

183. Luce, *supra* note 28, at 514–15, 520–23.

184. *Id.* at 523.

185. Bailey, *supra* note 169, at 6 (emphasis added).

186. *Id.*

187. Smith Dissertation, *supra* note 29, at 57–66.

188. Alice Tanner Boyer, *The "Olive Branch Petition,"* 22 U. KAN. CITY L. REV. 183, 185 (1953–1954); *see* 1 J. Cont. Cong. 104–06 (July 7, 1775) (Way & Gideon eds., 1823) (reporting on the adoption and dispatch of the Olive Branch Petition).

189. The Olive Branch Petition, *reprinted in* Boyer, *supra* note 188, at 189.

190. *Id.*

191. *Id.* at 186.

192. THE DECLARATION OF INDEPENDENCE para. 30 (July 4, 1776), *reprinted in* 5 THE FOUNDERS' CONSTITUTION, *supra* note 2, at 199.

193. *See* Mark, *supra* note 1, at 2192 ("Having met the sole precondition for reception by petitioning 'in the most humble terms,' the colonists felt entitled to consideration."); *see also* Stamp Act Congress, Declaration of Rights § 13 (1765), *reprinted in* 5 THE

FOUNDERS' CONSTITUTION, *supra* note 2, at 198 ("That it is the right of the British subjects in these colonies to petition the king or either house of parliament.")

194. *See* Mark, *supra* note 1, at 2199–2203; Smith, *supra* note 1, at 1174.

195. Smith Dissertation, *supra* note 29, at 67.

196. PENN. CONST., DECL. OF RIGHTS, art. xvi (1776).

197. CONST. OF VERMONT, ch. 1, art. xviii (1777) ("That the people have a right to assemble together, to consult for their common good—to instruct their representatives, and to apply to the legislature for redress of grievances, by address, petition or remonstrance.").

198. CONST. OF NORTH CAROLINA, DECL. OF RIGHTS, art. xviii (1776) ("That the people have a right to assemble together, to consult for the common good, to instruct their representatives, and to apply to the legislature for redress of grievances.").

199. Smith Dissertation, *supra* note 29, at 68.

200. Letter from James Mason to Thomas Jefferson, *reprinted in* 2 MAX FARRAND, RECORDS OF THE FEDERAL CONVENTION 1787, at 135–36 (1912).

201. *Id.* at 136.

202. For a discussion of the how the absence of a petition clause in the Constitution affected ratification debates in the state conventions, see Smith Dissertation, *supra* note 29, at 70–74. The absence of a provision protecting the right to petition arose in the ratification debates in Maryland, Massachusetts, North Carolina, South Carolina, and Virginia, *id.*; only North Carolina and Virginia included the right to petition in their proposed amendments to the Constitution, *see id.* at 74.

203. *See* Proceedings in the House of Representatives, June 8, 1789, *in* 1 ANNALS OF CONGRESS 424–51 (Joseph Gales ed., 1834), *reprinted in* BENNETT B. PATTERSON, THE FORGOTTEN NINTH AMENDMENT 100–127 (1955).

204. *Id.* at 434, *reprinted in* PATTERSON, *supra* note 203, at 110. Limiting petitioning to "the Legislature" was consistent with the early state protections of the right to petition. *See* Mark, *supra* note 1, at 2200–203 (attributing the limitation to "the republican faith in the legislature and the central role accorded that body in republican thought," and stating that it "did not mean that the petitioning of other branches of the state government was barred or left unprotected"). The change from "the Legislature" to "the government" in the final version of the amendment is, however, more consistent with British and colonial practice. *See* Spanbauer, *supra* note 1, at 40. For a discussion of Madison's use of the word "apply" rather than "petition," see Mark, *supra* note 1, at 2208–09.

205. This is not to say that the Petition Clause, as adopted, escaped debate among early American legal scholars. In his commentaries on Blackstone, St. George Tucker criticized the language of the clause as "savour[ing] of that stile of condescension, in which favours are supposed to be granted." 1 ST. GEORGE TUCKER, BLACKSTONE'S COMMENTARIES: WITH NOTES OF REFERENCE TO THE CONSTITUTION AND LAWS OF THE FEDERAL GOVERNMENT OF THE UNITED STATES AND OF THE COMMONWEALTH OF VIRGINIA App. 299 (1803). In reply, Joseph Story wrote: "Mr. Tucker has indulged himself in a disparaging criticism upon the phraseology of this clause. . . But this seems to be quite overstrained; since it speaks the voice of the people in the language

of prohibition, and not in that of affirmance of a right, supposed to be unquestionable, and inherent." 3 JOSEPH STORY, COMMENTARIES ON THE CONSTITUTION OF THE UNITED STATES § 1888 (1833).

206. *See* Proceedings in the House of Representatives, Aug. 15, 1789, *in* 1 ANNALS OF CONGRESS 704–49 (Joseph Gales ed., 1834), *reprinted in* PATTERSON, *supra* note 203, at 163–79.

207. *Id.* at 738, *reprinted in* PATTERSON, *supra* note 203, at 169.

208. *See* Proceedings in the House of Representatives, Sept. 24, 1789, *in* 1 ANNALS OF CONGRESS 913 (Joseph Gales ed., 1834), *reprinted in* PATTERSON, *supra* note 203, at 210.

209. John & Young, *supra* note 159, at 103.

210. William C. diGiacomantonio, *Petitioners and Their Grievances: A View from the First Federal Congress,* in Bowling & Kennon, *supra* note 159, at 29.

211. *Id.* at 31.

212. *Id.; see also* Anita Hodgkiss, Note, *Petitioning and the Empowerment Theory of Practice,* 96 YALE L.J. 569, 571 (1986) (citing early Supreme Court decisions that invoke assembly and petitioning as the natural rights of citizens and suggesting that "[t]hese early decisions suggest that, in theory, the right to petition would have been recognized even without the petition clause of the First Amendment and are further evidence that this right was thought to be a basic aspect of self-government"). Of course, given the actual practice of Congress from 1789 to 1791, a time before ratification of the First Amendment, we know that the Petition Clause was not required to ensure that Congress would receive, consider, and respond to petitions.

213. diGiacomantonio, *supra* note 210, at 32.

214. Christine A. Desan, *Contesting the Character of the Political Economy in the Early Republic: Rights and Remedies in* Chisholm v. Georgia, *in* Bowling & Kennon, *supra* note 159, at 178, 188–89.

215. Frederick, *supra* note 182, at 117 (internal citation omitted).

216. For a discussion of the wide scope of policy-oriented petitions and also those seeking justice in individual claims, see *id.* at 31–56; *see also* John & Young, *supra* note 159, at 168–69 ("In the Federalist era, Americans petitioned Congress for a variety of reasons. Some sought financial compensation for services performed or losses suffered in the War of Independence. Others protested the Jay Treaty, the government's financial policies, or the expansion of the military. Still others urged the suspension of the slave trade—and, in at least one instance, the abolition of the institution of slavery.").

217. 1 ANNALS OF CONG. 1182–83 (Feb. 11, 1790) (Joseph Gales ed., 1834). This was not the first antislavery petitioning effort. For example, on October 4, 1783, Quakers from Pennsylvania and Virginia had petitioned the Continental Congress, which existed under the Articles of Confederation, to abolish the slave trade. Katherine Hessler, *Early Efforts to Suppress Protest: Unwanted Abolitionist Speech,* 7 B.U. PUB. INT. L.J. 185, 207–08 (1998). Opponents of slavery also petitioned state legislatures in slave states, such as Virginia, for an end to the practice. *See id.* at 208. Needless to say, these efforts did not meet with much success.

218. 1 ANNALS OF CONG. 1184 (Feb. 11, 1790) (Joseph Gales ed., 1834).

219. *Id.* at 1192.
220. diGiacomantonio, *supra* note 210, at 36.
221. 1 ANNALS OF CONG. 1198 (Feb. 12, 1790) (Joseph Gales ed., 1834).
222. *Id.*
223. *Id.* at 1206.
224. *Id.* at 1472 (Mar. 23, 1790).
225. *Id.*
226. *Id.*
227. *Id.* at 1473.
228. *Id.* (Report of the Special Committee).
229. *Id.* at 1473–74.
230. *Id.*
231. *Id.* at 1474 (Report of the Committee of the Whole House).
232. Spanbauer, *supra* note 1, at 38; *see* ARTHUR MARCHAND, RIGHTS OF PETITION AND ASSEMBLY AND THEIR INTERPRETATION BY THE UNITED STATES JUDICIARY 48 (1955) (unpublished Colby College undergraduate thesis on file with author) ("A right presupposes a duty on the part of the government, and in the case of the right of petition the duty consists in receiving, hearing and considering the petition.").
233. *See* LUCETTA RALPHA SPURLOCK, THE CONTEST OVER THE RIGHT OF PETITION IN THE AMERICAN CONGRESS 1830–1844: AN EPISODE IN THE SLAVERY CONTROVERSY 15–17 (1930) (unpublished master's thesis on file with the author). Spurlock reports that the House refused to consider petitions submitted by enslaved African Americans in North Carolina in 1797 and also rejected petitions from emancipated former slaves in Philadelphia in 1799 on the grounds that consideration of the petitions would have "a tendency to create disquiet and jealousy." *Id.* at 15. In general, however, even petitions challenging the expansion of slavery were referred to a committee for consideration and a response. *See id.* at 16–17.
234. *Id.* at 17.
235. Note, *A Petition Clause Analysis of Suits against the Government: Implications for Rule 11 Sanctions,* 106 HARV. L. REV. 1111, 1117 (1993).
236. John & Young, *supra* note 159, at 106; *see* Frederick, *supra* note 182 at 118 (noting that "the normal practice in the decades between the ratification of the first amendment and the debates of the 1830s was for Congress to receive petitions and refer them to committees").
237. John & Young, *supra* note 159, at 106.
238. John P. Nields, *Right of Petition, in* LECTURES ON HISTORY AND GOVERNMENT: SERIES ONE 1923–1924, at 135 (University of Delaware Depts. of History & Political Science 1924).
239. *See id.* at 107–08.
240. *Id.* at 108–09.
241. Harlow, *supra* note 171, at 135.
242. *Id.* at 135 n.33.
243. 3 ANNALS OF CONG. 475 (Joseph Gales ed., 1834) (March 4, 1794).
244. *See* Harlow, *supra* note 171, at 152–54.

245. Frederick, *supra* note 182, at 118.
246. *See* Higginson, *supra* note 1, at 156; *see also* Andrews, *supra* note 1, at 642 n.292 ("Most commentators acknowledge that Congressional processing of petitions forever changed after abolitionists, beginning in the 1830s, inundated Congress with petitions urging it to end slavery in the District of Columbia.").
247. Higginson, *supra* note 1, at 157.
248. Mark, *supra* note 1, at 2216–17 (citations omitted). For an in-depth discussion of the gag rule and its effects on the right to petition, see *id.* at 2215–26; Higginson, *supra* note 1, at 155–65.
249. Mark, *supra* note 1, at 2216–17.
250. Frederick, *supra* note 182, at 118.
251. *See* U.S. CONST. art. V (providing general procedures governing adoptions of amendments to the Constitution, but also stating that "no Amendment which may be made prior to the Year One thousand eight hundred and eight shall in any Manner affect the first and fourth Clauses in the Ninth Section of the first Article"). If one consults the "first and fourth" clauses of Article I, section 9, one finds that the first clause protects the international and interstate slave trade, which might otherwise be thought to come within the scope of Congress's Article I, section 8, clause 3, powers to regulate commerce. *See* U.S. CONST., art. I, § 9, cl. 1 ("The Migration or Importation of such Persons as any of the States now existing shall think proper to admit, shall not be prohibited by the Congress prior to the Year one thousand eight hundred and eight, but a Tax or duty may be imposed on such Importation, not exceeding ten dollars for each Person."). The second provision, relating to direct taxes, also has its genesis in protecting the institution of human chattel slavery; if Congress could tax the ownership of human slaves, it could make the practice financially unsustainable. *See* U.S. CONST. art. I, § 9, cl. 4 ("No Capitation, or other direct, Tax shall be laid, unless in Proportion to the Census or enumeration herein before directed to be taken."). The early debates on the Quakers' antislavery petitions make clear that the framers included the prohibition against direct taxes at least in part to protect the institution of slavery. As Representative Abraham Baldwin, of Georgia, explained, the prohibition against federal direct taxes "was intended to prevent Congress from laying any special tax upon negro slaves, as they might, in this way, so burden the possessors of them as to induce a general emancipation." 1 ANNALS OF CONG. 1201 (Feb. 12, 1790) (Statement of Rep. Baldwin).
252. *See* U.S. CONST. art. I, § 8, cl. 17 ("The Congress shall have the Power . . . to exercise exclusive Legislation in all Cases whatsoever, over such District (not exceeding ten Miles square) as may, by Cession of particular States, and the acceptance of Congress, become the Seat of the Government of the United States, and to exercise like Authority over all Places purchased by the Consent of the Legislature of the State in which the Same shall be, for the Erection of Forts, Magazines, Arsenals, dock-Yards, and other needful Buildings.")
253. LEONARD FALKNER, THE PRESIDENT WHO WOULDN'T RETIRE 50 (1967).
254. *Id.*
255. *Id.* at 50–51.

256. *Id.* at 51.
257. *Id.*
258. *See* SUSAN ZAESKE, SIGNATURES OF CITIZENSHIP: PETITIONING, ANTISLAVERY, & WOMEN'S POLITICAL IDENTITY 35 (2003) ("Petitioning was endorsed by abolitionist leaders at the national level in December 1833 at the founding convention of the American Anti-Slavery Society."). The American Anti-Slavery Society did not rely solely on petitioning, however, as a means of advancing the cause of abolitionism. In addition, the society printed and distributed antislavery tracts, pamphlets, and books, and also published newspaper advertisements, often targeting the residents of slave states. *See* WILLIAM SHERMAN SAVAGE, THE CONTROVERSY OVER THE DISTRIBUTION OF SLAVE LITERATURE 1830–1860 (1968); Michael Kent Curtis, *The Curious History of Attempts to Suppress Antislavery Speech, Press, and Petition in 1835–37,* 89 NW. U. L. REV. 785, 804–05 (1995); Hessler, *supra* note 217, at 191–207. In July 1835, the American Anti-Slavery Society undertook a mass mailing of antislavery publications to Southern elites, prompting members of Congress from Southern states to propose closing the federal mails to such materials. *See* Curtis, *supra,* at 817–19. Although the proposal to close the mails to antislavery materials generated much heated debate, Congress declined to adopt legislation authorizing censorship of the federal mail service. *Id.* at 835–37. In fact, Congress instead enacted a bill that required local postmasters to refrain from declining to deliver properly mailed materials, thereby closing a loophole that some local postmasters had used to decline to deliver potentially controversial mailings in the South. Hessler, *supra* note 217, at 206. For an excellent and comprehensive overview of the antislavery mailings controversy, see Savage, *supra,* at 9–122.
259. 12 REGISTER OF DEBATES IN CONGRESS, pt. 1, at 471–498 (Feb. 12, 1836) (Joseph Gales & William Winston Seaton eds., 1836).
260. *Id.* at 483.
261. *Id.* at 484.
262. The debate on the admissibility of the antislavery petitions runs for more than a hundred pages, and took place over six days, from March 2, 1836, to March 9, 1836. *See* 12 REGISTER OF DEBATES IN CONGRESS, pt. 1, at 679–782 (Mar. 2–9, 1836).
263. *Id.* at 681.
264. *See id.* at 679–765 (antislavery petition debates of March 2, 3, 4, 7, and 8, 1836).
265. *See* William L. Van Deburg, *Henry Clay, the Right of Petition, and Slavery in the Nation's Capital,* 68 REG. KY. HIST. SOC'Y 132, 132–33 (April 1970).
266. 12 REGISTER OF DEBATES IN CONG., pt. 1, at 765 (Mar. 9, 1836) (statement of Sen. Calhoun).
267. *Id.* at 773.
268. Van Deburg, *supra* note 265, at 132.
269. *Id.* at 133.
270. 12 REGISTER OF DEBATES IN CONG., pt. 1, at 778 (March 9, 1836) (statement of Sen. Clay).
271. Van Deburg, *supra* note 265, at 134.

272. *Id.*

273. *Id.* at 134.

274. *Id.* at 135.

275. *See id.* at 137–40.

276. *Id.* at 142–44.

277. Moreover, this story has received repeated—and quite comprehensive—tellings. For a particularly thorough historical overview of the antislavery debate in the House of Representatives during the 1830s and 1840s, see WILLIAM LEE MILLER, ARGUING ABOUT SLAVERY: THE GREAT BATTLE IN THE UNITED STATES CONGRESS (1996). For a work focusing on Representative John Quincy Adams's role in advocating for the right of petition, see Falkner, *supra* note 253, at 51–53, 124–67, 246–63, 281–92.

278. Robert P. Ludlum, *The Antislavery "Gag-Rule": History and Argument*, 26 J. OF NEGRO HIST. 203, 205–06 (April 1941).

279. Frederick, *supra* note 182, at 130.

280. *Id.*

281. *Id.* at 132.

282. Ludlum, *supra* note 278, at 207; *see* 13 CONG. DEB. 1411 (1837) (providing text of the 1836 gag rule).

283. Ludlum, *supra* note 278, at 208.

284. *Id.* at 208–09.

285. *See* Falkner, *supra* note 253, at 281–84 (discussing Adams's presentation of anti-Texas annexation petitions as a means of avoiding the gag rule).

286. Ludlum, *supra* note 278, at 211.

287. *Id.* at 214; *see* 8 CONG. GLOBE 150 (1840) (Jan. 28, 1840).

288. Ludlum, *supra* note 278, at 215.

289. *Id.*

290. *Id.* at 216.

291. *See* 14 CONG. GLOBE 7 (Dec. 3, 1844).

292. Ludlum, *supra* note 278, at 221–22.

293. Frederick, *supra* note 182, at 139.

294. *Id.* at 140.

295. *See id.* at 119 (observing that "Congress devised means of thwarting the right of petition without drawing the scrutiny of the courts").

296. Mark, *supra* note 1, at 2226–28.

297. Note, *supra* note 235, at 1120.

298. As Frederick puts it, after the mass antislavery petition campaign of 1831–1844, "[n]ever again would any group exercise the right of petition on so grand a scale to engage in a dialogue with Congress on an important social issue." Frederick, *supra* note 182, at 119. With all due respect to Professor Frederick, mass petitioning campaigns did engage Congress with respect to women's suffrage, Prohibition, and even the income tax. *See infra* section III.E., text and accompanying notes 303–25.

299. Frederick, *supra* note 182, at 141.

300. Zaeske, *supra* note 258, at 173–84.

301. *Id.* at 179–80. In one of the less appealing aspects of the campaign to secure voting rights for women, Susan B. Anthony and Elizabeth Cady Stanton also circulated petitions opposing ratification of the Fourteenth Amendment because it failed to secure universal voting rights for all citizens, regardless of gender. *See* ELEANOR FLEXNER & ELLEN FITZPATRICK, CENTURY OF STRUGGLE: THE WOMEN'S RIGHTS MOVEMENT IN THE UNITED STATES 139 (1996). Their opposition was based not on racism but rather a sense that a great political opportunity to achieve equality had been squandered. "It would have been so easy, argued Mrs. Stanton and Miss Anthony, to have included the word 'sex' [in the Fourteenth or Fifteenth Amendment]; they failed to see that such a step was ahead of practical political possibilities." *Id.* at 141.

302. Zaeske, *supra* note 258, at 178. Moreover, petitioning in favor of women's rights was not limited to the federal government. For example, Susan B. Anthony's first campaign for women's rights involved an effort to secure legislation in New York that recognized the right of women to control their earnings, to enjoy guardianship of their children in case of a divorce, and to vote; she advanced these reforms through a well-organized statewide petition campaign in 1854. *See* Flexner & Fitzpatrick, *supra* note 301, at 80–81. Over a period of ten weeks, "they collected six thousand signatures" from across the state. *Id.* at 81. Anthony scheduled a convention of women's rights advocates for Albany, New York, to coincide with the meeting of the state legislature, with the petition to be "used to try to gain a hearing for the bills the women were supporting." *Id.*

303. Zaeske, *supra*, note 258, at 183.

304. *Id.*

305. *Id.*

306. *Id.* at 184.

307. *Id.* at 176.

308. *Id.* at 177.

309. *Id.*

310. U.S. CONST. amend. xviii, § 1 ("After one year from the ratification of this article the manufacture, sale, or transportation of intoxicating liquors within, the importation thereof into, or the exportation thereof from the United States and all territory subject to the jurisdiction thereof for beverage purposes is hereby prohibited.").

311. Smith Dissertation, *supra* note 29, at 140–41.

312. The Sherman Antitrust Act, ch. 647, 26 Stat. 209 (July 2, 1890) (codified as amended at 15 U.S.C. §§ 1–7 (2006)).

313. The Clayton Antitrust Act of 1914, ch. 323, 38 Stat. 730 (Oct. 15, 1914) (codified as amended at 15 U.S.C. §§ 12–27 & 29 U.S.C. §§ 52–53 (2006)).

314. Smith Dissertation, *supra* note 29, at 136.

315. *See* DAVID P. THELEN, THE NEW CITIZENSHIP: ORIGINS OF PROGRESSIVISM IN WISCONSIN, 1885–1900, at 130–31 (1972) ("Locating the basic evils in corporate arrogance, tax dodging, and unresponsive and undemocratic political machinery, the Progressives advocated a number of devices to regulate and tax corporations, to equalize the tax burden, and to make the political process more democratic.").

316. *Id.* at 137–38.

317. Marchand, *supra* note 232, at 60–61; *see* Manny Fernandez, *A Protest March or an Invasion?*, N.Y. TIMES, Oct. 3, 2010, at WK4 ("Coxey wanted Congress to put people to work building roads and public works projects with federally subsidized bonds.").

318. Marchand, *supra* note 232, at 61.

319. Fernandez, *supra* note 317, at WK4.

320. Marchand, *supra* note 232, at 61.

321. Fernandez, *supra* note 317, at WK4.

322. Smith Dissertation, *supra* note 29, at 144–46.

323. Marchand, *supra* note 232, at 61.

324. *Id.*

325. *Id.* at 62.

326. *Id.*

327. *Id.*

328. *See* TAYLOR BRANCH, PARTING THE WATERS: AMERICA IN THE KING YEARS, 1954–63, at 846–87 (1988).

329. *Id.* at 878, 881–83.

330. *See id.* at 883–87.

331. Speech of John Lewis, March on Washington for Jobs and Freedom, August 28, 1963, *available at* http://www.crmvet.org/info/mowjl2.htm (last visited on July 8, 2010).

332. *See* Branch, *supra* note 328, at 877–78. Branch writes that "[t]he stream of early marchers grew so thick that it required almost a military operation to create the illusion for posterity that King and the other sponsors had gone ahead of them all." *Id.*; *see also* CHARLES C. EUCHNER, NOBODY TURN ME AROUND: A PEOPLE'S HISTORY OF THE 1963 MARCH ON WASHINGTON 86 (2010) ("Originally, the March on Washington was to include a day of citizen lobbying on Capitol Hill, but march organizers had decided against bringing demonstrators to the Hill. Now, on the morning of the Great March, the Big Ten [i.e., the march's leaders, led by Dr. King] made the rounds on Capitol Hill."). In fact, the entire congressional leadership, including Speaker of the House John McCormack, House Majority Leader Carl Albert, House Minority Leader Charles Halleck, Senate Majority Leader Mike Mansfield, and Senate Minority Leader Everett Dirksen, met with the delegation of civil rights organization leaders the morning of the march. *See id.*

333. Branch, *supra* note 328, at 883–86. Kennedy was pleasant with Dr. King and the other leaders of the March on Washington, but he remained largely noncommital regarding pressing Congress for new comprehensive civil rights legislation. *See id.* at 885–86.

334. *See id.* at 876, 883.

335. *Id.* at 876. CBS provided live coverage from the beginning of the march, whereas ABC and NBC began their live national coverage at the rally in front of the Lincoln Memorial. *See id.* at 876, 881. Branch also notes that this live television coverage provided many viewers, including President Kennedy, with their first complete King speech delivered live. *Id.* at 883.

336. *See* John & Young, *supra* note 159, at 100–138.

337. *Id.* at 100.
338. *Id.* at 121–23.
339. *See,* e.g., Andrews, *supra* note 1, at 642 n.292 ("Most commentators acknowledge that
     Congressional processing of petitions forever changed after abolitionists, beginning
     in the 1830s, inundated Congress with petitions urging it to end slavery in the District
     of Columbia."); Frederick, *supra* note 182, at 140 ("The end of the gag rule brought
     neither an exhaustive discussion of slavery in the District of Columbia nor a full
     restoration of the right of petition as it had been practiced from 1789 to 1836."); *id.* at
     141 (describing the right of petition as "a right little exercised in the aftermath of the
     gag rule" and incorrectly asserting that "[b]y the twentieth century, when the
     Supreme Court began interpreting the first amendment, the practice of the petition
     right as a means of communicating grievances to government in the eighteenth cen-
     tury had long since been abandoned"); Higginson, *supra* note 1, at 144 (arguing that
     the gag rule "effectively abolished the right of petition"); Lawson & Seidman, *supra*
     note 1, at 751 ("The so-called gag rule, which prohibited receipt of petitions concern-
     ing slavery, brought this era of petitioning to an end. By the time the Supreme Court
     began interpreting the Petitions Clause, the eighteenth-century importance of the
     petition as a means of communicating grievances to government had significantly
     waned."); Christopher L. Sagers, *The Legal Structure of American Freedom and the
     Provenance of the Antitrust Immunities,* 2002 UTAH L. REV. 927, 938 (noting that "[i]t
     is frequently said that the petition as a genuine mode of political participation met its
     end in the so-called 'gag rule' controversy in the House of Representatives in the mid-
     nineteenth century" and observing that "it also seems generally agreed that even had
     the gag rule affair never happened, petitions would have waned, and at about the
     same time, due to the procedural strain of dealing with a growing populace, the rise
     of a strong and independent judiciary, the gradual change to a more and more repre-
     sentative democracy, the availability of better communications technology, and so
     on"); *id.* at 938 n.40 ("Ironically, by attempting to take advantage of the procedural
     strain imposed by their barrage of petitions, the abolitionists may well have killed the
     petition as a United States political institution.").
340. *See* Mark, *supra* note 1, at 2228 ("Petitioning did not die. General subject matter peti-
     tions—political petitions—were transformed from instruments that were part of the
     deliberative process to, in their nadir, marginal instruments of mass politics, often fringe
     politics."). I rather doubt that the women's suffragists, the Prohibitionists, supporters of
     federal antitrust legislation, or the advocates of a federal income tax would agree with
     this characterization of the utility of petitioning after the repeal of the gag rule.
341. John & Young, *supra* note 159, at 137.
342. *Id.* at 137–38.
343. *Id.* at 138.
344. *See supra* chapter 4, section II.C., text and accompanying notes 77–114.
345. John & Young, *supra* note 159, at 138.
346. Andrews, *supra* note 1, at 642 n.292 (emphasis added).
347. John & Young, *supra* note 159, at 138; *see also* Marchand, *supra* note 232, at 64 ("The
     right of petition no longer enjoys the important role it did in earlier times. In England

and in the United States previous to the development of modern communications, the right served an important function.").

348. Marchand, *supra* note 232, at 64 ("With the advent of new mediums of communication and more representative institutions of government, the right [of petition] has become relatively disused.").

349. ELLIS PAXSON OBERHOLTZER, THE REFERENDUM IN AMERICA TOGETHER WITH SOME CHAPTERS ON THE INITIATIVE AND THE RECALL 368 (1912).

350. *Id.*

351. *Id.* at 369.

352. *Id.*

353. *See* ALAN WATSON, LEGAL TRANSPLANTS: AN APPROACH TO COMPARATIVE LAW (1974); *see also* ALAN WATSON, SOCIETY AND LEGAL CHANGE (1977).

354. EDWARD A. JAKSHA, OF THE PEOPLE: DEMOCRACY AND THE PETITION PROCESS 69 (1988).

355. JOSEPH F. ZIMMERMAN, THE INITIATIVE: CITIZEN LAW-MAKING 3 (1999).

356. *Id.* at 3.

357. *Id.* at 2.

358. *See* Luce, *supra* note 28, at 565 ("Taking modern form, the Swiss Referendum first appeared in the German-speaking canton of Saint Gallen in 1831.").

359. STEVEN L. PIOTT, GIVING VOTERS A VOICE: THE ORIGINS OF THE INITIATIVE AND REFERENDUM IN AMERICA 3 (2003). Swiss cantons adopted referendum as a means of obtaining the voters' imprimatur on new laws in the 1830s, and the 1848 federal constitution mandated referendum for all cantons and for federal legislation. Zimmerman, *supra* note 355, at 3.

360. Piott, *supra* note 359, at 16.

361. *Id.* at 16–17, 29–30; *see* Zimmerman, *supra* note 355, at 3 (arguing that disaffection with existing forms of government, featuring a separation of powers, animated populist support for the initiative and that populists believed "[t]his governance system had broken down, and the farmers and industrial workers were at the mercy of an economic oligarchy"). For a description of the adverse economic conditions that helped lead to the progressive movement, see *id.* at 4–5.

362. Piott, *supra* note 359, at 51 n.1.

363. *Id.* at 32.

364. *Id.* at 40.

365. *Id.*

366. *Id.* at 51.

367. Zimmerman, *supra* note 355, at 6.

368. 125 CONG. REC. 1807 (1979) (statement of Sen. Mark O. Hatfield on the Voter Initiative Amendment).

369. *Id.*

370. *Id.* at 1808.

371. *Id.*

372. Luce, *supra* note 28, at 599.

373. *Id.* at 608–09.

374. Nields, *supra* note 238, at 153–54.
375. *Id.* at 154.
376. *Id.*
377. WILLIAM DENISON MCCRACKAN, THE RISE OF THE SWISS REPUBLIC: A HISTORY 340–41 (2nd ed. 1901).
378. *Id.* at 341.
379. *Id.*
380. *See id.* at 340 ("Nor must the right of the Initiative be considered as equivalent to the general privilege of petition, which is enjoyed by the inhabitants of every state which makes any pretentions [*sic*] whatever to political liberty.").
381. *Id.*
382. *Id.*
383. THEODORE D. WOOLSEY, 1 POLITICAL SCIENCE OR THE STATE: THEORETICALLY AND PRACTICALLY CONSIDERED, § 92, at 270–71 (1878).
384. John Parkinson, *Direct Democracy, in* NEW ZEALAND GOVERNMENT & POLITICS 547, 548 (Raymond Miller ed., 4th ed. 2006).
385. *Id.* at 548–49.
386. *See id.* at 556 ("In New Zealand, CIR [Citizens Initiated Referenda] are non-binding and the government can determine for itself how to respond to the outcome."). Since New Zealand's unicameral legislature adopted a statute permitting Citizens' Initiated Referendums in 1993, about three dozen petition-gathering efforts have taken place, leading to three national votes. *See id.* at 549–54. Of the three initiative petition drives that met the 10 percent threshold of all registered voters to secure a national vote, *see id.* at 555, two secured positive majorities and one failed; even so, the New Zealand Parliament declined to implement to provisions of the two initiatives that secured majority support with the voters.
387. 5 U.S.C. § 555(e) (2006) ("Prompt notice shall be given of the denial in whole or in part of a written application, petition, or other request of an interested person made in connection with any agency proceeding. Except in affirming a prior denial or when the denial is self-explanatory, the notice shall be accompanied by a brief statement of the grounds for denial.").
388. Massachusetts v. EPA, 549 U.S. 497, 510–12, 533–35 (2007).
389. *Id.* at 528–29.
390. *Id.* at 533.
391. *Id.*
392. Mark, *supra* note 1, at 2154.
393. *Id.* at 2155.
394. *Id.* at 2230.
395. *Id.*
396. Higginson, *supra* note 1, at 165.
397. Nicholls, *supra* note 107, at 51.
398. *Id.*
399. Lieber, *supra* note 54, at 122.
400. Woolsey, *supra* note 383, § 92, at 270.

401. *See* Loretta Chao, *Beijing Seeks to Put an End to Petitioning*, WALL ST. J., Aug. 22–23, 2009, at A9 ("Authorities in China are moving to snuff out petitioning, a centuries-old form of protest that brings thousands of aggrieved people to the capital each year seeking justice.").

402. Lieber, *supra* note 54, at 121 (emphasis added).

403. *Id.*

404. *Id.*

405. Woolsey, *supra* note 383, § 92, at 270.

406. *Id.*; *see* Hodgkiss, *supra* note 212, at 575 ("The petition clause is rooted in the idea that citizens should participate in government decisionmaking.").

407. Woolsey, *supra* note 383, § 92, at 271.

408. Note, *supra* note 235, at 1120.

409. *Id.* at 1121.

410. PHILIP A. JOSEPH, CONSTITUTIONAL AND ADMINISTRATIVE LAW IN NEW ZEALAND 32–35 (1993).

411. Constitution Act 1986, s. 2(1) (NZ) ("The Sovereign in right of New Zealand is the head of State in New Zealand, and shall be known by the royal style and titles proclaimed from time to time.").

412. *See* RAYMOND D. MULHOLLAND, INTRODUCTION TO THE NEW ZEALAND LEGAL SYSTEM 17 (1976) ("Unlike the United States, New Zealand has no written constitution.").

413. PHILIP A. JOSEPH, CONSTITUTIONAL AND ADMINISTRATIVE LAW IN NEW ZEALAND § 1.6.2, at 25 (3rd ed. 2007) ("The Constitution Act 1986 is New Zealand's premier constitutional statute.").

414. JOSEPH, *supra* note 410, § 1.61., at 21.

415. *Id.* at 22.

416. Constitution Act 1986, s. 6(1) (NZ) ("A person may be appointed and may hold office as a member of the Executive Council or as a Minister of the Crown only if that person is a member of Parliament.").

417. MULHOLLAND, *supra* note 412, at 16; *see* Joseph, *supra* note 413, § 1.5.16, at 20 ("The New Zealand Parliament in unicameral, having only the House of Representatives. New Zealand abolished its upper house, the Legislative Council, in 1950.").

418. MULHOLLAND, *supra* note 412, at 17 (noting that, in light of the principle of parliamentary supremacy and absence of a written entrenched constitution "it is not possible for the Courts in this country to declare Acts of the New Zealand Parliament invalid upon the ground that they are unconstitutional"); *see also id.* at 38 ("The legislative supremacy of Parliament is accepted by the Courts.").

419. JOSEPH, *supra* note 413, § 1.6.3, at 25. Joseph also notes that "[t]he doctrine of parliamentary sovereignty is historically grounded in customary common law, although the legal source of law-making power in New Zealand is statutory." *Id.*

420. New Zealand Bill of Rights Act 1990, s. 4.

421. *Id.* at s. 6 ("Wherever an enactment can be given a meaning that is consistent with the rights and freedoms contained in this Bill of Rights, that meaning shall be preferred to any other meaning.").

422. *See supra* chapter 4, section II.C.

423. David McGee, Parliamentary Practice in New Zealand 517 (3rd ed. 2005).
424. *Id.*
425. Mulholland, *supra* note 412, at 19.
426. McGee, *supra* note 423, at 517.
427. Frank Parsons, The Story of New Zealand 225 (1904).
428. *See id.* at 390–92 ("When the people want a new railway in any part of the country, they petition the Minister, and pledge their representatives in Parliament to work for it. . . Parliament acts on the initiative of the Minister, and he acts on the initiative of the people.").
429. *Id.* at 581.
430. *Id.* at 771.
431. *Id.*
432. *See Women's Petition to Parliament,* The Star (Wellington, N.Z.), Aug. 15, 1884, at 1.
433. Parsons, *supra* note 427, at 261.
434. *Id.* at 262.
435. 81 N.Z. Parliamentary Debates, 4th Sess. of the 11th Parliament, Legislative Council and House of Representatives 142 (August 18, 1893) (Council) (1898) ("I am given to understand that a petition containing thirty thousand names of women—being one-seventh of the whole number of adult women of the country—has been sent to Parliament in favor of this Bill.").
436. *Id.* at 144–45.
437. *Id.* at 145.
438. Parsons, *supra* note 427, at 263.
439. McGgee, *supra* note 423, at 517.
440. Te Ra o te Reo Maori, July 29, 2009, *available at* www.tki.org.nz/r/maori/trotrm_e.php (last visited on June 24, 2010). "This date remains an auspicious one in the history of the Māori language renaissance." *Id.*
441. Manapouri: Art, Power, Protest, 264,907 signatures, *available at* http://www.natlib.govt.nz/collections/online-exhibitions/manapouri/save-manapouri-petition (last visited on March 17, 2011).
442. *Id.*
443. McGee, *supra* note 423, at 525.
444. *Id.*
445. *Id.*
446. McGee, *supra* note 423, at 518.
447. *Id.*
448. *Id.* at 522 (citing Standing Order 362(a)).
449. *Id.* (citing Standing Order 362(b)).
450. Mulholland, *supra* note 412, at 31.
451. *Id.*
452. *See id.* at 31–32.
453. Letter from David Bagnall, senior parliamentary officer, Office of the Clerk, New Zealand House of Representatives, to Professor Ronald Krotoszynski, October 2, 2009, at 3 (on file with author).

454. McGee, *supra* note 423, at 525.

455. *Id.* at 525.

456. *See id.* at 525; *see also* Mulholland, *supra* note 412, at 19 (reporting that, as of 1976, a petition will initially be "heard by the Petitions Committee," with this committee making a recommendation to "a Cabinet sub-committee upon petitions" and finally to the House itself).

457. McGee, *supra* note 423, at 525.

458. *Id.* at 526.

459. *Id.*

460. *Id.*

461. Standing Orders 185(1) & 360.

462. McGee, *supra* note 423, at 527.

463. Bagnall Letter, *supra* note 453, at 3.

464. McGee, *supra* note 423, at 528.

465. *Id.*

466. Standing Order 253(1).

467. McGee, *supra* note 423, at 529.

468. *Id.*

469. Bagnall Letter, *supra* note 453, at 5.

470. *Id.*

471. *Id.*

472. *Id.*

473. *Id.*

474. *See* E. Allen Lind & Tom R. Tyler, The Social Psychology of Procedural Justice 60–92, 100–105 (1988); Tom R. Tyler, Why People Obey the Law 19–20, 57–68, 104–12, 125–57, 170–78, 234–35 (1990); Tom R. Tyler, *Citizen Discontent with Legal Procedures: A Social Science Perspective on Court Procedural Reform*, 45 Am. J. Comp. L. 871, 887–92 (1997).

475. Bagnall Letter, *supra* note 453, at 2.

476. *Id.*

477. *Id.*

478. *Id.*

479. *See* http://www.parliament.nz/en-NZ/PB/Presented/Petitions/Default.htm?p=2 (listing chronologically from most recent to oldest all public petitions submitted in the current legislative term) (last visited June 24, 2010).

480. *See* Petition of Maryan Street and 51,089 others, Requesting that the House of Representatives call on the National Government to reverse all expenditure cuts in Budget 2009 that affect Adult and Community Education Services for the 2009/2010 financial year with a reinstatement of these funds taking effect from 1 January 2010, *available at* http://www.parliament.nz/en-NZ/PB/Presented/Petitions/c/f/a/49DBHOH_PET2977_1-Petition-of-Maryan-Street-and-51–089-others-requesting.htm (last visited on June 25, 2010).

481. Petition 2008/41 of Maryan Street and 51,089 others, Petition 2008/42 of Damien O'Connor and 120 others, Petition 2008/43 of Kathryn Sclater and 776 oth-

ers, and Petition 2008/44 of Damien O'Connor, Report of the Education and Science Committee (May 31, 2010), *available at* http://www.parliament.nz/NR/ rdonlyres/F29E10F0-C53B-4CB3-B3CF-7D8A1B256E2B/144101/ DBSCH_SCR_4761_Petition2008410fMaryanStreetand5108.pdf (last visited June 26, 2010).

482. *Id.* at 3–5.

483. *Id.* at 2.

484. Petition 2008/9 of Juliet Pratt and 1,341 others, *available at* http://www.parliament.nz/ en-NZ/PB/Presented/Petitions/8/a/e/49DBHOH_PET2944_1-Petition-of-Juliet-Pratt- and-1341-others-requests.htm (last visited on June 27, 2010).

485. *See* Petition 2008/9 of Juliet Pratt and 1,341 others, Report of the Health Committee (September 4, 2009), *available at* http://www.parliament.nz/en-NZ/PB/SC/ Documents/Reports/6/a/a/49DBSCH_SCR4489_1-Petition-2008–9-of-Juliet-Pratt- and-1–341-others.htm (last visited on June 27, 2010).

486. *Id.* at 5.

487. *Id.* at 16.

488. *Id.*

489. Bagnall Letter, *supra* note 453, at 2.

490. *See* http://www.parliament.nz/en-NZ/ (last visited on June 25, 2010).

491. *See* http://www.parliament.nz/en-NZ/AboutParl/GetInvolved// (last visited on June 25, 2010).

492. *See* http://www.parliament.nz/en-NZ/PB/Presented/Petitions/Default.htm?p=2 (last visited on June 25, 2010).

493. McGee, *supra* note 423, at 525.

494. *See supra* note 474.

495. *See infra* chapter 5.

CHAPTER 5. THE JURISPRUDENTIAL CONTOURS OF THE PETITION CLAUSE

1. New York Times Co. v. Sullivan, 376 U.S. 254 (1964).

2. Harry Kalven Jr., *The* New York Times *Case: A Note on "The Central Meaning of the First Amendment,"* 1964 Sup. Ct. Rev. 191, 192–93.

3. U.S. Const., Amend. I (emphasis added).

4. *See infra* chapter 5, section II, text and accompanying notes 26–71.

5. *See supra* chapter 4 (discussing the history of the right to petition).

6. *See supra* chapter 3 (discussing the security rationale as a basis for circumscribing the exercise of expressive freedoms).

7. Kalven, *supra* note 2, at 209; *see also* Williams v. Wallace, 240 F. Supp. 100, 101–06 (M.D. Ala. 1965) (issuing an injunction to facilitate a civil rights march in protest of Alabama's discriminatory voter registration practices, noting that "[t]he law is clear that the right to petition one's government for a redress of grievances may be exercised in large groups," and holding that the conduct of Alabama's state government "had the effect of preventing and discouraging Negro citizens from exercising their right of citi-

zenship," notably, the right to "remonstrate with government authorities and petition for redress of grievances").

8. *See supra* chapter 2.

9. *See supra* chapter 4, sections II.–IV.

10. *See infra chapter* 5, section III.C., text and accompanying notes 91–107 (discussing petitioners' immunity from seditious libel prosecution).

11. *See* Mary M. Cheh, *Demonstrations, Security Zones, and First Amendment Protection of Special Places*, 8 D.C. L. REV. 53, 73 (2004).

12. *See infra* chapter 5, sections II.A. and B. (discussing the historical limitations on the right to petition).

13. *Cf.* Frisby v. Schultz, 487 U.S. 474, 479–81, 484–86 (1988) (rejecting on privacy grounds a right to protest at a person's home via a fixed picket).

14. ALEXANDER MEIKLEJOHN, FREE SPEECH AND ITS RELATION TO SELF-GOVERNMENT 22–27 (1948).

15. Chuck D, Hank Shocklee & William Drayton, Public Enemy, *Yo! Bum Rush the Show* (1987). The lyrics, which in part address an effort to gain unauthorized admission to a concert after being denied admission at the door, may be found at: http://www.metrolyrics.com/yo-bum-rush-the-show-lyrics-public-enemy.html (last visited August 23, 2010).

16. MEIKLEJOHN, *supra* note 14, at 24; *see also* Alexander Meiklejohn, *The First Amendment Is an Absolute*, 1961 SUP. CT. REV. 245, 261 ("Just as an individual, seeking to advocate some public policy may not do so, without consent, by interrupting a church service, or a classroom, or a sickroom, or a session of Congress or of the Supreme Court, or by ringing a doorbell and demanding to be heard, so meetings must conform to the necessities of the community, with respect to time, place, circumstance, and manner of procedure.").

17. *See, e.g.*, James E. Pfander, *Sovereign Immunity and the Right to Petition: Toward a First Amendment Right to Pursue Judicial Claims Against the Government*, 91 NW. U. L. REV. 899, 905 n.22 (1997); Julie M. Spanbauer, *The First Amendment Right to Petition Government for a Redress of Grievances: Cut From a Different Cloth*, 21 HASTINGS CONST. L.Q. 15, 51 (1993); Stephen A. Higginson, Note, *A Short History of the Right to Petition Government for the Redress of Grievances*, 96 YALE L.J. 142, 165–66 (1986). *But see* Smith v. Ark. State Highway Employees, Local 1315, 441 U.S. 463, 465 (1979) ("The public employee surely can associate and speak freely and petition openly... But the First Amendment does not impose any affirmative obligation on the government to listen [or] to respond."); Gary Lawson & Guy Seidman, *Downsizing the Right to Petition*, 93 NW. U. L. REV. 739, 740 (1999) ("[W]e do not agree that the Petitions Clause imposes on Congress a general obligation to consider or respond in any fashion to petitions that it receives."); Norman B. Smith, *"Shall Make No Law Abridging...": An Analysis of the Neglected, But Nearly Absolute, Right of Petition*, 54 U. CIN. L. REV. 1153, 1190–91 (1986) ("Such an extension of the right of petition ... could exceed the practical limitations of our system of government; with our present capacity for multiplying documents, the business of government could be halted if each paper produced in a massive petition campaign is addressed.").

18. *See supra* chapter 4, section III.

19. *See supra* chapter 2.

20. By "hybrid petitioning activity," I mean the exercise conjunctively of the rights of speech, assembly, association, and *petition*. When a protest, march, or demonstration seeks to communicate the fact of support or opposition to a particular government policy to an audience that includes either government officials with responsibility for the policy in question or party officials who control the means of election to such posts within the government, the expressive activity in question constitutes hybrid petitioning. Not all speech, assembly, and association, even related to questions of governance and public affairs, would come within the category of hybrid petitioning. For an example and extended discussion of hybrid petitioning, see *infra* chapter 6. *See also* HARRY KALVEN JR., THE NEGRO AND THE FIRST AMENDMENT 39–40, 143–44 (1965) (noting that protest activity can contain a petitioning element and suggesting that this petitioning element should affect the scope of its protection under the First Amendment); Kermit Lipez, *The Law of Demonstrations: The Demonstrators, the Police, the Courts*, 44 DENVER L.J. 499, 534–35 (1967) (arguing that although civil rights era protests "are not quiet preludes, and they do not conform to the ancient scheme perceived by Tucker and the Court in *De Jonge*," they nevertheless constitute petitioning activity, and that failing to recognize this fact "would be sadly formal").

21. By "petitioning speech," I mean speech that seeks the alteration—or continuation—of a particular government policy, whether or not this speech is directly addressed to an audience that includes a government official. This approach is consistent with existing Supreme Court jurisprudence that recognizes "indirect" forms of petitioning, such as mass media campaigns, which seek to affect public policy, but which might not involve direct communications with the government. *See infra* chapter 5, section III.A.; *see also* Lipez, *supra* note 20, at 535 ("Now, however, in the modern demonstration, the acts of assembly and petition occur simultaneously. But if the value of effective petition remains compelling, and it must, the fact of assembly, now, as then, must be protected.").

22. *See, e.g.*, Borough of Duryea v. Guarnieri, 131 S. Ct. 2488, 2494–98, 2501 (2011) (holding that the Petition Clause does not confer any special protection on complaints by government employees about their treatment by their employers because "[p]etitions, no less than speech, can interfere with the efficient and effective operation of the government" and noting that the rights of petition and free speech "share substantial common ground"); McDonald v. Smith, 472 U.S. 479, 482, 485 (1985) (holding that the Petition Clause does not create any greater right of public comment that contains false factual assertions than do the Free Speech or Free Press Clauses because the Petition Clause is "cut from the same cloth" as these parallel rights).

23. *See* Adderley v. Florida, 385 U.S. 39, 52 (1966) (Douglas, J., dissenting) ("We do violence to the First Amendment when we permit this 'petition for redress of grievances' to be turned into a trespass action. . . To say that a private owner could have done the same if the rally had taken place on private property is to speak of a different case, as an assembly and a petition for redress of grievances run to government."); Williams v. Wallace, 240 F. Supp. 100, 108 (M.D. Ala. 1965) ("[T]he extent of a group's constitutional right to protest peaceably and petition one's government for redress of

grievances must be, if our American Constitution is to be a flexible and 'living' document, found and held to be commensurate with the enormity of the wrongs being protested and petitioned against.").

24. *See supra* chapter 2, sections I. and III.

25. In the words of Professor Kalven:

> The concept of seditious libel strikes at the very heart of democracy. My point is not the tepid one that there should be leeway for criticism of the government. Political freedom ends when government can use its powers and its courts to silence its critics. It is rather that defamation of the government is an impossible notion for a democracy. In brief, I suggest that the presence or absence in the law of the concept of seditious libel defines the society. A society may or may not treat obscenity or contempt by publication as legal offenses without altering its basic nature. If, however, it makes seditious libel an offense, it is not a free society no matter what its other characteristics.

Kalven, *supra* note 2, at 205.

26. *See* Crandall v. Nevada, 73 U.S. (6 Wall.) 35, 43–44 (1867).

27. *See, e.g.,* United States v. Cruikshank, 92 U.S. 542, 552 (1876) ("The very idea of a government, republican in form, implies a right on the part of its citizens to meet peaceably for consultation in respect to public affairs and to petition for a redress of grievances.")

28. Thomas v. Collins, 323 U.S. 516, 530 (1945).

29. *See, e.g.,* Borough of Duryea v. Guarnieri, 131 S. Ct. 2488, 2494 (2011) ("It is not necessary to say that the two Clauses are identical in their mandate or their purpose and effect to acknowledge that the rights of speech and petition share substantial common ground."); Wayte v. United States, 470 U.S. 598, 610 n.11 (1985) ("Although the right to petition and the right to free speech are separate guarantees, they are related and generally subject to the same constitutional analysis.")

30. *See infra* chapter 5, section II.A., text and accompanying notes 55–68 (discussing the *Noerr-Pennington* doctrine).

31. McDonald v. Smith, 472 U.S. 479, 482 (1985).

32. Part of the problem may also be that litigants invoking the Petition Clause have not done a particularly good job of distinguishing claims under the Petition Clause from run-of-the-mill Speech or Assembly Clause claims. *See, e.g., Wayte,* 470 U.S. at 610 n.11 (1985) (refusing to consider Petition Clause claim independently where plaintiff failed to argue that the government's conduct "burdened each right differently" and treating speech and petition claims "as essentially the same"). With respect to a right to protest proximate to government officials, however, this chapter argues for an independent, Petition Clause–based claim. Indeed, because the lower federal courts have repeatedly rejected any right to protest proximate to an intended audience incident to the Speech and Assembly Clauses, the government's policy of banishing dissenters from areas physically proximate to incumbent officeholders does burden the Petition Clause "differently" than other First Amendment rights.

33. 472 U.S. 479 (1985).

34. McDonald v. Smith, 472 U.S. 479, 484–85 (1985); *cf.* Eric Schnapper, *"Libelous" Petitions for Redress of Grievances—Bad Historiography Makes Worse Law*, 74 Iowa L. Rev. 303 (1989) (arguing that the Court's historical analysis in *McDonald* is incorrect).

35. *McDonald*, 472 U.S. at 482. *But see* Spanbauer, *supra* note 17, at 17 ("This Article will demonstrate that, contrary to the Court's assertion, the right to petition was cut from a different cloth than were the rights of speech, press, and assembly.").

36. *McDonald*, 472 U.S. at 485.

37. *See supra* chapter 4.

38. *See generally* Schnapper, *supra* note 34, at 304–05, 312–16, 318, 328–29, 338, 343–48 (arguing that, historically, petitioners were immune from liability for both civil and criminal libel); *see also* Carol Rice Andrews, *A Right of Access to Court Under the Petition Clause of the First Amendment: Defining the Right*, 60 Ohio St. L.J. 557, 624 (1999) (describing the unique values protected by the Petition Clause).

39. *McDonald*, 472 U.S. at 485.

40. *Id.*

41. *See* Antonin Scalia, A Matter of Interpretation 14–18, 23–25, 29–32, 37–41 (1997); *see also* William N. Eskridge Jr., Dynamic Statutory Interpretation 268, 282, 324 (1994).

42. 131 S. Ct. 2488 (2011).

43. *See id.* at 2494–98, 2501. After the borough terminated Charles Guarnieri as the town's chief of police, Guarnieri invoked a union grievance proceeding to seek and obtain reinstatement; subsequent to his reinstatement, he filed a second grievance, alleging that the borough was retaliating against him for successfully challenging his termination. *Id.* at 2492. The U.S. Court of Appeals for the Third Circuit sustained Guarnieri's Petition Clause claim, notwithstanding the fact that the petitioning speech at issue did not relate to a matter of public concern. *See* Borough of Duryea v. Guarnieri, 364 Fed. Appx. 749, 752–53 (3rd Cir. 2010), *rev'd*, 131 S. Ct. 2488 (2011). The Supreme Court granted Duryea's petition for review and reversed this ruling. *See Guarnieri*, 131 S. Ct. at 2493, 2495–98.

44. *Guarnieri*, 131 S. Ct. at 2495.

45. *Id.* at 2498.

46. *Id.* at 2501. Justice Scalia objected to the use of more generic free speech principles to resolve this case, arguing that "[r]ather than shoehorning the 'public concern' doctrine into a Clause where it does not fit, we should hold that the Petition Clause protects public employees against retaliation for filing petitions unless those petitions are addressed to the government in its capacity as the petitioners' employer, rather than its capacity as their sovereign." *Id.* at 2506 (Scalia, J., concurring in part and dissenting in part).

47. *See id.* at 2495 ("There may arise cases where the special concerns of the Petition Clause would provide a sound basis for a distinct analysis; and if that is so, the rules and principles that define the two rights might differ in emphasis and formulation.").

48. *Id.* at 2494.

49. *See id.* at 2494–98. More specifically, Justice Kennedy observes that "[i]t is not necessary to say that the two Clauses are identical in their mandate or their purpose and

effect to acknowledge that the rights of speech and petition share substantial common ground." *Id.* at 2494.

50. *See* U.S. CONST. amend. I.

51. *See, e.g.,* Richmond Newspapers, Inc. v. Virginia, 448 U.S. 555 (1980) (press); Cohen v. California, 403 U.S. 15 (1971) (speech); Lemon v. Kurtzman, 403 U.S. 602 (1971) (establishment); Employment Div. v. Smith, 494 U.S. 872 (1990) (free exercise); De Jonge v. Oregon, 299 U.S. 353 (1937) (assembly).

52. *See, e.g.,* Rumsfeld v. Forum for Academic and Institutional Rights, Inc., 547 U.S. 47 (2006); Boy Scouts of Am. v. Dale, 530 U.S. 640 (2000); Roberts v. U.S. Jaycees, 468 U.S. 609 (1984); Healy v. James, 408 U.S. 169 (1972).

53. *See, e.g.,* United States v. Williams, 504 U.S. 36 (1992) (grand jury indictment); Fong Foo v. United States, 369 U.S. 141 (1962) (double jeopardy); Miranda v. Arizona, 384 U.S. 436 (1966) (self-incrimination); Mathews v. Eldridge, 424 U.S. 319 (1976) (due process); Phillips v. Wash. Legal Found., 524 U.S. 156 (1998) (takings).

54. *See, e.g.,* Doggett v. United States, 505 U.S. 647 (1992) (speedy trial); Duncan v. Louisiana, 391 U.S. 145 (1968) (impartial jury); Bartell v. United States, 227 U.S. 427 (1913) (nature and cause of the accusation); Crawford v. Washington, 541 U.S. 36 (2004) (confront witnesses); Washington v. Texas, 388 U.S. 14 (1967) (compulsory process); Gideon v. Wainwright, 372 U.S. 335 (1963) (assistance of counsel).

55. E.R.R. Presidents Conference v. Noerr Motor Freight, Inc., 365 U.S. 127 (1961).

56. United Mine Workers of Am. v. Pennington, 381 U.S. 657 (1965).

57. *Noerr,* 365 U.S. at 138–39; *Pennington,* 381 U.S. at 669–70.

58. *Noerr,* 365 U.S. at 129.

59. *Id.* at 128–30.

60. *Id.* at 143–44.

61. *Id.* at 140.

62. *Id.*

63. *Id.* at 138.

64. *Id.* at 137–38.

65. *See supra* chapter 4, sections II.–IV.

66. *See supra* chapter 4, section II.A., text and accompanying notes 6–26.

67. *See supra* chapter 4, sections III.D.–F.

68. *See supra* chapter 4, section III.E.

69. *See* Schnapper, *supra* note 34, at 347–49.

70. McDonald v. Smith, 472 U.S. 479, 485 (1985)

71. *Id.; cf.* Schnapper, *supra* note 34, at 304–05, 347–49 (arguing that, contrary to the *McDonald* Court's conclusion, long-standing Anglo-American common law tradition and consistent practice support a greater privilege for factual errors in the context of a petition).

72. Kalven, *supra* note 2, at 192–93.

73. *See, e.g.,* Bates v. Little Rock, 361 U.S. 516 (1960); NAACP v. Button, 371 U.S. 415 (1963); Edwards v. South Carolina, 372 U.S. 229 (1963); Henry v. Rock Hill, 376 U.S. 776 (1964) (per curiam); Brown v. Louisiana, 383 U.S. 131 (1966) (plurality opinion); Adderley v. Florida, 385 U.S. 39 (1966); Gregory v. Chicago, 394 U.S. 111 (1969).

74. *McDonald*, 472 U.S. at 488 n.2 (Brennan, J., concurring).

75. Gregory A. Mark, *The Vestigial Constitution: The History and Significance of the Right to Petition*, 66 FORDHAM L. REV. 2153, 2171 (1998). A nineteenth-century historian described the formalities of petitioning as follows: "It must be written, it must be free from erasures or interlineations, it must not be a simple memorial or remonstrance, but must conclude with a prayer. In matter it must be respectful of the privileges of the House, and free from disloyalty or expression of intention to resist the law. Beyond this the inclination of modern time is to allow the widest latitude to petitions." WILLIAM R. ANSON, THE LAW AND CUSTOM OF THE CONSTITUTION, PART I 349 (2d ed., 1892). Consistent with this view, Professor Mark argues that "had historical understandings been fully extended [in *McDonald*], the plaintiff would have had his claim dismissed by the trial court at the outset. Mr. McDonald's 'petitions' were not actually petitions at all, but rather letters to President Reagan (copied to others)." Mark, *supra*, at 2228 n.358. If the concept of "historical understandings" is limited to those derived from England, then this assessment is undoubtedly correct.

76. *A Coppie of the Liberties of the Massachusetts Collonie in New England* (December 1641), *reprinted in* 1 DOCUMENTS ON FUNDAMENTAL HUMAN RIGHTS: THE ANGLO-AMERICAN TRADITION 122, 124 (Zechariah Chafee Jr., ed. & compiler, 1963) (1951).

77. Andrews, *supra* note 38, at 624 (emphasis added).

78. *See* Lawson & Seidman, *supra* note 17, at 743, 751–52, 766.

79. *Id.* at 740.

80. *See id.* at 740.

81. *See supra* chapter 2, section III.

82. *See supra* chapter 4, sections II. and III.

83. *See* New York Times Co. v. Sullivan, 376 U.S. 254, 282 (1964); *see also* KALVEN, *supra* note 20, at 59–60 (discussing the need for citizens to be able to engage government officials without fear of tort liability for erroneous statements of fact and the corresponding privilege enjoyed by government officials against defamation liability).

84. *See* Nixon v. United States, 506 U.S. 224, 228–32, 236–38 (1993); Baker v. Carr, 369 U.S. 186, 209–18 (1962); *see also* Alexander M. Bickel, *The Supreme Court 1960 Term—Foreword: The Passive Virtues*, 75 HARV. L. REV. 40 (1961); Gerald Gunther, *The Subtle Vices of the "Passive Virtues": A Comment on Principle and Expediency in Judicial Review*, 64 COLUM. L. REV. 1 (1964); Henry P. Monaghan, *Constitutional Adjudication: The Who and When*, 82 YALE L.J. 1363 (1973); Robert J. Pushaw Jr., *Judicial Review and the Political Question Doctrine: Reviving the Federalist "Rebuttable Presumption" Analysis*, 80 N.C. L. REV. 1165 (2002); Martin Redish, *Judicial Review and the "Political Question,"* 79 NW. U. L. REV. 1031 (1984).

85. *See supra* chapter 4, sections II.C. and III.E.

86. The Supreme Court has held that organizations that voluntarily accept responsibility for the electoral process, including control of essential elements of that process, such as conducting primary elections and caucuses, are in consequence state actors, and subject to the strictures of the Bill of Rights and the Fourteenth and Fifteenth Amendments. *See* Terry v. Adams, 345 U.S. 461, 473–77 (1953). By parity of reasoning, it should also be possible to assert the right of petition against such entities. It

would make little sense to say that the Texas state Democratic Party, as a state actor, must honor the requirements of the Equal Protection Clause but is not subject to the requirements of the First Amendment, and the Petition Clause, at least with respect to its participation in the operational mechanics of local, state, and federal elections. The presidential nominating primaries and caucuses, and the national nominating conventions themselves, are no less integral to the selection of a president than a state primary election to the selection of a governor or member of Congress.

87. Professor Meiklejohn modified his initial position that only speech directly associated with self-government should enjoy the protection of the First Amendment and argued instead that expression associated with the arts, science, and literature should be protected as necessary elements for the creation and maintenance of an electorate capable of rational self-government; speech of this sort was not, however, to be valued as possessing intrinsic social value. *See* Meiklejohn, *The First Amendment Is an Absolute, supra* note 16, at 256–57, 262–63.

88. *See* MEIKLEJOHN, *supra* note 14, at 24–26.

89. *See id.*

90. *See* Cheh, *supra* note 11, at 73.

91. *His Majesty's gracious Declaration to all his loving subjects for Liberty of Conscience* (Apr. 1687 & May 1688), *reprinted in* 12 HOW. ST. TR. 234–39 (1812).

92. *See* Schnapper, *supra* note 34, at 313.

93. *Id.* at 313–14.

94. *Id.* at 314.

95. *Id.*

96. *See generally* Trial of the Seven Bishops for Publishing a Libel, 12 HOW. ST. TR. 183, 415 (1688), *reprinted in* 5 THE FOUNDERS' CONSTITUTION 189–96 (Philip B. Kurland & Ralph Lerner eds., 1987).

97. Smith, *supra* note 17, at 1160; *see also* Schnapper, *supra* note 34, at 314–15.

98. Bill of Rights, 1 W. & M., c. 2, § 5 (1689) (Eng.), *reprinted in* 5 THE FOUNDERS' CONSTITUTION, *supra* note 88, at 2.

99. Smith, *supra* note 17, at 1165.

100. *See, e.g.,* Spanbauer, *supra* note 17, at 29–31 (describing the restrictions, or lack thereof, on the right to petition in the colonies).

101. Smith, *supra* note 17, at 1176.

102. *Id.*

103. 376 U.S. 254 (1964).

104. *Id.* at 273–77 ("Although the Sedition Act was never tested in this Court, the attack upon its validity has carried the day in the court of history."); *see also* Kalven, *supra* note 2, at 209 (stating that after the Supreme Court's decision in *Sullivan,* "[t]he central meaning of the [First] Amendment is that seditious libel cannot be made the subject of government sanction.").

105. 378 F.3d 8 (1st Cir. 2004).

106. 477 F.3d 1212 (10th Cir. 2007).

107. *See supra* chapter 2, section II.

108. *See supra* chapter 2, sections II. and III; *see also* 2 WILLIAM STUBBS, THE CONSTITUTIONAL HISTORY OF ENGLAND 286–87 (1880) (describing the process for receiving and hearing petitions during the reign of Edward I). Some scholars would take the right to be heard a step further by also requiring a government response to every petition for redress of grievances. *See supra* chapter 5, section I., text and accompanying notes 17–18. Although this view is undoubtedly consistent with the history of the Petition Clause, I tend to agree with those who argue that such a requirement is simply too impractical in the modern era. This is particularly true with less formal forms of petitioning such as political protests, where, even if government officials were inclined to respond, the identities and contact information of those petitioning may not be readily ascertainable.

109. *See supra* chapter 2.

110. 2 STUBBS, *supra* note 108, at 602 (internal citation omitted).

111. The Tumultuous Petition Act, 13 Chas. 2, st. 1, c. 5, § 2 (1661) (Eng.), *reprinted in* 5 THE FOUNDERS' CONSTITUTION, *supra* note 96, at 191; *see also* 4 WILLIAM BLACKSTONE, COMMENTARIES *146–47 ("Nearly related to this head of riots is the offence of *tumultuous petitioning*; which was carried to an enormous height in the times preceding the grand rebellion. Wherefore by statute . . . no petition shall be delivered by a company of more than ten persons.").

112. *Trial of the Seven Bishops for Publishing a Libel,* 12 How. ST. TR. 183, 415 (1688), *reprinted in* 5 THE FOUNDERS' CONSTITUTION, *supra* note 96, at 192.

113. Smith, *supra* note 17, at 1158.

114. Spanbauer, *supra* note 17, at 23.

115. *Id.* at 28; *see also* Mark, *supra* note 75, at 2177 (noting that colonial practice included the right to present a petition in person to a legislative body).

116. Spanbauer, *supra* note 17, at 26 (stating that the right to petition "did not include a right to a personal audience").

117. Blackstone's few mentions of the right of petition discuss little else. *See* 1 BLACKSTONE, *supra* note 111, at *138–39 (discussing the security-based restrictions on the right to petition); 4 BLACKSTONE, *supra* note 111, at *146–47 (discussing "the offence of *tumultuous petitioning*").

118. Smith, *supra* note 17, at 1158.

119. *See id.* at 1158–59.

120. U.S. CONST. amend. I (emphasis added); *see also* WILLIAM RAWLE, A VIEW OF THE CONSTITUTION OF THE UNITED STATES 124 (2d ed. 1829), *reprinted in* 5 THE FOUNDERS' CONSTITUTION, *supra* note 96, at 207 ("It may, however, be urged, that history shows how those meetings and petitions have been abused. . . But besides the well known irrelevancy of the argument from the abuse of any thing against its use, we must remember that by requiring the assembly to be peaceable, the usual remedies of the law are retained, if the right is illegally exercised.").

121. 477 F.3d 1212, 1217–20 (10th Cir. 2007).

122. At an absolute minimum, these principles counsel that the outcome in *Citizens for Peace in Space* was a clear violation of the protestors' Petition Clause right to protest proximate to government officials to whom their intended protest was addressed.

Given that they had voluntarily agreed to limit the number of protestors to six and to submit to the same rigorous security screening applied to members of the press, there was simply no justification for denying their right to petition.

123. Although the litigants failed to invoke the Petition Clause in the federal court proceedings associated with speech bans proximate to the 2008 Democratic National Convention, the ACLU sought access for protestors that would be within the "sight and sound" of delegates, government officials, and the media. *See* ACLU of Colo. v. City and County of Denver, 569 F. Supp. 2d 1142, 1180–84 (D. Colo. 2008); *see also* Bl(a)ck Tea Soc'y v. City of Boston, 378 F.3d 8, 14 (1st Cir. 2004) (rejecting unequivocally the plaintiff's argument that the rights of speech, assembly, and association secured a right to protest within the "sight and sound" of the delegates attending the 2004 Democratic National Convention, in Boston, Massachusetts).

124. *Noerr*, 365 U.S. at 132–40 (sustaining a generic mass media campaign as protected petitioning activity because it was "a publicity campaign to influence governmental action").

125. *See supra* chapter 4, section IV.

126. *See supra* chapter 4, section III.B., text and accompanying notes 187–193.

127. *See supra* chapter 4, section III.G., text and accompanying notes 387–91.

128. *See* Schneider v. State, 308 U.S. 147, 161–63 (1939).

129. Of course, if government officials and agencies were to adopt easy to use *and effective* means for citizens to communicate their concerns, one would predict that resort to other, less convenient, less effective forms of petitioning activity would probably become less common. Thus, were the federal courts to recognize a right to access and engage government under the auspices of the Petition Clause, governments might well respond by creating effective and efficient means of communication that, as a matter of practice — but not law — would come to displace other kinds of petitioning speech. I obviously would have no objection to government officials and agencies creating such feedback systems, provided that their use is not the only constitutionally protected means of petitioning the government.

130. *See* Central Huson Gas & Elec. Co. v. Public Service Comm'n, 447 U.S. 557 (1980); *see also* Ronald J. Krotoszynski Jr., *Celebrating Selma: The Importance of Context in Public Forum Analysis*, 104 YALE L.J. 1411, 1424 (1995) ("The visceral aversion to context-specific applications of the First Amendment is somewhat puzzling. Contemporary First Amendment jurisprudence makes a number of fine distinctions based solely on the content of the speech at issue.").

131. *See* Miller v. California, 413 U.S. 15 (1973); *see also* Krotoszynski, *supra* note 130, at 1432 n.119 ("Current First Amendment jurisprudence divides speech into a number of such categories: political, religious, commercial, erotic or pornographic, and obscene.").

132. 372 U.S. 229 (1963).

133. *See id.* at 235–38; *see also* KALVEN, *supra* note 20, at 141–46 (discussing *Edwards* and endorsing the Supreme Court's holding in the case as advancing important First Amendment values and preventing a "hecklers' veto" to silence core petitioning speech).

134. *Id.* at 143–44.

135. *Id.* at 144.

136. *See, e.g.,* Adderley v. Florida, 385 U.S. 39, 49–52 (1966) (Douglas, J., dissenting); Brown v. Louisiana, 383 U.S. 131, 146–47 (1966) (Brennan, J., concurring); Edwards v. South Carolina, 372 U.S. 229, 235 (1963).

137. *See* Williams v. Wallace, 240 F. Supp. 100, 106 (M.D. Ala. 1965) ("The law is clear that the right to petition one's government for the redress of grievances may be exercised in large groups. Indeed, where, as here, minorities have been harassed, coerced and intimidated, group association may be the only realistic way of exercising such rights.").

138. *See, e.g.,* Timothy Zick, *Space, Place, and Speech: The Expressive Topography,* 74 Geo. Wash. L. Rev. 439 (2006) [hereinafter *Space, Place, and Speech*]; Timothy Zick, *Speech and Spatial Tactics,* 84 Tex. L. Rev. 581 (2006) [hereinafter *Speech and Spacial Tactics*].

139. 376 U.S. 254 (1964). For examples of the extension of the *Sullivan* doctrine, *see, e.g.,* Hustler v. Falwell, 485 U.S. 46 (1988) and Gertz v. Welch, 418 U.S. 323 (1974).

140. *See* Frisby v. Schultz, 487 U.S. 474, 479–86 (1988).

141. *See supra* chapter 2, section III.A., text and accompanying notes 169–78.

142. *See supra* chapter 2.

143. *Cf.* Bruce Ackerman, *The Emergency Constitution,* 113 Yale L.J. 1029 (2004) (arguing that limits must exist regarding the extent to which claims of national emergency may justify erosions of constitutional practices derived from the Constitution itself); Vincent Blasi, *The Pathological Perspective and the First Amendment,* 85 Colum. L. Rev. 449 (1985) (arguing forcefully that judges should enforce the First Amendment most aggressively in times of great national stress because it is precisely at those times that free speech comes under the greatest threat and also, paradoxically, the time at which full and free political discussion is most crucial).

144. *See* C. Edwin Baker, *Unreasoned Reasonableness: Mandatory Parade Permits and Time, Place, and Manner Regulations,* 78 Nw. U. L. Rev. 937, 941–44 (1983) (arguing that "reasonableness" often serves as a proxy for "the dominant viewpoint," that government officials are likely to undervalue both the importance and potential relevance of dissenting speech, particularly when "dissenting, disruptive" activities are at issue, and suggesting that "reasonableness is so much a matter of the dominant viewpoint that it may not even acknowledge the propriety of counting the dissidents' values [or] their evaluations of the needs of the community").

145. Bl(a)ck Tea Soc'y v. City of Boston, 378 F.3d 8, 14 (1st Cir. 2004).

146. *See id.* In this respect, Professor Zick's arguments about protecting spatial relationships have some relevance; Zick argues that the notion of space should also take into account the overall context of proposed speech activity, including the ability of a speaker to reach an intended audience. *See* Zick, *Space, Place, and Speech, supra* note 138, at 440–42, 466–87, 499–505; Zick, *Speech and Spatial Tactics, supra* note 138, at 583–87, 630–46. This certainly represents one way of addressing the problem: broadening the notion of spatial access to make it more context specific. From my perspective, the problem with this approach is that nothing in the existing legal

doctrine seems to take seriously the idea that audience access is a relevant consideration when testing reasonable time, place, and manner restrictions on speech in a public forum. On the contrary, the lower federal courts have routinely brushed aside arguments that alternative public forums were insufficient substitutes because the forums limited access to a preferred target audience. *See, e.g., Bl(a)ck Tea Soc'y*, 378 F. 3d at 13–14; Citizens for Peace in Space v. City of Colorado Springs, 477 F.3d 1212, 1217–20 (10th Cir. 2007). In fact, if *any* potential access to an audience is sufficient to meet the "reasonable alternative channels of communication" prong of the *Ward* test, then the ability to blog about the concerns on the Internet would potentially satisfy the existing time, place, and manner test. *See Bl(a)ck Tea Soc'y*, 378 F.3d at 14 (arguing that ability to reach target audience via the local media and Internet, rather than person-to-person, satisfies the alternative channels of communication requirement).

147. *See* FRANCIS LIEBER, ON CIVIL LIBERTY AND SELF-GOVERNMENT 121 (1875) (arguing that petitioning is "a sacred right, which in difficult times shows itself in its full magnitude, [and] frequently serves as a safety-valve, if judiciously treated by the recipients, and may give to the representatives or other bodies the most valuable information"); THEODORE D. WOOLSEY, 1 POLITICAL SCIENCE OR THE STATE: THEORETICALLY AND PRACTICALLY CONSIDERED, § 92, at 270–71 (1878) (arguing that the right of petition remains relevant because a regular exchange of information and ideas between citizens and their government improves the quality of government and suggesting that "[a]ll the people in all countries, citizens and foreigners, ought thus to have free access not only to courts but to legislatures and magistrates, either in reference to public affairs or to such as affect their own industry or calling").

148. For example, limits on the number of protestors permitted to demonstrate proximate to a venue might be permissible, as would a requirement of clearing a security check before reaching the demonstration area. For example, if a group of fifty protestors has been screened for noxious substances and weapons, and found to possess only placards and signs opposing a government policy, it is difficult to understand why such a group must be excluded entirely from the earshot or eyesight of the government officials attending the event as well as the invited guests at the event. By the same token, if a mass march of ten thousand persons attempted to invoke the right of petition by blocking the entrance to the meeting site of a national nominating convention, the Petition Clause should not stand as an obstacle to the government disallowing a protest of such a size and with such an objective.

149. *See* Schneider v. State, 308 U.S. 147, 161–63 (1939).

150. United States v. Harris, 347 U.S. 612, 635 (1954) (Jackson, J., dissenting).

CHAPTER 6. THE SELMA-TO-MONTGOMERY MARCH AS AN EXEMPLAR
OF HYBRID PETITIONING

Epigraph. Special Message to the Congress: The American Promise, 1965 PUB. PAPERS 281 (Lyndon B. Johnson, Mar. 15, 1965).

1. Martin Luther King Jr., *Our God Is Marching On!* (Mar. 25, 1965), in A TESTAMENT OF HOPE: THE ESSENTIAL WRITINGS OF MARTIN LUTHER KING, JR. 227, 228 (James M. Washington ed., 1986) [hereinafter A TESTAMENT OF HOPE].

2. As one prominent historian of the Civil Rights era has observed, "In the long saga of southern blacks' efforts to win free and equal access to the ballot, no one event meant more than the voting rights campaign in Selma, Alabama." DAVID J. GARROW, PROTEST AT SELMA: MARTIN LUTHER KING, JR. AND THE VOTING RIGHTS ACT OF 1965, at 1 (1978) [hereinafter GARROW, PROTEST AT SELMA].

3. 42 U.S.C. §§ 1973–1973p (2006). Historians have acknowledged the causal relationship between the Selma protests and passage of the Voting Rights Act. *See* JACK BASS, TAMING THE STORM: THE LIFE AND TIMES OF JUDGE FRANK M. JOHNSON, JR. AND THE SOUTH'S FIGHT OVER CIVIL RIGHTS 254–55 (1993); GARROW, PROTEST AT SELMA, *supra* note 2, at 133–78.

4. *See* U.S. COMM'N ON CIVIL RIGHTS, THE VOTING RIGHTS ACT: TEN YEARS AFTER 1–9, 39–52 (1975) (noting substantial increase in minority political participation and voting rates as result of Act); BERNARD GROFMAN ET AL., MINORITY REPRESENTATION AND THE QUEST FOR VOTING EQUALITY 1–3, 15–16, 21–23 (1992) (noting that direct barriers to electoral participation by minorities have largely fallen).

5. President Carter elevated Judge Johnson to the Fifth Circuit Court of Appeals in 1979.

6. 240 F. Supp. 100 (M.D. Ala. 1965).

7. *Id.* at 106.

8. *Id.*

9. *Id.*

10. *See, e.g.*, City of Ladue v. Gilleo, 512 U.S. 42, 59–60 (1994) (O'Connor, J., concurring) ("With rare exceptions, content discrimination in regulations of the speech of private citizens on private property or in a traditional public forum is presumptively impermissible, and this presumption is a very strong one."). For an academic treatment of content neutrality and freedom of speech, see Paul B. Stephan III, *The First Amendment and Content Discrimination*, 68 VA. L. REV. 203, 214–31 (1982) (reviewing the evolution of the Supreme Court's approach to content neutrality); *see also* Daniel A. Farber, *Content Regulation and the First Amendment: A Revisionist View*, 68 GEO. L.J. 727 (1980) (noting and justifying the Supreme Court's recent departures from content neutrality); Geoffrey R. Stone, *Restrictions of Speech Because of Its Content: The Peculiar Case of Subject Matter Restrictions*, 46 U. CHI. L. REV. 81 (1978) (analyzing recent cases in which the Supreme Court did not adhere to content neutrality).

11. *See* Frank M. Johnson, *Civil Disobedience and the Law*, 44 TUL. L. REV. 1, 4 (1969).

12. *See, e.g.*, National Socialist White People's Party v. Ringser, 473 F.2d 1010, 1014 n.4 (4th Cir. 1973); Collin v. Chicago Park Dist., 460 F.2d 746, 755 (7th Cir. 1972); *see also* LAURENCE H. TRIBE, AMERICAN CONSTITUTIONAL LAW § 12–10, at 853 n.22 (2nd ed. 1988) (citing *Williams* for proposition that public hostility to a speaker's point of view cannot serve as the basis for limiting the speaker's exercise of his free speech rights).

13. *See* HARRY KALVEN JR., THE NEGRO AND THE FIRST AMENDMENT 141–42, 145 (1965).

14. Another district court applied the proportionality principle when determining whether a municipal government's refusal to issue a parade permit for an antiwar

demonstration was "reasonable" in context. *See* Hurwitt v. City of Oakland, 247 F. Supp. 995, 1002–03 (N.D. Cal. 1965). The Fifth Circuit has never directly passed on the substance of Judge Johnson's *Williams* opinion. In *Wilkins v. United States*, 376 F.2d 552 (5th Cir. 1967), however, the court did uphold a conviction for a civil rights violation based in part on interference with the march. The court held that the protesters had a legal right to march but reserved judgment as to whether that authority stemmed from the district court's order. *Id.* at 560–61.

15. For criticism of the *Williams* decision, see Nicholas DeB. Katzenbach, *Protest, Politics and the First Amendment*, 44 Tul. L. Rev. 439, 443–44 (1969) (characterizing the proportionality test as an exercise in "interpreting existing doctrine imaginatively"); Burke Marshall, *The Protest Movement and the Law*, 51 Va. L. Rev. 785, 788–89 (1965) (noting the novelty of the proportionality test); Elliot Zashin, *Civil Rights and Civil Disobedience: The Limits of Legalism*, 52 Tex. L. Rev. 285, 300–01 (1974) (noting the controversial nature of Judge Johnson's opinion). *But see* Bass, *supra* note 3, at 252 (quoting Archibald Cox's description of Judge Johnson's approach as "novel, but sound"). One of the more recent discussions of the proportionality principle appearing in a law review appears to misconstrue Judge Johnson's opinion. *See* Donald A. Downs, *Skokie Revisited: Hate Group Speech and the First Amendment*, 60 Notre Dame L. Rev. 629, 675–76 (1985) (arguing that under the proportionality principle, Nazis would not be permitted to march in Skokie, Illinois, because Nazis are bad people). Downs's claim that Judge Johnson would look to the morality of the person or group seeking to exercise speech rights is plainly wide of the mark. *See infra* text accompanying notes 91–93.

16. *See* David J. Garrow, Bearing the Cross: Martin Luther King, Jr. and the Southern Christian Leadership Conference 412 (1986) [hereinafter Garrow, Bearing the Cross].

17. King, *supra* note 1, at 228.

18. *Id.* at 230.

19. Williams v. Wallace, 240 F. Supp. 100, 121 (M.D. Ala. 1965).

20. Selma March Petition, *reprinted in* John Kirshon, *King Leads March from Selma to Montgomery: Highlight of the Civil Rights Movement*, March 25, 2010, *available at* http://www.suite101.com/content/king-leads-marchers-from-selma-to-montgomery-a217939 (site last visited on October 19, 2010).

21. *See* Garrow, Protest at Selma, *supra* note 2, at 117.

22. Roy Reed, *Wallace Rebuffs Petitioners; White Rights Worker Is Slain*, N.Y. Times, Mar. 26, 1965, at 1.

23. *Id.*

24. *See id.*

25. *Id.*

26. *Id.*

27. *Id.*

28. Garrow, Protest at Selma, *supra* note 2, at 119 ("In Alabama on Wednesday [, March 31, 1965], Governor Wallace quietly received the marcher's petition of a week earlier during an eighty-five minute meeting with a sixteen-member delegation which

included James Bevel, Tuskegee Institute President L.H. Foster and Professor C.G. Gomillion, and Birmingham's Reverend Ellwanger.").

29. *See supra* chapter 4, section I., text and accompanying notes 4–6, and chapter 5, section I., text and accompanying notes 17–25.

30. KING, *supra* note 1, at 227.

31. Williams v. Wallace, 240 F.Supp. 100, 104, 112 (M.D. Ala. 1965).

32. *Id.*

33. In Perry County, 365 of 5,202 black residents were registered to vote, compared with 3,260 of the 3,441 white residents. *Id.* at 114. In Hale County, 218 of 5,999 black residents and 3,395 of 3,594 white residents were registered. *Id.* at 116. In Choctaw County, 284 of 3,982 black residents and 4,886 of 5,192 white residents were registered. *Id.* at 118.

34. *Id.* at 115.

35. *See* BASS, *supra* note 3, at 146–48, 152–53; GARROW, BEARING THE CROSS, *supra* note 16, at 380–81; *see also* KING, *supra* note 1, at 228.

36. MARTIN LUTHER KING JR., *Letter from Birmingham City Jail* (1963), *reprinted in* A TESTAMENT OF HOPE, *supra* note 1, at 289, 299.

37. Following the most notorious incident, which took place on May 3, 1963, the national media carried pictures of dogs attacking young children and fire hoses literally blowing the clothes off their bodies. GARROW, BEARING THE CROSS, *supra* note 16, at 249–50. These images left President John F. Kennedy "sick." *Id.* at 250; *see also* CHARLES WHALEN & BARBARA WHALEN, THE LONGEST DEBATE: A LEGISLATIVE HISTORY OF THE 1964 CIVIL RIGHTS ACT at xvii–xx (1985) (noting causal relationship between events in Birmingham, Alabama, and introduction of civil rights legislation). In the late spring of 1963, with President Kennedy's approval, the Justice Department drafted comprehensive legislation that would provide for the desegregation of all public accommodations. GARROW, BEARING THE CROSS, *supra* note 16, at 267–69. Ultimately, Congress approved the legislation, and President Lyndon B. Johnson signed it on July 2, 1964. WHALEN & WHALEN, *supra*, at 227–29. For a comprehensive history of the Birmingham civil rights protests in the spring of 1963, see TAYLOR BRANCH, PARTING THE WATERS: AMERICA IN THE KING YEARS 1954–63, at 673–802 (1988).

38. CHARLES E. FAGER, SELMA, 1965, at 8–10 (2nd ed. 1985); GARROW, BEARING THE CROSS, *supra* note 16, at 369–72.

39. GARROW, BEARING THE CROSS, *supra* note 16, at 371.

40. GARROW, PROTEST AT SELMA, *supra* note 2, at 3 (1978); *see also* FAGER, *supra* note 38, at 5.

41. *See* GARROW, PROTEST AT SELMA, *supra* note 2, at 3–4, 42–43.

42. *See id.* at 39–40; GARROW, BEARING THE CROSS, *supra* note 16, at 370–73.

43. *See* FAGER, *supra* note 38, at 9–10; GARROW, PROTEST AT SELMA, *supra* note 2, at 39.

44. *See* GARROW, PROTEST AT SELMA, *supra* note 2, at 42.

45. *Id.*

46. *See* GARROW, BEARING THE CROSS, *supra* note note 16, at 370–92; GARROW, PROTEST AT SELMA, *supra* note 2, at 42–67.

47. *See* FAGER, *supra* note 38, at 26–40, 49–56, 66–71; GARROW, PROTEST AT SELMA, *supra* note 2, at 42–73.

48. Williams v. Wallace, 240 F. Supp. 100, 104 (M.D. Ala. 1965); *see also* GARROW, PROTEST AT SELMA, *supra* note 2, at 73–77.

49. *See Williams*, 240 F. Supp. at 104–05; GARROW, BEARING THE CROSS, *supra* note 16, at 397–98; *see also* FAGER, *supra* note 38, at 150.

50. *Williams*, 240 F. Supp. at 105; GARROW, BEARING THE CROSS, *supra* note 16, at 398.

51. *Williams*, 240 F. Supp. at 105.

52. GARROW, BEARING THE CROSS, *supra* note 16, at 399.

53. FAGER, *supra* note 38, at 99; *see* GARROW, BEARING THE CROSS, *supra* note 16, at 399–400.

54. GARROW, BEARING THE CROSS, *supra* note 16, at 399.

55. *Id.* at 400.

56. *Id.* at 400, 412; GARROW, PROTEST AT SELMA, *supra* note 2, at 85–86.

57. FAGER, *supra* note 38, at 101.

58. *See* Williams v. Wallace, 240 F. Supp. 100, 102 (M.D. Ala. 1965).

59. GARROW, BEARING THE CROSS, *supra* note 16, at 317–37, 678 n.2.

60. *Williams*, 240 F. Supp. at 103. The Supreme Court later cited Judge Johnson's example as an appropriate refusal to provide relief on an ex parte basis. *See* Carroll v. President & Comm'rs, 393 U.S. 175, 184 n.11 (1968).

61. *Williams*, 240 F. Supp. at 103.

62. Many of the organizers from the Student Non-Violent Coordinating Committee (SNCC) argued, apparently quite fervently, that King should disregard the order. On the other hand, many of King's legal advisers counseled against such action. *See* Bernard G. Segal, *The Lawyer and Civil Rights*, Remarks at the Third Circuit Judicial Conference (Sept. 8, 1966), *in* 42 F.R.D. 442, 450–51 (1966); *see also* FAGER, *supra* note 38, at 101–03; GARROW, BEARING THE CROSS, *supra* note 16, at 401–03.

63. Professor David Garrow has suggested that King reached an agreement not to march beyond the Edmund Pettus Bridge through the intervention of former Florida governor Leroy Collins. *See* GARROW, BEARING THE CROSS, *supra* note 16, at 402–03; GARROW, PROTEST AT SELMA, *supra* note 2, at 84–86. Certainly, the apparent lack of detailed logistical preparations for a fifty-four-mile, multiday march suggests that King did not intend to go forward but rather was concerned with maintaining his leadership and authority over the direction of the civil rights movement. In particular, King and the leadership of SNCC were often in conflict over both questions of strategy and tactics regarding how best to advance the civil rights cause.

64. FAGER, *supra* note 38, at 102–03; GARROW, BEARING THE CROSS, *supra* note 16, at 403.

65. FAGER, *supra* note 38, at 103–04; FRANK SIKORA, THE JUDGE: THE LIFE AND OPINIONS OF ALABAMA'S FRANK M. JOHNSON, JR. 191 (1992).

66. FAGER, *supra* note 38, at 104.

67. *Id.*; GARROW, BEARING THE CROSS, *supra* note 16, at 403–04.

68. GARROW, PROTEST AT SELMA, *supra* note 2, at 87.

69. *See* BASS, *supra* note 3, at 239–42; FAGER, *supra* note 38, at 104–05.

70. *See* KING, *supra* note 36, at 293. King defined a "just law" as "a code that a majority compels a minority to follow that it is willing to follow itself. This is sameness made legal." *Id.* at 294. Conversely, an "unjust law" is "a code that a majority inflicts on a

minority that is not binding on itself [or that is] inflicted upon a minority which that minority had no part in enacting or creating because they did not have the unhampered right to vote." *Id.* Although King questioned the basic fairness of the order restraining the march, he apparently never intended to defy the court. *See* Bass, *supra* note 3, at 238–39; Garrow, Protest at Selma, *supra* note 2, at 84. Plainly, King was not prepared to challenge the law without a stronger showing that it was unjust.

Significantly, as defined by King, an "unjust" law will usually, if not always, be inconsistent with the equal protection and due process guarantees of the Fifth and Fourteenth Amendments, and therefore not be law at all. *See* Katzenbach, *supra* note 15, at 444–45; Marshall, *supra* note 15, at 794–800.

71. Segal, *supra* note 62, at 450–51. At the time of the march, Segal was an attorney for the Lawyers' Committee for Civil Rights Under Law.

72. For a historical perspective on the court proceedings, see Bass, *supra* note 3, at 241–49; Garrow, Bearing the Cross, *supra* note 16, at 406–11; Garrow, Protest at Selma, *supra* note 2, at 95–96.

73. Williams v. Wallace, 240 F. Supp. 100, 104 (M.D. Ala. 1965). Judge Johnson explained: "The evidence in this case reflects that, particularly as to Selma, Dallas County, Alabama, an almost continuous pattern of conduct has existed on the part of defendant Sheriff Clark, his deputies, and his auxiliary deputies known as 'possemen' of harassment, intimidation, coercion, threatening conduct, and, sometimes, brutal mistreatment toward these plaintiffs and other members of their class who were engaged in their demonstrations for the purpose of encouraging Negroes to attempt to register to vote and to protest discriminatory voter registration practices in Alabama." *Id.*; *see also* Garrow, Protest at Selma, *supra* note 2, at 99, 102, 108 (describing progress of hearings).

74. *Williams*, 240 F. Supp. at 104.

75. *Id.*

76. *Id.* at 105.

77. *Id.*

78. Judge Johnson's law clerk at the time observed that the judge knew that contemporary case law favored denial of the march, if only because of its proposed scope and the state's "duty to maintain the safety and commerce on those highways." Bass, *supra* note 3, at 243 (internal quotation marks omitted). Throughout his tenure on the bench, however, Judge Johnson was never one to shrink from deciding hard cases in ways that might prove controversial. *See, e.g.*, Jager v. Douglas County Sch. Dist., 862 F.2d 824 (11th Cir. 1989) (holding that a state-sponsored prayer before a high school football game violated the Establishment Clause); Hardwick v. Bowers, 760 F.2d 1202 (11th Cir. 1985) (holding that the constitutional right of privacy encompasses homosexual acts between consenting adults in their home), *rev'd*, 478 U.S. 186 (1986); Parducci v. Rutland, 316 F. Supp. 352 (M.D. Ala. 1970) (holding that the dismissal of high school teacher for assigning a controversial short story violated her right to academic freedom under the First Amendment); Lewis v. Greyhound Corp., 199 F. Supp. 210 (M.D. Ala. 1961) (desegregating interstate and intrastate motor carriers and bus terminals); Gilmore v. City of Montgomery, 176 F. Supp. 776 (M.D. Ala. 1959) (desegregating Montgomery, Alabama, public parks).

79. *Williams*, 240 F.Supp. at 106.
80. *Id.*
81. *Id.*
82. *Id.* (quoting Kelly v. Page, 335 F.2d 114 (5th Cir. 1964)).
83. *Id.*
84. Perry Educ. Ass'n v. Perry Local Educators' Ass'n, 460 U.S. 37, 46–47 & n.7 (1983).
85. *Id.* at 45.
86. *Id.* A similar standard applies to so-called designated public forums, although the government may limit the categories of speech permissible in such areas. *See id.* at 46 & n.7; Crowder v. Housing Auth., 990 F.2d 586, 590–91 (11th Cir. 1993).
87. *See* United States v. Kokinda, 497 U.S. 720, 736–37 (1990) (plurality opinion); Ward v. Rock Against Racism, 491 U.S. 781, 791–92 (1989); City Council v. Taxpayers for Vincent, 466 U.S. 789, 804 (1984); *Perry*, 460 U.S. at 45–49.
88. Judge Johnson's failure to employ public forum analysis did not indicate a lack of familiarity with the applicable law. From the 1930s through the 1960s, the Supreme Court relied on a rebuttable presumption that public property could be used for speech-related activities. *See, e.g.*, Hague v. Committee for Indus. Org., 307 U.S. 496, 515–16 (1939). Under the First Amendment, public property presumptively was available for speech activities, unless under particular circumstances the government established content-neutral, reasonable time, place, and manner restrictions on the use of the property. *See, e.g.*, Brown v. Louisiana, 383 U.S. 131 (1966) (holding, without undertaking forum analysis, that the First Amendment protected protest activity in a public library). It was not until the 1970s that the Supreme Court began engaging in formal "public forum" analyses. *See, e.g.*, Southeastern Promotions v. Conrad, 420 U.S. 546, 547, 552–58 (1975) (undertaking forum analysis to determine the scope of First Amendment rights in a public auditorium). Thus *Williams* might be understood in part as a reflection of the state of First Amendment jurisprudence in the mid-1960s.
89. Williams v. Wallace, 240 F. Supp. 100, 108 (M.D. Ala. 1965).
90. *Id.* at 109.
91. *Id.* at 108. It is worth noting that the plaintiffs' planned use of U.S. Highway 80 was not per se unlawful. Alabama state law clearly permitted pedestrians to walk along highways. *Id.* at 107 & n.5. Moreover, the court did not authorize the marchers to take over the highway incident to the march. On the contrary, the plan proposed by the marchers and approved by the court specifically limited the number of marchers permitted along the two-lane stretch of Highway 80, and included detailed plans for providing logistical support for the march. *Id.* at 107–08. It is also important to realize that much of the disruption that ultimately occurred was not inherent in the plan for the march but was rather a result of local hostility so intense that the protesters had to be protected by a phalanx of armed National Guard members. *See* Marshall, *supra* note 15, at 788 (noting that the march "necessitated the closing of half the highway, cost the taxpayers over $500,000 in the pay of National Guardsmen alone, caused innumerable traffic jams, and again exposed to world opinion the magnitude of the discrimination in the United States against Negro citizens").

92. *See, e.g.,* Downs, *supra* note 15, at 676 ("Johnson's 'commensurity theorem' is not legitimate because it incorporates the ends and substance of the speech.") (citation omitted); Zashin, *supra note* 15, at 300–301 (describing Judge Johnson's holding in *Williams* as "a slender reed on which to base the larger question of the socially tolerable amounts of disruption" caused by speech activities on public property); *cf.* Kingsley R. Browne, *Title VII as Censorship: Hostile Environment Harassment and the First Amendment,* 52 OHIO ST. L.J. 481, 536 & n.336 (1991) (arguing that the First Amendment requires "official agnosticism on questions of social policy").

93. 512 U.S. 753 (1994).

94. *Id.* at 784–85 (Scalia, J., concurring in part and dissenting in part); *cf.* NAACP v. Claiborne Hardware Co., 458 U.S. 886 (1982) (providing broad First Amendment protection to civil rights protesters engaged in an economic boycott of local merchants).

95. *Madsen,* 512 U.S. at 797–815.

96. *See, e.g.,* Vincent Blasi, *The Pathological Perspective and the First Amendment,* 85 COLUM. L. REV. 449, 449–52 (1985). Professor Blasi did not consider the implications that *Williams* might have for his theory.

97. *Id.* at 452–59, 512–14.

98. *Id.* at 456–59, 462–69.

99. *Id.* at 451, 484. Indeed, he describes such an approach as "antithetical to my thesis." *Id.* at 451.

100. *See* sources cited *supra* note 10.

101. In fact, Judge Johnson was highly skeptical that public protests would bring about meaningful reform. *See* Frank M. Johnson Jr., *Civil Disobedience and the Law,* 20 U. FLA. L. REV. 267, 267–68 (1968); *see also* TINSLEY E. YARBROUGH, JUDGE FRANK JOHNSON AND HUMAN RIGHTS IN ALABAMA 122–24 (1981).

102. Williams v. Wallace, 240 F. Supp. 100, 108–09 (M.D. Ala. 1965).

103. *See id.* at 103 ("Included in the rights plaintiffs seek and ask this Court to adjudicate is . . . petitioning their State government, particularly the chief executive officer—the Governor—for redress of grievances."); *id.* at 105 ("By these activities and by this conduct, the defendants, together with other members of their enforcement agencies, have intimidated, threatened and coerced Negro citizens in this section of Alabama for the purpose of interfering with these citizens and preventing them from exercising certain of their basic constitutional rights—i.e., the right to register to vote, peaceably assemble, remonstrate with governmental authorities and petition for redress of grievances."); *id.* ("The attempted march . . . on March 7, 1965, involved nothing more than a peaceful effort on the part of Negro citizens to exercise a classic constitutional right; that is, the right to assemble peaceably and to petition one's government for the redress of grievances."); *id.* at 106 ("The law is clear that the right to petition one's government for the redress of grievances may be exercised in large groups."); *id.* (noting that "the law in this country constitutionally guarantees that a citizen or group of citizens may assemble and petition their government, or their governmental authorities, for redress of their grievances, even by mass demonstrations as long as the exercise of these rights is peaceful"); *id.* at 108 (upholding as "reasonable" the plaintiffs' proposed march and rally as

an "exercise of a constitutional right of assembly and free movement within the state of Alabama for the purpose of petitioning their State government for a redress of their grievances"); *id.* ("As stated earlier in this opinion, the extent of a groups' constitutional right to protest peaceably and petition one's government for redress of grievances must be, if our American Constitution is to be a flexible and 'living' document, found and held to be commensurate with the enormity of the wrongs being protested and petitioned against."). Thus, Judge Johnson plainly viewed the petitioning function of the proposed march and rally as central to the strength of the plaintiffs' First Amendment claim. *See also* Robin Handley, *Public Order, Petitioning and Freedom of Assembly*, 7 J. LEGAL HIST. 123, 138 (1986) ("The right to petition and freedom of assembly are closely linked.").

104. *Williams*, 240 F. Supp. at 106–09.

105. *See id.* at 106, 108. To be sure, some of the language in *Williams* focuses on the "wrongs and injustices inflicted upon [the] plaintiffs." 240 F. Supp. at 108. Other parts of the opinion, however, make it clear that the court's holding rests on the legal wrongs established by the record evidence, not on a more generalized sense of justice or morality. *See id.* at 104–05, 109. Although Judge Johnson described a judge's role as one of "remov[ing] injustice," see Frank M. Johnson Jr., *Civilization, Integrity, and Justice: Some Observations on the Function of the Judiciary*, 43 SW. U. L. REV. 645, 647 (1989), he also said that a judge possesses only the limited tools provided by the law for accomplishing this task, see Frank M. Johnson, *In Defense of Judicial Activism*, 28 EMORY L.J. 901, 909 (1979) ("[I]t is one thing for a judge to adopt a theory of public morality because it is his own; it is another for him to exercise his judgment about what the public morality implied by the Constitution is."). Thus, a judge is bound in the first instance by law but can inform the application of particular laws with the broader policy choices reflected in the Constitution.

106. Kermit Lipez, *The Law of Demonstrations: The Demonstrators, the Police, the Courts*, 44 DENVER L.J. 499, 536 (1967).

107. Judge Johnson was quite explicit that the scope of his injunction in *Williams* was very much specific to the facts of the case: "What has been said in this opinion is not intended to declare or adjudicate the rights of citizens to assemble, petition, or protest within the City of Selma, Alabama, the City of Montgomery, Alabama, or any other municipal area since the exercise of such rights in each instance must be determined according to the facts and circumstances presented." *Williams*, 240 F. Supp. at 109. Thus, *Williams* was not intended to set down generic principles governing access to public property, including streets, highways, and sidewalks, for expressive activity, even of a petitioning cast.

108. *Cf.* Abrams v. United States, 250 U.S. 616, 624–31 (1919) (Holmes, J., dissenting). As Justice Holmes explains:

> To allow opposition by speech seems to indicate that you think the speech impotent, as when a man says that he has squared the circle, or that you do not care whole-heartedly for the result, or that you doubt either your power or your premises. But when men have realized that time has upset many fighting faiths, they

may come to believe even more than they believe the very foundations of their own conduct that the ultimate good desired is better reached by free trade in ideas— that the best test of truth is the power of the thought to get itself accepted in the competition of the market, and that truth is the only ground upon which their wishes safely can be carried out. That at any rate is the theory of our Constitution. It is an experiment, as all life is an experiment. Every year if not every day we have to wager our salvation upon some prophecy based upon imperfect knowledge. While that experiment is part of our system I think that we should be eternally vigilant against attempts to check the expression of opinions that we loathe and believe to be fraught with death, unless they so imminently threaten immediate interference with the lawful and pressing purposes of the law that an immediate check is required to save the country.

Id. at 630. Would federal judges permit speakers whose overall purpose is "fraught with death" to enjoy heightened access to preferred public forums on the same basis as groups whose aims seem to be less odious? A modicum of faith in the judiciary is certainly required if the proportionality principle is to be implemented. Indeed, our current First Amendment jurisprudence already presupposes a basic faith in the professionalism of federal judges. *See* WILLIAM VAN ALSTYNE, INTERPRETATIONS OF THE FIRST AMENDMENT 39–47 (1984).

109. *See, e.g.,* ALEXANDER MEIKLEJOHN, FREE SPEECH AND ITS RELATION TO SELF-GOVERNMENT 22–27 (1948) [hereinafter MEIKLEJOHN, FREE SPEECH]; ALEXANDER MEIKLEJOHN, POLITICAL FREEDOM: THE CONSTITUTIONAL POWERS OF THE PEOPLE 20–28 (1960); Owen M. Fiss, *Silence on the Street Corner,* 26 SUFFOLK U.L. REV. 1, 19–20 (1992).

110. *See Williams,* 240 F. Supp. at 105 (describing as "basic constitutional rights" the ability "to register to vote, peaceably assemble, *remonstrate with governmental authorities* and *petition for redress of grievances*") (emphasis added).

111. *See, e.g.,* Charles L. Black Jr., *The Problem of the Compatibility of Civil Disobedience with American Institutions of Government,* 43 TEX. L. REV. 492, 505 (1965) ("A radical catharsis through drastic civil disobedience may be the only alternative in some places to solutions infinitely more dreadful."). The desire for publicity is a significant motivation for many acts of terrorism. Blowing up the World Trade Center gets the world to pay attention to a political cause, albeit in a destructive, negative way. *See* Graham Zellick, *Spies, Subversives, Terrorists and the British Government: Free Speech and Other Casualties,* 31 WM & MARY L. REV. 773, 779–82, 819–21 (1990). *See generally* Sheldon L. Leader, *Free Speech and the Advocacy of Illegal Action in Law and Political Theory,* 82 COLUM. L. REV. 412, 418–20, 428–29 (1982).

112. *See* Connick v. Myers, 461 U.S. 138, 160–65, 170 (1982) (Brennan, J., dissenting); Garrison v. Louisiana, 379 U.S. 64, 74–75 (1964).

113. *See* 42 U.S.C. §§ 1973–1973p (2006).

114. BASS, *supra* note 3, at 255.

115. *Id.* On the effectiveness of the Voting Rights Act, see also sources cited *supra* note 4.

116. Bass, *supra* note 3, at 255; *see also* HAROLD W. STANLEY, VOTER MOBILIZATION AND

THE POLITICS OF RACE: THE SOUTH AND UNIVERSAL SUFFRAGE 1952–1984, at 94–99 (1987).

117. *See* Williams v. Wallace, 240 F. Supp. 100, 105 (M.D. Ala. 1965) ("The attempted march . . . on March 7, 1965, involved nothing more than a peaceful effort on the part of Negro citizens to exercise a classic constitutional right; that is, the right to assemble peaceably and to petition one's government for a redress of grievances."). Again, it bears noting that the submission of a traditional written petition to Governor Wallace was, in fact, the final element of the SCLC's planned march and protest rally. *See id.* at 121; *see also* GARROW, PROTEST AT SELMA, *supra* note 2, at 117 ("The rally concluded, the great crowd began to disperse and make its way home, and a small group of black Alabamians who had been designated to deliver the marchers' petition to Wallace, who had watched the gathering through his office blinds, were turned away by a staff member at the capitol door."); Reed, *supra* note 22, at 1 ("Gov. George C. Wallace sent word about 2 P.M. that he would receive a delegation from the marchers after the rally, but the delegation met twice with rebuffs when it tried to see him").

118. 347 U.S. 483 (1954).

119. *See, e.g.,* GERALD N. ROSENBERG, THE HOLLOW HOPE: CAN COURTS BRING ABOUT SOCIAL CHANGE?, at 1–30, 42–71 (1991); Derrick Bell, Brown v. Board of Education *and the Interest-Convergence Dilemma*, 93 HARV. L. REV. 518, 518–19 (1980) (arguing that *Brown* is "irrelevant" to most black children). *But see* Drew S. Days III, *The Other Desegregation Story: Eradicating the Dual School System in Hillsborough County, Florida*, 61 FORDHAM L. REV. 33, 37 (1992) (arguing that *Brown* was a relative success).

120. *See* ROSENBERG, *supra* note 119, at 42–54, 70–71.

121. Almost ten years after the *Brown* decision, less than 2 percent of Southern schools had been desegregated. RICHARD KLUGER, SIMPLE JUSTICE 758 (1975). Conversely, ten years after passage of the Voting Rights Act, the black voter registration rate equaled, and in some cases exceeded, that of white voters. *See* GARROW, PROTEST AT SELMA, *supra* note 2, at 179 211; STANLEY, *supra* note 116, at 94–99.

122. *See, e.g.,* International Soc'y for Krishna Consciousness v. Lee, 505 U.S. 672, 679–85 (1992) (holding that airports are not public forums); United States v. Kokinda, 497 U.S. 720, 726–30, 732–37 (1990) (holding that sidewalk and parking lots on post office property are not public forums).

123. For examples of cases in which courts have found areas used by the public to be nonpublic forums, see Hazelwood Sch. Dist. v. Kuhlmeier, 484 U.S. 260, 267–73 (1988) (public primary and secondary school buildings); Greer v. Spock, 424 U.S. 828, 837–39 (1976) (streets and sidewalks in a military base); Multimedia Publishing Co. v. Greenville-Spartanburg Airport Dist., 991 F.2d 154, 158 (4th Cir. 1993) (airport terminals); Crowder v. Housing Auth., 990 F.2d 586, 591 (11th Cir. 1993) (auditoriums in a public housing development); Kreimer v. Bureau of Police, 958 F.2d 1242, 1260–62 (3d Cir. 1992) (public libraries); United States v. LaValley, 957 F.2d 1309, 1314–15 (6th Cir. 1992) (grassy median strip between road and military base); Sentinel Communications Co. v. Watts, 936 F.2d 1189, 1203–04 (11th Cir. 1991) (interstate rest areas); United States v. Gilbert, 920 F.2d 878, 885 (11th Cir. 1991) (unenclosed plaza

outside federal office building); Young v. New York City Transit Auth., 903 F.2d 146, 161–62 (2d Cir. 1990) (subway stations); Alabama Student Party v. Student Gov't Ass'n of the Univ. of Ala., 867 F.2d 1344, 1345–47 (11th Cir. 1989) (public university property). Perhaps the best example of this trend are the "boxes" that appear in obscure locations in major airports. Although the federal courts were unwilling to banish speech activities from public airports completely, they marginalized speech activities in airports in order to ensure that the primary mission of such facilities would not be compromised. *See generally* Fiss, *supra* note 109, at 3, 8–9.

124. *See* Tribe, *supra* note 12, § 12–24, at 995–97; Curtis J. Berger, Pruneyard *Revisited: Political Activity on Private Lands*, 66 N.Y.U. L. Rev. 633, 690–91 (1991); Deborah A. Schmedemann, *Of Meetings and Mailboxes: The First Amendment and Exclusive Representation in Public Sector Labor Relations*, 72 Va. L. Rev. 91, 112–15 (1986).

125. Former Attorney General Nicholas DeB. Katzenbach has explained that "in the spirit of the first amendment, the government has an especially high duty to preserve, and even to welcome, dissent when it is government policy which is under attack." Katzenbach, *supra* note 15, at 450–51. The proportionality principle simply incorporates this idea.

126. Following the Rodney King verdict in May 1992, a group of University of Washington students marched down Interstate 5 in downtown Seattle to protest both the Los Angeles Police Department's treatment of Rodney King and the jury's subsequent verdict. The organizer of the march explained that "[w]e want[ed] to be peaceful, but at the same time, we want[ed] to be heard." *Students Say Their Peace—UW Senior Maintains Calm in 1–5 March to Downtown*, Seattle Times, May 2, 1992, at A5. The protest caused tremendous disruption to motorists on the highway and was patently unlawful, because most limited-access highways are closed to pedestrian traffic. *See, e.g.*, Wash. Admin. Code § 468-58-050(1). A similar protest occurred in San Diego, where a group of angry citizens marched down Interstate 5. *See* Tony Perry, *Keeping Lid On in San Diego*, L.A. Times, Apr. 2, 1993, at A3. These demonstrations were certainly preferable as a means of social protest to the riots that erupted in Los Angeles and other U.S. cities. Under the proportionality principle, however, protesters might have legal access to highways and similar forums in these circumstances. *See generally* Fiss, *supra* note 109, at 3–11, 18–20.

127. *See* Meikeljohn, Free Speech, *supra* note 109, at 22–27, 88–89.

128. *See* Alexander Meiklejohn, *The First Amendment Is an Absolute*, 1961 Sup. Ct. Rev. 245, 257; *see also* discussion *supra* note 126. Whether a mass protest in downtown Los Angeles could have averted the rioting in the South Central neighborhood is open to question. Nevertheless, the absence of an effective forum for expressing the rage and alienation caused by both the police department's treatment of Mr. King and the subsequent verdict was certainly a contributing factor to the community's choice of rioting as a means of expressing its disapproval of the police officers' behavior and the verdict.

129. Professor William Van Alstyne has suggested that the First Amendment's protection of speech activities can be described as a series of concentric circles, each farther away from a "core" of political speech. *See* Van Alstyne, *supra* note 108, at 41. This

conceptualization of the First Amendment demonstrates one shortcoming of existing doctrine: The model is two-dimensional rather than three-dimensional, and thus lacks the depth that consideration of context would provide.

130. *See* Valentine v. Chrestensen, 316 U.S. 52, 53–55 (1942).

131. This principle is inherent in the Preamble to the Constitution, which locates power in "We the People." U.S. CONST. PMBL.

132. *See, e.g.*, McCulloch v. Maryland, 17 U.S. (4 Wheat.) 316, 404–05 (1819) (noting that government is the agent of the people); HENRY S. COMMAGER, MAJORITY RULE AND MINORITY RIGHTS 4–5 (1958) (discussing the principle that "men make government" as fundamental to American policies); JOHN HART ELY, DEMOCRACY AND DISTRUST 77–78 (1980) (arguing that the framers of the Constitution viewed the ballot as the primary means of combating the tendency of power to separate the rulers from ruled).

133. First Amendment law already makes special accommodations for persons wishing to speak about the existence of government wrongdoing. *See* Rankin v. McPherson, 483 U.S. 378, 384–87 (1987); Connick v. Myers, 461 U.S. 138, 149 (1983); Perry v. Sinderman, 408 U.S. 593, 598 (1972); Pickering v. Board of Educ., 391 U.S. 563, 568–73 (1968). Thus, a government employee who speaks out about a matter of "public concern" is generally protected from retaliation by his government employer. Moreover, application of *Pickering* and its progeny requires courts to balance the public employer's interest in "promoting the efficiency of the public services it performs" against the "[employees'] opportunities to contribute to public debate." *Id.* at 573. At the same time, the Supreme Court has recognized that the general public has a constitutionally protected interest in receiving information, even information of a (mere!) commercial nature. *See* Virginia State Bd. of Pharmacy v. Virginia Citizens Consumer Council, 425 U.S. 748, 756–57 & n.15, 761–70 (1976). *Williams* simply applies this same value in the context of weighing the availability of a particular public forum for petitioning speech activities—that is to say, speech, assembly, and association activities that seek to convey a message of protest directly to a governmental officer or entity with some measure of responsibility for the government policy at issue.

134. Former Attorney General Nicholas DeB. Katzenbach has endorsed this approach in relatively strong terms: "My point is that if the objective of government is—as it should be—to maintain confidence in its processes, it may often have to go well beyond what is constitutionally required to prove its point. In the spirit of Judge Johnson's decision with respect to the Selma-Montgomery march, it may have to go to extremes of inconvenience to prove its fundamental dedication to free political processes. Where the government itself is the object of criticism, the obligation to tolerate dissent, to make available suitable public forums, and to refrain from even the appearance of repression is particularly important." Katzenbach, *supra* note 15, at 449.

135. *See Williams*, 240 F. Supp. at 106–09; *see also Rankin*, 483 U.S. at 384 88; *Pickering*, 391 U.S. at 568–69, 572.

136. *See, e.g.*, Pugh v. Locke, 406 F. Supp. 318 (M.D. Ala. 1976), *aff'd in part sub nom.* Newman v. Alabama, 559 F.2d 283 (5th Cir. 1977) (ordering the judicially supervised

reform of the Alabama prisons following the failure of state authorities to undertake meaningful reform notwithstanding a prior court order requiring action); Wyatt v. Stickney, 344 F. Supp. 373 & 344 F. Supp. 387 (M.D. Ala. 1972), *aff'd sub nom.* Wyatt v. Aderholt, 503 F.2d 1305 (5th Cir. 1974) (ordering the judicially supervised reform of state-operated mental institutions following the failure of state authorities to under-take meaningful reform notwithstanding a prior judicial order to do so).

137. *Williams,* 240 F. Supp. at 108.

138. This is not to say that such exclusion is a necessary condition for the application of the principle. Rather, when a group has been denied access to the political process, the need for an alternative means of registering dissent is particularly acute. Thus, if individuals or groups seeking enhanced access to public property for speech activities can establish the existence of a legal wrong, the proportionality principle should potentially apply, even if the individual or group has not been completely excluded from the political process.

139. It should not matter whether the speaker is the actual person or group that has suf-fered the wrongs; it is the existence of the wrong that is critical. Not permitting third parties to claim the benefit of the proportionality principle would effectively preclude some wrongs from being called to the community's attention through mass protest. For example, the prevailing conditions in a state's prisons or mental hospitals might be unconstitutional; obviously the persons suffering the wrongs—the prisoners and mental patients—would not be able to protest the wrongs themselves, although they might have other legal recourses. *See, e.g.,* Alabama v. Pugh, 438 U.S. 781 (1978); *Wyatt,* 503 F.2d at 1305. However, a third party (e.g., a family support group for prisoners) should be permitted to engage in speech activities calling the unconstitutional conditions to the community's attention, and in determining an appropriate venue for such activities, the gravity of the wrongs suffered by the prisoners or mental patients should be considered. *See generally* United States Parole Comm'n v. Geraghty, 445 U.S. 388, 403–07 (1980) (permitting third party to assert legal rights of another); Singleton v. Wulff, 428 U.S. 106, 117–18 (1976) (same). Thus, "the spokesman need not . . . be the victim. . . . An individual member of the victim group can be a spokesman, but there is no reason why individual mem-bership should be required, or for that matter even preferred." Owen E. Fiss, *The Supreme Court 1978 Term—Foreword: The Forms of Justice,* 93 Harv. L. Rev. 1, 19 (1979).

140. *See* Amoco Prod. Co. v. Village of Gambell, 480 U.S. 531, 546 n.12 (1987); Thornburgh v. American College of Obstetricians & Gynecologists, 476 U.S. 747, 817–18 (1986) (O'Connor, J., dissenting); University of Texas v. Camenisch, 451 U.S. 390, 392 (1981). In addition to establishing the probability of success on the merits, in order to qualify for a preliminary injunction, a petitioner must also show: (1) irreparable harm, (2) that the respondent will not suffer undue harm if the injunction issues, and (3) that issuance of the injunction would not be inconsistent with the public interest. *See, e.g.,* Thornburgh, 476 U.S. at 817–18.

141. *Williams,* 240 F. Supp. at 103–05.

142. *Id.* at 108–09.

143. For better or worse, constitutional law cannot entirely cabin judicial discretion. *See* Lawrence C. George, *King Solomon's Judgment: Expressing Principles of Discretion and Feedback in Legal Rules and Reasoning*, 30 HASTINGS L.J. 1549, 1559–66, 1573–75 (1979); Mark Tushnet, *Critical Legal Studies: A Political History*, 100 YALE L.J. 1515, 1524, 1538–39 (1991). Rather than reject a doctrine that requires the exercise of judgment in its application, we should attempt to find reasonable ways of limiting the scope of the discretion.

144. *See* Barnes v. Glen Theatre, 501 U.S. 560, 565–68 (1991).

145. *See* VAN ALSTYNE, *supra* note 108, at 47–49.

146. Perhaps the best proof of this is Justice Potter Stewart's famous "I know it when I see it" comment on the problem of identifying obscenity: "I have reached the conclusion, which I think is confirmed at least by negative implication in the Court's decisions since *Roth* and *Alberts*, that under the First and Fourteenth Amendments criminal laws in this area are constitutionally limited to hard-core pornography. I shall not today attempt further to define the kinds of material I understand to be embraced within that shorthand description; and perhaps I could never succeed in intelligibly doing so. But I know it when I see it, and the motion picture involved in this case is not that." Jacobellis v. Ohio, 378 U.S. 184, 197 (1964) (Stewart, J., concurring) (footnotes omitted); *see also* BOB WOODWARD & SCOTT ARMSTRONG, THE BRETHREN: INSIDE THE SUPREME COURT 192–204 (1979) (describing "movie days" at the Supreme Court).

147. *See* New York v. Ferber, 458 U.S. 747, 753–65 (1982); Miller v. California, 413 U.S. 15, 23–30 (1973).

148. In this regard, *Williams* is an easy case. Because the government's wrongdoing was so blatant and pervasive, and given the fundamental nature of the rights involved, the court's decision to permit a march on a massive scale was reasonable. Obviously, more difficult cases may arise. Such cases would necessarily require courts to engage in delicate balancing acts.

149. Johnson, *In Defense of Judicial Activism, supra* note 105, at 910. Courts have undertaken this task in a number of disparate areas, notably including reform of prisons, see Pugh v. Locke, 406 F. Supp. 318 (M.D. Ala. 1976), *aff'd sub nom.* Newman v. Alabama, 559 F.2d 283 (5th Cir. 1977), mental institutions, see Wyatt v. Stickney, 344 F. Supp. 373 & 344 F. Supp. 387 (M.D. Ala. 1972), *aff'd in part sub nom.* Wyatt v. Aderholt, 503 F.2d 1305 (5th Cir. 1974), and primary and secondary public education, see Missouri v. Jenkins, 495 U.S. 33, 50–58 (1990); Rose v. Council for Better Educ., 790 S.W.2d 186, 209–15 (Ky. 1989); Edgewood Indep. Sch. Dist. v. Kirby, 804 S.W.2d 491, 496–98 (Tex. 1991).

150. *See supra* chapter 5.

151. Indeed, Judge Johnson was quite emphatic that the scope of the injunction was specific to the facts of *Williams* and did not establish general rules regarding the use of public property for speech activity. *See* Williams v. Wallace, 240 F. Supp. 100, 109 (M.D. Ala. 1965).

152. *See* Johnson, *In Defense of Judicial Activism, supra* note 105, at 910–12; *see also* George, *supra* note 143, at 1573–75.

153. SIKORA, *supra* note 65, at 231–33.

CHAPTER 7. CONCLUSION

1. *See* ALEXANDER MEIKLEJOHN, FREE SPEECH AND ITS RELATION TO SELF-GOVERNMENT 12–27 (1948).
2. Ward v. Rock Against Racism, 491 U.S. 781, 790–91 (1989).
3. *See* Bl(a)ck Tea Soc'y v. City of Boston, 378 F.3d 8, 12–14 (1st Cir. 2004).
4. *See* Citizens for Peace in Space v. City of Colorado Springs, 477 F.3d 112, 1217–20 (10th Cir. 2007).
5. As Professor Ed Baker has aptly noted, "The daily orientation of [most government decision makers, including judges] predictably leads to a very restrictive view of the desirability and reasonableness of dissenting, disruptive, activities—a prediction that many people find confirmed in their attempts to have bureaucracies adopt or enforce less restrictive rules and policies." C. Edwin Baker, *Unreasoned Reasonableness: Mandatory Parade Permits, and Time, Place, and Manner Regulations*, 78 NW. U. L. REV. 937, 942 (1983).
6. *See supra* chapter 2. As Judge Kermit Lipez correctly observes, "Such analysis simply ignores the rights of assembly and petition, permitting the [federal courts] to treat a case of public assembly 'as if it were an ordinary trespass case or an ordinary picketing case.'" Kermit Lipez, *The Law of Demonstrations: The Demonstrators, the Police, the Courts*, 44 DENVER L.J. 499, 536–37 (1967) (quoting Adderley v. Florida, 385 U.S. 39, 49 (1966) (Douglas, J., dissenting).
7. Anita Hodgkiss, Note, *Petitioning and the Empowerment Theory of Practice*, 96 YALE L.J. 571, 576 (1987).
8. In all probability, federal judges would resist entirely reviewing the adequacy of a governmental response a petition, absent extraordinary circumstances, on political question grounds. *See* Nixon v. United States, 506 U.S. 224, 228–32, 236–38 (1993); Baker v. Carr, 369 U.S. 186, 209–18 (1962). Alternatively, even if the federal courts were to hold that failure to respond to a petition constitutes a justiciable constitutional injury, it seems highly like that the federal courts would simply hold that a meaningless, pro forma response, e.g., a form e-mail or letter stating, "Thank you for sharing your concerns. We will do our best to consider them," would satisfy the requirements of the Petition Clause. On the other hand, however, the federal courts have been willing to police federal agencies that fail to honor the APA's requirement that federal agencies respond in some fashion to petitions from the public. *See* Massachusetts v. EPA, 549 U.S. 497, 510–12, 533–35 (2007) (reviewing an EPA response to a petition for rulemaking on greenhouse gasses and finding it to be legally inadequate).
9. MEIKLEJOHN, *supra* note 1, at 12.
10. *See* Hodgkiss, *supra* note 7, at 575 (arguing that "[p]resent doctrine . . . fails to recognize that the concept of petitioning implies a government duty to respond" and that this failure impedes the process of democratic self-government).
11. *See* Lipez, *supra* note 6, at 534–36.
12. *See, e.g.*, Snyder v. Phelps, 131 S. Ct. 1207, 1224 (2011) (Alito, J., dissenting) (noting that Fred Phelps and the Westboro Baptist Church, in addition to protesting at military funerals, also have "picketed the funerals of police officers, firefighters, and the

victims of natural disasters, accidents, and shocking crimes" in order to obtain media coverage of their social causes). As Justice Alito notes in his dissent, "The more outrageous the funeral protest, the more publicity the Westboro Baptist Church is able to obtain." *Id.* at 1224. In his view, however, this interest in securing national media attention for their various social crusades is largely, if not wholly, illegitimate: "In order to have a society in which public issues can be openly and vigorously debated, it is not necessary to allow the brutalization of innocent victims like petitioner." *Id.* at 1229. He suggests, instead, that Phelps and his followers "write and distribute books, articles, and other texts," "create and disseminate video and audio recordings," "circulate petitions," "speak to individuals and groups in public forums and in any private venue that wishes to accommodate them," "picket peacefully in countless locations," "appear on television and speak on the radio," and "post messages on the Internet and send out emails." *Id.* at 1222. However, they may not "intentionally inflict severe emotional injury on private persons by launching vicious verbal attacks that make no contribution to the public debate." *Id.*

13. Of course, the "reasonableness" of a particular cause, or protest in support of a cause, is very much in the eye of the beholder. *See* Baker, *supra* note 5, at 942–44. As Professor Baker has observed, "[R]easonableness is so much a matter of the dominant viewpoint that it may not ever acknowledge the propriety of counting the dissidents' values, their evaluations of the needs of the community, or their conclusions about what opportunities society ought to make available to people for expressing their dissenting views." *Id.* at 944.

14. *See Phelps*, 131 S. Ct. at 1222–25 (Alito, J., dissenting); *but cf. id.* at 1218 ("Simply put, the church members had a right to be where they were."); *id.* at 1220 ("As a Nation we have chosen . . . to protect even hurtful speech on public issues to ensure that we do not stifle public debate. That choice requires that we shield Westboro from tort liability for its picketing in this case").

15. *See* Williams v. Wallace, 240 F. Supp. 100, 106–08 (M.D. Ala. 1965); *see also* Ronald J. Krotoszynski Jr., *Celebrating Selma: The Importance of Context in Public Forum Analysis*, 104 YALE L.J. 1411, 1412–20 (1995).

16. *See supra* chapter 4, section III.

17. Adderley v. Florida, 385 U.S. 39, 52 (1966) (Douglas, J., dissenting).

18. *See* Gary Lawson & Guy Seidman, *Downsizing the Right to Petition*, 93 Nw. U. L. REV. 739, 740, 743, 751–52, 766 (1999).

19. *Adderley*, 385 U.S. at 50–51 (Douglas, J., dissenting).

20. Lipez, *supra* note 6, at 535.

21. *See supra* chapter 4, section III.

22. *See supra* chapter 4, section IV.

23. Alexander Meiklejohn, *The First Amendment Is an Absolute*, 1961 SUP. CT. REV. 245, 255.

24. *Id.* at 260.

25. *Id.*

26. *See* Menotti v. City of Seattle, 409 F.3d 1113 (9th Cir. 2005).

27. *See* REPUBLICAN NATIONAL CONVENTION PUBLIC SAFETY AND IMPLEMENTATION REVIEW COMMISSION, REPORT OF THE REPUBLICAN NATIONAL CONVENTION PUBLIC

SAFETY PLANNING AND IMPLEMENTATION REVIEW COMMISSION, EXECUTIVE SUMMARY 1–3, 9–14 (Jan. 14, 2009) (copy on file with author) (providing a historical account of the running street melees that occurred in St. Paul during the 2008 Republican National Convention between federal, state, and local law enforcement personnel and about a thousand "self-declared violent anarchists" bent on disrupting the convention proceedings).

28. Meiklejohn, *supra* note 23, at 260–61.

29. *See* Letter from Thomas Jefferson to Joseph Cabell, Sept. 9, 1817, in 17 WRITINGS OF THOMAS JEFFERSON 417, 423–424 (Mem. ed. 1904); THOMAS JEFFERSON AND EDUCATION IN A REPUBLIC (Charles Finn Arrowood ed., 1930); *see also* Wisconsin v. Yoder, 406 U.S. 205, 225–26 & 226 n.14 (1972); Lisa Krall, *Thomas Jefferson's Agrarian Vision and the Changing Nature of Property*, 36 J. ECON. ISSUES 131, 131–32 (2002).

30. Hodgkiss, *supra* note 7, at 575.

31. *See supra* chapter 4, section III., and chapter 6.

32. *See, e.g.*, ACLU of Colo. v. City and County of Denver, 569 F. Supp. 1142, 1181–89 (D. Colo. 2008); Coalition to March on the RNC & Stop the War v. City of St. Paul, 557 F. Supp. 1014, 1028–31 (D. Minn. 2008); Mary M. Cheh, *Demonstrations, Security Zones, and First Amendment Protection of Special Places*, 8 D.C. L. Rev. 53, 54–63 (2004); Susan Rachel Nanes, Comment, *"The Constitutional Infringement Zone": Protest Pens and Demonstration Zones at the 2004 National Political Conventions*, 66 LA. L. REV. 189, 215–18 (2005); Joshua Rissman, *Put It on Ice: Chilling Free Speech at National Conventions*, 27 LAW & INEQ. 413, 416–20, 439–40 (2009); Nick Suplina, Note, *Crowd Control: The Troubling Mix of First Amendment Law, Political Demonstrations, and Terrorism*, 73 GEO. WASH. L. REV. 395, 402 (2005).

33. *See supra* chapter 3.

34. *See* John R. Emshwiller, Devlin Barrett, & Charles Forelle, *Suspect Fixated on Giffords*, WALL ST. J., Jan. 10, 2011, at A1, A4; Marc Lacey & David M. Herszenhorn, *Arizona Suspect: "I Planned Ahead,"* STAR-TRIBUNE (Minneapolis, MN), Jan. 11, 2011, at A1; *see also* Sam Dolnick, Katharine Q. Seelye, & Adam Nagourney, *In Giffords's District, a Long History of Tension*, N.Y. TIMES, Jan. 11, 2011, at A1. Using a Glock 9 mm semi-automatic pistol, Loughner shot U.S. Rep. Giffords at point-blank range, and then proceeded to shoot nineteen others, killing six, including a federal judge, Judge John Roll, and a nine-year-old girl, Christina Green. *See* Emshwiller, Barrett, & Forelle, *supra*; Darren Everson & Angel Gonzalez, *Sorrow Racks Tucson After Killings*, WALL ST. J., Jan. 10, 2011, at A4.

35. *See supra* chapter 3.

36. *See* Eric Lipton, Charlie Savage, & Jennifer Steinhauer, *Congress Weighs Enhanced Security*, N.Y. TIMES, Jan. 11, 2011, at A18.

37. Paul E. Kanjorski, *Why Politicians Need to Stay Out in the Open*, N.Y. TIMES, Jan. 11, 2011, at A23.

38. *See* Cheh, *supra* note 32, at 73, 75 (arguing that protests should be permitted proximate to those holding government power and that the "rule should be: whenever there are expressive activities such as marches, protests or demonstrations directed at government officials or policies, such activity is presumptively permitted to take place at a

time and at a place proximate to the object of the protest and in such manner as to be seen and heard by the object of the protest" because otherwise security concerns can and will largely displace all expressive activities in any context involving protest proximate to public officials or buildings).

39. Harry Kalven Jr., *The* New York Times *Case: A Note on "The Central Meaning of the First Amendment,"* 1964 SUP. CT. REV. 191, 205.

40. *Id.*

41. *See* New York Times Co. v. United States, 403 U.S. 713, 723–24 (1971) (Douglas, J., concurring) ("The dominant purpose of the First Amendment was to prohibit the widespread practice of governmental suppression of embarrassing information.").

42. *See supra* chapters 3 and 5.

43. Williams v. Wallace, 240 F. Supp. 100, 106 (M.D. Ala. 1965).

INDEX

abolition, 10, 17, 86, 89–90, 102, 104, 111–13
165, 211, 213, 266n258; petitions, 89
abolitionists, 10–11, 89–90, 92, 114–29
Abrams v. United States, 241n232, 295n108
access: to government officials and
political party leaders, 54, 166–67,
174; to the media, 167; to a particular
audience, 39, 156; to public
property, 209
accountability, 175
Ackerman, Bruce, 286n143
active petitioning culture, 148
Adams, John, 115
Adams, John Quincy, 115–16, 119–20
Adams, Michelle, 231n68
Adams administration, 6, 8, 66, 70, 76, 113
administrative offices, and petitions,
134–35
Administrative Procedure Act (APA),
134, 152, 175–76; Section 555(e), 134
Alabama Project, 190
Allen, W. L., 188
alternative channels of communication,
15, 22, 27–29, 33, 36, 38, 44, 53, 168, 176,
181, 194, 227n17, 236n128, 286–87n146
American Anti-Slavery Association, 114,
116, 119, 168, 266n258
American Civil Liberties Union of

Colorado v. City and County of Denver,
39–42
American Nazi Party, 58, 65–67,
289n15
American Revolution, 88
Amnesty International, 46–49
Amnesty International, USA v. Battle,
46–50
anarchist protests, 44, 212
Anderson, David A., 77, 250n118
Andrews, Carol, 129, 164–65
annexation of Texas, 119
Anthony, Susan B., 122, 268nn301–2
antiprotest policies, 56
Anti-Saloon League, 123
antislavery petitioning, 115–16, 119,
265n251; crisis of 1836–1844, 114–20; gag
rule, 128
antitrust law, 127, 129; and Petition Clause,
10, 160, 162–63
Arizona, 131
Article I, Section 5, 114
Article V, 115
Ashcroft v. ACLU, 230n53
*Attorney General (Quebec) v. Irwin Toy
Ltd.*, 244n30
*Australian Capital Tele. v.
Commonwealth*, 224n67, 240n225